Reshaping Journalism and Communications With AI

Bünyamin Ayhan
Selcuk University, Turkey

Zehra Özkeçeci
https://orcid.org/0000-0002-2921-7831
Necmettin Erbakan University, Turkey

IGI Global
Scientific Publishing
Publishing Tomorrow's Research Today

Vice President of Editorial Melissa Wagner
Director of Acquisitions Mikaela Felty
Director of Book Development Jocelynn Hessler
Production Manager Mike Brehm
Cover Design Jose Rosado

Published in the United States of America by
IGI Global Scientific Publishing
701 East Chocolate Avenue
Hershey, PA, 17033, USA
Tel: 717-533-8845 | Fax: 717-533-7115
Website: https://www.igi-global.com E-mail: cust@igi-global.com

Library of Congress Cataloging-in-Publication Data

Names: Ayhan, Bünyamin editor | Özkeçeci, Zehra, 1984- editor
Title: Reshaping journalism and communications with AI / edited by Bünyamin Ayhan, Zehra Özkeçeci.
Description: Hershey, PA : IGI Global Scientific Publishing, 2025. | Includes bibliographical references and index. | Summary: "This book examines how artificial intelligence is transforming the phenomenon and discipline of journalism and communication"-- Provided by publisher.
Identifiers: LCCN 2025029423 (print) | LCCN 2025029424 (ebook) | ISBN 9798337329604 hardcover | ISBN 9798337329611 paperback | ISBN 9798337329628 ebook
Subjects: LCSH: Journalism--Technological innovations | Communication--Technological innovations | Artificial intelligence | LCGFT: Essays
Classification: LCC PN4784.T34 R468 2025 (print) | LCC PN4784.T34 (ebook)
LC record available at https://lccn.loc.gov/2025029423
LC ebook record available at https://lccn.loc.gov/2025029424

British Cataloguing in Publication Data
A Cataloguing in Publication record for this book is available from the British Library.

Table of Contents

Detailed Table of Contents

This study evaluates the feasibility of AI-assisted content analysis and the agreement between two large language models in local journalism. We analyze Hurses and Istanbul Gazetesi from May 13th, 2025. PDFs were converted with PDF.js to plain text, then unitized into segments of approximately 1000 characters. Each segment was labeled under Boydstun and colleagues' 15 Generic Frames by a PHP web application using gpt-4o-mini-2024-07-18 and by the ChatGPT 5 interface. The primary labels were compared. For Hurses, observed agreement was 0.577, Cohen's κ 0.458, and Krippendorff's α 0.432. For Istanbul Gazetesi, observed agreement was 0.551, κ 0.473 and α 0.459. With ChatGPT 5 as reference, micro F1 was 0.577 for Hurses and 0.551 for Istanbul. The web app overassigned economics and underassigned quality of life. The single day design, fixed segmentation, and absence of a human gold standard limit inference. Results have shown that human validation and RAG-supported prompts are recommended for more potential reliable findings.

Digital transformation is leading to radical changes, especially in the field of communication; artificial intelligence and data analysis have become key components of this transformation. Traditional communication practices are being replaced by big data analytics, algorithms, and AI-powered content production processes. This change is profoundly affecting communication disciplines such as media, journalism, advertising, and marketing. This section comprehensively examines the role of artificial intelligence and data analysis in the field of communication, exploring how these technologies are used in many areas, from news production to digital marketing, social media management, and target audience analysis. It also addresses critical issues such as the ethical problems, privacy violations, and data security risks that these technologies bring with them.

In the digital age, where new communication technologies are developing rapidly, continuous change and transformation are taking place in many areas. This study aims to reveal the effects of artificial intelligence-supported journalism on the future of journalism, the benefits and risks it will provide to journalists, and how it will affect the media and journalism sector. In this context, data were collected through face-to-face interviews with 15 participants between January 1, 2025, and February 20, 2025, through a form consisting of semi-structured questions.The study found out how artificial intelligence is used in business, what the pros and cons are, what the participants thought about AI-supported journalism, how AI might change the future of journalism, what the pros and cons are for journalists in newsrooms, how AI will change the news industry, and how AI relates to the ideas of "fake news," "disinformation," "deepfake," and "ethics."

The present chapter considers how artificial intelligence (AI) uses algorithmic personalisation, trust mechanisms, and attention capture to influence consumer behaviour. It outlines the development of recommendation systems using AI such as deep learning and reinforcement learning, explaining how they personalise content and predict preferences to influence decisions. One of the observed changes in the AI approach occurs through rise of "thinking" with predict preferences and "feeling" with simulating empathy for uninterrupted conversations. It also defines "filter bubbles" for another impact of recommendation engines, search filters, and chatbots with their personalised experiences by predicted preferences, so that users could only face with similar and "relevant" options during their journey. Higher engagement could manipulate a user's preference through the given predictions and direct the user to complete a purchase even at higher prices.

The integration of computer technology into journalistic processes brought journalism into the digital age with the widespread use of the Internet in the 1990s. The digitalisation of journalism has led to changes in production, consumption and distribution processes, leaving traditional journalistic practices behind. As in the past, some news can be produced with information gathered in the field, some can be produced with data quickly gathered at a desk, news can be presented individually, and even false/fake news can be verified by artificial intelligence tools. On the other hand, the fact that images and sounds can be created or modified using artificial intelligence-based deep learning algorithms has led to the need to evaluate artificial intelligence technologies from different angles. Based on this context, this study used content analysis to identify trends in scientific research on deepfake technologies and journalism, and to guide those who will conduct new research on the topic.

This study argues that AI technologies, as exemplified by DeepSeek, must be examined not only in terms of economic efficiency and cost advantages but also through the lenses of data ownership, surveillance, ethical responsibility, and global inequalities. Rather than adopting a merely critical perspective, the study embraces a critical stance to analyze the societal implications of DeepSeek and similar AI applications. It draws upon current academic research in critical theory, political economy, and communication studies to explore how the rapid adoption of AI is deeply intertwined with broader social, economic, and political dynamics. In this context, the future of AI is not merely a technological issue, but a normative one, the protection of data privacy, the design of systems for the public good, and the fair distribution of benefits must be safeguarded through democratic governance. The impacts of DeepSeek and similar systems will ultimately be shaped by how these fundamental questions are addressed.

Recent technological advances have significantly transformed media, replacing traditional one-way communication with interactive digital structures. However, this shift has also accelerated the spread of fake news, posing serious social and political risks. Artificial intelligence (AI) technologies—such as machine learning and natural language processing—offer promising tools to detect and limit disinformation. Yet, these systems face limitations, including bias, ethical concerns, and misclassification risks. This chapter explores both the opportunities and threats of AI in combating fake news, emphasizing that effective solutions require not only technology but also enhanced media literacy to foster critical, informed news consumption.

The viral spread of fake news on social media platforms has become a significant concern. Detecting and mitigating the spread of fake news pose a major challenge, requiring extensive effort from fact-checkers, governments, and organizations. However, the speed and volume of disinformation on social media reach far beyond the capacity of manual efforts to prebunk it. In recent years, various automatic fake news detection mechanisms have been proposed, ranging from models focusing on linguistic cues to approaches analyzing network characteristics. While these methods produce successful results, ever-evolving techniques of deception often outpace them. AI-based approaches offer a new opportunity in the subject matter. Especially deep learning-based detection systems provide substantial new ways to understand the context while adapting well to the evolving patterns of fake news. In this study, we explore the evolution of fake news detection. We discuss conventional and automatic fake news detection methods and the state-of-the-art deep learning approaches.

This chapter explores deepfake technology's ethical and legal implications across business, politics, and society. Deepfakes, utilizing advanced AI techniques, pose

Preface

INTRODUCTION

With the rapid development of artificial intelligence, humanity and societies have entered a new stage of transformation. Emerging from broader processes of digitalisation, this stage has introduced new structures, practices, and modes of interaction into everyday life, reshaping how individuals, institutions, and societies function. Communication, as both a social phenomenon and an academic discipline, has been profoundly affected by this transformation. Alongside technological change, new concepts, questions, and challenges have come to the forefront, compelling scholars and practitioners alike to rethink established frameworks.

This edited reference book, *Reshaping Journalism and Communications with AI*, is grounded in the conviction that artificial intelligence is not merely an auxiliary tool but a transformative force redefining communication in fundamental ways. The chapters brought together in this volume analyze how AI reshapes communication processes, journalism practices, media production, and audience experiences. Particular attention is given to methodological shifts, emerging conceptual debates, and the changing direction and content of communication at key points of transformation.

The contributions in this volume explore how various sub-dimensions of communication—journalism, media industries, digital platforms, audiences, and institutional communication—are implicated in the age of artificial intelligence. The book also addresses the innovations and opportunities enabled by AI, while critically examining the problems, risks, and ethical concerns it introduces. Issues such as trust, responsibility, power, regulation, and social impact are discussed within the broader relationship between the individual, society, and communication systems.

Looking ahead, this volume seeks to offer insights into how the future of communication may evolve alongside artificial intelligence. It examines the changing nature of communication tools and platforms, as well as what audiences, viewers, and consumers encounter within increasingly automated and data-driven environments. By bringing together diverse perspectives, the book aims to contribute to an informed and balanced understanding of AI's role in reshaping journalism and communication.

This reference work is intended for a wide readership, including academics, students, media professionals, business practitioners, policymakers, and executives, as well as representatives of government, the private sector, and non-governmental organizations connected to the field of communication. Above all, it is designed for anyone seeking to understand, critically engage with, and thoughtfully navigate the evolving intersection of artificial intelligence and communication.

ORGANIZATION OF THE BOOK

Chapter 1: Implementing AI-Assisted Coding for Content Analysis in Journalism: An Empirical Study on Local Newspapers in Istanbul

This empirically grounded chapter evaluates the feasibility of AI-assisted content analysis in journalism research. Focusing on local newspapers in Istanbul, the study compares the performance of large language models in applying generic news frames. By reporting agreement metrics and methodological limitations, the chapter provides a transparent assessment of AI's analytical potential and constraints. As Editors, we regard this chapter as an important methodological contribution, demonstrating both the promise of AI-assisted research and the continuing necessity of human validation, critical oversight, and carefully designed research frameworks.

Chapter 2: Artificial Intelligence and Data Analysis in Communication: New Dynamics of Digital Transformation

This chapter broadens the discussion by focusing on artificial intelligence and data analysis as core drivers of digital transformation across communication disciplines. It examines how traditional practices in journalism, media, advertising, and marketing are being reshaped by big data, algorithms, and AI-powered content production. The chapter offers a comprehensive overview of AI applications ranging from newsrooms to digital marketing and social media management, while also foregrounding ethical concerns such as privacy, data security, and surveillance. From an editorial perspective, this contribution highlights the structural depth of AI's impact and underscores the need for critical awareness alongside technological adoption.

Chapter 3: Artificial Intelligence-Supported Journalism and Approaches to Journalism

Grounded in empirical research, this chapter explores how journalists themselves perceive and experience AI-supported journalism. Based on in-depth interviews conducted in early 2025, the study reveals how artificial intelligence is integrated into newsroom practices, outlining both its perceived advantages and limitations. The chapter also addresses pressing concerns surrounding ethics, disinformation, deepfakes, and professional identity. As Editors, we consider this chapter particularly valuable for linking abstract debates to lived professional realities, offering insight into how AI reshapes journalistic labor, decision-making, and future expectations within the media sector.

Chapter 4: AI-Driven Media Influence on Consumer Behavior: Algorithmic Personalization, Trust, and Attention

This chapter shifts attention to the audience side of communication, examining how AI-driven personalization systems influence consumer behavior. By analyzing recommendation algorithms, attention capture mechanisms, and simulated empathy in human–machine interaction, the chapter reveals how predictive systems shape preferences, trust, and decision-making. Concepts such as filter bubbles and engagement-driven manipulation are critically discussed. From the Editors' standpoint, this contribution deepens the book's engagement with power, persuasion, and agency in AI-mediated communication environments, highlighting how personalization can subtly redefine choice and autonomy.

Chapter 5: An Academic Perspective on Deepfake Technologies in AI-Powered Journalism

This chapter addresses one of the most disruptive outcomes of AI in journalism: deepfake technologies. Through content analysis of academic research, the study maps key trends and debates surrounding deepfakes and journalistic practice. It situates deepfakes within broader processes of digitalization, verification, and misinformation, highlighting both technological capabilities and emerging risks. As Editors, we see this chapter as an essential scholarly guide for researchers, offering a systematic overview that informs future studies on AI-generated manipulation and media credibility.

Chapter 6: The Political Economy of Artificial Intelligence: A Critical Assessment of DeepSeek

This chapter offers a critical political economy perspective on artificial intelligence through the case of DeepSeek. It situates AI development within broader issues of data ownership, surveillance, inequality, and democratic governance. Rather than treating AI as a neutral efficiency tool, the chapter frames it as a normative and societal challenge. As Editors, we view this final contribution as a fitting conclusion, reminding readers that the future of AI in communication will ultimately be shaped not only by innovation, but by collective choices concerning ethics, power, and the public good.

Chapter 7: Combating Fake News with Artificial Intelligence: A Hope or a Threat?

Building on prior discussions, this chapter critically examines whether AI represents a solution or a new risk in the fight against fake news. While highlighting the potential of machine learning and natural language processing, the chapter also addresses ethical concerns, bias, and the dangers of overreliance on automated systems. Importantly, it emphasizes media literacy as a necessary complement to technological tools. From the Editors' perspective, this chapter reinforces the book's central argument: technological responses must be embedded within broader social and educational strategies.

Chapter 8: Evolution of Fake-News Detection: Conventional, Automatic and AI-Based Methods

This chapter traces the evolution of fake-news detection methods, from conventional manual approaches to automated and AI-based systems. It critically reviews linguistic, network-based, and deep learning models, emphasizing their strengths and limitations in an environment of rapidly evolving deception. As Editors, we consider this chapter a technically informed yet accessible synthesis that demonstrates why artificial intelligence has become indispensable in combating large-scale disinformation, while also acknowledging that no single solution can fully address the problem.

Chapter 9: Deepfakes: Ethical and Legal Implications Across Business, Politics, and Society

Expanding the deepfake discussion beyond journalism, this chapter examines ethical and legal challenges across business, politics, and society. By analyzing regulatory approaches in different global contexts and proposing mitigation strategies such as detection tools and media literacy initiatives, the chapter underscores the societal stakes of synthetic media. From our editorial perspective, this contribution powerfully illustrates the need for cross-sector collaboration and governance frameworks that balance innovation with accountability and public trust.

Chapter 10: Artificial Intelligence, Digital Media, and the Future of Journalism

In the concluding chapter, the volume establishes its conceptual foundation by examining how artificial intelligence–driven digital media tools signal a new era for journalism. The chapter situates contemporary journalistic transformation within the accelerated digitalization of the post–COVID-19 period, emphasizing shifts in news production, dissemination, and verification. Drawing on the theoretical contributions of Zuboff, Castells, and McLuhan, the author critically interrogates algorithmically generated news, personalization, and automated editorial decision-making. As Editors, we view this chapter as a crucial starting point, as it frames journalism's future as a hybrid model that must carefully balance technological innovation with democratic responsibility and ethical accountability.

Chapter 11: Exploring Transparency in Data Journalism in the United Kingdom Through Ethical Tensions, Practical Challenges, and Organizational Influences

Focusing on transparency as a core ethical principle, this chapter examines how data journalists in the United Kingdom navigate professional responsibility within AI- and data-driven journalism. Drawing on practitioners' perspectives, the study highlights the tension between ideals of openness and practical constraints such as time pressure, data privacy, and organizational resources. The chapter also emphasizes collaboration, training, and institutional support as key enablers of transparent journalism. From an editorial viewpoint, this contribution reinforces the enduring relevance of ethical norms in technologically advanced news production.

CONCLUSION

As the Editors of *Reshaping Journalism and Communications with AI*, we conclude this reference work with a recognition that artificial intelligence is no longer a distant or speculative force within communication, but a defining element of its present and future. The chapters in this volume collectively demonstrate that AI is reshaping not only the tools and practices of journalism and communication, but also their underlying logics, values, and social responsibilities. What emerges is a complex landscape in which technological innovation intersects with cultural, ethical, economic, and political dimensions.

Throughout the book, contributors have shown that the transformation brought by artificial intelligence is neither uniform nor unidirectional. Instead, it unfolds across multiple layers of communication—from production and distribution to consumption and regulation—challenging established paradigms while simultaneously creating new possibilities. Methodological reconfigurations, conceptual expansions, and interdisciplinary approaches highlighted in this volume underscore the need to rethink how communication research and practice are conducted in the age of intelligent systems.

At the same time, this book has emphasized that the opportunities enabled by AI are inseparable from the risks and challenges it introduces. Questions of transparency, accountability, bias, trust, labor, and governance remain central to ongoing debates. The relationship between individuals, society, and communication systems is being recalibrated, requiring careful reflection and responsible decision-making from scholars, professionals, and policymakers alike. Artificial intelligence, as the contributions illustrate, amplifies both the creative and problematic dimensions of communication, making critical engagement indispensable.

Looking forward, we do not propose a single vision of the future of journalism and communication. Rather, this volume offers a framework for understanding possible trajectories and for navigating uncertainty with informed judgment. By addressing communication tools, audience experiences, institutional transformations, and regulatory considerations, the book aims to support thoughtful adaptation in a rapidly evolving environment.

We hope this reference work serves as a lasting resource for academics, students, media practitioners, business professionals, and decision-makers across public, private, and civil society sectors. More importantly, we hope it encourages continued dialogue, research, and collaboration at the intersection of artificial intelligence and communication. As Editors, we believe that the future of journalism and communication will be shaped not only by technological capabilities, but by the values, choices, and responsibilities that guide their use.

Chapter 1
Implementing AI-Assisted Coding for Content Analysis in Journalism:
An Empirical Study on Local Newspapers in Istanbul

Suat Gezgin
Yeditepe University, Turkey

Ali Efe Irali
https://orcid.org/0000-0001-5332-1367
Mimar Sinan Fine Arts University, Turkey

ABSTRACT

This study evaluates the feasibility of AI-assisted content analysis and the agreement between two large language models in local journalism. We analyze Hurses and Istanbul Gazetesi from May 13th, 2025. PDFs were converted with PDF.js to plain text, then unitized into segments of approximately 1000 characters. Each segment was labeled under Boydstun and colleagues' 15 Generic Frames by a PHP web application using gpt-4o-mini-2024-07-18 and by the ChatGPT 5 interface. The primary labels were compared. For Hurses, observed agreement was 0.577, Cohen's κ 0.458, and Krippendorff's α 0.432. For Istanbul Gazetesi, observed agreement was 0.551, κ 0.473 and α 0.459. With ChatGPT 5 as reference, micro F1 was 0.577 for Hurses and 0.551 for Istanbul. The web app overassigned economics and under-

DOI: 10.4018/979-8-3373-2960-4.ch001

assigned quality of life. The single day design, fixed segmentation, and absence of a human gold standard limit inference. Results have shown that human validation and RAG-supported prompts are recommended for more potential reliable findings.

INTRODUCTION

The changes observed in technology have begun to influence academia's field approaches in both theoretical and practical terms. In this sense, it can readily be said that artificial intelligence (AI) is one of the key components of this transformation, both on the user side and as a research domain. Its contributions to automation processes and data-analytics structures in many areas have, ultimately, reached the social sciences as well. Especially methods that are both quantitative and qualitative, such as content analysis that requires long periods of time, can be evaluated differently thanks to AI. Under this assumption, the reliability and accessibility of the technology are also important. Indeed, AI has opened the window to a very significant change. However, whether it can be made completely independent of human control remains a matter of debate. When we address this specifically within journalism, we continue to ask the same questions. Rather than removing the human entirely from the process, if we position them as an operator, can we observe that it helps shorten the process; understanding this is quite important. At this point, it is evident that AI is following a strongly rising trend globally in the field of communication. According to the World Association of News Publishers report, 87% of publishers worldwide view AI and automation as a major area of investment (Athens Technology Center, 2025). However, views also exist that anticipate negative effects in relation to AI. For example, studies indicate that 50% of adults in the United States think AI will negatively affect the quality of news people receive over the next 20 years (Lipka, 2025). This topic similarly intersects with the fake news discourse and the erosion of trust in news in Western contexts (Özkececi, 2018:355-356). At the same time, AI has begun to find a place even in checking the content of news. For example, in the Digital News Report 2025 prepared by the Reuters Institute and the University of Oxford, it is reported that the weekly use of chatbots for news is 7% globally, and 15% in the under-25 group. It is also stated that 13% of users aged 18–34 and 7% of those over 35 are currently engaging with AI bots to check news (Newman et al., 2025). As noted by Yapar Gönenç (2012: 88), news does not equal reality, it sometimes mediates it through constructed representation. As the emerging picture shows, we face a different dynamic both in terms of trust and in terms of adoption. Differentiation also manifests itself, independently of AI, in many types of news content. For example, it is known that a gray area has formed between content produced by citizen journalism and that produced by professional publishers. The reintegration of user-generated content on social media into institutional channels' news flows increasingly blurs the space in between. Therefore, the analysis process likewise comes under a different kind of influence (Özkeçeci, 2019). As technology continues to develop, the production and consumption of content change. Accordingly, we may assume that analytical capacity regarding the re-presentation of content has been reshaped for this reason. Within this framework, our study focuses on the differentiation occurring in analysis in the context of AI. We seek to test the capacity of rising AI in the field of communication to measure its reflections in news flows as an analytical tool in the academic context. Rather than the accuracy or acquisition of news, we will propose an automatable system that can conduct content analysis in terms of categories. The reason is that, as content analyses in the field of communication are quite new and have multiplied especially in 2024 and thereafter, a gap has been identified concerning the processes to be followed as a roadmap. The study does not include human coding. We measure, in the context of inter-model agreement, the consistency between the labels produced by our web-based application developed directly on the gpt-4o-mini-2024-07-18 API and the ChatGPT 5 web interface outputs at default settings. Therefore, the reported values are not accuracy but agreement coefficients. However, before that, it is necessary to focus both on the concepts within the textual dimension of AI and on the studies previously conducted in the literature. Accordingly, the study is divided into three main sections. The first section begins with a literature review built in the context of a traditional compilation. This literature-review process is built on a delimited sample within the context of qualitative research methods and communication studies. In the second section, drawing also on examples from the literature, we address a proposed application system that we think can automate content analysis on the web. In the third section, in the context of general inferences, a sample comparison is provided at the scale of local newspapers in Istanbul through the application mentioned in the second section.

USING AI IN TERMS OF CONTENT ANALYSIS

Before addressing the response mechanism of artificial intelligence at its intersection with content analysis, we need to touch on its conceptual counterpart in order to understand it much better. Merritt (2025) explains, in this sense, the large language model and the process by which these models obtain information from external sources at a very basic level. A large language model is essentially a system fed by a large number of texts that produces fluent responses by predicting the next word. It retains knowledge internally in a pre-learned form. The system called retrieval-augmented generation or also known as RAG, is appended to the large language model (LLM) as a source-search module. As Merritt (2025) also notes, Lewis et al. (2020) were among the first teams to bring the RAG system to the fore. The main objective is to convert the LLM's parametric knowledge into controllable answers with citations to external sources (Lewis et al., 2020). First, it converts the question to be asked to the AI into numbers in a vector space that the computer can interpret. This embedding, that is, vectorization process, stores words and sentences in a multi-dimensional numerical space and, by scanning according to various similarity search algorithms, tries to match those with similar meanings. In other words, it converts texts into a multi-dimensional numeric system and positions similar ones close to each other (Google, 2025; Mikolov et al., 2013). It attempts to match the most relevant pieces in an external knowledge base to the question by scoring, and based on the higher score, tries to surface the most appropriate one as the answer. Various measures are taken, according to prompts and similarity ratios, to reduce the model's hallucination rate. In a study comparing an LLM evaluated together with a RAG system, Nurzhanov and Sharipbay (2025) state that, for example in ChatGPT, the RAG model can pull information from external data sources to produce more up-to-date and comprehensive answers and can process long texts better, but that it is disadvantaged in terms of increased response time.

If we consider artificial intelligence in the context of content analysis, we can say that it has found room to spread largely through systems also defined as large language models. The analytical processes of communication media are likewise influenced in this context. One example appears in the study by Stromer-Galley et al. (2025) on content analysis in political communication. The study states that, by using a comparative content analysis method, research was conducted both with student and crowd-sourced coder groups and across different large language model architectures. Based on comparisons across different APIs of ChatGPT, they concluded that any LLM requires validation before being used for coding tasks and may not have sufficient capacity to examine human communication. In another study focusing on politics, Heseltine and Clemm von Hohenberg (2024) analyzed tweets and news from the United States, Chile, Germany, and Italy using an experimental comparison method. In that study, which reported two separate rounds of coding with ChatGPT 4, they stated that ChatGPT achieved high accuracy on short texts. At this point, in their final results, they indicate that LLM-supported content analysis coding processes represent a cost-effective and feasible approach.

Of course, when an analytical process is undertaken at the textual level, it should not be forgotten that each sentence may carry different meanings across different language groups. In this sense, the presence of structures that appear as latent meaning and add irony to the existing meaning also needs to be underscored. In one study that can be given as an example, Bojić et al. (2025) focused on comparing large language models with human evaluators in analyzing hidden content in texts. This can be considered a highly important line of inquiry because it is assumed that texts may bear different meanings in different linguistic structures and that irony may be of critical importance. Under this assumption, in the study comparing models such as ChatGPT, Gemini, Llama and Mixtral, it is reported that Krippendorff's alpha was used for reliability and t-tests and ANOVA analyses were conducted for between-group differences. The results highlight that large language models can replace human evaluators in certain content analysis tasks, but that humans may still be needed in terms of emotional differences.

In another example, Törnberg (2024), who compared large language models with expert coders and supervised classifiers using social media messages, examined a sample composed of social media posts by political figures from 11 different countries. Törnberg reports results suggesting that text analysis in the social sciences can sustain the coding process with natural-language instructions without requiring training data. This matter of the training set is also quite important. Because LLMs are, by nature, pre-trained systems, they may be closed off to real-time data. Today, many models such as ChatGPT, DeepSeek, Gemini, Claude, and Grok can perform real-time scanning. However, in embedded, closed-loop systems, if data flow is not provided dynamically, operations will continue based on previously learned data. Tai et al. (2024) sought to approach large language models as a supportive method for qualitative research in traditional deductive coding. At this point, they subjected different interview transcripts to iterative analysis through different conceptual codes. Their findings report that LLM results are consistent with traditional coding and that LLMs may help identify implicit biases. From this, they also indicate that LLMs can be used as a validation tool in terms of qualitative research methods. Another study examining large language models in the context of qualitative coding processes was conducted by Than et al. (2025). In an experimental comparison across Llama, Gemma and ChatGPT, they report attempting the conceptual identification of socio-economic inequality in 1,253 articles published in U.S. news magazines between 1980 and 2012. The results, similar to other studies, indicate that LLMs have the ability to emulate traditional qualitative methods and point to their potential to transform qualitative research methodology.

In the study by Vu et al. (2024), a process was advanced that aimed to boost the performance of large language models with search-engine support so they can adapt to changing world knowledge. At this point, their results draw attention to the importance of measuring the degree to which LLM-derived information can be purged of hallucination. On the other hand, they report that LLM architectures without access to real-time information may fall short on topics that require up-to-date knowledge. This real-time feeding and training process is linked to access to new texts. Here, the processes of reaching information, interpreting it once accessed, and producing meaningful new data outputs also need to be properly defined. This occurs through

RAG. Embedded items or vectorized sentences, are stored in the database. Thereafter, the vectors of the questions asked are compared with the structures in this database. Of course, there are also processes for updating the old datasets of existing language models, which can be examined within the framework of fine-tune systems. In the literature, fine-tuning is defined as reweighting the classification layers of models previously trained with various datasets and retraining and refreshing the model with a new dataset. Naturally, this system has many different methods for scoring and classification (Church et al. 2021, as cited in Liu, 2024: 925).

One of the fundamental systems that enabled the development of large language models is based on BERT. Developed in 2018 by Google's AI Language research team as a machine-learning model built on natural language processing, BERT is an acronym formed from the initial letters of Bidirectional Encoder Representations from Transformers. With its ability to perform tasks across many different languages, it has assumed a highly pivotal role going forward (Devlin et al., 2019; Muller, 2022). Building on this system, there are also many different studies focusing on the Turkish language. Among the studies that hold an important place in communication research are those by Najafi and Varol (2024), conducted via TurkishBERTweet on Turkish tweets from social media and addressing two separate tasks: sentiment classification and hate-speech detection. In their work, they compared existing systems such as BERTurk, mBERT, and TurkishAlbert with products such as ChatGPT, Llama, and Gemini. Other studies addressing communication research with a Turkish focus also exist. In the study by Türkmen and Koçlu Maman (2024), a process was carried out using the ChatGPT-4o model for AI-assisted news text generation and for evaluating the levels of neutrality and ideological manipulation in these texts. In the methodology where descriptive analysis was preferred, postgraduate theses and scholarly articles on AI and news translation between 2004 and 2024 also constituted the sample of their study. According to their findings, AI is an important facilitator in the news production process; however, it exhibits a structure that resists requests for ideological manipulation.

As is apparent, artificial intelligence and news continue to appear as two key stakeholders moving in same direction. We also observe that this partnership and companionship is enriched by diverse topics that contribute to each other in a multifaceted and multidisciplinary manner. The fact that content analysis forms an intersection set offers quite important clues in this regard. However, to evaluate the issue through a full category and code analysis, we can say that it is also important to understand the structures in which AI is used within news-analysis processes. Rather than evaluations based solely on codes and categories in the context of content analysis, we may assume that, in a more objective sense, measuring performance in the analysis process under specific categories will yield more significant results. In other words, it is considered meaningful to design an objective method to better see the strength of content analysis which varies for each piece of content, in the context of AI. On this basis, the view has emerged that it would be appropriate to use frameworks previously applied in the field in a scientific sense. To make better sense of this, it is quite important to learn what similar studies have been conducted in existing research carried out within a framing approach.

METHODOLOGY

Within the scope of our study, the focus has been placed on the impact of AI's analytical power in content analyses to be conducted on newspaper articles at the textual level. We encountered many different studies in which AI is situated within the news context through framing. Rather than building a foundation from scratch directly in the code–category sense, these studies prefer approaches that are already widely used in scientific practice. In the studies reviewed, we observe different approaches in which AI is both the subject of research and used as an analytical tool. As an example of studies in which it is the research subject, Lupano (2025) can be cited. In that study, an analysis process focusing on the period after the release of ChatGPT was conducted to examine the change in AI discourse in China. Seventy-three opinion pieces were examined with SketchEngine software through Semetko and Valkenburg's five-frame model. Examples of its use as an analysis tool are found in the work of Bazlutckaia and Sytnik (2023). In their study, they tested Entman's framing approach by using ChatGPT instead of traditional manual coding. In their research on Russian-language tweets, they shared results indicating that ChatGPT reduced researcher bias in frame analysis. In another study, it is observed that Tagle (2025) used AI as a supportive tool. Processing the media reflections of the social events that took place in Chile in 2019 through Semetko and Valkenburg's general framing model, as also preferred in Lupano (2025), they used ChatGPT for Spanish translation and appear to have compared communication media with each other in their study.

As we can say, prior work has frequently relied on Semetko and Valkenburg's five-frame template which includes economic consequences, attribution of responsibility, conflict, human interest, and morality for cross-national news comparisons (Semetko & Valkenburg, 2000). Additionally, another framework we observed similarly used in artificial intelligence studies, was Entman's framing. Entman (1993) defines framing as the selection and salience of aspects of perceived reality that promote problem definitions, causal interpretations, moral evaluations, and treatment recommendations. Based on this, it was considered that a different framing categorization not encountered in literature reviews could be tested within the AI process. Building on this tradition while seeking greater granularity, we adopt different framing which is Boydstun et al.'s 15 Generic Frames to broaden topical coverage and enable finer distinctions in local news (Boydstun et al., 2013; Card et al., 2015). The system created by Boydstun et.al (2013), with its 15 distinct framing dimensions, was preferred. These dimensions are: economic, capacity and resources, morality, fairness and equality, legality, constitutionality and jurisprudence, policy prescription and evaluation, crime and punishment, security and defense, health and safety, quality of life, cultural identity, public opinion; political, external regulation and reputation and other (Card et al. 2015; Boydstun et.al, 2013). The explanations attached to these dimensions were later introduced to the AI as prompts within the system that we will describe as a PHP endpoint. Accordingly, during our research, a coding process was built through this framing system. However, rather than comparing a human and an LLM here, a comparison of two different models was carried out. The reason is that many up-to-date studies in the literature already test AI directly in the context of content analysis. Differing from that, the question we seek to answer is the level of agreement between a structured PHP application across AI models and a model open to general use, and, if agreement exists, whether this agreement is consistent. The point at which it diverges from systems comparing different AI APIs and models (Stromer-Galley et al., 2025) is that it is conducted within a much broader categorization focused on framing. In this context, our main hypothesis derived from the literature is based on the assumption that there is significant agreement (Krippendorff's $\alpha>0.667$) between Boydstun et al (2013) framing dimensions and AI coders. To test this hypothesis, we developed a basic-level web application that calls ChatGPT API.

The technical flow of our web application was designed to consist of an HTML/JS-based front end and a PHP server endpoint. On the front end, which uses the PDF.js library, the May 13, 2025 PDFs of Hurses and Istanbul Gazetesi were converted to plain text, and the texts were split into units of approximately $1{,}000 \pm 200$ characters. Each news segment was sent to the PHP endpoint with a JSON payload (action, paper, date, articles, classify). Our PHP endpoint supported three actions. The first, called the init step, saved the text segments as TXT files and created a CSV file for the results. The second, called status, handled progress tracking. Here, by returning the current TXT list and the "completed" items according to the CSV, a structure was set up to allow resuming from where it left off if no response was received from ChatGPT or if the process was interrupted for another reason. The third is the batch, i.e., bulk generation section. In this step, once the classification was defined, a structure was prepared that sent each TXT to the ChatGPT API to classify according to 15 Generic Frames of Boydstun et al. (2013) and received only JSON-formatted outputs in four fields: primary, secondary, confidence, and brief rationale. These fields were written row-wise to the same CSV, and in cases of classification errors, only a blank row was produced for monitoring purposes.

All agreement and performance metrics reported in the Findings were derived from the workflow built within this TXT-CSV-JSON triangle. The general workflow diagram is as shown in Figure 1.

Figure 1. Workflow applied by authors for labeling generic frames

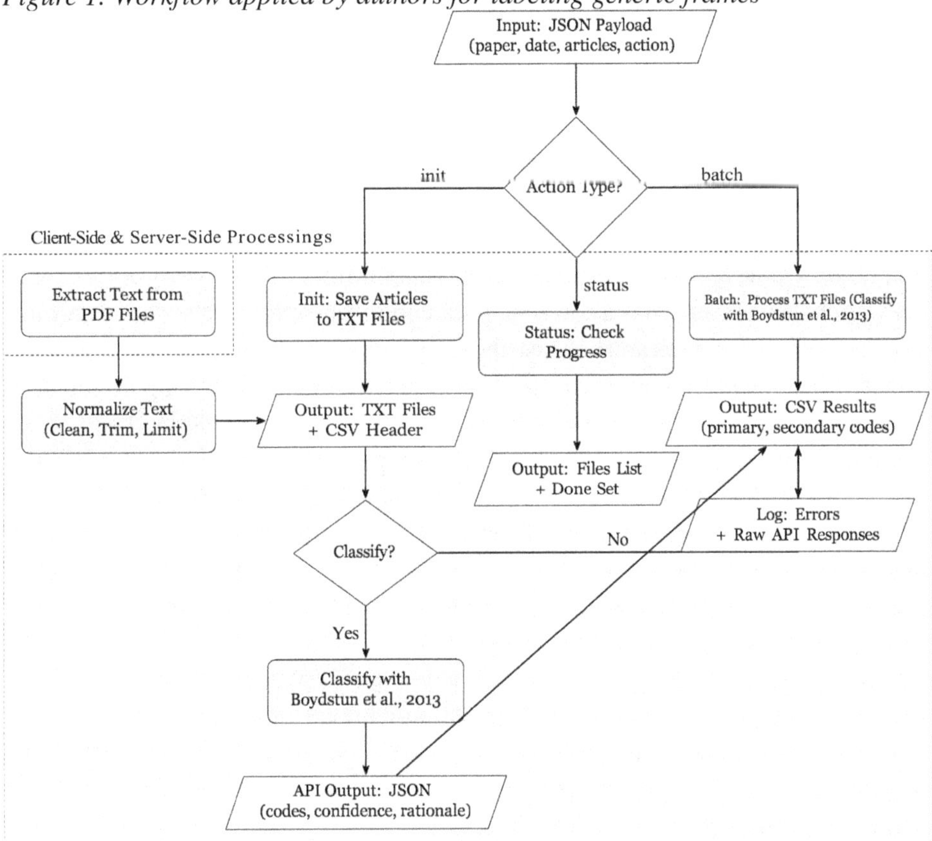

(Boydstun et al., 2013)

The raw texts obtained via PDF.js were subjected to uniform processing prior to content analysis. All characters and words including page titles, subheadings, page numbers, announcement and advertisement blocks, and the texts of tables and tables of contents, were individually parsed on the front end. However, no additional correction was applied. Processes such as word concatenation in Turkish or intra-paragraph line breaks were left as they were. In addition, for all requests made to the server side, ChatGPT parameters such as model ID, prompt version, temperature, top_p, and max_tokens, as well as the timestamp, response time, HTTP status, and token usage were logged. If classification failed, a blank row was written to the CSV containing the results table to preserve research consistency. Conversely, the relevant error code and raw response were stored in the log files, ensuring later auditability and the ability to resume from where the process left off. ChatGPT 5 was chosen as the system against which the web application would be compared. The same text segments converted to TXT on the same front end were manually sent to ChatGPT 5 one by one and processed.

FINDINGS

The PDF editions of the May 13, 2025 issues of Hurses and Istanbul Gazetesi were converted to plain text using the JavaScript-based PDF.js library and, to ensure comparability, the texts were segmented into approximately fixed-length units; this date was chosen because it is a common publication day within the scope of permissions for both newspapers and because the sample size was anticipated to be suitable in terms of data sufficiency. The target length of each unit was set at approximately 1,000 ± 200 characters (maximum 400 words). Each unit was defined as a news segment during analysis and labeled with a single primary category according to the Boydstun et al. (2013) topic classification. Coding was carried out independently by two large language models. As a result of these procedures, N = 163 news segments were obtained for Hurses and N = 167 for Istanbul Gazetesi. All computed accuracy, agreement, and F1 metrics, as well as reliability coefficients Cohen's κ (1960) and Krippendorff's α (2004), were calculated based on this unitization.

Dimensions are analyzed using Generic Frames as defined by Boydstun et al. (2013). Texts were preprocessed identically without any sentimental reflection or prioritization, unified into fixed-length segments. Each segment was independently labeled by researchers and the PHP endpoint based system that uses ChatGPT's gpt-4o-mini-2024-07-18 as large language model we described in methodology. Using 163 Hurses items dated 13 May 2025, we compared primary topic assignments between our web app and ChatGPT 5. We observed 94 exact matches out of 163 (Po=0.577). Treating ChatGPT 5 as the reference, we obtained micro-F1=0.577, macro-F1=0.610 and weighted F1=0.533. Reliability coefficients indicated moderate agreement: Cohen's κ=0.458 and Krippendorff's α (nominal with two coders)=0.432. Substantively, our web app tended to over-assign economics relative to the ChatGPT 5. We then applied the same coding and evaluation pipeline to Istanbul Gazetesi from the same date to assess cross-outlet consistency under a common protocol. This parallel design helps to clarify whether any API based-general usage based divergences are outlet-specific or reflect general tendencies of our web app. Using 167 Istanbul Gazetesi items dated 13 May 2025, we found 92 exact matches out of 167 (Po=0.551). As same as Hurses, with ChatGPT 5 as the reference, we obtained micro-F1=0.551, macro-F1=0.611 and weighted F1=0.486. Agreement was again moderate with Cohen's κ=0.473 and Krippendorff's α (nominal with two coders) = 0.459. Relative to the ChatGPT 5 distribution, our web app shows a systematic tilt: higher assignment to economics and lower to quality of life.

Table 1. Comparison in between PHP web app using GPT API and ChatGPT 5

Metric	HURSES	ISTANBUL
N	163	167
Exact matches	94	92
Observed agreement (Po)	0.577	0.551
Cohen's κ	0.458	0.473
Krippendorff's α	0.432	0.459
Micro-F1	0.577	0.551
Macro-F1	0.610	0.611
Weighted F1	0.533	0.486

Instead of attributing this similarity to any outlet-specific property, we note that it may partly reflect shared preprocessing and unitizing choices such as fixed-length segments, identical prompts possibilities, model and other ChatGPT specific parameters. We therefore interpret cross-outlet similarity cautiously as a possible design effect rather than evidence of generalizability. On the other hand, approximate κ results stay between 0.46 and 0.47 indicates moderate agreement under Landis and Koch's benchmarks (from 0.41 to 0.60 which means moderate according to Landis & Koch, 1977), while Krippendorff's α is around 0.43-0.46 sits below commonly recommended adequacy thresholds for content analysis (more than 0.667 for tentative conclusions and more than 0.800 for strong conclusions recommended by Krippendorff, 2004: 241). The relatively lower α is expected with many categories, class-imbalance, prevalence and fine-grained boundaries. According to the distribution from ChatGPT 5, the most frequent categories were economics by 28.8%, cultural identity by 16.0%, health and safety by 14.1% for Hurses, and economics by 20.4%, health and safety by 19.2% and quality of life by 13.2% for Istanbul Gazetesi.

DISCUSSION

Within the scope of the study, content analysis was conducted by two different large language models based on the 15-dimensional framing system proposed by Boydstun et al. (2013). Human coding or validation was not included in the process.

The findings were evaluated on the basis of inter-model consistency, and the Krippendorff's α results remained in the 0.43–0.46 range. Since these values fall below the α = 0.667 threshold, the main hypothesis was rejected (Krippendorff, 2004, s. 241; Krippendorff, 2018). By contrast, the Cohen's κ value yielded results in the 0.46–0.47 range. This result indicates a moderate level of agreement according to Landis and Koch (1977). Although our results do not directly represent a need due to the absence of human coding, the low level of agreement points to a process that necessitates human validation. In other words, they resemble prior studies in the literature that emphasize the need for validation before using LLMs for coding and that point to the necessity of human oversight (Stromer-Galley et al., 2025; Bojić et al., 2025). Based on this, reading the results with a focus on consistency, we should note the emergence of a point indicating that LLMs be used as supportive tools in processes such as content analysis (Tagle, 2025).

Alongside the findings obtained in the study, the limitations of the research that we believe affected these findings also need to be mentioned. The analysis during the study was limited to a single day and two newspapers. While this choice offers advantages in terms of the alignment of access and permission conditions and the auditability of workload, it restricts the temporal and institutional generalizability of the findings. Additionally, it was observed that the character-based fixed-length approach we used to segment the news that defined as 1000 ± 200 characters, could at times split natural news boundaries and weaken frame signals. This can lead us to the conclusion that it may introduce a bias causing topics of different lengths to stand out more. It is considered that sensitivity analyses using paragraph- and headline-based natural units or sentence-level alternatives could improve the performance reported here. Therefore, it is assumed that benefiting from AI on the front end when processing news text, rather than simple JavaScript systems, would be important. Another limitation is that using the same preprocessing, the same prompt, and the same model parameters for both newspapers may have produced a design effect that increases cross-environment similarity. In addition, the RAG system was not preferred in the study in order to test the model's ability to assign to the Boydstun et al. (2013) framework solely on the basis of the internal structure of the text. However, for future studies, it is thought that repeating the process together with a RAG system on the axis of a larger data pool would be beneficial both to reduce context loss between articles, to address any potential unfair rises among frame dimensions independent of the character limit, and to produce more auditable responses. Finally, it is recommended that the Boydstun et al. (2013) dimensions be revisited with an expanded code set whose reliability–validity process has been completed scientifically. It is assumed that a code–category library to be built in the context of RAG with a larger sample will yield much higher agreement results.

RESULTS

While artificial intelligence changes the perspective on the communication environment, it also affects academic evaluation processes. Within this inevitable process, it appears that, for now, it is not very feasible to approach studies from a fully human-free perspective. The low agreement observed between different models based on the same architecture suggests that, at present, it is not possible to establish a system that is reproducible or generalizable. However, it can be said that overcoming various limitations that particularly by employing structures that can be fed with broad code–category libraries such as RAG systems, would correspondingly raise agreement rates. On the other hand, special care is required in complex analyses such as content analysis, where subjective judgments also come into play. Still, it is evident that a substantial time saving is achieved. Yet this saving must likewise be supported by additional measurements. Moreover, it should be assumed that erroneous results may generate costs significant enough to necessitate repeating the studies.

ACKNOWLEDGEMENT

The authors acknowledge administrations of Hurses and Istanbul Gazetesi for granting permission to use their publication materials for research purposes. All necessary permissions were obtained prior to data collection and analysis.

REFERENCES

Athens Technology Center. (2025, February 26). World Press Trends Outlook 2024–2025: How News Publishers Are Adapting to Change and Embracing AI-Driven Growth. Retrieved September 1, 2025, from https://www.atc.gr/wan-ifras-latest-world-press-trends-2024-2025-report/

Bazlutckaia, M., & Sytnik, A. (2023, June 28-July 1). Frame analysis in Russian with ChatGPT. Science Media International Forum, Saint-Petersburg, Russia.

Boydstun, A. E., Gross, J. H., Resnik, P., & Smith, N. A. (2013, September 16). Identifying media frames and frame dynamics within and across policy issues [Conference paper]. New Directions in Analyzing Text as Data Workshop, London, United Kingdom.

Bojić, L., Zagovora, O., Zelenkauskaite, A., Veseljević Jerković, S., Vuković, V., Čabarkapa, M., & Jovančević, A. (2025). Comparing large language models and human annotators in latent content analysis of sentiment, political leaning, emotional intensity and sarcasm. *Scientific Reports, 15*, 11477.

Card, D., Boydstun, A. E., Gross, J. H., Resnik, P., & Smith, N. A. (2015). The Media Frames Corpus: Annotations of frames across issues. In *Proceedings of the 53rd Annual Meeting of the Association for Computational Linguistics and the 7th International Joint Conference on Natural Language Processing* (Vol. 2, pp. 438-444). Association for Computational Linguistics.

Cohen, J. (1960). A coefficient of agreement for nominal scales. *Educational and Psychological Measurement, 20*(1), 37–46.

Devlin, J., Chang, M.-W., Lee, K., & Toutanova, K. (2019). BERT: Pre-training of deep bidirectional transformers for language understanding. *NAACL-HLT, 2019*, 4171–4186.

Entman, R. M. (1993). Framing: Toward clarification of a fractured paradigm. *Journal of Communication, 43*(4), 51–58.

Google. (2025). Embeddings (Machine Learning Crash Course). Retrieved September 1, 2025, from https://developers.google.com/machine-learning/crash-course/embeddings

Heseltine, M., & Clemm von Hohenberg, B. (2024). Large language models as a substitute for human experts in annotating political text. *Research and Politics*, *11*(1), 1–10.

Krippendorff, K. (2004). *Content Analysis: An Introduction to Its Methodology* (2nd ed.). Sage Publications.

Krippendorff, K. (2018). *Content Analysis: An Introduction to Its Methodology* (4th ed.). SAGE.

Landis, J. R., & Koch, G. G. (1977). The measurement of observer agreement for categorical data. *Biometrics*, *33*(1), 159–174.

Lewis, P., Perez, E., Piktus, A., Petroni, F., Karpukhin, V., Goyal, N., Küttler, H., Lewis, M., Yih, W.-T., Rocktäschel, T., Riedel, S., & Kiela, D. (2020). Retrieval-augmented generation for knowledge-intensive NLP tasks. Advances in Neural Information Processing Systems, 33, 9459–9474. Retrieved September 3, 2025, from https://proceedings.neurips.cc/paper/2020/file/6b493230205f780e1bc26945df7481e5-Paper.pdf

Lipka, M. (2025, April 28). Americans largely foresee AI having negative effects on news, journalists. Pew Research Center. Retrieved September 1, 2025, from https://www.pewresearch.org/short-reads/2025/04/28/americans-largely-foresee-ai-having-negative-effects-on-news-journalists/

Liu, Z. (2024). Fine-tuning technologies for reducing the FER bias across various distributions. In Y. Wang (Ed.), Proceedings of the 2024 2nd International Conference on Image, Algorithms and Artificial Intelligence (ICIAAI 2024) (Advances in Computer Science Research, Vol. 115). Atlantis Press.

Lupano, E. (2025). Of Pride and Patriotism. The Representation of Artificial Intelligence in Chinese Official and Media Discourse. In Lupano, E., & Orrù, P. (Eds.), *Artificial Intelligenceand Human Perception Media Discourse and Public Opinion* (pp. 83–109).

Merritt, R. (2025, January 31). What is retrieval-augmented generation, aka RAG? NVIDIA Blog. Retrieved September 1, 2025, from https://blogs.nvidia.com/blog/what-is-retrieval-augmented-generation/

Mikolov, T., Chen, K., Corrado, G., & Dean, J. (2013). Efficient estimation of word representations in vector space. arXiv. Retrieved September 1, 2025, from https://arxiv.org/abs/1301.3781

Muller, B. (2022, March 2). BERT 101, State Of The Art NLP Model Explained. Hugging Face, Retrieved September 3, 2025, from https://huggingface.co/blog/bert-101

Najafi, A., & Varol, O. (2024). TurkishBERTweet: Fast and reliable large language model for social media analysis. *Expert Systems with Applications*, *255*(Part C), 124737.

Newman, N., Ross Arguedas, A., Robertson, C. T., Fletcher, R., & Nielsen, R. K. (2025). Digital News Report 2025. Reuters Institute for the Study of Journalism, University of Oxford. Retrieved September 1, 2025, from https://reutersinstitute.politics.ox.ac.uk/digital-news-report/2025

Nurzhanov, A., & Sharipbay, A. (2025). Modern AI models for text analysis: A comparison of ChatGPT and RAG. *Journal of Data Analytics and Artificial Intelligence Applications*, *1*(1), 1–13.

Özkececi, Z. (2018). Die Perspektiven des türkischen Journalismus: Ein Drahtseilakt zwischen eingeschränkter Pressefreiheit und begrenzten Alternativen. *SWS-Rundschau*, *58*(3), 349–371.

Özkeçeci, Z. (2019). Citizen journalism-opportunities and challenges. Asya Studies-Academic Social Studies/Akademik Sosyal Araştırmalar, (8), 33-39.

Semetko, H. A., & Valkenburg, P. M. (2000). Framing European politics: A content analysis of press and television news. *Journal of Communication*, *50*(2), 93–109.

Stromer-Galley, J., McKernan, B., Zaman, S., Maganur, C., & Regmi, S. (2025). The Efficacy of Large Language Models and Crowd Annotation for Accurate Content Analysis of Political Social Media Messages. *Social Science Computer Review*.

Tagle, F. (2025). Why Radio is More Reliable Than Television During Social Protests: An Explanation Through Framing Theory. *Journal of Radio & Audio Media*, 1–15.

Tai, R. H., Bentley, L. R., Xia, X., Sitt, J. M., Fankhauser, S. C., Chicas-Mosier, A. M., & Monteith, B. G. (2024). An examination of the use of large language models to aid analysis of textual data. *International Journal of Qualitative Methods*, *23*, 1–14.

Than, N., Fan, L., Law, T., Nelson, L. K., & McCall, L. (2025). Updating "the future of coding": Qualitative coding with generative large language models. *Sociological Methods & Research*, *54*(3), 849–888.

Törnberg, P. (2024). Large language models outperform expert coders and supervised classifiers at annotating political social media messages. *Social Science Computer Review*, *0*(0), 1–15.

Türkmen, B., & Koçlu Maman, S. (2024). Yapay zeka destekli haber metni üretimi ve çevirilerinin karşılaştırmalı bir analizi: ChatGPT-4o örneği. İstanbul Üniversitesi Çeviribilim Dergisi, 21, 212-229.

Vu, T., Iyyer, M., Wang, X., Constant, N., Wei, J., Wei, J., Tar, C., Sung, Y.-H., Zhou, D., Le, Q., & Luong, T. (2024). FreshLLMs: Refreshing large language models with search engine augmentation. In *Findings of the Association for Computational Linguistics* (pp. 13697–13720). ACL.

Yapar Gönenç, A. (2012). Medya ve Haber. İstanbul Üniversitesi İletişim Fakültesi Dergisi, 14, 77-89.

Chapter 2
Artificial Intelligence and Data Analysis in Communication:
New Dynamics of Digital Transformation

Berrin Aslan Öztezcan
https://orcid.org/0000-0002-8781-735X
Doğuş University, Turkey

ABSTRACT

Digital transformation is leading to radical changes, especially in the field of communication; artificial intelligence and data analysis have become key components of this transformation. Traditional communication practices are being replaced by big data analytics, algorithms, and AI-powered content production processes. This change is profoundly affecting communication disciplines such as media, journalism, advertising, and marketing. This section comprehensively examines the role of artificial intelligence and data analysis in the field of communication, exploring how these technologies are used in many areas, from news production to digital marketing, social media management, and target audience analysis. It also addresses critical issues such as the ethical problems, privacy violations, and data security risks that these technologies bring with them.

1. INTRODUCTION

Today, with the impact of digitalization, there is an incredible flow of data in the digital world every minute. According to Domo's Data Never Sleeps 12.0

DOI: 10.4018/979-8-3373-2960-4.ch002

report (2024), Google AI's Gemini receives 8,574 visitors per minute, while 5.9 million Google searches are made worldwide. Netflix users consume 362,962 hours of content, 16,000 new videos are uploaded on TikTok and 3,472,222 videos are viewed on YouTube. Facebook and Instagram Reels content was viewed 138.9 million times, while Snapchat users sent 3.3 million snaps. Voice assistants also play an important role in this busy ecosystem; for example, Siri answers 1,041,666 questions per minute Communication and collaboration platforms also contribute to massive data generation. Every minute, 251.1 million emails are sent, 18.8 million text messages are sent and 9,000 people apply for jobs on LinkedIn. Microsoft Teams users generate a total of 229 million meeting minutes per minute, while the Zoom app is downloaded 288 times per minute.

These striking statistics show how much digitalization is integrated into the daily lives of individuals and how huge amounts of data are generated every minute. As seen in Figure 1, digitally generated data is expected to reach approximately 175 zettabytes in 2025 (Reinsel, Gantz, & Rydning, 2018).

Figure 1. Growth rate of digital data over the years

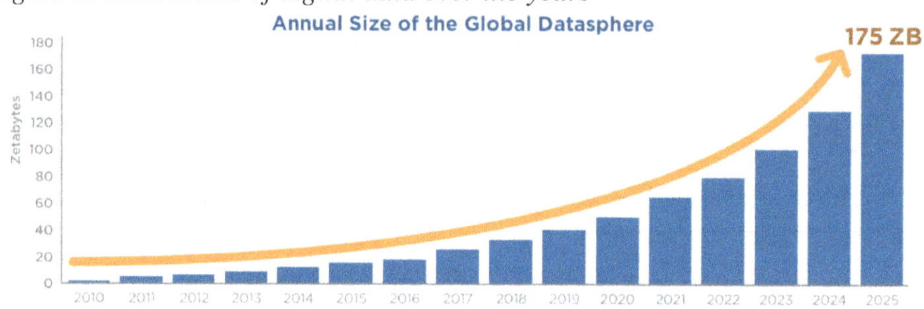

This ever-increasing flow of data shows that the digital ecosystem is constantly expanding and data-driven technologies are becoming increasingly central.

Digital transformation is leading to fundamental changes, especially in the field of communication, with artificial intelligence and data analytics becoming key components of this transformation. Traditional communication practices are being replaced by content production processes supported by big data analytics, algorithms and artificial intelligence. This change deeply affects communication disciplines such as media, journalism, advertising and marketing.

This chapter provides a comprehensive overview of the role of artificial intelligence and data analytics in the field of communication and examines how these technologies are being used in various fields ranging from news production to digital marketing, from social media management to audience analysis. In addition, critical issues such as ethical issues, privacy violations and data security risks that these technologies bring with them are also covered.

2. DIGITAL TRANSFORMATION AND PARADIGM SHIFT IN COMMUNICATION

With the impact of digitalization and internet technologies, radical transformations have taken place in people's daily lives. The way individuals use language, their bodily reactions, mental activities and behaviors have changed significantly when interacting with smart devices. Technology has not only transformed relations between individuals and societies; it has also reshaped the human relationship with space, nature and objects. This transformation enabled by digitalization has transformed the human body and the way of communication through interaction with smart objects, as well as economic and cultural organizations. Today, interaction with artificial intelligence allows people to use their fingers, gestures and voices in ways they never could before. As technology becomes an extension of the body, symbolic and physical meanings are attached to these tools, creating a two-way need in the human-technology relationship (Kaplan & Kaplan, 2020, s. 191).

This change has profoundly affected communication processes and pushed the limits of classical communication theories. The classical communication model developed by Shannon and Weaver defines communication as a linear process between sender, message, channel and receiver (Shannon & Weaver, 1963). This model treats communication as a technical problem and focuses on the correct transmission of the message. However, it left out more complex dimensions such as the meaning, context and subject of the message.

With the digital transformation, this linear and human-centered understanding has been replaced by a multi-actor, multi-layered and interactive communication model. Communication is no longer just an exchange of meaning between humans, but has become a network of multiple relationships involving technological subjects such as software, algorithms and artificial intelligence. Especially in computer-mediated communication, the assumption that the other party is human has lost its validity. This is because communication today often takes place in the form of man-machine or machine-machine (Wiener, 1989, p. 16).

This situation has led to the necessity of reconsidering technology in the field of communication not only as a tool but also as an active subject of communication. In this context, artificial intelligence should be considered not only as a system that processes information, but also as a communicative entity that can construct meaning, initiate and sustain interaction. Therefore, the basic concepts in communication science should also be rethought with this perspective; and the human-centered understanding should be moved beyond (Guzman & Lewis, 2019) .

The main driving force of this structural transformation is technological advances. In particular, the Fourth Industrial Revolution is being shaped by knowledge-based technologies such as artificial intelligence, information technologies and robotic-sensor systems. These technologies, combined with knowledge-intensive approaches, ensure the continuity of digital transformation. Today, there is a consensus not only among scientists but also among the general public that the fundamental energy of this transformation is "information". Artificial intelligence stands out at the center of this process with its capacity to process information (Öztemel, 2020, pp. 100-101).

The integration of advances in media and communication technologies with artificial intelligence has made digital transformation more visible in Turkey and the world (Kırık & Özkoçak, 2023, p. 73) . This transformation covers not only interpersonal communication, but also many professional fields, from restructuring marketing strategies to digital journalism to shaping social media algorithms according to user behavior. Therefore, it seems that a radical paradigm shift in the field of communication is inevitable.

In the light of all these developments, the applicability of artificial intelligence in the field of communication is becoming increasingly evident. Machines that can produce articles as if they were written by human hands, machines that interact naturally, algorithms that can perform effective competitor analysis and systems that automatically generate news texts offer innovative solutions in the field of communication. Thus, artificial intelligence stands out as a transformative and decisive force in communication (Yıldız, 2021, p. 609).

3. DATA SCIENCE AND DATA ANALYTICS

Data science is an interdisciplinary field that aims to obtain meaningful information by analyzing large and complex data sets. In this field, data are processed and interpreted using methods such as statistics, machine learning and data visualization (Sağlam & Cengiz, 2023) .

Although the term data science is new, in fact, the definitions we make today as data science cover definitions that already exist but for different fields. For example, statistical analysis of datasets has a long history as a field. Again, data visualization was a field that was studied in the past. Or studies and discussions on data ethics are just as old. So why the need for a new definition of "data science" today? It can be said that "convergence" is at the heart of this need. Components such as statistics, methodology, computer science, and domain knowledge were integrated with the need to extract meaningful information from big data, and the convergence that occurred in this way, together with the systematic structure of science trying to reach generalizations, led to the conceptualization of data science (Sütcü & Aytekin, 2018).

This transformation has not only remained at the theoretical level, but also transformed data analysis practices with technological developments. Although statistical analyses are still among the basic methods in data analysis today, the advancement of technology, the proliferation of data sources, the increase in the amount of data produced and the differentiation of data types have led to the development and diversification of analysis methods. Due to these developments, the strict boundaries between research fields have become increasingly blurred, and interdisciplinary interaction and information exchange have increased (Emre & Erol, 2017, p. 166) . Thus, data science has become a product of interdisciplinary interaction rather than just an analysis tool.

In this context, it is also necessary to mention concepts such as artificial intelligence, machine learning and deep learning, which are frequently mentioned together with data science. Although they are related to each other, these concepts represent different disciplines. While data science works with big data, artificial intelligence aims to develop systems that can make human-like decisions using this data (Amazon Web Services, 2023). Machine learning, as a sub-branch of AI, involves the process of learning from data. Deep learning, on the other hand, is the most advanced form of machine learning and functions to extract meaning from large and complex data sets (Amazon Web Services, 2023) . The relationship between these concepts is shown in Figure 2 (Coderspace, 2024) .

Figure 2. The relationship between artificial intelligence, machine learning, deep learning, and data science

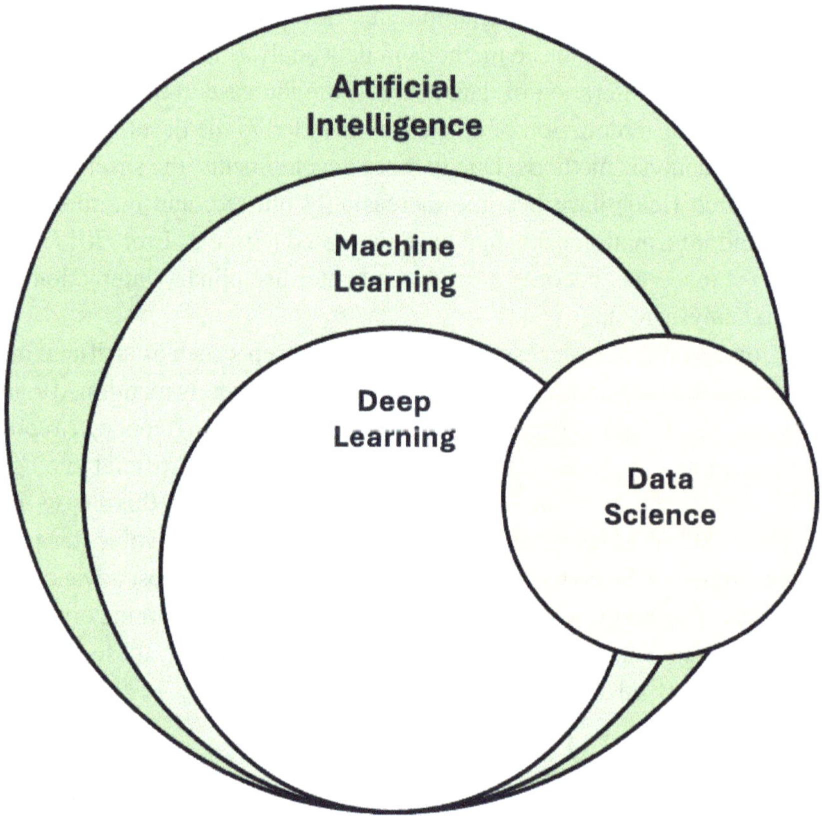

The complementarity of these technological structures has visibly increased the practical impact of data science in different sectors. Today, data in finance, health, education and many other fields are stored in large databases. Today, data in many fields such as finance, health, education and many more are collected in large databases, and data science aims to process this raw data and transform it into meaningful outputs. While raw data by itself has no meaning, processing it with the right analysis techniques provides predictable and useful results in many areas from marketing strategies to medical diagnostics. Properly analyzed databases are no longer mere storage spaces; they become dynamic sources of information that feed strategic decision processes (Fayyad, Piatetsky-Shapiro, & Smyth, 1996) .

The practical implications of data science are far-reaching. For example, applications that advise doctors in the treatment processes of patients and predict health threats such as cancer risk become possible through in-depth analysis of data. Algorithms that detect sentiment in social media posts can measure the mood of the public using natural language processing and sentiment analysis. Likewise, systems that match the right employees with the right companies use data mining and machine learning techniques to make the labor market more efficient. In addition, applications that can recognize people through biometric data and written content play an important role in security. In factories, predictive maintenance methods increase production efficiency by predicting machine failures with IoT and data-driven analytics. Personalized electricity tariffs make it possible to use energy more economically and efficiently by analyzing the consumption data of individuals. These examples show how data science can transform everyday life and make it more personalized, efficient and secure (Kılınç & Başeğmez, 2022) .

4. ARTIFICIAL INTELLIGENCE AND COMMUNICATION

In 1950, Alan Turing, in his article "Computing Machinery and Intelligence", questioned the ability of machines to think and introduced the concept of Turing Test (Turing, 1950) . The basic question Turing asked at this point was "Can machines think?". According to him, if a computer can imitate human behavior to such an extent that it cannot distinguish whether the person in front of it is a human or a machine during written communication with a human, this computer should be considered intelligent. With this idea, although the concept of artificial intelligence was not directly defined, the idea that such a system could exist began to be seriously discussed in the 1950s (Demirel, 2023, p. 9843) .

Following these discussions, the Dartmouth Conference held in 1956 was an important turning point where the term artificial intelligence was used for the first time and this field was defined as an independent research discipline. This conference, attended by pioneering scientists such as John McCarthy, Marvin Minsky, Nathaniel Rochester and Claude Shannon, gave a systematic direction to artificial intelligence studies (Mutlu, 2024) .

Developments in the field of artificial intelligence have not only been limited to technical calculations, but have also profoundly affected human-machine interaction. In his 1960 article "Man-Computer Symbiosis", Licklider emphasized that human-computer interaction should be similar to human-human interaction. According to Licklider, just as people's reactions to each other depend on the other person's attitude, similar dynamics should be created in interaction with computers (Çağıltay, 2018) .

Today, this view has become a concrete reality thanks to developing technologies. Artificial intelligence systems have reached the capacity to communicate more naturally and harmoniously by better understanding human reactions. In this context, artificial intelligence is defined not only as a system that processes information, but also as a technological structure that can perform human-specific skills such as thinking, decision-making and interacting (Can & Sezgin, 2024, p. 105) . Artificial intelligence, which includes technologies such as natural language processing, machine learning, deep learning and computer vision, has a wide range of applications (Haleem, Javaid, Qadri, Singh, & Suman, 2022, p. 120) .

While artificial intelligence refers to computer systems that have the ability to think and make decisions like humans, communication is a multidimensional process that enables the exchange of information. At this point, there is an inseparable link between artificial intelligence and communication. Today, artificial intelligence can communicate effectively with humans through chatbots, virtual assistants and natural language processing techniques, and help overcome communication barriers through translation or sign language applications. Thus, communication between people becomes faster, easier and more efficient; artificial intelligence facilitates information sharing by acting as a bridge (Koçyiğit & Darı, 2023, p.432). This situation reveals the importance of artificial intelligence both as a tool equipped with technical skills and as an effective intermediary in human interactions.

In a study conducted by Hohenstein et al. (2023), the effects of AI-supported intelligent response suggestions on interpersonal communication were examined. According to the research findings, participants tend to use the response suggestions provided by artificial intelligence. This increases the speed of communication and makes the emotional tone of the language more positive.

The rise of AI-enabled technologies in the field of communication is not limited to interpersonal interaction. Robot journalism applications in news reporting, personalized campaigns in digital marketing and algorithms analyzing user behavior on social media show that artificial intelligence is radically transforming communication processes on both individual and mass scales. However, this transformation also brings with it certain risks and responsibilities. Issues such as ethical principles, privacy protection and data reliability are areas that should not be ignored when evaluating the social impacts of AI-enabled communication systems.

Therefore, the role of artificial intelligence in communication should be considered not only as a technological development, but also from social, cultural and ethical perspectives, and its multifaceted nature should be placed at the center of scientific research.

5. ARTIFICIAL INTELLIGENCE AND DATA ANALYTICS IN NEWS PRODUCTION

The rapid development of artificial intelligence and data analysis technologies has ushered in a new era in news production processes, different from traditional methods. These technologies profoundly transform the practice of journalism both technically and ethically, offering significant advantages in terms of speed and scope in the collection, analysis and presentation of news (Böyük, 2024, p. 49) . One of the most concrete examples of this transformation is robot journalism.

Robot journalism emerged when artificial intelligence algorithms integrated into social media platforms or various data sources imitated human-specific processes such as reasoning, inference, generalization and learning from past experiences. This new type of journalism creates human-like narratives by shaping the communication between data through algorithms; however, the issue of how this mechanical and hybrid structure will construct new human narratives has still not been adequately addressed (Tellan, 2022) .

Looking at the technical workings of robot journalism, Diakopoulos (2014) summarized this process in five basic steps:

1- Collecting data,
2- Analyzing newsworthy elements in data,
3- Identify and prioritize relevant perspectives,
4- To relate these perspectives to the main points of the news story,
5- Producing the final news text.

These processes systematically demonstrate how robot journalism can produce news without human intervention. Today, artificial intelligence firms such as Automated Insights, Narrative Science and Yseop are putting robot journalism into practice by developing chatbots, automated reporting systems and news production algorithms. These systems not only fulfill existing journalistic tasks but also have the potential to reach areas that traditional journalism cannot. By analyzing content published in different languages, these systems can produce multidimensional and comprehensive summaries of events, synthesize information from text and visuals, and bridge the gap between two worlds (Gülleb, 2022, p. 172) .

However, although AI-based systems have the capacity to accelerate and diversify the news production process, current technologies are not yet capable of replacing human judgment. It is not yet possible in today's technology for artificial intelligence to replace humans in journalism, especially in cases where there are no figures, thought production, discussion or social analysis is required (Ay, 2023, p. 431) . Therefore, while robotic journalism systems are powerful in terms of fast data access and content production, human judgment is still indispensable for social and ethical dimensions.

In terms of the journalism profession, the proliferation of artificial intelligence in the field of journalism means that the role of journalists is changing. Instead of just gathering and writing news, there is a need for journalists who can analyze data, control algorithms and use technology ethically (Beckett & Yaseen, 2023) . This shows that ethical supervision has become an indispensable element in journalism as much as digital literacy.

News platforms based on artificial intelligence and human collaboration offer practical examples of this transformation. For example, organizations such as Knowhere News are taking important steps to use AI to ensure news objectivity and restore public trust. By combining artificial intelligence with human collaboration, Knowhere identifies the most talked-about news stories on social media and analyzes news headlines from different political tendencies to produce objective, balanced content. This method clearly demonstrates the role of data-driven journalism in credible journalism (Inverse, 2018) .

On the other hand, the increasing effectiveness of artificial intelligence technologies in the production and circulation of information brings with it various problems in terms of ethics and security. In particular, presenting texts, images and videos produced through artificial intelligence to the public in a way that distorts the perception of reality can lead to disinformation becoming a systematic tool (Bekar, 2024) . As Özkeçeci (2019) notes, technical innovations have made it possible for fake news to spread much easier and faster. Such content violates individual rights, undermines social trust and damages the information ecosystem.

In conclusion, the rise of artificial intelligence and data analysis technologies in journalism is radically changing the nature of the journalism profession and the way news is produced and consumed. In this process, it is of great importance for journalists to gain technological literacy and to develop algorithms in accordance with transparent and ethical principles. While the potential of artificial intelligence in news production is undeniable, the social impacts of this transformation should be constantly reviewed and the human-centered journalism approach should be preserved.

6. ARTIFICIAL INTELLIGENCE AND DATA ANALYTICS IN DIGITAL MARKETING

Artificial intelligence is a term that is frequently heard today and is generally associated with positive sciences. However, with the impact of Industry 4.0, this concept is not only limited to positive sciences but has started to affect many different branches of science (Binbir, 2021, p. 314) . In this transformation process, especially the field of marketing has become one of the sectors that feel the impact of artificial intelligence intensely.

In today's competitive environment, brands use marketing strategies with artificial intelligence technologies in order to establish a healthy communication with existing and potential customers and direct them to purchase. With its interdisciplinary and constantly evolving structure, artificial intelligence marketing is becoming one of the main communication tools to respond to customer expectations and create user-oriented strategies (Kavut, 2022, p. 542) .

In this context, artificial intelligence can be integrated into marketing under seven main headings (Zeydan, 2024, p. 434):

1. Content production
2. Personalization
3. Search engine optimization (SEO)
4. Customer behavior analysis
5. Chatbots and customer service
6. Data Analytics
7. Automation

Each of these areas is supported by different types of AI technologies. For example, advanced machine learning algorithms underpin recommendation systems on platforms such as Amazon and Netflix, while deep learning techniques enable the automatic analysis and tagging of billions of images on social media platforms. In addition, automated bidding algorithms instantly evaluate users' profiles and present the most appropriate ad offer, while chat bots aim to increase customer loyalty through human-like interactions. In addition, AI-powered applications such as social media mining, sentiment analysis and churn prevention improve the accuracy of marketing decisions by processing large and complex data in real time. All these applications significantly improve the overall performance of businesses (Ma & Sun, 2020, p. 482) .

Kavut's (2022) research shows that artificial intelligence is effective not only in technology companies but also in different fields such as the food sector. In the case of Domino's Pizza, it was found that AI algorithms significantly increased marketing success and customer satisfaction (p.549). This clearly demonstrates the strategic role and growing importance of AI in different sectors.

The use of AI in marketing also brings some disadvantages. One of these disadvantages is the threats to data privacy and security. While AI applications make it necessary to provide and share data in marketing processes, they also become a potential threat. In addition, the risk of misuse of information is also an important problem. In addition, the fact that machines make decisions on behalf of humans and become autonomous over time raises important questions in terms of ethics and control (Zeydan, 2024, p. 442) .

Çeber's (2024, June) research on the advertising sector in the context of artificial intelligence ethics supports these concerns. According to the research findings, the majority of the participants evaluated artificial intelligence applications as problematic in terms of data security and privacy and stated that these applications are insufficient in terms of transparency (p.79). Harari (2018) makes the following assessment:

They capture our attention by offering us free information, services and entertainment, and then sell it to advertisers. But the data giants probably have much bigger ambitions than the old attention merchants. Their main business is certainly not selling advertising. By capturing our attention, they manage to collect an inordinate amount of data about us, which is more valuable than the total revenue from advertising. We are their product, not their customer.

Therefore, the use of artificial intelligence in marketing represents not only a technological transformation but also a multi-layered change that needs to be addressed with its ethical, social and legal dimensions.

7. ARTIFICIAL INTELLIGENCE POWERED SOCIAL MEDIA ALGORITHMS

With the increasing amount of content on social media platforms, it has become increasingly impossible for users to consume all content individually. This forces users to choose between content. Changing social media algorithms over time have also affected this process; while initially users saw the content of the accounts they followed sorted according to the time of sharing, today algorithms offer personalized content in accordance with their interests, expectations and habits in line with the data obtained from users' behavior on the internet (Bilgici, 2023, p. 223) .

At this point, efforts to personalize the experience offered by social media platforms make large-scale data processing techniques inevitable. The collected user data has reached a volume too large to be analyzed by manual methods. Artificial intelligence systems come into play in the process of classifying and making sense of this data; they not only analyze data, but also learn user habits and create personalized content streams (Koçyiğit & Koçyiğit, Artificial Intelligence and New Media: Opportunities, Threats and Future Perspectives, 2024, p. 77) . Thus, the social media experience is shaped in a more fluid, fast and interesting way.

Artificial intelligence-supported algorithms used in social media platforms differ according to the purpose of the platform and the user audience. For example, the Facebook algorithm focuses more on interactions around family and friends, while LinkedIn algorithms emphasize employee interactions through professional connections. Twitter ranks content based not only on user interest, but also on historical timing and current events. Instagram, on the other hand, ranks posts by analyzing engagement signals such as interest level, content popularity, likes, comments, saves and shares in order to show the user as much content as possible throughout the day (Karaman, 2021, p. 1345) . These platforms learn user behavior through artificial intelligence-supported algorithms and aim to provide the most relevant content to the user.

Although the algorithmic structure of social media seems to facilitate users' access to information, in the long run it turns into a structure that limits the intellectual diversity of individuals, feeds one-way perspectives and weakens critical thinking skills. The fact that algorithms present content according to user habits reduces the visibility of different opinions, thus confining access to information to a narrow framework. This process, which is carried out under the name of personalization, unwittingly leads users into a digital uniformity, creating individuals trapped in echo chambers. As a result, artificial intelligence-supported algorithms, rather than enriching the digital experience of individuals, make them dependent on certain content and pave the way for deepening information pollution and social polarization (Sarı, 2025, p. 51) . Therefore, reshaping the algorithms of social media platforms in a way that encourages the intellectual diversity of users and includes content with a wide range of perspectives is critical for creating a healthier information ecosystem in the digital world.

8. ARTIFICIAL INTELLIGENCE AND ETHICAL ISSUES

Artificial intelligence is a broad and multidimensional field where different techniques and forms of application come together. The diversity in its areas of use makes it necessary to address the ethical problems arising from artificial intelligence in a field-specific manner. As a matter of fact, the ethics of artificial intelligence differs in every field where it is applied and brings context-specific ethical evaluations. Especially in the field of communication, ethical issues such as data privacy and privacy violations, algorithmic bias and discrimination, lack of transparency and accountability come to the fore.

The new online environment has transformed into a structure that deeply affects society and individuals with dynamics shaped by artificial intelligence and algorithms. All individuals and organizations in this environment must strike a fine balance between freedom and privacy. Issues such as how and by whom online data will be processed, for what purpose it will be used, and where ethical boundaries begin and end are not just technical issues, but are of great social, legal and ethical importance. In this context, the privacy and security of digital data becomes a deep and complex issue that cannot be left to the conscience of algorithms (Işık, Ölçekçi, & Koz, 2022, p. 1266) .

Data, which is the basic building block of artificial intelligence systems, mostly contains personal information of individuals. The unauthorized collection, storage or use of this data for commercial purposes may lead to significant ethical violations. As a matter of fact, security vulnerabilities and privacy concerns increase when individuals' voice, image, location, identity or financial information are compromised by malicious individuals. With the development of artificial intelligence technologies, the number and impact of such violations are increasing significantly (Darı & Koçyiğit, 2024, p. 254) . If necessary precautions are not taken during the collection, storage, analysis and use of data sets, serious problems such as privacy, security, algorithmic biases, discrimination and manipulation may arise within the scope of data ethics (Çeber, 2024, p.17).

Artificial intelligence is not inherently ethical or unethical; however, how it is used can lead to various ethical problems. Indeed, examples such as artificial intelligence discriminating on the basis of race or gender have already been recorded (Tünalp, 2024, p. 1042) . AI's failure to provide algorithmic neutrality may create inequality between different groups, which may reinforce discrimination.

The lack of accountability and transparency of AI technologies causes users to lack sufficient information about the functioning of algorithms. This undermines trust in AI systems, especially in critical areas such as combating disinformation (Sarı, 2025, p. 58) . Non-transparent structures restrict users' access to inquiry and audit mechanisms on AI, which poses serious ethical problems.

In Turkey, the Personal Data Protection Authority (KVKK) published a report titled "Recommendations on the Protection of Personal Data in the Field of Artificial Intelligence" to determine the ethical framework in artificial intelligence applications. According to the report, key ethical and security considerations in AI systems include preventing discrimination, collecting only necessary personal information, and processing data in a way that cannot be associated with identity. It is also emphasized that algorithms should be designed to be transparent, traceable and accountable. Giving users the right to access, correct, delete and object to the processing of their data is also seen as part of ethical responsibility. In addition to all these, it is stated that necessary technical measures should be taken for the security of personal data, protection against unauthorized access and data security should be integrated into the design of the system from the very beginning. In this framework, it is essential to develop artificial intelligence systems in a safe and responsible manner that respects human rights (KVKK, 2025) .

Similarly, in the document titled 'Ethical Principles for Trustworthy Artificial Intelligence' published by the European Commission, seven basic requirements are defined to ensure the trustworthiness of artificial intelligence systems: (AI HLEG, 2019):

1. Human Factors and Oversight: AI systems should support individuals to make informed decisions and promote the protection of fundamental rights. In this process, appropriate oversight mechanisms should also be provided.
2. Technical Robustness and Security: Systems should be resilient, secure and equipped with backup plans in case of potential failure. Unintentional damage should be minimized by ensuring accurate, reliable and repeatable operation.
3. Privacy and Data Governance: In addition to full compliance with confidentiality principles, adequate arrangements should be in place for data governance, protecting data quality and integrity and ensuring only legitimate access to data.
4. Transparency: AI systems and their decision-making processes should be transparent, supported by traceability mechanisms to ensure that users are aware that they are interacting with the system.
5. Diversity, Non-Discrimination and Fairness: Systems should be accessible to all individuals and designed to be free from bias. In this process, vulnerable groups should not be excluded and all stakeholders should be included.
6. Social and Environmental Welfare: Artificial intelligence systems should be environmentally sustainable and eco-friendly in a way that will benefit not only today's individuals but also future generations. To this end, the environmental and social impacts of systems should be carefully evaluated.
7. Accountability: Responsibility and accountability mechanisms should be established for AI systems, and it should be ensured that algorithms, data and design processes are auditable, especially in critical applications. Users should also be provided with adequate means of appeal and redress.

Research reveals that current artificial intelligence systems have various shortcomings in terms of these ethical principles. According to Küçükvardar et al. (2020), AI technologies have various deficiencies in terms of basic ethical criteria such as accountability, privacy, data governance and transparency. The fact that large companies that dominate data are not subject to any supervisory authority, do not carry out data management processes transparently, and violate the privacy and confidentiality rights of individuals keeps ethical and moral debates about artificial intelligence on the agenda (Küçükvardar, Aslan, & Bayrakcı, 2020, p. 1073) .

Asıl (2025) points out that biases and lack of transparency in artificial intelligence algorithms may increase social inequalities. He recommends transparent, user-friendly systems and diversified data sets against these problems. It also emphasizes the need for global regulations, training programs and community-oriented oversight mechanisms on data privacy, accountability and ethical awareness (p.170).

The rapid development of artificial intelligence technologies brings ethical issues to the agenda at the same pace. Issues such as personal data security, non-discrimination, transparency and accountability form the basis of AI ethics. Both national regulatory bodies and international organizations publish various principles and reports to address the gaps in these areas. However, the practical realization of these principles is not only technical, but also ethical and socially responsible. Therefore, interdisciplinary cooperation, legal regulations and ethical awareness are of great importance for the development of AI systems in a human-centered, safe and fair manner.

9. CONCLUSION

With the rapid development of technology and data science, digitalization continues to transform every aspect of life today. This transformation is reshaping the digital experiences of individuals as well as sectoral changes such as communication, marketing and media production. Technological advances, especially when supported by tools such as artificial intelligence and data analysis, make all these processes much more efficient, faster and personalized.

In the world of communication, digital transformation has made communication processes more dynamic and multifaceted, centering on the use of big data analytics, artificial intelligence-supported systems and algorithms. Traditional communication methods have been replaced by a new understanding based on multi-actor interactions, which has led to radical changes, especially in the fields of media, journalism, advertising and marketing. Artificial intelligence offers more effective and customized solutions in every field from content production to data analysis, significantly increasing the speed and scope of interactions in the digital world.

In the field of journalism, digital transformation has radically changed news production processes. Robotic journalism applications offer artificial intelligence and data science-supported solutions at many stages from news gathering to analysis, enabling faster and more comprehensive content production. This transformation makes traditional journalistic practice more efficient and allows journalists to produce more informed and objective news with data-driven content. However, this process brings with it new responsibilities regarding the accuracy and reliability of news, and reveals that technology should be used not only for speed, but also in line with ethical principles.

Changes in digital marketing are enabling brands to develop more targeted and personalized marketing strategies. Artificial intelligence-supported recommendation systems, innovations in social media algorithms and data analytics enable brands to run more efficient campaigns by increasing customer interaction. This process improves the user experience and makes marketing processes more dynamic.

Social media platforms have undergone a major transformation in personalizing users' content experiences. Artificial intelligence-supported algorithms have made digital interaction more efficient by organizing content streams according to users' interests, behaviors and preferences. However, these developments also have some negative effects. Personalization of content can sometimes lead to digital polarization by restricting individuals' access to different views. This highlights the importance of having a broader perspective on access to information.

In conclusion, the effects of digital transformation and artificial intelligence have led to a complete paradigm shift in the field of communication. While the proper use of data and technology can bring great benefits in every field, from business processes to social media, from digital marketing to news production, it is also a fact that ever-evolving technologies raise issues such as ethics, security and transparency. Digital transformation should be shaped not only by technology and tools, but also by a human-centered approach. The future success of this transformation will be directly proportional to ethical responsibilities, transparency and sustainability principles.

REFERENCES

AI HLEG. (2019). Ethics guidelines for trustworthy AI. Temmuz 2025 tarihinde https://digital-strategy.ec.europa.eu/en/library/ethics-guidelines-trustworthy-ai adresinden alındı

Amazon Web Services. (2023). Makine Öğrenimi ve Derin Öğrenme Arasındaki Fark Nedir? Şubat 2025 tarihinde https://aws.amazon.com/tr/compare/the-difference-between-machine-learning-and-deep-learning/ adresinden alındı

Amazon Web Services. (2023). Veri Bilimi ve Yapay Zeka arasındaki fark nedir? Şubat 2025 tarihinde https://aws.amazon.com/tr/compare/the-difference-between-data-science-and-ai/ adresinden alındı

Asıl, S. (2025). Yapay Zekâ Etiği: Temel İlkeler, Sorunlar ve Disiplinlerarası Yaklaşımlar. *İNİF E- Dergi, 10*(1), 152-175.

Ay, A. (2023). Gazetecilik 4.0: Yapay Zekâ Haberciliğinin Güncel Örneklerine Yönelik Bir İnceleme. *Süleyman Demirel Üniversitesi Vizyoner Dergisi, 14*(38), 412–435. DOI: 10.21076/vizyoner.1141093

Beckett, C., & Yaseen, M. (2023). Generating Change: A global survey of what news organisations are doing with artificial intelligence. JournalismAI, London School of Economics and Political Science.

Bekar, S. (2024). Yeni Medyada Yapay Zekâ Aracılığıyla Dezenformasyon Oluşturulması: Trump Örneği. *Uluslararası Batı Karadeniz Sosyal ve Beşeri Bilimler Dergisi, 8*(1), 40–66. DOI: 10.46452/baksoder.1448805

Bilgici, C. (2023). Yapay Zekâ ve Algoritmik Kültür Bağlaminda Sosyal Medya Deneyiminin Geleceği Üzerine Bir Değerlendirme. *Yeni Medya Elektronik Dergisi, 7*(3), 216–237. DOI: 10.17932/IAU.EJNM.25480200.2023/ejnm_v7i3003

Binbir, S. (2021). Pazarlama Çalışmalarında Yapay Zeka Kullanımı Üzerine Betimleyici Bir Çalışma. *e-Journal of New Media, 5*(3), 314-328.

Böyük, M. (2024). Dijital Çağda Haber: İnsan ve Yapay Zeka Üretimi Haber İçeriklerinin Karşılaştırmalı Analizi. *Akdeniz İletişim*, (46), 44–72.

Çağıltay, K. (2018). *İnsan Bilgisayar Etkileşimi ve Kullanılabilirlik Mühendisliği*. Seçkin.

Can, Ö., & Sezgin, M. (2024). Yapay Zeka Teknolojilerinin Kurumsal İletişimdeki Rolünün Değerlendirilmesi. *Uluslararası Sosyal Bilimler Akademik Araştırmalar Dergisi, 8*(15), 103–114. DOI: 10.58201/utsobilder.1497333

Çeber, B. (2024). Haziran). Yapay Zekâ Etiği Bağlamında Reklamcılık Sektörü Üzerine Uygulamalı Bir Araştırma. *Intermedia. International Journal (Toronto, Ont.), 11*(20), 63–84.

Çeber, B. (2024). *Yapay Zekayı Sorgulamak: Veri Etiği ve Dijital Reklamcılığın Kesişimi. B. Çeber içinde, Yapay Zekâ Etiği ve İletişim: Sorunlar, Sınırlar ve Zorluklar*. Nobel Akademik Yayıncılık.

Coderspace. (2024, Temmuz 8). *Derin Öğrenme Nedir? - Deep Learning Nasıl Çalışır?* Şubat 2025 tarihinde https://coderspace.io/blog/derin-ogrenme-nedir-deep-learning-nasil-calisir/ adresinden alındı

Darı, A. B., & Koçyiğit, A. (2024). Yapay Zekâ ve Etik: Yeni Medyanın Dönüşümünde Sorumluluk ve Sınırlar. *İletişim ve Toplum Araştırmaları Dergisi, 4*(2), 246-261.

Demirel, E. S. (2023). İletişim Alanında Yapay Zekâ: İletişim Fakültelerinde Yapay Zekâ. *International Social Sciences Studies Journal, 9*(118), 9842–9852. DOI: 10.29228/sssj.74032

Diakopoulos, N. (2014, Haziran 12). *The Anatomy of a Robot Journalist.* Haziran 2025 tarihinde https://medium.com/tow-center/the-anatomy-of-a-robot-journalist-1aa879bc6769 adresinden alındı

DOMO. (2024). *Data Never Sleeps 12.0.* Şubat 2025 tarihinde https://www.domo.com/learn/infographic/data-never-sleeps-12 adresinden alındı

Emre, İ. E., & Erol, Ç. S. (2017). Veri Analizinde İstatistik mi Veri Madenciliği mi? *Bilişim Teknolojileri Dergisi, 10*(2), 161–167. DOI: 10.17671/gazibtd.309297

Fayyad, U., Piatetsky-Shapiro, G., & Smyth, P. (1996). The KDD Process for Extracting Useful Knowledge from Volumes of Data. *Communications of the ACM, 39*(11), 27–34. DOI: 10.1145/240455.240464

Gülleb, O. (2022). *Algoritmaların Haber Alma Biçimlerine Etkileri: Veri Gazeteciliği ve Algoritmalar. N. E. Dilmen, & C. T. Şahoğlu içinde, Sosyal Medya ve Algoritmalar*. Kriter Yayınevi.

Guzman, A. L., & Lewis, S. C. (2019). Artificial intelligence and communication: A Human– Machine Communication research agenda. *New Media & Society, 22*(1), 70–86. DOI: 10.1177/1461444819858691

Haleem, A., Javaid, M., Qadri, M. A., Singh, R. P., & Suman, R. (2022). Artificial intelligence (AI) applications for marketing: A literature-based study. *International Journal of Intelligent Networks, 3*, 119–132. DOI: 10.1016/j.ijin.2022.08.005

Harari, Y. N. (2018). *21. Yüzyıl İçin 21 Ders.* Kolektif Kitap.

Hohenstein, J., Kizilcec, R. F., DiFranzo, D., Aghajari, Z., Mieczkowski, H., Levy, K., Naaman, M., Hancock, J., & Jung, M. F. (2023). Artificial intelligence in communication impacts language and social relationships. *Scientific Reports*, *13*(5487), 5487. DOI: 10.1038/s41598-023-30938-9

Inverse. (2018, Temmuz 15). *How 'Knowhere' Uses Artificial Intelligence to Eliminate News Bias*. Haziran 2025 tarihinde https://www.inverse.com/article/46286-how-knowhere-uses-artificial-intelligence-to-eliminate-news-bias adresinden alındı

Işık, U., Ölçekçi, H., & Koz, K. A. (2022). Eylül). Yapay Zeka ve Algoritma Ekseninde Gazeteciliğin Geleceği ve Toplum İçin Anlamı. *Gümüşhane Üniversitesi İletişim Fakültesi Elektronik Dergisi*, *10*(2), 1248–1275.

Kaplan, A. B., & Kaplan, F. (2020). Haziran). Yeni İletişim Teknolojileri ve Yapay Zekâ Uygulamaları Bağlamında İhtiyaç Olgusunun Değişimi ve Toplumsal Dönüşüm. *Akademik Sosyal Araştırmalar Dergisi*, (46), 178–193.

Karaman, Ö. (2021). Yapay Zeka Destekli Kişiselleştirme Algoritmalarının Tüketici Zihninde Filtre Balonu Yaratma Etkisinin İncelenmesi. *Vizyoner Dergisi*, *12*(32), 1339–1351. DOI: 10.21076/vizyoner.896059

Kavut, S. (2022). Yapay Zekâ Pazarlaması ve Yapay Zekâ Algoritmaları: Domino's Pizza Yapay Zekâ Uygulamaları. *9.Uluslararası İletişim Günleri Dijital Çağda İletişim Çalışmaları Sempozyumu*, (s. 537-552). İstanbul.

Kılınç, D., & Başeğmez, N. (2022). *Uygulamalarla Veri Bilimi*. Abaküs Yayınları.

Kırık, A. M., & Özkoçak, V. (2023). Medya ve İletişim Bağlamında Yapay Zeka Tarihi ve Teknolojisi: ChatGPT ve Deepfake ile Gelen Dijital Dönüşüm. *Karadeniz Uluslararası Bilimsel Dergi*, (58), 73–99. DOI: 10.17498/kdeniz.1308471

Koçyiğit, A., & Darı, A. B. (2023). Temmuz). Yapay Zekâ İletişiminde ChatGPT: İnsanlaşan Dijitalleşmenin Geleceği. *Stratejik ve Sosyal Araştırmalar Dergisi*, *7*(2), 427–438.

Koçyiğit, A., & Koçyiğit, M. (2024). Yapay Zekâ ve Yeni Medya: Fırsatlar, Tehditler ve Gelecek Perspektifi. *5.* [Akdeniz Üniversitesi.]. *Uluslarası Medya Çalışmaları Sempozyumu IMS*, *2024*, 26–31.

Küçükvardar, M., Aslan, A., & Bayrakcı, S. (2020). Yapay Zekâ Ve Etik Üzerine Bir Araştırma. *Atras Journal*, *6*(36), 1065–1077.

KVKK. (2025, Nisan 27). *Yapay Zeka Alanında Kişisel Verilerin Korunmasına Daire Tavsiyeler*. Haziran 2025 tarihinde http://www.kvkk.gov.tr/Icerik/7048/Yapay-Zeka-Alaninda-Kisisel-Verilerin-Korunmasina-Dair-Tavsiyeler adresinden alındı

Ma, L., & Sun, B. (2020, September). Machine learning and AI in marketing – Connecting computing power to human insights. *International Journal of Research in Marketing, 37*(3), 481–504. DOI: 10.1016/j.ijresmar.2020.04.005

Mutlu, E. (2024). Yaratıcılığın Sınırları: Yapay Zeka Yaratıcılığına Bir Bakış. *Hacettepe Üniversitesi İletişin Fakültesi Kültürel Çalışmalar Dergisi, 11*(2), 422–446.

Özkeçeci, Z. (2019). Citizen Journalism-Opportunities And Challenges. *Asya Studies-Academic Social Studies, 2*(8), 33–39. DOI: 10.31455/asya.565973

Öztemel, E. (2020). *Yapay Zekâ ve İnsanlığın Geleceği. M. Şeker, Y. Bulduklu, C. Korkut, & M. Doğrul içinde, Bilişim Teknolojileri ve iletişim: Bircy ve Toplum Güvenliği.* Türkiye Bilimler Akademisi.

Reinsel, D., Gantz, J., & Rydning, J. (2018). *The Digitization of the World From Edge to Core*. IDC.

Sağlam, F., & Cengiz, M. A. (2023). Sosyal Bilimlerde Veri Bilimi Kullanımı. *Avrasya Sosyal ve Ekonomi Araştırmaları Dergisi, 10*(4), 1375–1407.

Sarı, E. (2025). Sosyal Medyada Dezenformasyonla Mücadelede Yapay Zekâ: Olanaklar ve Sınırlılıklar. *Van Yüzüncü Yıl Üniversitesi Sosyal Bilimler Enstitüsü Dergisi*, (67), 49–61. DOI: 10.53568/yyusbed.1583326

Shannon, C., & Weaver, W. (1963). *The Mathematical Theory of Communication*. University of Illinois Press.

Sütcü, C. S., & Aytekin, Ç. (2018). *Veri Bilimi*. Paloma.

Tellan, T. (2022). *Yapay Zeka, Robot Gazetecilik ve Dijitalleşen İletişimin Doğasını Tartışmak. 9.Uluslararası İletişim Günleri*. Üsküdar Üniversitesi.

Tünalp, B. F. (2024). Yapay Zeka Sistemlerine Etik Değerlerin Entegrasyonu-Kavramsal Çerçevede Bir Tartışma. *Uluslararası Akademik Birikim Dergisi, 7*(5), 1041–1052.

Turing, A. (1950). Computing Machinery and Intelligence. *Mind, 59*(236), 433–460. DOI: 10.1093/mind/LIX.236.433

Wiener, N. (1989). *The Human Use Of Human Beings: Cybernetics and Society*. Free Association Books.

Yıldız, E. (2021). İletişim Alanındaki Yapay Zeka Konulu Tezlerin İncelenmesi. *İstanbul Aydın Üniversitesi Sosyal Bilimler Dergisi, 13*(3), 605 - 618.

Zeydan, İ. (2024). Yapay Zeka Pazarlama Entegrasyonu: Örnek Uygulamalar. *International Journal of Management Economics and Business, 20*(ICMEB'24 Special Issue), 423-446.

Chapter 3

Artificial Intelligence-Supported Journalism and Approaches to Journalism

Duygu Dumanlı Kürkçü
https://orcid.org/0000-0002-3425-2826
İstanbul Arel University, Turkey

Mehmet Murat Mengü
İstanbul Arel University, Turkey

ABSTRACT

In the digital age, where new communication technologies are developing rapidly, continuous change and transformation are taking place in many areas. This study aims to reveal the effects of artificial intelligence-supported journalism on the future of journalism, the benefits and risks it will provide to journalists, and how it will affect the media and journalism sector. In this context, data were collected through face-to-face interviews with 15 participants between January 1, 2025, and February 20, 2025, through a form consisting of semi-structured questions.The study found out how artificial intelligence is used in business, what the pros and cons are, what the participants thought about AI-supported journalism, how AI might change the future of journalism, what the pros and cons are for journalists in newsrooms, how AI will change the news industry, and how AI relates to the ideas of "fake news," "disinformation," "deepfake," and "ethics."

DOI: 10.4018/979-8-3373-2960-4.ch003

INTRODUCTION

In the age of digitalisation, algorithms and artificial intelligence technologies are radically transforming journalistic practices. The role of artificial intelligence in processes such as news production, verification, content recommendations, and reader interactions is increasing day by day. This change and transformation, which emerges with the integration of algorithms and artificial intelligence into newsrooms, affects not only how information is created and distributed but also how audiences interact with news content and ultimately reshapes the nature of journalism (Brennan, 2018). The rise of generative AI models, especially after 2023, has accelerated this transformation, leading to a reassessment of journalistic competencies and training (Lopezosa et al., 2023). News organisations are increasingly leveraging AI to analyse large datasets, detect trends, and efficiently create personalised content (Sharadga et al., 2022). However, while these developments promise greater reach and productivity, they also raise critical concerns about transparency, biases, and the ethical use of technology in news production. The growing use of AI in journalism has caused different reactions among media workers (Sánchez-García et al., 2023) and has led to mixed definitions of AI in the media, showing wider confusion in society (Zhai et al., 2020; Nguyen and Hekman, 2022; Sun et al., 2020). On the other hand, traditional news dissemination models, which suffer from problems such as information filtering and bias, are struggling to meet the changing information needs of the public. The more effective dissemination of fake news through digital channels further complicates the situation and responsible integration.

This study aims to reveal opportunities and challenges through in-depth interviews with academics, journalists, and artificial intelligence experts about the applications of algorithms and artificial intelligence in journalism, their positive and negative aspects, their effects on the news industry, the potential effects of the use of artificial intelligence on the future of journalism, and the benefits and risks that the use of artificial intelligence will provide to journalists.

In the first part of the study, the structure and characteristics of algorithms and artificial intelligence and the opportunities and challenges they present to journalistic practices are presented. In the second part, the effects of artificial intelligence-supported journalism on the news industry, the purposes of using artificial intelligence tools in journalistic activities, changing journalistic practices, and the advantages offered by artificial intelligence-supported journalism are explained. In the research part of the study, in-depth interviews were conducted with journalists, artificial intelligence developers, academics, and ChatGPT, an artificial intelligence chat tool, in order to draw attention to the potential effects of artificial intelligence-supported journalism on the future of journalism, its effects on newsrooms and the news industry, and the negative developments that may arise in the near future on 'fake news,' 'disinformation,' 'deepfake,' and 'ethics,' as well as the positive aspects of the use of artificial intelligence.

Within the scope of the study, research questions were asked to the participants to reveal their views on the use of artificial intelligence in business processes, the positive and negative aspects of the use of artificial intelligence, their views on artificial intelligence-supported journalism, the potential effects of artificial intelligence on the future of journalism, the benefits and risks that the use of artificial intelligence in newsrooms will provide to journalists, their views on how the use of artificial intelligence will affect the news industry, and their views on 'fake news,' 'disinformation,' 'deepfake,' and 'ethics' in artificial intelligence-supported journalism. This study is important due to the limited studies in the literature on the effects of artificial intelligence-supported journalism on newsrooms, the news industry, and the future of journalism, and the advantages and challenges it will present to journalists.

ALGORITHMS, ARTIFICIAL INTELLIGENCE, AND JOURNALISM

The introduction of artificial intelligence and algorithmic technologies has significantly changed the entire journalistic chain and its governing rules, including the creation, distribution, and consumption of information within media ecosystems.

Zhou (2024), who conducted an empirical study in terms of news content quality, dissemination efficiency, objectivity, and dissemination cost to verify the usefulness of AI and big data in overcoming the challenge of news distribution, found that when tactics based on big data and AI were applied, an improvement of 4.76 percent in news content quality and 3.63 percent in distribution efficiency was achieved. The findings suggest that AI and big data can improve news content quality and distribution efficiency by fulfilling various public information needs.

According to Marer et al. (2024), AI offers a competitive advantage to modern businesses by automating processes, making pay practices fairer, and identifying improvements suggested by AI. However, businesses face four major obstacles when implementing AI solutions: timing and method, ensuring fairness, identifying the source of AI-recommended improvements, and being strategically smart. In this context, organisations need to address internal, external, and individual equity; maintain transparency; and adopt a strategic mindset.

In a study by Ufarte et al. (2023), Videre AI (Spain), JX Press Corp (Japan), Reuters News Tracer (UK), and News Republic (France) were sampled to categorise the current state of artificial media organisations, explain how newsrooms without journalists function, shed light on the content they produce, and determine whether they are temporary exceptions or the beginning of a larger trend away from journalistic control. In this context, semi-structured, in-depth interviews were conducted with the heads of communication and technology at the three European projects, in addition to analysing the news content on their respective websites. Since there was no human staff in the Japanese project, the only method for obtaining information was the chatbot. This study aims to understand better the news production processes of these initiatives, their impact on the journalism profession, and their applicability. It is thought that this study demonstrates how extensively the media industry is using AI and how communication agencies are leading established media organisations in creating and disseminating artificial content.

Larrondo and Grandi (2021) point out that while AI has the potential to be a useful tool in policing fake news and violent content, the risk of censorship may arise when used without human intervention to provide context and accurate translations. Due to the inability of artificial intelligence to put what it monitors into perspective, it is considered an indiscriminate pre-censorship tool rather than a tool to protect freedom of expression. In conclusion, after analysing relevant international laws, reports from international organisations, and the policies of Facebook and Twitter, Larrondo and Grandi propose five changes to content moderation:

First, they call on states to harmonise their domestic laws while protecting universally recognised rights to freedom of expression. They also recommend that public policies enact laws guaranteeing the conditions of employment for human moderators involved in automated content removal decisions. They also emphasise that social media platforms should be transparent about the use of AI in content removal and dissemination, have clear and consistent terms and conditions, and assess the potential impact of AI on human rights before implementation (Larrondo and Grandi, 2021: 168).

Noting that social media has made news more accessible, cheaper, and faster than ever before, but that this change is increasingly threatened by misleading material such as fake news shared by social media users, Özbay and Alataş (2019) present a strategy that combines text mining techniques with supervised artificial intelligence algorithms to detect fake news on social media and suggest that researching new methods, combining existing ones, or incorporating intelligent optimisation algorithms into future studies could improve this work.

Recently, there have been attempts to use blockchain and AI technologies to identify and minimise fake news. Seong-Kyu et al. (2024), who conducted a study to develop an algorithm that can predict the future spread of fake news by utilising artificial intelligence technology, state that a blockchain-based news media platform has not yet received the expected market response. At this point, they also point out that it is unclear whether the obstacles to the rapid expansion of the blockchain news media platform are due to consumers' reluctance to trust new technologies, consumers' lack of expectations for innovative news media platforms, or some other factor.

In this study, a verification study was conducted using blockchain, and fake news predictions were created with artificial intelligence. Seong-Kyu et al. predict that the integration of artificial intelligence and blockchain technologies will be crucial.

PURPOSE OF THE STUDY AND RESEARCH QUESTIONS

The aim of this study is to analyse the use of artificial intelligence in business processes, the positive and negative aspects of the use of artificial intelligence, the opinions of sector professionals, academics, and journalists who are experts in the field of artificial intelligence, and the potential effects of the use of artificial intelligence on the future of journalism. This study aims to seek answers to research questions such as the benefits and risks that the use of artificial intelligence in newsrooms will provide to journalists, their views on how the use of artificial intelligence will affect the news industry, and their views on 'fake news,' 'disinformation,' 'deepfake,' and 'ethics' in AI-supported journalism through in-depth interviews conducted in Turkey.

In this context, the research questions are as follows:

AS 1: What are your opinions about the use of artificial intelligence in business processes?
AS 2: What do you think are the positive and negative aspects of the use of artificial intelligence?
AS 3: What are your opinions about artificial intelligence-supported journalism?
AS 4: What are the potential effects of the use of artificial intelligence on the future of journalism?
AS 5: What are the benefits and risks of using artificial intelligence in newsrooms for journalists?
AS 6: How do you think the use of AI will impact the media and the news industry in particular?
AS 7: What are your views on the concepts of 'fake news,' 'disinformation,' 'deepfake,' and 'ethics' in AI-supported journalism?

This study is important because it reveals the potential effects of AI-supported journalism on business processes, newsrooms, and the news industry; it also discusses the future of journalism and outlines the benefits and risks that AI-supported journalism may present to journalists, as well as its impact on 'fake news,' 'disinformation,' 'deepfakes,' and 'ethics.'

SCOPE AND METHOD OF THE STUDY

The population of the study consists of journalists, reporters, editors, and lecturers working in the field of communication sciences; artificial intelligence experts and developers; and ChatGPT artificial intelligence chat tool users between the ages of 25 and 45 in Turkey. In the study, 15 participants who are predicted to represent the universe well were determined as the sample group by the convenience sampling method. To draw attention to the potential effects of artificial intelligence-supported journalism on the future of journalism, its effects on newsrooms and the news industry, and the negative developments that may arise in the near future on 'fake news,' 'disinformation,' 'deepfake,' and 'ethics,' as well as the positive aspects of the use of artificial intelligence, journalists, artificial intelligence developers, academics, and ChatGPT, an artificial intelligence chat tool, were interviewed with in-depth interview technique.

As a data collection technique, in-depth interviews are described as obtaining detailed and qualitative information about the research topic by asking the interviewees detailed and qualitative questions. This type of interview is referred to as an "in-depth interview" (Aziz, 2003, pp. 84-85). In-depth interviews are defined as the process of asking open-ended research questions to learn about the views, thoughts, perspectives, and experiences of individuals in the sample, recording the obtained responses, and examining the research topic in detail with additional questions related to the subject (Kümbetoğlu, 2008, pp. 71-81).

In this context, participants were asked research questions to uncover their views on the use of artificial intelligence in business processes, the positive and negative aspects of using artificial intelligence, their opinions on AI-supported journalism, the potential impacts of AI usage on the future of journalism, the benefits and risks of using AI in newsrooms for journalists, their views on how AI usage will affect the news industry, and their opinions on topics such as "fake news," "disinformation," "deepfake," and "ethics" in AI-supported journalism.

FINDINGS

The information about the participants in the study sample, which includes artificial intelligence developers and experts, journalists, editors, reporters, ChatGPT artificial intelligence chat tool users, and academics in the field of communication science, is presented in Table 1.

Table 1. Information on the participants with whom in-depth interviews were conducted

Participant Code	Institution	Department/Title & Position	Gender
K1	İstanbul Arel University	Department of Journalism (Assoc. Prof. Dr.)	F
K2	24 Hours Newspaper	Internet Editor	M
K3	-	Freelance Journalist & Independent Verifier	F
K4	Yeni Gün Newspaper	Journalist-Sports Reporter	M
K5	-	Serbest Gazeteci	M
K6	Necmettin Erbakan University	Department of Radio, Television, and Cinema (Assoc. Dr.)	F
K7	İstanbul Arel University	Department of Journalism (Research Assist.)	F
K8	Sözcü Newspaper	Journalist-Sports Reporter	M
K9	VSY Biontechnology	Marcom Specialist	F
K10	Chat GPT	Artificial Intelligence Chat Tool	-
K11	-	Freelance Journalist & Independent Verifier	M
K12	-	Artificial Intelligence Expert & GPT Developer	M
K13	İstanbul University	Technology Transfer Application and Research Centre Specialist (Lecturer)	F
K14	İstanbul Aydın University	Department of Journalism (Assoc. Prof. Dr.)	M
K15	Yeni Yüzyıl University	New Media and Communication (Dr. Lecturer)	F

Table 1 contains information on the participants' gender, the institutions they work for, their departments, and their titles. In the study sample, in addition to academics specialising in communication sciences, journalism, and new media technologies, interviews were conducted with industry professionals who are well-versed in developments in artificial intelligence and their impact on the media and journalism fields, including journalists, reporters, editors, artificial intelligence experts, and technology transfer and research centre specialists working in news organisations and as freelancers. When examining the literature on artificial intelligence, there is no study reflecting the views of media professionals, academics, artificial intelligence experts, and developers on AI-supported journalism, the effects of AI tools on newsrooms, the media industry, and the future of journalism, as well as the issues of "fake news," "disinformation," "deepfake," and "ethics" that the use of artificial intelligence in journalism brings.

Therefore, the study will be beneficial in providing information and recommendations about the future of journalism with artificial intelligence technologies, the positive and negative contributions to journalistic practices, and the potential impacts on the news industry, particularly to students studying journalism, artificial intelligence developers and experts, and journalists working in news organisations or as freelancers. The data obtained from the participants through in-depth interviews were analysed under seven headings by categorising the research question contents based on keywords.

THE USE OF ARTIFICIAL INTELLIGENCE IN BUSINESS PROCESSES

The views of academics and artificial intelligence experts on the use of artificial intelligence in business processes have focused on the fact that AI will enable the rapid execution of business processes, provide automation and efficiency, facilitate data analysis and content production, become more widespread in the future, and significantly change some professions. Additionally, it was emphasised that artificial intelligence should be considered with both its positive and negative aspects and that it should be used under human control as merely an assistant in business processes.

The participants coded K2 (internet editor), K3 (freelance journalist/independent verifier), K12 (artificial intelligence expert/GPT developer), and K11 (freelance journalist/independent verifier) and respectively explained their thoughts on the advantages of using artificial intelligence in business processes, such as automation, efficiency, speed, translation, and visual creation, as follows:

"The importance of artificial intelligence is undeniably significant technology..." Artificial intelligence serves as a kind of automation in the production of ideas. Thanks to artificial intelligence tools, the processes in intellectual production (video editing, animation creation, drawing, etc.) have been shortened.

"Artificial intelligence is useful in the work process like an assistant with features such as transcription, summarisation, and translation." By reducing menial tasks, it allows the work to be prepared in a more qualitative manner. In this regard, I think it is a useful tool when used correctly.

"Artificial intelligence, especially in tasks that require intense thinking, increases productivity." While contributing to the faster execution of tasks, it may reduce the need for human labour in some areas. This could lead to job losses over time.

"AI technologies can create materials such as foreign language translation, visual creation and editing, video creation, and voiceover, which journalists use every day in every news report." This, frankly, makes journalists' jobs particularly easier. As someone who has worked in journalism both before and after the era of AI, I can say that I use it. I use it, and I think it is quite helpful."

Participants coded K4 (sports journalist) and K13 (technology transfer application research centre expert), who expressed their views on the potential advantages of effectively using artificial intelligence tools in business processes as well as the negative aspects such as ethics, privacy, data security, employment issues, and misinformation, explained their thoughts as follows:

"Artificial intelligence is creating a significant transformation in business processes and providing important advantages to companies by increasing efficiency." However, this transformation has both positive and negative aspects. Therefore, it is necessary to be very conscious. While artificial intelligence offers great opportunities in the business world, it needs to be used within the framework of careful planning and ethical rules. Businesses' ability to adapt their employees to new technologies and use artificial intelligence in the right areas will provide a significant advantage.

"In general, I think that artificial intelligence should be addressed with both its positive and negative aspects." From a positive perspective, artificial intelligence provides a beneficial contribution to increasing efficiency in business processes and using time more effectively... On the other hand, artificial intelligence is still a subject of debate regarding issues such as disinformation and plagiarism. After all, artificial intelligence compiles information based on the data available in the system, and the information it uses may lack truth, be manipulated, or contain falsehoods. Additionally, it can present the compiled information without showing its source. Therefore, its use in business processes still poses a concern in terms of ethics and truthfulness.

As can be understood from the opinions expressed by the participants, the use of artificial intelligence in business processes offers positive contributions such as performing time-consuming tasks quickly and efficiently, providing journalists with the opportunity to create more creative content, analysing large data sets, creating personalised content by considering reader algorithms, enhancing the accuracy of news, ensuring neutrality, etc. However, it can also pave the way for negative aspects such as data security, manipulation caused by automated content creation, unethical use, privacy violations, and employment issues. Therefore, it can be said that it is necessary to be cautious against these potential drawbacks when using artificial intelligence in business processes.

POSITIVE AND NEGATIVE ASPECTS OF ARTIFICIAL INTELLIGENCE

The use of artificial intelligence tools in business processes, especially in fields like journalism that involve creativity and ethical responsibility in informing the public, should particularly consider the risks as well as the benefits these tools bring, and precautions should be taken. Within the scope of the study, research questions were directed not only to professionals such as academics, journalists, freelance journalists, editors, reporters, artificial intelligence experts, GPT developers, freelance fact-checkers, and technology transfer application research centre experts, but also to ChatGPT, and the impartiality of its responses was also analysed within the study.

In this context, regarding the positive and negative aspects of artificial intelligence, ChatGPT with the code K10 explained its views as follows:

Positive Aspects:

- *Efficiency and Time Savings: Artificial intelligence automates repetitive and time-consuming tasks, leaving journalists with more creative space.*
- *Fast Content Production: Artificial intelligence, which processes large amounts of data quickly and extracts meaningful results, especially ensures the rapid dissemination of urgent news.*
- *Personalised Experiences: Artificial intelligence analyses users' preferences to offer more customised content suggestions.*
- *Data Analysis and Research Support: Journalists may struggle to manually analyse large data sets, but artificial intelligence can quickly scan large data sets to provide useful information. This strengthens investigative journalism.*
- *Reducing Inaccuracy and Misleading Content: Artificial intelligence can help detect inaccuracies, misleading information, or potentially manipulative content in news articles. Thus, more accurate and reliable news is produced.*

Negative Aspects:

- *Bias and Ethical Issues: Since artificial intelligence systems operate based on training data, biases in this data can also create biases in the content produced by the AI.*
- *Risk of Job Loss: Artificial intelligence can reduce the workforce by automating some journalistic tasks.*
- *Manipulation and Security Issues: Artificial intelligence can be used by malicious individuals for manipulation purposes.*
- *Addiction and Decreased Creativity: Continuous production of AI-based content may lead journalists to think less creatively.*
- *Data Security and Privacy: Artificial intelligence can analyse personal information using large data sets.*

When examining ChatGPT's response regarding the positive and negative aspects of artificial intelligence, it is possible to say that it answered impartially, especially by detailing and explaining the negative aspects. Notable points in ChatGPT's response include the emphasis that in the context of bias and ethical issues, the responsibility for potential negative outcomes arising from AI systems' reliance on training data is due to the training data itself. Regarding employment and job loss, it has been stated that journalists working in low-level jobs will face this issue.

Additionally, it has been neutrally stated that there are risks of manipulation and security regarding fake news and deepfakes by malicious individuals, and that excessive use of artificial intelligence could lead to laziness and a decrease in creativity among journalists. In this context, it is necessary to take precautions against the risks mentioned by ChatGPT regarding the negative aspects that the use of artificial intelligence may bring and to use AI tools as assistants, meaning to ensure that the control remains under human supervision rather than completely delegating work processes to them.

AI-POWERED JOURNALISM

AI-supported journalism is important for the radical transformations it brings to the media sector. The positive aspects brought by the use of artificial intelligence tools in the media sector include the faster execution of journalistic activities, the opportunity for journalists to create creative news stories and content, the production of personalised news content, etc., which enhance efficiency and accessibility in journalistic practices.

The participants coded K1 (academic), K3 (freelance journalist/independent verifier), and K5 (freelance journalist) and explained their thoughts as follows: They believe that AI-supported journalism will bring significant changes to journalistic practices, that it should be used in accordance with ethical principles under editorial control, and that journalists and journalism students should receive training in this area to acquire new skill sets for the effective use of AI tools.

> *"Especially for young people studying journalism, being able to integrate artificial intelligence tools into the news production process will be an important requirement in the media industry." Therefore, journalism students need to be educated on the use of artificial intelligence and AI tools and develop their skills to incorporate AI applications into the news production process.*
>
> *"If used in a controlled and ethical manner from an editor's perspective, it ensures the production of highly qualified work." Especially in data journalism, the effective use of artificial intelligence produces higher-quality news. Additionally, its speed, especially when time is limited, can increase the pace of tasks while maintaining quality, compared to a human.*
>
> *"Artificial intelligence can increase efficiency in journalism and allow journalists to conduct more in-depth work." However, within the framework of ethical principles, it should be a necessity for it to remain a supportive tool rather than replacing human journalism. There is a need to establish transparency, oversight mechanisms, and ethical rules regarding how artificial intelligence is used by journalists.*

As can be understood from the opinions expressed by the participants, AI-supported journalism is being increasingly and intensively used by news organisations around the world and in our country due to the advantages it provides. Therefore, journalists, editors, and journalism candidates working in the media sector should quickly adapt to artificial intelligence technologies and tools in order to effectively and efficiently perform tasks such as translation, visual creation, news accuracy verification, voiceover, video creation, data analysis, news content personalisation, and automation. Additionally, in the field of AI-supported journalism, while benefiting from the speed and capabilities of these tools, journalistic practices should prioritise human oversight and ethical principles.

THE EFFECTS OF ARTIFICIAL INTELLIGENCE ON THE FUTURE OF JOURNALISM

The potential impacts of artificial intelligence usage in the media industry on the future of journalism are extensive. AI-supported journalism has the potential to bring about radical transformations in a wide range of areas, from news production processes in journalism to the interaction of journalism with society and employment conditions, when considering the future of journalism. Some of these potential impacts include the automation of news production processes, personalised news content experiences, the increase of data-driven journalism, the rapid production and dissemination of news, the quick detection of false news content and the prevention of its spread, as well as potential risks such as security threats, disinformation, deepfakes, and ethical violations.

Participants coded K9 (Marcom Specialist) and K4 (sports reporter), who stated that artificial intelligence could lead to an evolution in the journalism profession, expressed their thoughts as follows:

> *"In the future, the development of artificial intelligence could lead to a significant evolution in the field of journalism." The production of news by advanced robots can accelerate the news flow while reducing the role of journalists. This situation has the potential to offer readers personalised news tailored to their interests, while also bringing along algorithmic risks such as malware and misinformation. "Artificial intelligence is fundamentally changing and transforming the future of journalism." Speed and efficiency are important in journalism. Artificial intelligence can quickly analyse large data sets and prepare news in a shorter time. For example, in data-driven news such as finance, sports, and weather, automated content generation is becoming widespread... Artificial intelligence and algorithms can personalise news according to readers' interests. This way, readers can more easily access the content that is most suitable for them.*

The user coded as K3 (freelance journalist/independent verifier), who stated that journalists who can integrate artificial intelligence technologies into their profession may be preferred by the media industry and those who cannot adapt to the use of artificial intelligence may face job loss, explained their views as follows:

"I think we have entered a process where those who can effectively integrate artificial intelligence into their profession will undergo natural selection." If we continue to see artificial intelligence as a tool that will take our jobs, of course it will. But instead, if we use it as an assistant to do more qualitative work, we will understand that our concern is unfounded."

On the other hand, a participant coded K8 (sports reporter) who expressed the opinion that developments in the field of artificial intelligence would not affect the future of journalism explained their thoughts as follows:

"I don't think it will affect journalism." I see it as an addition to the innovation experienced during the transition from traditional media to digital media. In this context, artificial intelligence can be used to transmit incorrect images or audio recordings to people, potentially leading to misinformation. However, a reporter will always be needed to convey the news. This has not changed even with the advent of digital media. What has changed is the speed of news transmission and the possibilities for rapid dissemination.

Regarding the potential impacts of artificial intelligence on the future of journalism, the vast majority of participants expressed the view that AI technologies will bring evolutionary changes and transformations to the media industry and the future of journalism. It has been stated that artificial intelligence can pose both positive and negative risks to the future of journalism. Among the positive impacts on the future of journalism are automation, personalised news content, the increase of data-driven journalism, the rapid production and dissemination of news, the quick detection of false news content, and the greater accessibility of journalism. On the other hand, potential negative impacts such as ethical violations and workforce changes have been emphasised. Additionally, a participant who expressed the opinion that artificial intelligence would not affect the future of journalism likened the process to the transition from traditional media to digital media and stated that the change would occur in terms of speed.

THE BENEFITS AND RISKS OF ARTIFICIAL INTELLIGENCE FOR JOURNALISTS

The benefits and risks of using artificial intelligence in newsrooms for journalists can vary depending on how this technology is integrated into journalism, how it is used, and for what purposes. However, in general, artificial intelligence offers both great opportunities and some potential dangers to the media sector and journalists. Among the benefits mentioned by the participants regarding this topic are time savings and efficiency in work processes, automated content production, data analysis, rapid detection of incorrect content, and personalised news presentation; while potential risks include bias and ethical issues, distancing from the human element and employment concerns, manipulation, and disinformation.

Explaining the benefits and risks of using artificial intelligence for journalists with examples from reputable media organisations, participants coded K15 (academic) and K7 (academic) and expressed their thoughts as follows:

"Nowadays, many reputable media and news organisations effectively use artificial intelligence in their newsrooms." For example, The New York Times summarises long news articles using artificial intelligence, making it easier for users to read. The Washington Post, on the other hand, utilises artificial intelligence tools to verify the data in news content. Thus, the use of artificial intelligence as a verification tool, especially in combating fake news, offers journalists a benefit in the fight against disinformation... However, there are also certain risks that AI-supported journalism brings to journalism. At the forefront of these are the ease of spreading fake news and disinformation, ethical violations, copyright issues, and employment and unemployment problems.

"The use of artificial intelligence will further enable the proliferation of newsrooms integrated with digitalisation." When considering journalists, it is expected that they will have gained multiple skills, being able to produce news for every medium and mastering technologies related to the use of artificial intelligence alongside their traditional areas of expertise. The concept of workflow for journalists will change, and they will be able to use artificial intelligence like an assistant and focus on investigative journalism themselves. Journalists will be exposed to a faster flow of information and will encounter more news that they need to verify. Additionally, the number of human journalists in newsrooms will decrease, the newsrooms will shrink, and some will be replaced by robot journalists. It will also be necessary for journalists to adopt a more creative and continuously self-improving mindset in order to make their profession sustainable."

While artificial intelligence offers significant benefits to journalists in newsrooms, it also carries some potential risks that need to be considered. While advantages such as efficiency, speed, accurate content production, and personalised experiences have the potential to transform journalism, ethical issues, bias, reduced creativity among journalists, diminished human control, and security threats should also be taken into account. In order for artificial intelligence to be successfully integrated, it should be considered that the ethical use of artificial intelligence, centred around human oversight and in accordance with ethical principles and rules, should be emphasised by academics and press professional organisations.

POTENTIAL IMPACTS OF ARTIFICIAL INTELLIGENCE ON THE NEWS INDUSTRY

The way artificial intelligence will impact the media and especially the news industry will be quite extensive. Artificial intelligence appears as a technology that can transform journalism and lead to fundamental changes in the media sector. At this point, the use of artificial intelligence in newsrooms, by media organisations and journalists, will offer opportunities as well as present some challenges to journalistic practices and the news industry. As possible effects of artificial intelligence on the media and news industry, it can be noted that it may accelerate news production processes, enable personalised news content creation and targeting of news consumers, improve efficiency in data journalism and investigative journalism, facilitate automated news writing and routine news content production, aid in detecting fake news and combating disinformation, produce visual content, pose risks of automated workforce and job loss, reduce creativity and downplay the human factor, and raise ethical and security issues.

As a contribution of artificial intelligence to the news industry, the participant coded as K12 (AI expert and GPT developer) explained their thoughts as follows:

> *"In the media sector, artificial intelligence can pave the way for independent journalists and democratise news production." However, if large organisations require less manpower due to automation, mass layoffs may occur. This could also increase the trend towards smaller teams and individual work in the industry.*

K3 (freelance journalist/independent verifier), K8 (reporter), and coded participants explained their thoughts on the impact of artificial intelligence on the news industry in terms of employment and the expectation of new skill sets from journalists as follows:

> *"With the faster editing of news from agencies using artificial intelligence, journalists who know how to use artificial intelligence will be preferred more." In addition to this, I think that some institutions will also provide training to their reporters on this matter.*
>
> *"The news industry will have to operate with fewer employees." Because artificial intelligence will do the work of several journalists alone, and it will do it more perfectly. Media moguls will continue to earn more. He will do this thanks to artificial intelligence. However, as long as the journalist who influences the masses does not improve themselves, they will lose their job to artificial intelligence!"*

A participant coded as K13 (expert at the Technology Transfer Application Research Centre) explained their thoughts as follows, stating that the use of artificial intelligence is likely to standardise the language and style of the media industry:

> *"It is likely that the use of artificial intelligence will standardise the language and style of the media and news industry." Ultimately, generative artificial*

intelligence technologies operate on existing inputs, and therefore, unless there is an improvement in this area, production will remain within certain patterns. In addition, the ease it provides in news and video editing will accelerate the news production processes. However, alongside this, there remains a need for a human-centred tool for issues of truth and ethics. Therefore, I think it will affect the news and media industry both positively and negatively." Honestly, I am undecided about taking a clear side, but I am concerned about the disinformation and ethical aspects."

Artificial intelligence will lead to significant changes in the media and news industry, making the sector faster, more efficient, and more personalised. Benefits such as increased efficiency, automated content production, data analysis, and fake content detection can offer significant advantages to media companies. However, negative impacts such as the reduction of creative processes, workforce loss, ethical issues, security risks, and misinformation should also be taken into account. Therefore, establishing a balance where artificial intelligence and human journalism work together and prioritising human journalist oversight in the use of artificial intelligence is of critical importance for the future of the media sector.

"FAKE NEWS," "DISINFORMATION," "DEEPFAKE," AND "ETHICS" IN ARTIFICIAL INTELLIGENCE-SUPPORTED JOURNALISM

AI-enabled journalism offers many opportunities to the media sector but also poses serious responsibilities and challenges related to concepts such as 'fake news,' 'disinformation,' 'deepfake,' and 'ethics.' These concepts are directly related to the fundamental principles of journalism and are critical to providing accurate information and maintaining public trust. It is necessary to correctly analyse how AI-supported journalism activities interact with concepts such as 'fake news,' 'disinformation,' 'deepfake,' and 'ethics.' It should be considered that the relationship of AI-supported journalism with these concepts is both a threat and a solution.

The participants coded P5 (freelance journalist), P6 (academician), and P8 (sports reporter), who drew attention to the point that concepts such as 'fake news,' 'disinformation,' 'deepfake,' and 'ethics' in artificial intelligence-supported journalism can be produced by artificial intelligence due to the training of artificial intelligence with incorrect data sets, and explained their thoughts, respectively, as follows:

'AI-enabled journalism poses serious threats to critical issues such as fake news, disinformation, deepfakes, and ethics. When trained with the wrong data sets, this technology can produce erroneous or deliberately misleading news, accelerating the spread of disinformation. Deepfake technology can manipulate public

opinion with fake video and audio content, posing a great threat, especially in times of crisis and election processes. At this point, the concept of ethics becomes one of the most critical elements of AI-supported journalism. In this direction, it should be transparent about how artificial intelligence is used in news production processes, and human journalists should supervise the content.'

'Even if AI is used in the detection of these phenomena, it is also AI that contributes to their production. AI is both poison and antidote. Since news production will be too much with AI, disinformation, ethical problems, and fake news will increase. With AI, information pollution is increasing, with digitalisation will increase even more. Therefore, AI will further reduce the trust in journalism.'

'Whatever data you enter into artificial intelligence, it gives you the equivalent. It serves you in a simpler and more target-oriented way... Artificial intelligence can be used as an easily manipulable tool to create fake news by violating ethical values.'

The participants coded K9 (Marcom Specialist) and K12 (artificial intelligence specialist/GPT developer), who emphasised that in order to prevent the risks related to concepts such as 'fake news,' 'disinformation,' 'deepfake,' and 'ethics' in artificial intelligence-supported journalism, human control and artificial intelligence should be utilised and confirmation mechanisms should be given importance, respectively, and explained their views as follows:

'In artificial intelligence-supported news, journalist control should be kept in hand. News confirmation must be made... Strong protective mechanisms and legal regulations are required to prevent ethical violations and protect individual rights.'

'Since there is a risk of artificial intelligence producing false information in news texts, confirmation mechanisms must be established. Recently, the capacity of artificial intelligence to produce videos from scratch has also developed; content reflecting events that do not exist can emerge. Therefore, AI literacy is important. In terms of ethics, artificial intelligence should not be allowed to work completely independently; at least the final control should be done by human hands. This would clarify the responsibility for damages arising from erroneous news.'

The views of the participants regarding the interaction of concepts such as 'fake news,' 'disinformation,' 'deepfake,' and 'ethics' in terms of artificial intelligence-supported journalism are united in the view that artificial intelligence should be used as a tool and should be used under human control. ChatGPT, an artificial intelligence chat tool, is also included in the participant group of the study. In this context, K10 ChatGPT explained his views on concepts such as 'fake news,' 'disinformation,' 'deepfake,' and 'ethics' in AI-supported journalism as follows:

'AI's data analysis and language processing capabilities provide a great advantage in detecting fake news. By analysing texts and sources, AI can identify news whose accuracy is questionable or suspicious. AI is also a powerful tool

for combating disinformation. By analysing large data sets, AI can quickly identify the source, spread, and impact of disinformation. AI can detect subtle anomalies in videos and audio recordings. The development of AI in this area makes it easier for media organisations to quickly recognise deepfake content and take the necessary measures to ensure accuracy. Ethical journalism should be a fundamental principle in the use of AI. Media organisations should use AI not only in content production but also in ethical verification processes.'

When ChatGPT's views are evaluated, negative effects such as fake news, disinformation, and deepfakes can be combated by leveraging the features offered by AI-supported journalism activities. When using AI technologies, media organisations and journalists must focus on accuracy, reliability, impartiality, and ethical values. Artificial intelligence-supported journalism, when used as a tool and under human control, offers important solutions for informing the public and combating fake news and disinformation.

CONCLUSION

Artificial intelligence-supported journalism brings about a significant transformation for both the media sector and journalists. The use of artificial intelligence technologies in journalistic practices and newsrooms offers great opportunities but also brings risks such as fake news, deepfakes, ethical violations, and disinformation. For this reason, the effective use of artificial intelligence requires a careful approach centred on human control. While taking advantage of the opportunities offered by artificial intelligence, a more balanced approach should be adopted, taking into account the creativity, ethical responsibilities, and social ties of human journalists. AI-supported journalism has the potential to transform both the news content production processes of journalists and the interaction of journalism with society. Artificial intelligence technologies offer important opportunities to shape the future of journalism. In addition to many benefits, such as increasing the speed of journalism, reaching more people by personalising news content, ensuring accuracy, and creating news stories from large datasets, some risks require a careful approach, such as ethics, reliability, disinformation, fake news, and deepfakes.

In this study, in-depth interviews were conducted with journalists, artificial intelligence developers, academics, and ChatGPT, an artificial intelligence chat tool. The aim was to highlight the potential effects of artificial intelligence-supported journalism on the future of the field, including its implications for newsrooms and the broader news industry. Additionally, the study addresses potential negative developments that may emerge in the near future, such as 'fake news', 'disinformation', 'deepfakes', and ethical concerns, while also considering the positive aspects associated with the use of artificial intelligence. The opinions of academics and artificial intelligence experts on the use of artificial intelligence in business processes are focused on the fact that artificial intelligence will enable rapid execution of business processes, provide automation and efficiency, facilitate data analysis and content production, become more widespread in the future, and strongly change some professions. It was also emphasised that artificial intelligence should be handled together with its positive and negative aspects, and that artificial intelligence should only be used as an assistant in business processes with human control. The use of artificial intelligence tools in business processes, especially in areas such as the journalism profession, which is creative and carries ethical responsibility in terms of informing the public, should take into account that these tools carry risks as well as the benefits they will bring, and caution should be taken. When ChatGPT's response regarding the positive and negative aspects of artificial intelligence is analysed, it is possible to say that ChatGPT responded impartially, especially in terms of including and explaining the negative aspects in detail. The noteworthy points in ChatGPT's response: In the title of bias and ethical problems, it was emphasised that the responsibility for the negativities that may occur due to the fact that artificial intelligence systems are based on educational data is due to the uploaded educational data. Regarding employment and job loss, it was stated that journalists working in low-level jobs would face this problem.

Artificial intelligence-supported journalism is being used intensively by more and more news organisations in the world and in our country due to the advantages it provides. For this reason, journalists, editors, and journalist candidates working in the media sector should adapt to artificial intelligence technologies and tools as soon as possible and have the skills to perform processes such as translation, visual creation, news accuracy verification, voice-over, video creation, data analysis, personalisation, and automation of news content effectively and efficiently. Regarding the potential effects of artificial intelligence on the future of journalism, the majority of the participants stated that it will bring evolutionary changes and transformations to the future of the media industry and journalism. It was stated that artificial intelligence may pose some risks to the future of journalism, both positive and negative. Among the positive effects on the future of journalism, automation, personalised news content, an increase in data-driven journalism, rapid production and dissemination of news, rapid detection of false news content, and making journalism more accessible are listed. On the other hand, ethical violations and labour force change were emphasised among the potential negative effects. In addition, a participant who stated that artificial intelligence will not affect the future of journalism likened the process to the transition from traditional media to digital media and stated that the change that may occur will be in the field of speed.

While AI offers significant benefits to journalists in newsrooms, it also carries some potential risks that need to be considered. While advantages such as efficiency, speed, accurate content production, and personalised experiences have the potential to transform journalism, ethical issues, bias, decreased creativity in journalists, reduced human control, and security threats should also be considered. In order for AI to be successfully integrated, academics and media professional organisations should take into account that the ethical use of AI should be in accordance with ethical principles and rules that centre on human control. Artificial intelligence will lead to major changes in the media and news industries, making them faster, more efficient, and more personalised. Benefits such as increased efficiency, automated content production, data analytics, and fake content detection can offer significant advantages to media companies. However, negative impacts such as reduced creative processes, loss of labour, ethical issues, security risks, and disinformation should also be considered. Therefore, it is critical for the future of the media sector to establish a balance where artificial intelligence and human journalism work together and to prioritise human journalists' supervision in the use of artificial intelligence. Artificial intelligence, as a powerful tool in the media world, can both create negative effects such as fake news, disinformation, and deepfakes and offer powerful solutions to combat these negativities. When using this technology, it is critical to focus on accuracy, reliability, impartiality, and ethical values. It is essential for media organisations to use AI responsibly, both in terms of protecting public trust and maintaining a knowledge-based, ethical journalistic approach. When used correctly, AI-supported journalism has enormous potential to inform the public and combat misleading content.

REFERENCES

Aziz, A. (2003). *Araştırma yöntemleri teknikleri ve iletişim. Ankara.* Turhan Kitabevi.

Kümbetoğlu, B. (2008). *Sosyolojide ve antropolojide niteliksel yöntem ve araştırma. İstanbul.* Bağlam Yayınevi.

Larrondo, E., & Grandi, N. (2021). Artificial Intelligence, algorithms and freedom of expression. *Universitas (Accra), 34*(2), 169–186. DOI: 10.54517/met.v2i2.1790

Lopezosa, C., Codina, L., Pont-Sorribes, C., & Vállez, M. (2023). Use of generative artificial intelligence in the training of journalists: Challenges, uses and training proposal. *El Profesional de la Información, 32*(4), e320408. DOI: 10.3145/epi.2023.jul.08

Nguyen, D., & Hekman, E. (2022). The news framing of artificial intelligence: A critical exploration of how media discourses make sense of automation. *AI & Society, 39*(2), 437–451. Advance online publication. DOI: 10.1007/s00146-022-01511-1

Özbay, F., & Alataş, B. (2019). Fake news detection within online social media using supervisedartificial intelligence algorithms. *Physica A, 540*, 123174. DOI: 10.1016/j.physa.2019.123174

Sharadga, T., Tahat, Z., & Safori, A. (2022). Journalists' Perceptions towards Employing Artificial Intelligence Techniques in Jordan TV's Newsrooms. *Studies in Media and Communication, 10*(2), 239. Advance online publication. DOI: 10.11114/smc.v10i2.5749

Sun, S., Yujia, Z. S., & Yibei, C. (2020). Newspaper coverage of artificial intelligence: A perspective of emerging technologies. *Telematics and Informatics, 53*, 101433. Advance online publication. DOI: 10.1016/j.tele.2020.101433

Ufarte, R. M. J., Verdú, F. J., & Túñez-López, J. M. (2023). Use of artificial intelligence in synthetic media: First newsrooms without journalists. *El Profesional de la Información, 32*, e320203. Advance online publication. DOI: 10.3145/epi.2023.mar.03

Zhai, Y., Yan, J., Zhang, H., & Lu, W. (2020). Tracing the evolution of AI: Conceptualization of artificial intelligence in mass media discourse. *Information Discovery and Delivery, 48*(3), 137–149. DOI: 10.1108/IDD-01-2020-0007

Zhou, W. (2024). Dilemma and coping strategies of news communication based on artificial intelligence and big data. *Heliyon, 10*(3), e25398. DOI: 10.1016/j.heliyon.2024.e25398 PMID: 38352794

Chapter 4
AI-Driven Media Influence on Consumer Behavior:
Algorithmic Personalization, Trust, and Attention

Burak Pekun
https://orcid.org/0000-0002-8480-0202
Muğla Sıtkı Koçman University, Turkey

ABSTRACT

The present chapter considers how artificial intelligence (AI) uses algorithmic personalisation, trust mechanisms, and attention capture to influence consumer behaviour. It outlines the development of recommendation systems using AI such as deep learning and reinforcement learning, explaining how they personalise content and predict preferences to influence decisions. One of the observed changes in the AI approach occurs through rise of "thinking" with predict preferences and "feeling" with simulating empathy for uninterrupted conversations. It also defines "filter bubbles" for another impact of recommendation engines, search filters, and chatbots with their personalised experiences by predicted preferences, so that users could only face with similar and "relevant" options during their journey. Higher engagement could manipulate a user's preference through the given predictions and direct the user to complete a purchase even at higher prices.

DOI: 10.4018/979-8-3373-2960-4.ch004

INTRODUCTION

There is a move toward media consumption mediated by AI. Artificial intelligence (AI) is taking an increasingly active place in forming what people see and how they engage, affecting the decisions they make. Media systems therefore change from mass broadcasting mass of undifferentiated content to curated streams generated by AI to adjust content flows adapted to individual behaviour. Kaplan and Haenlein (2019) describe the change as the rise of "thinking" AI where recommendation systems predict preferences and "feeling" AI such as chatbots simulating empathy for continuing engagement. The forms dominate contemporary media platforms such as Netflix and TikTok.

The technology changes have modified business logics, Zuboff (2019) outlining how platforms monetise the behavioural data users generate alongside content they distribute. Platforms extract data to predict and influence future actions, often leaving users unaware of AI's influence over their engagement. The economic model treats attention as a resource to be mined.

Empirical research illustrates such dynamics, with Kang and Lou (2022) showing that TikTok users rely on "For You" feeds generated by AI to an extent leading users to report time distortion and habitual scrolling. Some users attempt to "train" the algorithm to regain control, yet machine agency is dominant. Liang (2022) shows how TikTok's Chinese counterpart Douyin organises attention based on algorithmic tags instead of social networks. Douyin's 600 million daily users exemplify how "algorithmic capitalism" lead to vast audiences and revenues being channelled through systems made to capture and monetise users' attention.

In this line, the key concepts to consider in this chapter should be introduced briefly. First of all, Kaplan and Haenlein (2019) distinguish mechanical, thinking, and feeling AI, out of which thinking and feeling systems are most relevant in media contexts. Recommendation engines, search filters, and chatbots personalise experiences by predicting preferences or simulating responsiveness.

The process depends on algorithmic personalisation, Pariser (2011) warning that personalisation narrows informational exposure and creates "filter bubbles" in which users encounter only what algorithms predict they will like. Gillespie (2014) notes that algorithms embed cultural and economic priorities into what is deemed "relevant" as they sort content, advantaging advertising goals at the expense of diversity. Such systems increase engagement and convenience, yet Mohsin (2024) shows them to do so by manipulating preferences and pushing consumers toward purchases at higher prices or which are not necessary to them, significantly affecting satisfaction and loyalty. Yeung (2017) discusses personalisation evolved into "hypernudging" (continuous digital environment adjustment using AI) with live environment adaptations based on monitoring behaviours in the moment, making influence dynamic and harder to detect.

Teodorescu et al. (2023) finds trust in AI systems to require transparency and familiarity, both of which strongly predict such trust. Ribes et al. (2021) find interface designs to influence perceived credibility and comprehension, with technical explanations less certain to achieve such results, as the research shows excessively detailed explanations to sometimes reduce understanding and obstruct trust-building.

After a brief look at the key concepts, it is of importance to review connecting trust, attention, and personalisation. Trust, attention, and personalisation influence each other through consumer behaviour influences, Cheung and Ho (2025b) showing perceived explainability to enhance trust in the human engineers behind AI systems and signal competence and integrity. Trust rarely arises from only technical quality, with Swart (2021) noting that people who do not grasp algorithmic process may fill gaps with "folk theories" drawn from media or personal experience. Such "folk theories" build trust or create scepticism.

The dynamics are amplified due to platform designs, and Bucher (2018) argues that algorithms form influence visibility and attention invisibly by privileging metrics based on engagement. Noble (2018) shows how such influence can reproduce societal biases to undermine trust further. Cotter (2019) finds that users seek to adapt to such systems by "playing the visibility game" and that their success in that depends on their literacy and awareness levels. Reisdorf and Blank (2021) find algorithmic literacy to be highly uneven, 17% of users being well below average, with low literacy users remaining active but sceptical, which leads to gaps in trust distributions.

When it comes to consumer behaviour, AI systems' behavioural effects range from benign to highly intrusive, Mohsin (2024) exemplifying the former through AI system recommendations increasing convenience and loyalty, contributing to 35% of Amazon's revenue. Yeung's (2017) hypernudges are an example of the latter, eroding autonomy by dynamically influencing decisions which users do not make consciously.

Kahneman (2011) explains such effectiveness through cognitive science, showing that humans use fast and intuitive System 1 thinking which makes open to biases and emotional triggers. AI personalisation uses salient and emotionally charged options to exploit such thinking models by prompting impulsive decisions. Kim et al.'s (2021) cognitive shortcuts example is precise numbers used to increase trust in AI recommendations and increase adoption.

McStay (2018) points to the evolution in emotional AI, reading facial, vocal, and behavioural cues allowing platforms to tailor content to users' moods. Such deepened engagement raises concerns related to subconscious manipulation. Swart (2021) notes that users' welcoming of precision is limited because highly accurate and intrusive recommendations create discomfort which outweighs the benefits from relevance.

The purpose and the structure of the present chapter is provided in the following. The present chapter considers modes in which media systems using AI influence consumer behaviour by managing attention and seeking trust or personalising content. It draws on theories including surveillance capitalism, behavioural economics, attention economy, medium theory, and cognitive science, contextualised through empirical studies on user trust, literacy, agency, and platform practices.

The chapter first traces the history of AI in media and outlining theories informing the analysis. It then explains how AI systems personalise and target content, followed by examining how attention is extracted and managed. The subsequent section explores how platforms build or undermine trust and authenticity, followed by a discussion of agency and resistance looking into user adoption or struggle in opaque systems. The chapter then considers the interactions between attention, trust, and personalisation on AI-driven platforms, continuing to discuss future and regulatory implications. It concludes on findings and their significance for consumer autonomy and media ethics.

HISTORICAL AND THEORETICAL BACKGROUND

There is a change from rule-based recommenders to deep learning. Recommendation systems trace back to early rule-based tools in the mid-1990s, such as Web Watcher and Amazon's first collaborative filtering engines increasing sales by delivering simple matches between users and items (Li & Cao, 2025). Initial simpler systems used models recommending products through content- and behavioural data. Hybrid approaches including collaborative and content filtering were introduced after the late 2000s to deal with sparsity and cold-start problems (Chakraborty et al., 2021). Deep learning became dominant after 2016 as convolutional and recurrent neural networks with factorisation machines and attention-focused architectures improved accuracy and scalability (Han et al., 2023; Jiang & Qin, 2025). Knowledge graphs, reinforcement learning, and transformer-based large language models such as UniLLMRec are used in recent systems which adapt to dynamic user preferences and sparse data (Xu et al., 2024). Such developments built the foundation for current large scale AI recommendation platforms predicting preferences and modulating behaviour in e-commerce and media, such as Amazon and TikTok whose recommendation engines increase engagement and in Amazon's case over a third of their sales (Necula & Păvăloaia, 2023).

Digital environments as behavioural economics with nudging; it is gainful to understand the systems' influence through behavioural economics highlighting the psychological mechanisms they exploit. Choice architecture and nudging show defaults, framing, and social cues to steer decisions without having to remove free choice. Kahneman's (2011) dual process model shows why the strategies work, as the intuitive System 1 is open to biases including loss aversion and anchoring, in contrast to the slow and deliberative System 2 which is less likely to engage in environments with high pace. Digital personalisation exploits System 1 by presenting emotionally charged or salient content inciting impulsive responses where notifications and default recommendations subtly guide behaviour through nudges. Yeung's (2017) 'hypernudging' concept describes how systems using AI adapt interfaces 'on the go,' using behavioural data to recalibrate what users see or are prompted to do based on constant monitoring and prediction. It is effective for engagement yet such adaptivity raises concerns about autonomy because users may not detect and be able to resist such steering mechanisms (Ewert, 2020; Santos Silva, 2022).

It is also important to review the attention economy and cognitive load. The attention economy contextualises how media using AI influence consumer behaviour. Wu (2016) charts successive waves of media from print and broadcast to algorithmic platforms intensifying the move to capture and monetise attention that culminated in systems predicting and moulding habits by using notifications, feeds, and adaptive recommendations. Bhargava and Velasquez (2021) argue that such systems form addictive patterns distinct from other forms of compulsion by using variable rewards, social validation, and infinite scroll, where platforms optimise over time as they learn how to maximise individual users' engagement. Nguyen et al. (2020) draw on Cognitive Theory of Multimedia Learning to show how personalisation reduces cognitive load by tailoring formats to users' preferences and increasing attention and recall. The findings taken together show personalisation with AI to operate by filtering information and influencing the intensity and persistence of user engagement.

When it comes to surveillance capitalism and data colonialism, Zuboff (2019) structurally situates such dynamics as part of surveillance capitalism in which behavioural data becomes raw material for predictive and interventionist models eroding user autonomy. Corporations predict behaviour and modify it for engagement and revenue goals, Zuboff describing the process as "instrumentarian power." Couldry and Mejias (2019) equate the extraction and behavioural steering with "data colonialism" and argue that users' everyday actions are appropriated as profitable resources for in ways deepening power asymmetries. Andrejevic (2014) calls the imbalance the "big data divide" and highlights how people with analytic capacity can predict and influence behaviour in contrast to individuals who continue to be subjects of opaque profiling. The perspectives see media using AI for influence as being about more than convenience and efficiency, reflecting entrenched economic and political interests commodifying trust and attention.

Medium theory and socio-technical perspectives are another way of conceptualising the issues. McLuhan (1964) argued that a medium's form in terms of speed, interactivity, and sensory reach forms culture and cognition irrespective of the specific content. Gillespie (2014) and Bucher (2018) show algorithms to take a gatekeeper role and embed commercial and institutional logics into what is visible, relevant, or promoted. The "folk theories" about such systems discussed by Gillespie (2014) are one response, as is adapting behaviour to ensure visibility (Bucher, 2018), resulting in systems' influence being entrenched and their operations being obscured.

Having in mind the above discussion, it is important to review how the theories matter. The considered theories frame the way media driven by AI influences consumers, behavioural economics and nudging explaining why personalisation may steer decisions by exploiting cognitive shortcuts and biases. The attention economy and cognitive load theory highlight how engagement may become compulsive and how tailoring reduces cognitive barriers. Surveillance capitalism and data colonialism show such mechanisms exist within economic structures intended to extract value from user behaviour and undermining autonomy and trust in doing so. Medium theory and socio-technical perspectives show influence to exceed content and include platforms' structural qualities and embedded logics to influence attention and behaviour.

Understanding consumer influence of AI solutions requires an integrated view. Recommendation systems which used to be matching tools have become adaptive predictive engines embedded in economic models profiting from behavioural steering. Exploiting cognitive tendencies and optimising attention capture, as well as operating in infrastructures normalising data extraction and behavioural control are their sources of power. The frameworks can be used to analyse how trust and attention are cultivated and commodified in digital economies, sometimes eroding them.

HOW AI INFLUENCES CONSUMER EXPERIENCE

In order to understand how AI influences consumer experience, it is important to first review new generation personalisation engine types. Recommendation systems' scale and complexity has changed significantly since the discussed early models. Modern architectures use deep learning, reinforcement learning, and transformer-based approaches to predict changing interests and behaviours alongside static ones. Models including the LightGBM-factorisation deep neural network (LFDNN) model (Han et al., 2023), fusing Light Gradient Boosting Machine (LightGBM), factorisation machines, and deep neural networks, and Jiang and Qin's (2025) hybrid long short-term memory-convolutional neural network (LSTM-CNN) framework process billions of interactions by analysing temporal changes and structural content patterns in parallel, with architectures adapting to user interest changes and outperforming collaborative filtering on area under the curve (AUC) and recall metrics.

Scaling such systems requires infrastructure that can handle data flows on the population-level. Xu et al. (2024) show how UniLLMRec (a transformer-based large language model recommender) drawing on ChatGPT-4 uses elastic cloud computing for recommendations with high accuracy with limited data. Such architectures process heterogeneous inputs from browsing, purchases, demographic and contextual signals at low latency to enable highly profitable live personalisation in ecommerce and on social media (Xu et al., 2024; Li & Cao, 2025).

Reinforcement learning adds depth by optimising for long-term engagement over quick clicks, with Pseudo Dyna-Q (Zou et al., 2020) and the reinforcement learning -based recommender family surveyed by Afsar et al. (2022) using offline logs and simulated environments to train policies. Such systems learn from synthetic interactions generated by "world models" to reduce user risk to select strategies for longer term usage. Platforms use such methods to dynamically prioritise recommendation sequences prolonging engagement, as it fits their retention and monetisation goals.

Following the discussion above, affect and behavioural shaping should be considered. Emotional AI is another personalisation layer inferring users' affective states from multimodal data, but ethical issues around its potential to exploit emotional states raises issues (Pusztahelyi, 2020). Artificial empathy systems are created through such capabilities, with social and emotional cues close to human ones in their responses (Liu-Thompkins et al., 2022). Such systems combine reinforcement learning for perspective-taking, multimodal emotion recognition, and simulated emotional mirroring to increase social presence and rapport. They can make AI agents seem warmer and more trustworthy, yet their commercial function is to strengthen bonds that increase conversions or time on platform (McStay, 2018).

Such adaptive systems influence cognitive shortcuts in the way indicated by Kahneman's (2011) dual-process framework, including through precision cues (Kim et al., 2021) presenting data as "74.975% accurate" instead of "75%" as trust signals. Emotional AI can nudge decisions by tailoring content to users' moods or subtly shifting those moods to make advertising more effective (Pusztahelyi, 2020). Such effects may bypass reflective scrutiny and continually steer behaviour.

There is also dynamic feedback loops and network effects to consider. Modern personalisation uses recursive loops where system outputs influence user inputs, narrowing exposure over time. Michiels et al. (2023) show personalised news feeds to gradually have around 5.5% lower topic diversity over 13 weeks, with stable political diversity suggesting algorithms stabilise engagement by focusing attention without creating complete informational isolation.

Relatively minor parameter changes can create significant consequences in networks, as Chitra and Musco (2020) show small weighting adjustments in recommender systems to amplify polarisation by orders of magnitude up to 700-fold on Reddit networks when connections between groups weaken. Regularisation can mitigate such effects, yet commercial implementations may not be focused on such safeguards if engagement benefits from clustering.

Survey reviews by Interian et al. (2023) emphasise interventions reducing polarisation including modifying edges to connect across clusters or altering collaborative filtering weights to promote diversity. Such strategies are most effective if used before polarisation solidifies, as systems generally default to designs prioritising retention, even when such choices increase homophily and repetition in content.

When it comes to commercial imperative and consumer impact, the techniques are persistent due to their alignment with the dominant model of the digital economy, driven by advertisement. Platforms monetise engagement by optimising for time on site, clicks, and conversions, meaning technical innovations and affective systems converge on keeping users engaged. Session-based recommenders (Wang et al., 2021) and hypernudging architectures (Yeung, 2017) respond to behavioural feedback through adjusted feeds and interfaces to reduce disengagement harder.

As Bhargava and Velasquez (2021) show, behavioural addiction rates increase from 8.6% to 36.9% for young users subjected to infinite scroll, variable rewards, and algorithmically tuned validation cues. Longitudinal evidence shows such factors to predict later harms such as depression, impaired cognition, and reduced life satisfaction. Platforms supported by ads rather than subscriptions have profit incentives to deepening such dependency, making emotional AI and reinforcement learning tools commercially rational despite associated social costs.

Using advanced AI systems on consumer-facing media has taken personalisation away from aligning offers to preferences, using hybrid and reinforcement learning systems to predict and guide behaviour over the long term, with emotional AI tuning engagement at a subconscious level, and adaptive network dynamics upholding platform goals with high costs in terms of narrowing or polarising effects. The consumer experience is engineered to align attention and action with platform revenue imperatives over individual intent.

ATTENTION AS A MANAGED RESOURCE

Monetising attention is no novelty in media industries, and Wu (2016) shows the trend starting with print and broadcast and intensifying with algorithmic media. The current phase with AI systems predicting and directing habits via recommendation engines, notifications, and engagement metrics is a further development of such attention economies where attention is turned into a continuous revenue stream.

Zhu and Lerman (2016) study loss and concentration of attention on Twitter, showing the top 20% users capture 97% of followers and 93% of retweets, most influence with the top 1%. Attention value as a resource is increased by platforms rewarding those who are already visible.

Such practices fit Zuboff's (2019) surveillance capitalism framework, where behavioural data is collected and used to intervene in decisions to align user behaviour with commercial priorities.

When it comes to extraction with AI, there is scroll, notification and targeted feeds. Platforms including TikTok and Douyin are examples of attention extraction using AI, Kang and Lou (2022) showing it through TikTok's "For You" feed creating automatic scrolling and a distorted sense of time. Bhargava and Velasquez (2021) see such mechanics as part of behavioural addiction through noted designed mechanisms. Liang (2022) shows Douyin to use digital tags and algorithmic metrics to replace social networks with a centralised attention economy drawing on data, allowing even small creators to be surfaced while ultimately depending on rules they have little control over.

It is also important to review cognitive and temporal effects of managed attention. Engagement mechanisms using AI keep users online longer and change how people think and perceive time, feeds dominated by fast, emotionally charged content push users into intuitive, impulsive responses, reducing reflective decision-making under Kahneman's dual-process model. Kang and Lou (2022) identify a "time loss" effect as infinite scroll removes cues to stop and dynamic feeds mix predictable and surprising elements for continued focus. Lv, Li, and Wang (2024) note the use of over-recommendation where feeds feel redundant and overly narrow, leading to cognitive dissonance and disengagement intentions even in users who continue to actively use the media.

Another dimension is the addiction, harm and behavioural consequences. Algorithmic media maximises engagement through compulsive usage patterns resembling behavioural addiction. Fogg (2003) shows notifications, default options, reward loops, and other interface features to nudge users toward repeated interactions. The medium is the message, as suggested by McLuhan (1964).. Beer (2009) describes it as a "technological unconscious" where engagement logics such as popularity and speed are part of systems not fully open to user perceptions.

The mechanisms exploit psychological and behavioural traits. Nyrhinen et al.'s (2024) study finds young consumers with low self-control to be vulnerable to targeted advertising and social media cues and therefore to impulsive buying and indebtedness. Winter et al. (2021) similarly find that ads personalised to traits such as susceptibility to scarcity or authority increase engagement intentions significantly, especially when combined with social validation or urgency cues. The practices are commercially effective yet increase compulsive and financially harmful behaviour risks.

The same algorithmic systems concentrate attention and power which compounds harms, as pointed out in relation to Zhu and Lerman's (2016) study of Twitter users. The outcome is a "rich get richer" effect where the most visible voices attract more engagement at the expense of diversity and increased elite dominance. The phenomenon links to Andrejevic's (2014) "big data divide" where platforms draw on behavioural profiles to steer users, increasing power asymmetries by withholding equivalent insight or control. Couldry and Mejias (2019) consider algorithmic targeting a form of "data colonialism" commodifying human activity for profit.

Such systems create cognitive and emotional consequences, McStay (2018) noting that emotional AI enables platforms to infer and act on users' affective states for persuasive potential which erodes autonomy. Lv, Li, and Wang (2024) find Chinese short video platforms to 'over-recommend,' with resulting information overload and cognitive dissonance manifested through frustration and leaving the platforms. In the same vein, Helberger (2019) shows algorithmic news recommenders to cause fragmentation in shared informational spaces, undermining civic and contributing to social isolation.

Regulatory responses to curb such effects by increasing transparency and accountability have been developed, and Genovesi, Kaesling, and Robbins (2023) outline obligations for very large platforms to disclose recommender logic and mitigate systemic risks in the EU Digital Services Act (DSA). Koene et al. (2019) argue that further measures including algorithmic literacy, watchdogs, and pre-market approval systems are needed to restrict addictive and manipulative dynamics. Meaningful oversight will depend on regulators' ability to enforce such tools effectively (Söderlund et al. 2024).

There are also structural and societal implications to consider. The changes have individual consequences that are implemented widely and bring about structural and societal issues. Couldry and Mejias (2019) use the "data colonialism" concept to highlight everyday behaviour being harvested as profit-generating data, reinforcing corporate power, with Andrejevic's (2014) "big data divide" concept addressing a similar change where analytic elites become able to predict and shape behaviour as users become subjects of opaque profiling. Bucher's (2018) and Gillespie's (2014) thinking about visibility in commercial logics and "folk theories" affects the "technological unconscious" influence discussed by Beer (2009), as users adapt without realising how structures influence their behaviour. The cultural costs are significant, Wu (2016) and Pariser (2011) noting growing attention fragmentation, filter bubbles, and sensationalism as engagement is prioritised over diversity and shared discourse.

TRUST AND AUTHENTICITY FOR MEDIA MEDIATED BY AI

Design and communication choices on platforms that use AI to curate and generate media affect trust, as transparency, familiarity, and interface structure have predicted confidence reliably. Teodorescu et al. (2023) show students informed about when e-commerce sites use AI to be 43% to be more likely to trust such systems, with previous AI experience raising trust and unfamiliarity lowering it by 53%. AI recommendations' perceived usefulness is the strongest predictor of trust in their study, highly satisfied students being 90% more likely to indicate trust.

Interface presentation was considered by Ribes et al. (2021) who found layouts for AI-driven news feeds based on sources (trust $M = 5.28$ as compared to $M = 3.74$ for ranked feeds, $p < .001$) to increase perceived credibility, users preferring visible source citations (6.58 as compared to 0.30, $p = .048$). Detailed technical explanations reduce comprehension to colour-coded matching rate number score $M = 2.38$, as compared to $M = 2.66$ with short explanations ($p = .04$). Clarity induces more trust than exhaustive detail in the light of Ribes et al.'s (2021) study.

Oyekunle et al. (2024) considered organisational context, identifying technological transparency ($\beta = .256$), perceived usefulness ($\beta = .392$), and organisational integrity understood as leadership support and ethics to be the most important sources for trust. Technological, psychological, and institutional factors between them explain over 54% of source trust variance, suggesting that interface design is insufficient to overcome weak organisational credibility.

As another dimension, cognitive shortcuts and user discomfort should be reviewed. Heuristics affect trust, Kim et al. (2021) showing precise numerical outputs to increase perceived AI competence and trust. Their five experiments ($N = 993$) showed trust to mediate higher attitudes and behavioural intentions for high-quality products and when AI outputs diverged from expectations.

Invasive personalisation unsettles users, as shown by Swart (2021) who finds that Dutch users aged 16 to 26 appreciate accurate recommendations but become uneasy with feeds that they see as overly tailored, prompting privacy and bias concerns. Glikson and Woolley's (2020) results confirm such findings as immediacy behaviours such as personalisation are found to enhance cognitive trust but also to create emotional discomfort when systems feel too human.

Such results align with Kahneman's (2011) dual-process theory in that precision and relevance appeal to intuitive responses while perceived manipulation threatening autonomy triggers more scrutiny.

When it comes to bias, synthetic media and eroding trust relationship, bias and manipulation threaten trust, and Noble (2018) shows that search engine algorithms amplify racial and gender stereotypes, with returning harmful pornographic content for queries about marginalised groups. The patterns are not programmed into the algorithm but arises from ranking logics based on engagement.

Such problems are aggravated by synthetic media, and as Karnouskos (2020) shows, cheaply produced deepfakes threaten politics, journalism, and gendered harms such as revenge porn. In the absence of detection tools, provenance tracking, and legal frameworks, such media can cause "truth decay" and public cynicism. Vaccari and Chadwick (2020) find deepfake deception to be rare with 16% belief, but uncertainty rises to 35-37% with deceptive clips as compared to 27.5% for revealed fakes, uncertainty on its own lowering trust in news, with indirect b being –0.175 ($p < .001$).

Trust risks arise from text generated with AI too, Kreps et al. (2022) showing GPT-2 text to match stories written by humans in credibility at 58-83%, potentially scaling misinformation, with inconsistent believability reduction from disclaimers. Partisan alignment influences trust as Republican and Democrat participants in their study rate ideologically aligned outputs higher.

As another dimension, explainability, perception and public confidence should also be considered. Explainable AI (XAI) has been proposed as a trust solution, yet its outcomes are mixed. Cheung and Ho (2025b) show explainability to increase trust in engineers' ability ($\beta = .15$), benevolence ($\beta = .13$), and integrity ($\beta = .28$) which exceeds system trust. Their other study (Cheung & Ho, 2025a) shows explainability improves trust in AI performance ($\beta = .50$), purpose ($\beta = .61$), and process ($\beta = .61$), mediating over 50% of news exposure effects on public trust.

Liu (2021) finds real and informative transparency to reduce uncertainty ($B = .90$, $p < .001$, $d = .64$) and offsets low social presence in autonomous AI, while shallow, "placebic" explanations help little.

Whether AI can be "trusted" at all has also been questioned on theoretical grounds, Ryan (2020) considering AI to satisfy only rational reliance but not providing affective or normative trust as it cannot hold moral responsibility or goodwill. He advocates replacing "trustworthy AI" with "reliable AI" to hold organisations and developers accountable rather than artefacts.

Following the discussion on design and trust, the concepts of authenticity and human perception come to mind. User authenticity perception is a strong factor behind responses to content mediated by AI, with Kirk and Givi (2025) showing that consumers penalise emotional marketing produced by AI, reducing positive word of mouth by 1-1.3 points and loyalty by ~1 point, which was mediated by lower authenticity (B = -0.17) and moral disgust (B = -0.33). Such effects were not found for factual content or for content edited rather than written by AI. Brüns and Meißner (2024) showed similar patterns as users who could not visually detect AI in Instagram posts reported reduced authenticity ($M = 4.13$ and 5.24 respectively, $p < .001$), credibility, and brand attitudes when AI use was disclosed.

There are solutions for transparency, as Burrus et al. (2024) recommends process labelling using metadata clarifying AI's role without stigmatising creators or overwhelming users. They find AI is distrusted in news but accepted for influencer marketing, users being more accepting of subtle auto-enhancements than overt edits. Provenance standards such as Coalition for Content Provenance and Authenticity and legal frameworks such as the European Union Artificial Intelligence Act (AI Act) may improve transparency and trust trade-offs.

Such issues have been identified in journalism too, Kolo et al. (2022) showing news generated by AI to match journalism in credibility yet receiving unreadability scores at a level with fake news ($p < .05$). High-trust audiences rate AI-labelled content as even less readable ($M = 3.38$ and 3.75 respectively, $p < .05$), with low-trust audiences being indifferent. Kolo et al. (2022) recommend improving prose style and segmenting audiences by trust levels to sustain credibility.

Optimism is mixed in the long term, Feher et al. (2024) drawing on media expert predictions that despite bias and deepfake risks, AI will underpin more accessible, personalised, and fair information flows by 2050, with AI-to-AI systems mitigating disinformation, as long as critical oversight is maintained for trust.

AGENCY, POWER, AND RESISTANCE

This section first discusses structural power: surveillance capitalism and the user as data. Platforms using AI rely on significant data extraction, behavioural prediction, and monetisation to create systems in which users are a raw material for profit. Zuboff (2019) calls this 'surveillance capitalism', where behavioural data underpins algorithmically personalised feeds and advertising which reduces exposure to different perspectives and steers trust and engagement toward commercial aims. Couldry and Mejias (2019) frame the process as "data colonialism" where user actions are converted into monetizable profiles that give corporations control over how personalisation and recommendations are used, without a parallel power for individuals. The mechanisms reduce autonomy by transforming user participation into inputs for behavioural prediction and manipulation.

Such asymmetries grow in the attention economy, where Wu (2016) shows media industries from print to digital having intensified the commodification of attention, with algorithmic personalisation being the most intrusive phase. Algorithms analyse behavioural signals to sustain engagement, creating self-reinforcing consumption cycles at the cost of users' critical engagement (Wu, 2016). Tufekci (2015) shows algorithms optimised for engagement privileging sensational and emotionally charged content to influence public discourse, users remaining largely unaware of nudges steering their attention. Napoli (2011) notes that audiences which used to be conceived as collective publics are now treated as measurable micro-segments with each interaction feeding live adjustments to the media and advertising that they encounter. Those who possess the means to collect, analyse, and use data control predictive and persuasive powers, leaving most users passive profiling and targeting subjects (Andrejevic, 2014).

The power concentration is embedded in the algorithmic media architecture, Bucher (2018) and Gillespie (2014) characterising algorithms as socio-technical actors invisibly deciding whose content is promoted and which values are embedded into media flows, creating asymmetries without explicit user awareness. According to Noble (2018), such systems reproduce and grow social inequalities by including cultural and commercial biases monetising engagement, neglecting fairness and diversity concerns. Service industries have similar dynamics with predictive analytics leading to coercion, proxy discrimination, and predatory data cultures eroding privacy and autonomy (Breidbach & Maglio, 2020).

Infrastructure and tools being under corporate control, Luitse and Denkena (2021) show large language models (LLMs) to increase monopolistic power through enormous data, computing, and cloud infrastructure resource demands which are largely controlled by large firms including Google and Microsoft. Such models' closed distribution with application programming interfaces (APIs) increases dependency and makes independent deployment or research unfeasible for smaller entities. Simon (2022) notes that journalism AI tools supplied by platform companies create vendor lock-in and black-box decision-making, harming editorial oversight and embedding platforms' commercial logics into news production. AI personalisation and automation prioritise corporate control in different sectors, positioning users and institutions as data sources with low influence over systems influencing outcomes.

When it comes to user strategies and adaptations, users and creators try to control or influence algorithmic systems despite the asymmetries between them and the system. Espinoza-Rojas, Siles, and Castelain (2022) show that multi-platform users are more aware of algorithms than single-platform users do. They call it 'rhetorical awareness' and practising 'mutual domestication' by training algorithms to shield their profiles from unwanted signals and compare outputs on different platforms. Swart (2021) shows young people's literacy to be fragmented and experiential. It is in many cases triggered by surprising recommendations or privacy controversies, leading some to attempt muting, unfollowing or other interventions to correct feeds. They are unable to sustain engagement due to low perceived agency and entrenched habits.

Adaptations take on creative and tactical forms on content-driven platforms, Cotter (2019) showing Instagram influencers to "play the visibility game" by changing aesthetics, post timing, and engagement tactics in response to platform logics where algorithmic rules frequently change. Kang and Lou (2022) note how

TikTok users curate feeds by skipping unwanted videos and following trends, selectively engaging with content to develop 'algorithmic imaginaries' despite opaque mechanisms. Liang (2022) analyses how Douyin creators and marketing networks exploit algorithmic preferences using rigid specialisation, surrogate operations, or mass account strategies to maximise reach, which emphasises creators' active and precarious visibility metrics manipulation.

Ordinary users seek agency through transparency and control features. Dogruel, Facciorusso, and Stark (2020) find that feelings of diminished autonomy increase awareness around algorithmic influence and leads to calls for measures to increase transparency. Reisdorf and Blank (2021) investigate algorithmic literacy, which they separate from general internet skills, finding it to be uneven but associated with trust and online engagement. Many users are unable to influence recommendations meaningfully (Agner et al., 2020). Control and transparency may help in such situations, Huang, Jiao, and Zhu (2025) showing them to enhance personal agency and trust on travel platforms, Van Drunen, Zarouali, and Helberger (2022) showing that news consumers value disclosure and tangible options such as selecting data inputs, adjusting algorithmic goals, or disabling personalisation entirely.

Such adaptive practices may benefit platform priorities, Beer (2009) arguing that users' behavioural adjustments tend to fit algorithmic incentives and embed commercial logics into participatory spaces. Tactical engagement can enhance individual outcomes, yet it rarely challenges underlying power and control asymmetries.

Following the discussion above, it is important to look at who benefits and who struggles. Personalisation advantages and harms in AI environments are unevenly distributed under influence of literacy, resources, and social capital disparities. Users with higher algorithmic literacy who are often younger, wealthier, or more educated manipulate systems to optimise their feeds and recommendations, which gives them relevance, discovery, and efficiency benefits (Reisdorf & Blank, 2021). People not possessing the relevant skills find such systems to be opaque, causing scepticism and resignation with diminished autonomy (Dogruel et al., 2020). Many heavy users would need tools and vocabulary for challenging algorithmic influence, and in their absence default to habitual use, resigning to opaque curation (Swart, 2021).

Creators too have such different outcomes, as exemplified by Douyin's algorithmic attention model which enables small accounts to monetise but comes with volatility, unpredictable view counts and incentives for homogenised content (Liang, 2022). Lv, Li, and Wang (2024) show Chinese video apps' over-recommendation to lead to cognitive dissonance and discontinuance intentions in vulnerable groups. On Twitter, as noted, attention inequality is extreme in favour of the top quintile and particularly the top 1% (Zhu & Lerman, 2016). Posting actively and visibility from retweets can help users with less influence grow audiences, yet there are structural factors benefitting elite and celebrity accounts.

The considered phenomena are part of the 'big data divide' (Andrejevic, 2014), giving significant benefits to those able to collect and analyse data and leaving others primarily as data suppliers without such advantages. Targeted literacy initiatives and systemic reforms may be required to counter such risks that would entrench economic outcome and informational autonomy disparities.

As another concept to discuss under this section, there is the black box problem and its impact on agency. Opaque AI systems in the so-called "black box" constrain user and institutional agency and for the latter, Simon (2022) shows black-box AI tools in newsrooms to erode editorial scrutiny, with vendor lock-in preventing oversight and customisation. Opacity causes uncertainty and resignation in individual users, Agner et al. (2020) finding that Netflix users struggle to identify how recommendations are generated despite having engaged for a long time, leaving them do content discovery through social networks or external sources. Bucher (2018) notes engagement fluctuations and visibility changes to be indirect ways for users to experience algorithms, as it is rare for them to explicitly understand them.

As noted, the practice of users to construct 'folk theories' around such gaps leads to often inaccurate ideas hampering useful engagement (Gillespie, 2014). Success of transparency initiatives meant to address such issues has been varied. The EU's DSA requires horizontal transparency through platform disclosures to users and vertical transparency through audits and reporting systemic risk, as well as researcher access to equalise power and mitigate harms (Cole et al., 2023; Söderlund et al., 2024). Yet Shah et al. (2024) show transparency to be unable to alone restore trust if data collection practices are perceived as unethical, suggesting moral acceptability is needed alongside explainability. Koene et al. (2019) argue that co-regulation, public literacy campaigns, and certification schemes are needed to operationalise accountability beyond disclosure.

Yeung's (2017) critique of hypernudging shows further problems where AI systems adapt digital environments live, based on behavioural feedback, making influence fluid and hard to detect. Such systems are commercially effective yet undermine informed consent and self-determination by steering users without overt coercion. Without robust oversight, participatory design, and enforceable rights, controlling and contesting algorithmic influence from black-box systems will be hard, restricting user and institutional agency.

SYNTHESIS

AI driven media influences consumer behaviour through mutually reinforcing algorithmic personalisation, attention capture, and trust in systems built for engagement and revenue maximisation. Platforms use behavioural data and predictive models to keep users active, building trust only where it supports retention and steering choices using techniques blurring lines between service and manipulation. Convenience and relevance are consumer benefits on AI platforms, yet for consumers they include trade-offs in the form of dependency and lost autonomy.

Personalisation systems using reinforcement learning and deep learning draw on browsing histories, social signals, and contextual data to adapt to user behaviours by editing feeds and recommendations (Han et al., 2023; Xu et al., 2024). Behavioural manipulation methods also change with the discussed emotional AI. Relevance increases and reduced friction are benefits that can be considered illusory in the sense that they drive decisions that users would not otherwise make, and which are primarily in the platforms' commercial interest. AI nudges consumers to make unnecessary and costly purchases (Mohsin, 2024), subtly hypernudging systems adjusting environments continuously and undetectably (Yeung, 2017).

Platforms use infinite scroll and variable rewards with live feedback loops to extract and exploit attention for behavioural control and push users to compulsive engagement (Bhargava & Velasquez, 2021). Platforms use feeds to distort time and reduce reflective decision-making (Kang & Lou, 2022; Liang, 2022), exploiting what Kahneman's (2011) dual-process model explains as fast intuitive responses leading to impulsive actions. Too 'in the face' and repetitive recommendations however cause cognitive dissonance and disengagement (Lv, Li, & Wang, 2024).

Teodorescu et al. (2023) and Oyekunle et al. (2024) find that users trust AI recommendations if they perceive them as useful, transparent, and ethical. Too accurate and intrusive AI recommendations unsettle users and erode trust (Swart, 2021; Kim et al., 2021), which is also the case for deepfakes and algorithmic biases (Noble, 2018; Vaccari & Chadwick, 2020). Explainable AI increases users' trust in engineers and systems (Cheung & Ho, 2025a; Cheung & Ho, 2025b), yet the transparency must be part of perceived ethical data extraction to engender trust (Shah et al., 2024).

Workings of such systems differ by platform and previously discussed social video platforms optimise attention by creating self-reinforcing consumption loops. Helberger (2019) warns about news environment fragmentation as recommender systems narrow shared informational spaces. Convenience drives e-commerce sales (Necula & Păvăloaia, 2023) which exploit behavioural biases to increase consumer spending (Mohsin, 2024). The dominant fact is the commercial incentive to monetise attention, with outcomes that may include manipulation as well as satisfaction.

Ethically, the environment changes because AI driven media systems are not neutral intermediaries but behavioural environments where trust, attention, and personalisation create systems enhancing user experiences at the expense of autonomy. Regulatory tools such as the DSA are required to redress the power and control asymmetries through user controls over data and recommendations and norms mitigating addictive mechanics. The historical trajectory and commercial incentives suggest that AI-driven media is likely to continue to move toward maximising engagement and profit at the cost of consumer independence and broader media ethics, if regulatory measures are not adopted to mitigate the trend.

IMPLICATIONS

In the future, AI-driven media may continue its development arch from recommendation engines to autonomous agents and immersive environments, as generative AI systems already produce adaptive video and interactive narratives. If platforms integrate such agents into social, retail, and news media with highly integrated interactions anticipating needs and simulating human qualities, current convenience and engagement benefits may become more pronounced. The same is however also true for deeper behavioural steering risks, even more concerning as emotional AI becomes better at immediately reading and responding to affective cues.

Regulation has moved significantly slower than technology and commerce, but some beginnings can be seen in the EU AI Act and DSA which are the current most advanced frameworks requiring risk assessments, transparency, and oversight. The DSA requires large platforms to disclose recommender system logic and grant researcher access to algorithmic data. The AI Act categorises systems by risk, where high-risk AI including personalised advertising targeting vulnerable groups is subject to documentation, monitoring, and potential prohibition. Such regulation seeks to balance innovation with protection but will depend on political will and ability to enforce them, as global firms may move or change operations to exploit regulatory gaps.

Design principles are required for harm mitigation, and transparency must not be seen as solely about superficial disclosures but instead clearly provide explanations of how systems collect and use behavioural data in layered and user-friendly formats avoiding overload. Explainability would benefit from focusing on clarifying system purpose and decision criteria over technical logic, considering research showing detailed explanations to reduce comprehension and trust (Ribes et al., 2021). Protecting autonomy requires structural choices including meaningful default options and limits on manipulative mechanics such as infinite scroll, as well as user controls for turning off or adjusting personalisation. It would seem sensible to set strict limits on emotional AI and affect-based targeting to avoid exploitation aggravating cognitive biases arising from Kahneman's (2011) System 1 thinking.

There are open questions about journalism using efficiency benefits from automation without vendor lock-in and diminished editorial independence (Simon, 2022). Communication research must assess how audiences perceive authenticity and credibility when AI mediates or produces content, given evidence of moral discomfort with emotional marketing (Kirk & Givi, 2025). Consumer research must address unequal impacts, as literacy and resources determine who benefits from AI-enhanced media and who becomes vulnerable to manipulation. Future scholarship should seek to track how AI changes consumption, public discourse, and power structures.

CONCLUSION

AI has crated media into behavioural environments with personalisation, trust, and attention as core influences on the consumer experience. Current recommendation systems cannot be compared to early static filters as they have become adaptive engines predicting, guiding, and often overriding user preferences. Emotional AI and hypernudging intensify engagement as they align content with moods and cognitive shortcuts that bypass reflective decision-making. Platforms have commercial retention and monetisation incentives which produce environments in which user satisfaction intersects with dependency and manipulation.

The chapter shows such dynamics to best be interpreted as structural, stemming from the economic logics of surveillance capitalism and data colonialism (Zuboff, 2019; Couldry & Mejias, 2019), in which behavioural data is raw material for predictive models. Platforms hold most of the informational and operational power, users supplying data and being steered through opaque systems. Trust is fragile because transparency, explainability, and organisational integrity are uneven, and because algorithmic biases, synthetic media, and invasive personalisation erode confidence. Efforts to build trust tend to be motivated by sustaining engagement and are rather rarely rather about redistributing control.

The bigger question is how societies will balance AI-mediated media benefits such as convenience, relevance, and access against dangers around autonomy, diversity, and democratic discourse. Evidence considered in this chapter suggests that left to commercial logics alone, AI-driven systems will continue to deepen behavioural steering and attention commodification. Regulatory frameworks such as the DSA and AI Act are early attempts to counterbalance such forces, but oversight must match the technical and economic scale of the firms deploying them.

The path forward must use compliance as a baseline and rethink AI media system designs ambitiously. Defaults preserving autonomy, human-in-the-loop oversight, provenance tracking for synthetic media, and limitations on exploitative engagement mechanics could prevent media from becoming mere behavioural marketplaces. Addressing algorithmic literacy and access disparities is a required step for informational inequality reduction to ensure AI does not widen the "big data divide" (Andrejevic, 2014).

Ethical and civic consequences from passivity may be significant as media only trivially is about conveying messages and as medium theory suggests also forms cognition and culture through its structures. Media enhanced by AI now does so by embedding corporate incentives into information and interaction flows. The policy, research, and design challenge, is, to ensure that such systems provide benefits to consumers and societies that rely on them, alongside current benefits to platforms, that build them.

REFERENCES

Afsar, M. M., Crump, T., & Far, B. (2022). Reinforcement learning based recommender systems: A survey. *ACM Computing Surveys*, *55*(7), 1–38. DOI: 10.1145/3543846

Agner, L., Necyk, B., & Renzi, A. (2020). Recommendation systems and machine learning: Mapping the user experience. In A. Marcus & E. Rosenzweig (Eds.), *Design, user experience, and usability: Design for contemporary interactive environments* (LNCS, vol. 12201). Springer. DOI: 10.1007/978-3-030-49760-6_1

Andrejevic, M. (2014). Big data, big questions| The big data divide. *International Journal of Communication*, *8*, 1673–1689. https://ijoc.org/index.php/ijoc/article/view/2161/1163

Beer, D. (2009). Power through the algorithm? Participatory web cultures and the technological unconscious. *New Media & Society*, *11*(6), 985–1002. DOI: 10.1177/1461444809336551

Bhargava, V. R., & Velasquez, M. (2021). Ethics of the attention economy: The problem of social media addiction. *Business Ethics Quarterly*, *31*(3), 321–359. DOI: 10.1017/beq.2020.32

Breidbach, C. F., & Maglio, P. (2020). Accountable algorithms? The ethical implications of data-driven business models. *Journal of Service Management*, *31*(2), 163–185. DOI: 10.1108/JOSM-03-2019-0073

Brüns, J. D., & Meißner, M. (2024). Do you create your content yourself? Using generative artificial intelligence for social media content creation diminishes perceived brand authenticity. *Journal of Retailing and Consumer Services*, *79*, 103790. DOI: 10.1016/j.jretconser.2024.103790

Bucher, T. (2018). *If...then: Algorithmic power and politics*. Oxford University Press. DOI: 10.1093/oso/9780190493028.001.0001

Burrus, O., Curtis, A., & Herman, L. (2024). Unmasking AI: Informing authenticity decisions by labeling AI-generated content. *Interactions (New York, N.Y.)*, *31*(4), 38–42. https://interactions.acm.org/archive/view/july-august-2024/unmasking-ai-informing-authenticity-decisions-by-labeling-ai-generated-content. DOI: 10.1145/3665321

Chakraborty, S., Hoque, M. S., Rahman Jeem, N., Biswas, M. C., Bardhan, D., & Lobaton, E. (2021). Fashion recommendation systems, models and methods: A review. *Informatics (MDPI)*, *8*(3), 49. DOI: 10.3390/informatics8030049

Cheung, J. C., & Ho, S. S. (2025a). Explainable AI and trust: How news media shapes public support for AI-powered autonomous passenger drones. *Public Understanding of Science (Bristol, England)*, *34*(3), 344–362. DOI: 10.1177/09636625241291192

Cheung, J. C., & Ho, S. S. (2025b). The effectiveness of explainable AI on human factors in trust models. *Scientific Reports*, *15*(1), 23337. DOI: 10.1038/s41598-025-04189-9

Chitra, U., & Musco, C. (2020, January). Analyzing the impact of filter bubbles on social network polarization. In *Proceedings of the 13th international conference on web search and data mining* (pp. 115–123). Association for Computing Machinery. DOI: 10.1145/3336191.3371825

Cole, M. D., Etteldorf, C., Schmitz, S., & Ukrow, J. (2023). Algorithmic transparency and accountability of digital services. *IRIS Special 2023-2*. European Audiovisual Observatory. Retrieved July 01, 2025, from https://rm.coe.int/iris-special-2023-02en/1680aeda48

Cotter, K. (2019). Playing the visibility game: How digital influencers and algorithms negotiate influence on Instagram. *New Media & Society*, *21*(4), 895–913. DOI: 10.1177/1461444818815684

Couldry, N., & Mejias, U. A. (2019). *The costs of connection: How data is colonizing human life and appropriating it for capitalism*. Stanford University Press.

Dogruel, L., Facciorusso, D., & Stark, B. (2020). 'I'm still the master of the machine.' Internet users' awareness of algorithmic decision-making and their perception of its effect on their autonomy. *Information Communication and Society*, *25*(9), 1311–1332. DOI: 10.1080/1369118X.2020.1863999

Espinoza-Rojas, J., Siles, I., & Castelain, T. (2022). How using various platforms shapes awareness of algorithms. *Behaviour & Information Technology*. Advance online publication. DOI: 10.1080/0144929X.2022.2078224

Ewert, B. (2020). Moving beyond the obsession with nudging individual behaviour: Towards a broader understanding of behavioural public policy. *Public Policy and Administration*, *35*(3), 337–360. DOI: 10.1177/0952076719889090

Feher, K., Vicsek, L., & Deuze, M. (2024). Modeling AI trust for 2050: Perspectives from media and info-communication experts. *AI & Society*, *39*(6), 2933–2946. DOI: 10.1007/s00146-023-01827-6

Fogg, B. J. (2003). *Persuasive technology: Using computers to change what we think and do*. Morgan Kaufmann., DOI: 10.1016/B978-155860643-2/50011-1

Genovesi, S., Kaesling, K., & Robbins, S. (2023). Introduction: Understanding and regulating AI-powered recommender systems. In Genovesi, S., Kaesling, K., & Robbins, S. (Eds.), *Recommender systems: Legal and ethical issues* (Vol. 40, pp. 1–18). Springer., DOI: 10.1007/978-3-031-34804-4_1

Gillespie, T. (2014). The relevance of algorithms. In Gillespie, T., Boczkowski, P. J., & Foot, K. A. (Eds.), *Media technologies: Essays on communication, materiality, and society* (pp. 167–194). MIT Press., DOI: 10.7551/mitpress/9042.003.0013

Glikson, E., & Woolley, A. W. (2020). Human trust in artificial intelligence: Review of empirical research. *The Academy of Management Annals*, *14*(2), 627–660. DOI: 10.5465/annals.2018.0057

Han, H., Liang, Y., Bella, G., Giunchiglia, F., & Li, D. (2023). LFDNN: A novel hybrid recommendation model based on DeepFM and LightGBM. *Entropy (Basel, Switzerland)*, *25*(4), 638. DOI: 10.3390/e25040638

Helberger, N. (2019). On the democratic role of news recommenders. *Digital Journalism (Abingdon, England)*, *7*(8), 993–1012. DOI: 10.1080/21670811.2019.1623700

Huang, Y., Jiao, J., & Zhu, D. (2025). Empowering the traveler: The impact of algorithm transparency and customer control on customer experience. *Asia Pacific Journal of Tourism Research*, •••, 1–19. DOI: 10.1080/10941665.2025.2523339

Interian, R., Marzo, R. G., Mendoza, I., & Ribeiro, C. C. (2023). Network polarization, filter bubbles, and echo chambers: An annotated review of measures and reduction methods. *International Transactions in Operational Research*, *30*(6), 3122–3158. DOI: 10.1111/itor.13224

Jiang, C., & Qin, F. (2025, February). Research on algorithm of intelligent recommendation system in the era of big data. In *Proceedings of the 2025 international conference on digital analysis and processing, intelligent computation (DAPIC)* (pp. 358–362). IEEE. DOI: 10.1109/DAPIC66097.2025.00072

Kahneman, D. (2011). *Thinking, fast and slow*. Farrar, Straus and Giroux.

Kang, H., & Lou, C. (2022). AI agency vs. human agency: Understanding human-AI interactions on TikTok and their implications for user engagement. *Journal of Computer-Mediated Communication*, *27*(5), zmac014. Advance online publication. DOI: 10.1093/jcmc/zmac014

Kaplan, A. M., & Haenlein, M. (2019). Siri, Siri, in my hand: Who's the fairest in the land? On the interpretations, illustrations, and implications of artificial intelligence. *Business Horizons*, *62*(1), 15–25. DOI: 10.1016/j.bushor.2018.08.004

Karnouskos, S. (2020). Artificial intelligence in digital media: The era of deepfakes. *IEEE Transactions on Technology and Society*, *1*(3), 138–147. DOI: 10.1109/TTS.2020.3001312

Kim, J., Giroux, M., & Lee, J. C. (2021). When do you trust AI? The effect of number presentation detail on consumer trust and acceptance of AI recommendations. *Psychology and Marketing*, *38*(7), 1140–1155. DOI: 10.1002/mar.21498

Kirk, C. P., & Givi, J. (2025). The AI-authorship effect: Understanding authenticity, moral disgust, and consumer responses to AI-generated marketing communications. *Journal of Business Research*, *186*, 114984. DOI: 10.1016/j.jbusres.2024.114984

Koene, A., Clifton, C., Hatada, Y., Webb, H., Patel, M., Machado, C., LaViolette, J., Richardson, R., & Reisman, D. (2019). *A governance framework for algorithmic accountability and transparency.* European Parliamentary Research Service, Panel for the Future of Science and Technology (STOA). Retrieved July 01, 2025, from https://www.europarl.europa.eu/RegData/etudes/STUD/2019/624262/EPRS_STU(2019)624262_EN.pdf

Kolo, C., Mütterlein, J., & Schmid, S. A. (2022, January). Believing journalists, AI, or fake news: The role of trust in media. In *Proceedings of the 55th Hawaii international conference on system sciences* (pp. 3202–3211). Retrieved July 01, 2025, from https://hdl.handle.net/10125/79727

Kreps, S., McCain, R. M., & Brundage, M. (2022). All the news that's fit to fabricate: AI-generated text as a tool of media misinformation. *Journal of Experimental Political Science*, *9*(1), 104–117. DOI: 10.1017/XPS.2020.37

Li, Y., & Cao, J. (2025). The role of recommendation algorithm in online social platforms. *Procedia Computer Science*, *261*, 674–681. DOI: 10.1016/j.procs.2025.04.320

Liang, M. (2022). The end of social media? How data attraction model in the algorithmic media reshapes the attention economy. *Media Culture & Society*, *44*(6), 1110–1131. DOI: 10.1177/01634437221077168

Liu, B. (2021). In AI we trust? Effects of agency locus and transparency on uncertainty reduction in human-AI interaction. *Journal of Computer-Mediated Communication*, *26*(6), 384–402. DOI: 10.1093/jcmc/zmab013

Liu-Thompkins, Y., Okazaki, S., & Li, H. (2022). Artificial empathy in marketing interactions: Bridging the human-AI gap in affective and social customer experience. *Journal of the Academy of Marketing Science*, *50*(6), 1198–1218. DOI: 10.1007/s11747-022-00892-5

Luitse, D., & Denkena, W. (2021). The great transformer: Examining the role of large language models in the political economy of AI. *Big Data & Society*, *8*(2), 1–14. DOI: 10.1177/20539517211047734

Lv, X., Li, J., & Wang, Q. (2024). The dark side of recommendation algorithms in Chinese mass short video apps: Effect of perceived over-recommendation on users' cognitive dissonance and discontinuance intention. *International Journal of Human-Computer Interaction*, *41*(11), 6701–6715. DOI: 10.1080/10447318.2024.2383038

McLuhan, M. (1964). *Understanding media: The extensions of man*. McGraw-Hill.

McStay, A. (2018). Emotional AI: The rise of empathic media. *Sage (Atlanta, Ga.)*. Advance online publication. DOI: 10.4135/9781526451293

Michiels, L., Vannieuwenhuyze, J., Leysen, J., Verachtert, R., Smets, A., & Goethals, B. (2023, September). How should we measure filter bubbles? A regression model and evidence for online news. In *Proceedings of the 17th ACM conference on recommender systems* (pp. 640–651). ACM. DOI: 10.1145/3604915.3608805

Mohsin, S. (2024). The influence of AI-driven personalization on consumer decision-making in e-commerce platforms. *Al-Rafidain Journal of Engineering Sciences*, *2*(2), 249–261. DOI: 10.61268/ajs54s12

Napoli, P. M. (2011). *Audience evolution: New technologies and the transformation of media audiences*. Columbia University Press.

Necula, S. C., & Păvăloaia, V. D. (2023). AI-driven recommendations: A systematic review of the state of the art in e-commerce. *Applied Sciences (Basel, Switzerland)*, *13*(9), 5531. DOI: 10.3390/app13095531

Nguyen, M. H., Bol, N., & King, A. J. (2020). Customisation versus personalisation of digital health information: Effects of mode tailoring on information processing outcomes. *European Journal of Health Communication*, *1*(1), 30–54. DOI: 10.47368/ejhc.2020.003

Noble, S. U. (2018). *Algorithms of oppression: How search engines reinforce racism*. NYU Press. DOI: 10.18574/nyu/9781479833641.001.0001

Nyrhinen, J., Sirola, A., Koskelainen, T., Munnukka, J., & Wilska, T. A. (2024). Online antecedents for young consumers' impulse buying behavior. *Computers in Human Behavior*, *153*, 108129. DOI: 10.1016/j.chb.2023.108129

Oyekunle, D., Matthew, U. O., Preston, D., & Boohene, D. (2024). Trust beyond technology algorithms: A theoretical exploration of consumer trust and behavior in technological consumption and AI projects. *Journal of Computer and Communications*, *12*(6), 72–102. DOI: 10.4236/jcc.2024.126006

Pariser, E. (2011). *The filter bubble: What the Internet is hiding from you*. Penguin Press.

Pusztahelyi, R. (2020). Emotional AI and its challenges in the viewpoint of online marketing. *Curentul Juridic, 81*(2), 13-31. Retrieved July 01, 2025, from https://ideas.repec.org/a/pmu/cjurid/v81y2020p13-31.html

Reisdorf, B. C., & Blank, G. (2021). Algorithmic literacy and platform trust. In *Handbook of digital inequality* (pp. 341–357). Edward Elgar Publishing. DOI: 10.4337/9781788116572.00032

Ribes, D., Henchoz, N., Portier, H., Defaycs, L., Phan, T. T., Gatica-Perez, D., & Sondereger, A. (2021). Trust indicators and explainable AI: A study on user perceptions. In *Proceedings of the 18th IFIP conference on human-computer interaction (INTERACT)* (pp. 662–671). Springer. DOI: 10.1007/978-3-030-85616-8_39

Ryan, M. (2020). In AI we trust: Ethics, artificial intelligence, and reliability. *Science and Engineering Ethics*, *26*(5), 2749–2767. DOI: 10.1007/s11948-020-00228-y

Santos Silva, M. (2022). Nudging and other behaviourally based policies as enablers for environmental sustainability. *Laws*, *11*(1), 9. DOI: 10.3390/laws11010009

Shah, M. U., Rehman, U., Parmar, B., & Ismail, I. (2024). Effects of moral violation on algorithmic transparency: An empirical investigation. *Journal of Business Ethics*, *193*(1), 19–34. DOI: 10.1007/s10551-023-05472-3

Simon, F. M. (2022). Uneasy bedfellows: AI in the news, platform companies and the issue of journalistic autonomy. *Digital Journalism (Abingdon, England)*, *10*(10), 1832–1854. DOI: 10.1080/21670811.2022.2063150

Söderlund, K., Engström, E., Haresamudram, K., Larsson, S., & Strimling, P. (2024). Regulating high-reach AI: On transparency directions in the Digital Services Act. *Internet Policy Review*, *13*(1). Advance online publication. DOI: 10.14763/2024.1.1746

Swart, J. (2021). Experiencing algorithms: How young people understand, feel about, and engage with algorithmic news selection on social media. *Social Media + Society*, *7*(2), 20563051211008828. DOI: 10.1177/20563051211008828

Teodorescu, D., Aivaz, K. A., Vancea, D. P. C., Condrea, E., Dragan, C., & Olteanu, A. C. (2023). Consumer trust in AI algorithms used in e-commerce: A case study of college students at a Romanian public university. *Sustainability (Basel), 15*(15), 11925. DOI: 10.3390/su151511925

Tufekci, Z. (2015). Algorithmic harms beyond Facebook and Google: Emergent challenges of computational agency. *Colorado Technology Law Journal, 13*, 203-218. Retrieved July 16, 2025, from https://ctlj.colorado.edu/wp-content/uploads/2015/08/Tufekci-final.pdf

Vaccari, C., & Chadwick, A. (2020). Deepfakes and disinformation: Exploring the impact of synthetic political video on deception, uncertainty, and trust in news. *Social Media + Society, 6*(1), 1–13. DOI: 10.1177/2056305120903408

Van Drunen, M., Zarouali, B., & Helberger, N. (2022). Recommenders you can rely on: A legal and empirical perspective on the transparency and control individuals require to trust news personalisation. *Journal of Intellectual Property, Information Technology and E-Commerce Law, 13*, 302. Retrieved July 16, 2025, from https://heinonline.org/HOL/LandingPage?handle=hein.journals/jipitec13&div=29&id=&page=

Wang, S., Cao, L., Wang, Y., Sheng, Q. Z., Orgun, M. A., & Lian, D. (2021). A survey on session-based recommender systems. *ACM Computing Surveys, 54*(7), 1–38. DOI: 10.1145/3465401

Winter, S., Maslowska, E., & Vos, A. L. (2021). The effects of trait-based personalization in social media advertising. *Computers in Human Behavior, 114*, 106525. Advance online publication. DOI: 10.1016/j.chb.2020.106525

Wu, T. (2016). *The attention merchants: The epic scramble to get inside our heads.* Alfred A. Knopf.

Xu, K., Zheng, H., Zhan, X., Zhou, S., & Niu, K. (2024). Evaluation and optimization of intelligent recommendation system performance with cloud resource automation compatibility. *Applied Computing Engineering, 87*(1), 228–233. DOI: 10.54254/2755-2721/87/20241620

Yeung, K. (2017). 'Hypernudge': Big data as a mode of regulation by design. *Information Communication and Society, 20*(1), 118–136. DOI: 10.1080/1369118X.2016.1186713

Zhu, L., & Lerman, K. (2016). Attention inequality in social media. *arXiv.* https://doi.org//arXiv.1601.07200DOI: 10.48550

Zou, L., Xia, L., Du, P., Zhang, Z., Bai, T., Liu, W., Nie, J.-Y., & Yin, D. (2020, January). Pseudo Dyna-Q: A reinforcement learning framework for interactive recommendation. In *Proceedings of the 13th international conference on web search and data mining* (pp. 816–824). Association for Computing Machinery. DOI: 10.1145/3336191.3371801

Zuboff, S. (2019). *The age of surveillance capitalism: The fight for a human future at the new frontier of power*. PublicAffairs.

ADDITIONAL READING

Castells, M. (2009). *Communication power*. Oxford University Press.

Foucault, M. (1977). *Discipline and punish: The birth of the prison*. Vintage Books.

Habermas, J. (1989). *The structural transformation of the public sphere*. MIT Press.

McChesney, R. W. (2013). *Digital disconnect: How capitalism is turning the Internet against democracy*. The New Press. DOI: 10.2307/jj.26193195

Postman, N. (1985). *Amusing ourselves to death: Public discourse in the age of show business*. Penguin Books.

Schiller, H. I. (1989). *Culture, Inc.: The corporate takeover of public expression*. Oxford University Press.

Sunstein, C. R. (2017). *Republic: Divided democracy in the age of social media*. Princeton University Press. DOI: 10.1515/9781400884711

Tufekci, Z. (2017). *Twitter and tear gas: The power and fragility of networked protest*. Yale University Press.

Williams, R. (1974). *Television: Technology and cultural form*. Schocken Books.

Winner, L. (1986). *The whale and the reactor: A search for limits in an age of high technology*. University of Chicago Press.

KEY TERMS AND DEFINITIONS

Algorithmic Literacy: is users' understanding of ways in which algorithms steer information flows, personalisation, and visibility, which affects users' ability to engage or intervene.

Algorithmic Personalisation: tailors automated content and recommendations to user behaviours and preferences or inferred user traits for the platform's interest in engagement and monetisation.

Attention Economy: an economic model treating user attention as a scarce resource to monetise through advertising and design for engagement.

Emotional AI: is artificial intelligence detecting or simulating emotions using behavioural, facial, or vocal cues to personalise interactions and influence consumer responses.

Hypernudging: is the continuous dynamic adjustment of digital environments through behavioural monitoring to steer user choices without overt coercion or user awareness.

Recommendation Systems: are tools using AI such as deep learning and reinforcement learning to filter, rank, and suggest content or products by predicting user preferences.

Surveillance Capitalism: is an economic system described by Zuboff in which behavioural data is collected and used to predict and modify human behaviour for profit.

Chapter 5
An Academic Perspective on Deepfake Technologies in AI-Powered Journalism

Duygu Dumanlı Kürkçü
https://orcid.org/0000-0002-3425-2826
İstanbul Arel University, Turkey

Duygu Neşeli
İstanbul Arel University, Turkey

ABSTRACT

The integration of computer technology into journalistic processes brought journalism into the digital age with the widespread use of the Internet in the 1990s. The digitalisation of journalism has led to changes in production, consumption and distribution processes, leaving traditional journalistic practices behind. As in the past, some news can be produced with information gathered in the field, some can be produced with data quickly gathered at a desk, news can be presented individually, and even false/fake news can be verified by artificial intelligence tools. On the other hand, the fact that images and sounds can be created or modified using artificial intelligence-based deep learning algorithms has led to the need to evaluate artificial intelligence technologies from different angles. Based on this context, this study used content analysis to identify trends in scientific research on deepfake technologies and journalism, and to guide those who will conduct new research on the topic.

DOI: 10.4018/979-8-3373-2960-4.ch005

INTRODUCTION

The current state of journalism—digitalized and integrated with artificial intelligence technologies—has emerged as the result of a transformative process shaped by multilayered and time-spanning technological developments. The first stage of this process began with the use of optical and telegraph technologies, which enabled information to be transmitted to desired locations at desired times. In the 1950s and 1960s, the integration of satellite and space technologies into the field of communication constituted developments that accelerated this process. Particularly in the 1970s, with the widespread adoption of personal computers, information not only became transmittable but also acquired a structure that could be produced, processed, and stored entirely in digital environments. This marked one of the most critical technological advancements forming the foundation of digitalization (Değirmencioğlu, 2016: 592). It should be noted that the most significant development impacting today's journalism practices occurred in the 1990s, when internet technologies began to be used for individual purposes in addition to military applications. Just as journalism was once transformed by the introduction of audio-visual technologies, the integration of internet technologies led to a structural transformation, detaching journalism from its traditional identity and ushering it into a digital form.

The process that began with computer technologies and continued with the internet eventually accelerated the full integration of artificial intelligence technologies—originally gaining prominence after the Second World War—into all areas of modern life. In this sense, this technological development, much like other emerging technologies that have entered our lives, has given rise to a new domain of debate and critical inquiry.

When examining the positive implications of artificial intelligence in journalism, it appears that the use of AI in news production not only increases the speed of content creation but, as algorithms become more advanced, also enables the generation of news with fewer errors. AI's capacity to personalize content, allowing it to be produced in multiple languages and from diverse perspectives, as well as its ability to generate various types of news content based on user demands and data analysis, are among the prominent benefits it brings to the field of journalism (Ay, 2022: 923). Moreover, the use of artificial intelligence for fact-checking, audience analysis, and summarizing current developments demonstrates that AI contributes to journalism as a supportive and enhancing tool.

However, there are also aspects in which artificial intelligence negatively affects journalism—a profession that speaks directly to society. These concerns generally revolve around ethical issues (such as who bears responsibility in the face of an ethical dilemma, or the use of data without consent), legal regulations, the dependency of newsrooms that cannot develop their own AI technologies on corporations that produce them, and employment-related matters (Zinderen, 2024: 663–664). Beyond these, the fact that algorithms may contain inherent biases and lack the capacity to interpret new phenomena or exhibit truly human characteristics are among the critical limitations of AI use in journalism.

In recent discussions of AI-supported journalism, deepfake technology has emerged as one of the most frequently debated and controversial topics. Derived from the combination of "deep learning" and "fake," deepfake refers to a type of artificial intelligence used to produce fabricated images, videos, and audio recordings (Yasar, Barney, & Wigmore, n.d.). It is most often discussed in terms of its risks and potential for misuse. According to the *Oxford English Dictionary* (2025), the term *deepfake* is defined as: "various types of digitally manipulated media, especially used maliciously to convincingly replace one person's likeness with another, often to depict them doing something they did not do."

Before addressing the drawbacks, it is worth noting the potential applications of deepfake technology in journalism. Within the field, deepfakes can be used to create visual reconstructions in news reports, to detect and expose fake news, or to simulate events—enhancing the realism and narrative depth of a story. In addition to these features, deepfake technology can increase accessibility by offering news content in multiple languages and can even serve as a protective tool by helping conceal identities when reporting sensitive stories (Ebba Lundberg & Peter Mozelius, 2023: 2163). Nevertheless, despite its positive capabilities, deepfake technology is more often witnessed in malicious contexts. In an era where the distinction between real and fake, or true and false, has become increasingly blurred, technologies like deepfakes significantly contribute to this confusion. The fact that such technologies continue to evolve and enable the creation of increasingly realistic content only intensifies the problem. The widespread appearance of deepfake-generated videos, visuals, or audio in social media and news outlets today serves as strong evidence of this growing concern.

The process that began in 2017 with a fake video shared for entertainment purposes by a Reddit user soon evolved with the proliferation of similar content. Although initially perceived as harmless or amusing, this phenomenon has increasingly blurred the line between fiction and reality. Over time, it has also been used with malicious intent, aiming to deceive or cause harm. Unfortunately, this development has had a profound impact on the field of journalism, which plays a crucial role in shaping public opinion, informing society, and serving as a trusted source of news. A striking example is the case of a video that surfaced ahead of the 2014 U.S. elections, featuring CNN anchor Anderson Cooper seemingly speaking unfavorably about Donald Trump (Dupré, 2023). This incident served as a stark reminder—especially during election periods—of the heightened vigilance required by journalists and news producers in the age of synthetic media.

The trust-based nature of journalism and its strong influence on public opinion further complicate the challenges posed by this situation. Deepfake content presented in highly realistic ways not only makes it more difficult to reliably distinguish truth from fabrication but also carries the potential to seriously erode public trust in journalism. Any manipulated video presented by the media can deeply undermine confidence in news outlets and journalism as a whole. Beyond the general public, deepfake technologies also impose significant difficulties on media institutions and journalistic practices. Traditional methods of news verification are becoming insufficient for journalists, making it imperative to adopt and learn advanced technological tools. Moreover, even unintentionally publishing manipulated content may place media outlets in legally and ethically precarious positions (Fitzgerald, 2024). For all these reasons, both journalists and media organizations bear a considerable responsibility—not only for their own reputations but also for protecting public trust—when it comes to preventing the spread of deepfakes.

As seen, deepfake technology—an advanced form of artificial intelligence that deserves critical attention in the fields of media and journalism—is not only a sectoral concern but also a significant subject for academic inquiry. Especially in the context of communication and media studies, deepfake technology must be addressed with seriousness under themes such as trust, media ethics, disinformation, manipulation and perception, and critical media literacy.

USE OF ARTIFICIAL INTELLIGENCE IN JOURNALISM AND DISCUSSIONS

The term artificial intelligence was first coined in 1956 by John McCarthy, known as the father of artificial intelligence, and defined as 'the science and engineering of making intelligent machines' (HAI, Stanford, 2025). In general terms, artificial intelligence is defined by John McCarthy, the founder of the discipline, as the process of enabling a machine to behave in a way that would be considered intelligent if exhibited by a human (Kaplan, 2016: 1). Thus, it is predicted that artificial intelligence technologies, which emerged by modelling human intelligence, will be able to complete the tasks assigned to them without the need for any human in time.

Once limited to the realm of science fiction novels and films, artificial intelligence has now become integrated into nearly every aspect of life, ranging from everyday routines to complex business processes. According to data from Artificial Intelligence (AI) Worldwide – Statistics & Facts published by Statista (Thormundsson, 2024), the artificial intelligence technologies market has grown into a massive industry, reaching nearly 200 billion USD in 2023. And this market is estimated to grow to over $1.8 trillion by 2030. This clearly indicates that artificial intelligence is a rapidly expanding market, and its potential impact in the future is expected to be substantial. Artificial intelligence technologies, which are now widely used in various sectors such as advertising, retail, finance, transportation, insurance, healthcare, education, entertainment, and media, play a complementary role to human activities in numerous tasks. These include diagnosing diseases, detecting fraud, voice and image recognition, identifying creditworthy customers, recommending products to consumers, generating content, and creating visuals. However, such intensive use of artificial intelligence technologies causes some debates on artificial intelligence and these debates are generally centred around 5 views (Knickrehm, 2020: 158-161):

* Dystopian Vision: As a result of the struggle between man and machine, machines will win and people will lose their jobs and unemployment will increase dramatically.
* Utopian Vision: Artificial intelligence will be able to do everything that humans can do, and humans will be able to use their skills differently, and there will be no economic decline.
* Technological Optimists: There will be an increase in productivity and this increase will lead to economic growth and increase living standards.
* Sceptics about Productivity: AI technologies will lead to limited increases in productivity, but only to stagnant growth.
* Realistic Optimists: Artificial intelligence technologies will have an impact like the technology revolutions of the past. Demand for some people will increase while demand for others will decrease.

Under the umbrella of these diverse perspectives, the use of artificial intelligence in the field of journalism—and the impacts it creates—has also become a subject of debate, particularly in terms of its advantages and disadvantages. Journalism, fundamentally defined as the collection and dissemination of news about current events to inform the public and present factual information, continues today not only in traditional media but also as a widely practiced profession within digital media environments. Journalism, which has traditionally combined human effort and technological tools, has in recent years begun to evolve into a new form that incorporates artificial intelligence technologies—driven by the accelerating pace of digitisation and ongoing advances in computer technologies.

The use of artificial intelligence in journalism is categorized under three main headings, as outlined in the report *"New Power, New Responsibilities."* (Beckett, 2019: 20):

* News Gathering: Developing content, generating news ideas, finding news sources, identifying trends in the agenda, researching, monitoring events or topics.
* Producing News: Creating content, adapting content to different formats, organising content, producing visuals, videos, text, recreating content for different target audiences.
* News Distribution: Generating revenue, playing a role in subscription processes, personalisation, finding target audiences and understanding their behaviour, marketing.

As outlined above, the widespread use of artificial intelligence in various aspects of journalism—including news production, structure, and presentation to readers—has led to a fundamental transformation of the profession. This transformation extends not only to the organization of media institutions and the demand for journalists, but also to the roles and responsibilities of journalists themselves. This transformation has not only given rise to new areas of specialization such as mobile journalism, social media journalism, and multimedia journalism—emerging alongside digital journalism—but has also paved the way for the emergence of robotic journalism and, more broadly, artificial intelligence journalism. Robotic journalism (Narin, 2017: 82), is defined as the process by which algorithms analyze and store news patterns on specific topics and generate similar automated news texts using real-time data. At this point, robotic journalism enables journalists to produce news automatically with certain news patterns in routine news such as sports, finance and weather. On the other hand, artificial intelligence journalism refers to a journalistic practice in which human journalists, relying on their professional expertise (such as media literacy), take part in the production, analysis, verification and distribution of news. This is particularly the case when automated news generation alone is insufficient (Büyükafşar & Yıldırım, 2022: 326). In this context, what kind of opportunities and threats the transformation caused by artificial intelligence in the professional practices of journalism creates is an issue that needs to be discussed.

Assoc. Prof. Dr. Hülya Gökbel (Gökbel, 2024: 155-156), examines the role of artificial intelligence in journalistic practices—from news production to presentation and distribution—under categories such as metaverse journalism, drone journalism, robotic journalism, internet journalism, X Platform journalism, citizen journalism, YouTube journalism, and data journalism. According to Gökbel, the greatest advantage of artificial intelligence in journalism lies in its speed and efficiency. She emphasizes that AI can analyze large datasets to offer new story ideas and sources, save time by automating routine tasks, and allow journalists to focus on more in-depth reporting. Moreover, she notes that readers benefit from AI through access to personalized content tailored to their specific needs and interests. However, in the same study, Gökbel also highlights the potential negative impacts of artificial intelligence on journalism. She points out that AI may contribute to the production of biased news based on disinformation and could lead to ethical violations in areas such as data privacy, accountability, and transparency. Interviews with professionals representing various branches of the Turkish news media indicate that while AI tools such as ChatGPT can be useful when applied in line with journalistic principles, they also raise concerns about the possible neglect of ethical codes, the risk of unemployment and job displacement, and a perceived decline in the professional standards of journalism (Kırık, Göksu, & Yegen, 2024: 103). Moreover, the constant need to keep up with rapid technological developments can pose significant challenges for journalistic organizations. The inability of some institutions—particularly smaller media outlets—to afford the costs of adaptation further deepens the technological gap and inequality between large and small media organizations (Newman et al., 2020: 23). In this context, ethical guidelines that media organizations and journalists around the world must follow in their work involving artificial intelligence were established for the first time in 2023 with the *Paris Charter on Artificial Intelligence and Journalism*. The ethical principles defined under the leadership of Reporters Without Borders (RSF) by 17 press professional organizations are grouped under ten main headings. These principles are as follows (Merkezi, 2023):

* Journalistic ethics guide how media organizations and journalists use technology.
* Media organizations prioritize human agency.
* AI systems used in journalism must be subject to independent evaluation in advance.
* Media organizations are always responsible for the content they publish.
* Media organizations must maintain transparency when using AI systems.
* Media organizations ensure the traceability and sourcing of content.
* Journalism draws a clear line between original and AI-generated content.
* AI-assisted content development and recommendations should promote diversity and informational integrity.
* Journalists, media organizations, and journalism support groups should participate in AI governance.
* Journalism preserves its ethical and economic foundations in its relationships with AI companies.

In Turkey, Anadolu Agency has also addressed the ethical use of artificial intelligence in journalism by publishing the *Ethical Guidelines for the Use of Artificial Intelligence in Media* (Durdak, 2024) which outlines key considerations for journalists.

The guideline emphasizes that journalists should adhere to professional principles and press ethics when using artificial intelligence in news production. It warns against the use of algorithms that violate fundamental human rights and freedoms, and calls for the avoidance of practices such as deepfakes, disinformation, and manipulation. It highlights the importance of using AI not for commercial gain, but for delivering transparent, accurate, and timely news to the public for social benefit. The guideline also stresses the need to respect copyright and licensing when using digital twins, requires editorial oversight of AI-generated content to prevent biased information, and calls for the ethical implementation of automation to ensure that human creativity, employment, and journalists' rights are not undermined.

As can be seen, while AI technologies offer significant contributions to journalism, they also raise ethical concerns. Efforts are being made to ensure the sustainability of truthful journalism through clearly defined rules within the framework of ethical principles.

On the other hand, artificial intelligence also brings numerous unresolved challenges to the field of journalism, particularly through the creation of misleading content such as disinformation and fabricated images. In the so-called post-truth era—widely discussed since 2016—the increasing use of AI technologies like deepfakes in journalism has contributed to a rise in fake news, making this issue a subject that requires further investigation.

DEEPFAKE AND JOURNALISM

Deepfake, one of the most prominent artificial intelligence technologies, has become one of the most controversial topics of our time—especially in the post-truth era, where the distinction between what is real and fake is increasingly blurred. In order to better understand the current situation, it is essential to first explain the concept of post-truth. The term post-truth was first used in 1992 in an article written by Steve Tesich for The Nation magazine. While discussing the Iraq War and the Watergate Scandal, Tesich argued that we had come to accept living in a post-truth era—an era in which facts are concealed and lies are told indiscriminately. Although the term was introduced in 1992, its conceptual development was shaped later by Ralph Keyes in his 2004 book The Post-Truth Era (Camacho, 2019). The selection of post-truth as the Word of the Year by the Oxford Dictionary in 2016 further amplified public and academic attention to the concept, leading to increased discussions around fake news and the accuracy and authenticity of journalistic content. The selection of post-truth as the Word of the Year by the Oxford Dictionary in 2016 further amplified public and academic attention to the concept, leading to increased discussions around fake news and the accuracy and authenticity of journalistic content.

In this era, the increasing production of news—whether by professional journalists, political figures, or through social media platforms—based on information that is not grounded in truth has led to greater public skepticism toward news content. In this regard, the campaign period during Donald Trump's candidacy for the U.S. presidency, as well as the Brexit process, significantly accelerated the dynamics of the post-truth era (Şener, 2020: 231). In 2018, it was revealed that Claas Relotius, an award-winning journalist at *Der Spiegel*, had fabricated numerous articles (BBC, 2018). Other widely circulated fake news stories, such as the claim that a retired postman had fathered 1,300 children (Çavuş, 2017), or that a pastor attempting to walk on water was eaten by crocodiles (Timur, 2017), further demonstrate how prevalent fake news has become—even within some of the most reputable news organizations. These examples highlight the difficulty of verifying information in today's media environment. The integration of AI technologies—particularly deepfake applications—into journalistic processes further blurs the boundaries between truth and fabrication in the post-truth era.

The term deepfake, a combination of the words deep and fake, refers to a technology that combines deep learning with the ability to simulate reality, ultimately producing synthetic and highly convincing fake content that is difficult to distinguish from the real (Kılıç & Kahraman, 2023: 307). According to the Encyclopedia Britannica, deepfake is a type of artificial intelligence technology and synthetic media that creates fabricated audio, images, or videos of events or people that never actually existed (Payne, 2025). The emergence of deepfakes dates back to 2017, when a Reddit user created a category titled "deepfakes" and began publishing pornographic videos in which the faces of celebrities were swapped using face replacement technology.

In a study examining the current application areas of deepfake technology, four key fields in which deepfakes are most prominently used have been identified: communication and media, advertising and marketing, the film industry, arts and entertainment, and political communication (Kılıç & Kahraman, 2023: 307). Deepfake technology, which enables the alteration of data and the manipulation of time and place to reconstruct a fabricated version of reality, can be used as a tool of manipulation by taking advantage of deep learning and AI-based software, potentially causing harm to others. According to Büyükafşar and Yıldırım (Büyükafşar & Yıldırım, 2022: 321-313) this falsification creates significant challenges in the field of communication by allowing content to be disconnected from its original context, by modifying existing visuals, combining or removing elements, or even generating entirely fabricated content. In this context, almost everyone is now exposed to numerous deepfake-based materials through various media platforms.

Deepfake technology, which can be created by almost anyone, may be used for both positive and negative purposes. From a positive perspective, it can be applied in various beneficial areas such as reenacting historical events, digitally recreating deceased actors, generating voices for patients who have lost their ability to speak, detecting fake content, and creating virtual brand ambassadors in advertising. On the other hand, its negative uses include fraud, cyberbullying, the pornographic misuse of individuals' faces, cybercrimes, violations of privacy, and the manipulation of the public through false information. The most significant threat posed by deepfake to the field of journalism lies in its use for producing disinformation and fake news. Numerous real-life cases reported in the media illustrate the extent of this issue.

One notable example among the reported incidents occurred in 2023. One of the most widely discussed deepfake images of that year was a photo appearing to show Pope Francis, the spiritual leader of the Catholic world, wearing a puffy white jacket. The image quickly spread across social media and made headlines. However, it was later revealed that the photo had been generated using the artificial intelligence tool Midjourney AI.

Figure 1. 'Pope Francis wearing a white coat' claim

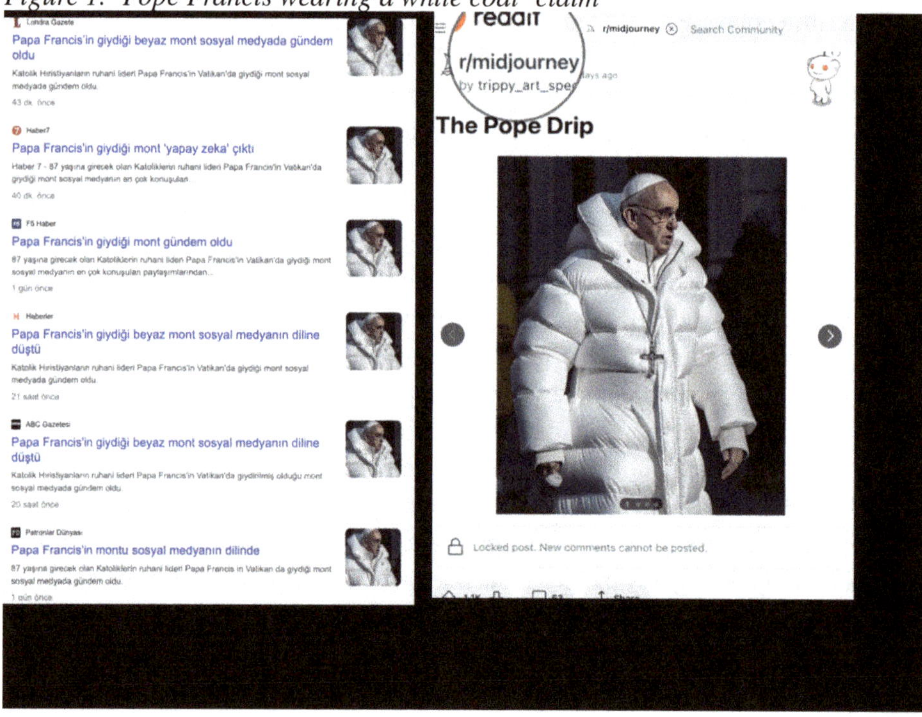

(AA teyithattı, 2023)

Another recent incident involved a video that appeared to show Ukrainian President Volodymyr Zelensky dancing to music. However, the video was a deepfake, originally shared by a user on the X platform. It was later reposted by Donald Trump

Jr., the son of former U.S. President Donald Trump, with the apparent intent of targeting Zelensky.

Figure 2. The deepfake video showing Zelensky dancing

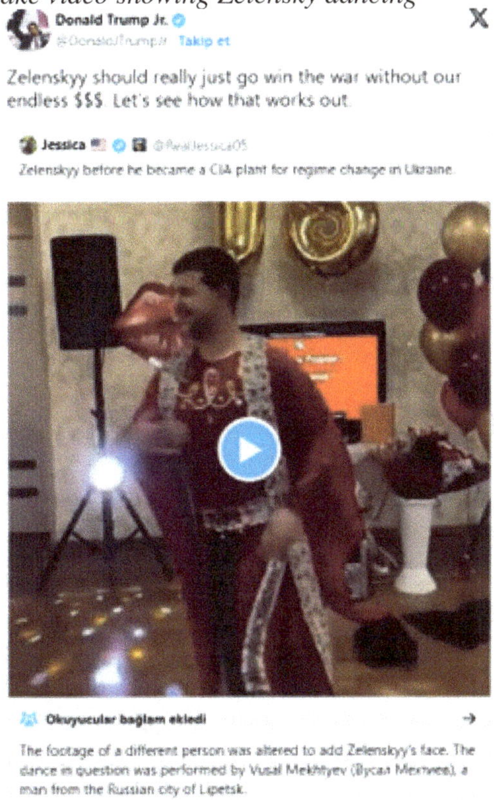

(Oksijen, 2025)

Perhaps the most alarming aspect of deepfake technology—of which countless examples already exist—is its rapid self-improvement, gradually eliminating the flaws that once made it distinguishable from reality. For instance, in 2018, researchers in the United States identified that faces generated by deepfake technology did not blink. However, shortly after this discovery was made public, the issue was resolved, and deepfake-generated faces began to blink (Sample, 2020). As a result, it appears increasingly likely that deepfake content will soon become virtually indistinguishable from real footage to the naked eye.

At this point, several artificial intelligence tools have emerged as verification systems designed to detect deepfakes. Among these are programs such as Sensity AI, which identifies falsifications in digital documents and verifies visual content; Deepware, which detects fake videos; and DeepFak-o-meter, which performs retrospective scanning (Büyükafşar & Yıldırım, 2022: 327–328). At this point, several artificial intelligence tools have emerged as verification systems designed to detect deepfakes. Among these are programs such as Sensity AI, which identifies falsifications in digital documents and verifies visual content; Deepware, which detects fake videos; and DeepFak-o-meter, which performs retrospective scanning (Büyükafşar & Yıldırım, 2022: 327-328). Another crucial aspect is the necessity for journalists to develop competence in using these technologies effectively, ensuring that they can detect AI tools into their professional practices.

The literature review indicates that artificial intelligence technologies, especially deepfake, are increasingly shaping journalism by impacting processes such as news production, distribution, and verification. Deepfake-generated content poses significant risks to journalistic credibility and public perception, underscoring the need for in-depth academic analysis.

RESEARCH METHODOLOGY

The concept of bibliometrics refers to the quantitative analysis of publications produced by individuals or institutions within a specific field, during a specific period, and in a specific region, as well as the relationships among these publications. In bibliometric analysis studies, various statistical data—such as country comparisons, comparisons of scientific disciplines, contributions to global science, the shares of public and private sectors in publication output, and patterns of international co-authorship—are collected cumulatively across specific time intervals and analyzed to interpret trends related to the research area yöntemidir (Ulakbim, 2025). Bibliometric analysis reveals the trends, dimensions, potential research topics, and limitations within a given field, while also identifying the academic impact of existing publications and the overlooked aspects of the subject under investigation (Ruhanen, Weiler, Moyle & McLennan, 2015).

Bibliometric analysis has emerged as a significant research method for quantifying scientific findings related to various academic elements—such as studies, authors, keywords, concepts, journals, institutions, and countries—within a given research area. It enables the examination of the intellectual, scientific, and social structures of a field, as well as their changes and development over time, by analyzing the interactions and relationships among these elements and identifying critical areas for attention (Aria & Cuccurullo, 2017: 960).

This study aims to examine the academic work conducted by researchers in the field of AI-assisted journalism, particularly focusing on deepfake applications, due to the increasing use of artificial intelligence in professional life and specifically within journalism in the digital age. The study also seeks to identify proposed solutions related to the application of AI and deepfake technologies in journalism.

For this purpose, analyses were conducted on the Web of Science database as of February 1, 2025, targeting academic research published between 2020 and 2024 with the terms "Deepfake and Journalism" and "Deepfake" in their titles. The sample of the study includes 28 scientific studies on deepfake and journalism published between 2020 and the date of analysis. To narrow the scope of the study and due to time constraints, the Scopus database was excluded from the analysis. Limiting the sample to only the Web of Science database and excluding studies published after February 1, 2025, represent the study's main limitations.Within the scope of the study, the sample includes articles and conference proceedings related to deepfake and journalism. These studies were analyzed using bibliometric analysis based on the following criteria: year of publication, publication types, Web of Science categories, meso and micro citation topics, distribution by Web of Science indexes, distribution by universities and university departments, publication titles, country distributions, and research areas.

FINDINGS AND INTERPRETATION

Research on deepfake and journalism was obtained from the Web of Science database. In line with the data obtained from Web of Science, 28 academic researches in the field of journalism and deepfake were identified.

Table 1. Distribution of research on deepfake in artificial intelligence supported journalism by years

YEAR OF PUBLICATION	NUMBER OF STUDIES PUBLISHED
2020	5
2021	5
2022	2
2023	5
2024	11
TOTAL	28

Source: Created by the author using the Web of Science database.

As shown in Table 1, the quantitative distribution of studies on the topic of deepfake in journalism extends back only as far as 2020. This suggests that, as a relatively new communication technology, research on deepfake within the context of artificial intelligence and journalism is of recent origin. According to data obtained from the Web of Science database, although there was a decrease in the number of studies in 2022, a notable increase occurred in 2024. This rise can be attributed to the growing prevalence of artificial intelligence technologies and applications across various sectors, including journalism. Since the analysis was conducted in the second month of 2025 and the year is not yet complete, the number of publications for 2025 may reasonably be expected to increase.

Table 2. Distribution of studies on deepfake in AI-assisted journalism by type of publication

PUBLICATION TYPES	NUMBER OF PUBLICATION	FREQUENCY (%)
Journal articles	21	75,00%
Conference proceedings	7	25,00%
TOTAL	28	100,00%

Source: Compiled by the author using data from the Web of Science database

According to Table 2, three-quarters (75%) of the studies on deepfake in the field of journalism are journal articles, while one-quarter (25%) are conference proceedings. Among the 21 journal articles, two articles each were published in Cyberpsychology, Behavior and Social Networking, Digital Journalism, and Media and Communication. The seven conference proceedings were presented at events such as the 2020 IEEE International Conference on Artificial Intelligence and Virtual Reality (AIVR 2020), the 36th Annual Computer Security Applications Conference (ACSAC 2020), and the Annual Computer Security Applications Conference Proceedings.

Table 3. Distribution of studies on deepfake in AI-assisted journalism by web of science categories

Web of Science Categories			Web of Science Categories		
Communication	8	28,57%	Engineering, Multidisciplinary	1	3,57%
Computer Science and Information Systems	8	28,57%	Film Radio Television	1	3,57%
Computer Science and AI	6	21,43%	Information Science & Library Science	1	3,57%
Computer Science, Theory & Methods	5	17,86%	Materials Science, Multidisciplinary	1	3,57%
Computer Science, Interdisciplinary Applications	3	10,71%	Neurosciences	1	3,57%
Computer Science, Software Engineering	2	7,14%	Physics, Applied	1	3,57%
Electrical & Electronic Engineering	2	7,14%	Psychology, Applied	1	3,57%
Social Psychology	2	7,14%	Social Sciences, Interdisciplinary	1	3,57%

continued on following page

Table 3. Continued

Web of Science Categories			Web of Science Categories		
Chemistry, Multidisciplinary	1	3,57%	Sociology	1	3,57%
Computer Science, Cybernetics	1	3,57%	Telecommunications	1	3,57%

Source: Compiled by the author using data from the Web of Science database.

According to Table 3, the distribution and frequency values of studies on deepfake in journalism span across 20 different scientific fields as classified by Web of Science categories. The fields of Communication and Computer Science, Artificial Intelligence rank first, each comprising 28.57% of the total. Computer Science, Theory & Methods follows in second place with 21.43%, and Computer Science, Information Systems ranks third with 17.86%. In fourth place is Computer Science, Interdisciplinary Applications, accounting for 10.71%.

In fifth place, Computer Science, Software Engineering, Electrical & Electronic Engineering, and Social Psychology each appear with a frequency of 7.14%. These findings indicate that most studies related to artificial intelligence and deepfake technology are concentrated in fields such as computer science, information systems, artificial intelligence, software engineering, and electrical & electronic engineering.

Given that the focus of this study is deepfake in journalism, it is noteworthy that the Communication category ranks highest. Meanwhile, fields such as Computer Science, Cybernetics, Engineering, Multidisciplinary, Film, Radio, Television, Information Science & Library Science, Social Sciences, Interdisciplinary, and Sociology are represented at relatively low rates—around 3%. This highlights the need for more studies on deepfake in journalism-related fields such as Journalism, New Media, Communication, Artificial Intelligence, Sociology, and Interdisciplinary Social Sciences.

Table 4. Distribution of studies on deepfake in AI-assisted journalism by meso-level citation topics

Meso-level Citation Topics	Sayı	Frekans (%)
Communication	14	51,85%
Security, Encryption and Coding	9	33,33%
Dietetics and Nutrition	1	3,70%
Digital Signal Processing	1	3,70%
Human Computer Interaction	1	3,70%
Social Psychology	1	3,70%
TOTAL	27	100,00%

Source: Compiled by the author using data from the Web of Science database.

According to Table 4, an analysis of meso-level citation topics for studies on deepfake in AI-assisted journalism reveals that *Communication* ranks first, accounting for 51.85% of the citations. This is primarily due to the strong focus of existing studies on how deepfake technology is integrated into communication-oriented journalism practices and workflows.

In second place is the field of *Security, Encryption, and Coding*, which is closely linked to deepfake technology due to its heavy reliance on encoding and encryption methods. Other meso-level citation topics include *Dietetics and Nutrition*, *Digital Signal Processing*, *Human-Computer Interaction*, and *Social Psychology*.

The inclusion of *Dietetics and Nutrition* among the cited topics is particularly noteworthy. Meanwhile, *Digital Signal Processing*, *Human-Computer Interaction*, and *Social Psychology* can be considered interdisciplinary areas that interact with deepfake technology in various capacities.

Table 5. Distribution of studies on deepfake in AI-assisted journalism by micro-level citation topics

Micro-level Citation Topics	Number	Frequency (%)
Journalism	12	44,44%
Watermarking	9	33,33%
Fake News Detection	2	7,41%
Eating Disorders	1	3,70%
Speech Recognition	1	3,70%
Augmented Reality (AR)	1	3,70%
Evolutionary Psychology	1	3,70%
TOTAL	27	100,00%

Source: Compiled by the author using data from the Web of Science database.

According to Table 5, the distribution of studies on deepfake in AI-assisted journalism by micro-level citation topics reveals that *Journalism* ranks first with 44.44%, followed by *Watermarking* at 33.33%, and *Fake News Detection* at 7.41%. These top three areas—*Journalism*, *Watermarking*, and *Fake News Detection*—are directly related to the use of deepfake technology in AI-supported journalism workflows and are therefore of particular importance.

Notably, *Eating Disorders* ranks fourth, despite not being directly related to the research subject, which makes its presence among the citation topics noteworthy. On the other hand, *Speech Recognition* and *Augmented Reality* are important as enabling technologies for deepfake applications. The inclusion of *Evolutionary Psychology* as a micro-level citation topic can be interpreted as reflecting concerns about how exposure to deepfake-generated content may influence news consumers' memory, perception, and psychological responses.

Table 6. Distribution of studies on deepfake in AI-assisted journalism by web of science index

Web of Science Index	Number	Frequency (%)
Social Sciences Citation Index (SSCI)	11	37,93%
Conference Proceedings Citation Index	7	24,14%
Science Citation Index Expended (SCI-EX)	6	20,69%
Emerging Sources Citation Index (ESCI)	4	13,79%
Arts & Humanities Citation Index (A&HCI)	1	3,45%
TOTAL	29	100,00%

Source: Compiled by the author using data from the Web of Science database.

Table 6 presents the distribution of studies on deepfake in AI-assisted journalism according to their indexing in the Web of Science. The *Social Sciences Citation Index (SSCI)* ranks first with 11 publications, followed by the *Conference Proceedings Citation Index (CPCI)* with 7 publications, the *Science Citation Index Expanded (SCI-EXPANDED)* with 6 publications, and the *Emerging Sources Citation Index (ESCI)* with 4 publications.

Since Web of Science is a subscription-based platform offering comprehensive citation data across various academic disciplines, it indexes academic journals from a wide range of fields. Given that the subject of this study falls within the domain of social sciences, it is expected that social science-oriented indexes are more prominently represented in the results.

Table 7. Distribution of studies on deepfake in AI-assisted journalism by university

List of Universities	Number of Links
PANJAB UNIVERSITY	2
ROCHESTER INSTITUTE OF TECHNOLOGY	2
UNIVERSITY OF ALABAMA SYSTEM	2
UNIVERSITY OF ALABAMA TUSCALOOSA	2
UNIVERSITY OF HAWAII MANOA	2
UNIVERSITY OF HAWAII SYSTEM	2
UNIVERSITY OF SOUTH CAROLINA COLUMBIA	2
UNIVERSITY OF SOUTH CAROLINA SYSTEM	2

continued on following page

Table 7. Continued

List of Universities	Number of Links
UNIVERSITY OF TEXAS SYSTEM	2
ASUTOSH COLL	1
BALL STATE UNIVERSITY	1
BUDAPEST UNIVERSITY OF TECHNOLOGY ECONOMICS	1
CORP RADIOTELEVIS ESPANOLA RTVE	1
COUNCIL SCI IND RES CSIR	1
HADASSAH ACAD COLL	1
HALIC UNIVERSITY	1
ISLAMIC UNIV	1
ISTANBUL NISANTASI UNIVERSITY	1
JADAVPUR UNIVERSITY	1
KADIR HAS UNIVERSITY	1

Source: Compiled by the author using data from the Web of Science database.

Table 7 shows the distribution of studies on deepfake in AI-assisted journalism by university affiliation. It can be observed that universities in the United States, India, Spain, and China have been particularly active in publishing research in the fields of artificial intelligence, deepfake, and journalism. Additionally, universities in the Netherlands, Australia, Hungary, the United Kingdom, and Turkey have also contributed to studies on the use of deepfake technologies in journalism practices.

According to the findings, the majority of publications in this field have been produced by U.S.-based universities and academics. A review of studies conducted by these institutions reveals the publication of the following nine articles: "Capturing the Persistence of Facial Expression Features for Deepfake Video Detection", "A Novel Blockchain-Based Deepfake Detection Method Using Federated and Deep Learning Models", "The Effect of Deepfake Video on News Credibility and Corrective Influence of Cost-Based Knowledge about Deepfakes", "Recurrent Convolutional Structures for Audio Spoof and Video Deepfake Detection", "Dungeons & Deepfakes: Using Scenario-Based Role-Play to Study Journalists' Behavior Towards Using AI-Based Verification Tools for Video Content", "To Believe or Not to Believe: Framing Analysis of Content and Audience Response of Top 10 Deepfake Videos on YouTube", "Something That They Never Said: Multimodal Disinformation and Source Vividness in Understanding the Power of AI-Enabled Deepfake News", "Video Normalization in Identifying Fake Videos Using a Long Short-Term Memory Model", and "NoiseScope: Detecting Deepfake Images in a Blind Setting."

In the case of Turkey, it has been found that Haliç University, Istanbul Nişantaşı University, and Kadir Has University have conducted studies in the area of AI-assisted journalism and deepfake. Among the Turkish contributions, the article titled "A Novel Blockchain-Based Deepfake Detection Method Using Federated and Deep Learning Models" stands out. This study is significant as it addresses the challenge of countering deepfake threats and preserving the authenticity of visual content in an increasingly digital environment.

Table 8. Distribution of studies on deepfake in AI-assisted journalism by university departments

List of Universities	Number of Links
The University Of Alabama College Of Communication And Information Sciences	2
The University Of Alabama Department Of Journalism And Creative Media	2
University Institute Of Engineering And Technology	2
Ball State University College Of Communication Information And Media	1
Ball State University Department Of Journalism	1
Jadavpur University Department Of Computer Science And Engineering	1
King Abdulaziz University Faculty Of Computing And Information Technology	1
National University Of Singapore Centre For Trusted Internet And Community	1
National University Of Singapore Department Of Communications And New Media	1
National University Of Singapore Faculty Of Arts Social Sciences	1
Oxford Internet Institute	1
Seoul National University College Of Social Sciences	1
Seoul National University Department Of Communication	1
The University Of Texas At San Antonio College Of Sciences	1
The University Of Texas At San Antonio Department Of Computer Science	1
Tsinghua University School Of Journalism And Communication	1
University Of Haifa School Of Business Administration	1
University Of Haifa The Herta And Paul Amir Faculty Of Social Sciences	1
University Of Oslo Department Of Media And Communication	1
University Of Oslo Faculty Of Humanities	1

Source: Compiled by the author using data from the Web of Science database.

Table 8 presents the distribution of studies focusing on the use of AI-generated audio and video content in journalism, based on the university departments where these studies were conducted. The analysis shows that 7 studies were produced by Faculties of Communication, New Media, and Information Sciences; 4 studies were affiliated with Departments of Journalism and Creative Media; and another 4 came from Faculties of Arts and Social Sciences. This indicates that the highest number of publications were conducted within Communication Faculties—particularly in the fields of Journalism, Media, and New Media.

In addition, given that the topic of AI-assisted journalism and deepfake involves emerging AI technologies, 2 studies were found to be conducted by Institutes of Engineering and Technology, and another 2 by Departments of Computer Science and Engineering. Other university departments contributing with a single study each include: the Trustworthy Internet and Community Center, the Internet Institute, and the School of Business Management.

Table 9. Distribution of studies on deepfake in AI-assisted journalism by publication titles

Title of Publications	Number of Links
CYBERPSYCHOLOGY BEHAVIOR AND SOCIAL NETWORKING	2
DIGITAL JOURNALISM	2
MEDIA AND COMMUNICATION	2
2020 IEEE INTERNATIONAL CONFERENCE ON ARTIFICIAL INTELLIGENCE AND VIRTUAL REALITY AIVR 2020	1
36TH ANNUAL COMPUTER SECURITY APPLICATIONS CONFERENCE ACSAC 2020	1
AI SOCIETY	1
ANNUAL COMPUTER SECURITY APPLICATIONS CONFERENCE PROCEEDINGS	1
APPLIED SCIENCES BASEL	1
COGNITIVE COMPUTATION	1
COMPUTERS	1
CONVERGENCE THE INTERNATIONAL JOURNAL OF RESEARCH INTO NEW MEDIA TECHNOLOGIES	1
EUROPEAN JOURNAL OF COMMUNICATION	1
FORENSIC SCIENCE INTERNATIONAL DIGITAL INVESTIGATION	1
GOVERNMENT INFORMATION QUARTERLY	1
IEEE CONFERENCE ON EVOLVING AND ADAPTIVE INTELLIGENCE SYSTEMS	1
IEEE CONFERENCE ON EVOLVING AND ADAPTIVE INTELLIGENT SYSTEMS 2024 IEEE EAIS 2024	1
IEEE JOURNAL OF SELECTED TOPICS IN SIGNAL PROCESSING	1
INFORMATION AND COMMUNICATIONS SECURITY ICICS 2019	1

continued on following page

Table 9. Continued

Title of Publications	Number of Links
INFORMATION SCIENCES	1
JOURNALISM AND MEDIA	1

Compiled by the author using data from the Web of Science database.

An analysis of Table 9, which presents the distribution of studies by publication titles in the field, reveals that 6 studies were published in journals focused on computer security applications, 4 in digital journalism publications, 3 in media and communication journals, 3 in artificial intelligence and virtual reality publications, and 2 in journals related to social networks. Given that the topic of the study revolves around the use of AI and deepfake technologies in journalism, it is unsurprising that most publications fall within the fields of computer science, information technology, and digital journalism.

On the other hand, it is noteworthy that only one study was published in journals focused on cognitive computing and new media technologies. This highlights the need for increased research on AI-assisted journalism and deepfake within the domain of new media technologies.

Table 10. Distribution of studies on deepfake in AI-assisted journalism by country

Country	Number of Publications	Country	Number of Publications
USA	9	ISRAEL	1
INDIA	4	NEW ZEALAND	1
SPAIN	4	NORWAY	1
PEOPLES R CHINA	3	SAUDI ARABIA	1
NETHERLANDS	2	SINGAPORE	1
AUSTRIA	1	SOUTH AFRICA	1
BRAZIL	1	SOUTH KOREA	1
ENGLAND	1	TAIWAN	1
HUNGARY	1	TURKIYE	1

Source: Compiled by the author using data from the Web of Science database.

Table 10 presents the distribution of studies on deepfake in AI-assisted journalism by country. The analysis reveals that 9 publications originated from the United States, 4 from India, 4 from Spain, 3 from China, and 2 from the Netherlands. Additionally, one publication each was found from Australia, Brazil, the United

Kingdom, Hungary, Israel, New Zealand, Norway, Saudi Arabia, South Africa, South Korea, Taiwan, and Turkey.

It is noteworthy that contributions from highly developed countries such as the United Kingdom and Norway are relatively limited in this research area. These findings indicate the need for further research on AI-assisted journalism and deepfake technology across a wider range of countries.

DISCUSSION AND CONCLUSION

Artificial intelligence technologies are now widely used in many fields, including journalism. In particular, technologies like deepfake, which are often employed to produce manipulative content, pose a serious threat to the credibility of journalism and its core mission of informing the public. This study aims to examine the academic literature on deepfake technologies in AI-assisted journalism and to analyze proposed solutions regarding news credibility. For this purpose, a total of 28 academic publications published between 2020 and 2024—bearing the terms "Deepfake and Journalism" or "Deepfake" in their titles—were analyzed using the Web of Science database.

In 2024, a noticeable increase in academic publications on deepfake and journalism has been observed, particularly due to the growing use of artificial intelligence technologies across various sectors, especially journalism. Among the analyzed studies, 75% are peer-reviewed journal articles and 25% are conference proceedings; however, the absence of book chapters, review articles, or editorials indicates a need for greater diversity in publication types within this field. According to Web of Science data, the research is distributed across 20 different scientific fields, with a concentration in Communication, Computer Science, and Artificial Intelligence. This reflects a strong focus on the technological aspects of the topic, while also highlighting the need for more research in fields such as Journalism, New Media, Sociology, and Interdisciplinary Social Sciences. Geographically, the highest number of publications originates from universities in the United States, India, Spain, and China, whereas the relatively low contribution from technologically advanced countries such as the United Kingdom and Norway is noteworthy. Most of the studies have been conducted within departments of Communication, Journalism, and New Media, and the publications have primarily appeared in journals related to computer security, digital journalism, media, and artificial intelligence. In terms of research topics, there is significant interest in deepfake detection, video and audio content, fake news production, and AI-based journalism. This trend suggests that areas such as news credibility and the ethical implications of AI-generated content have not yet been thoroughly explored and warrant further investigation.

RECOMMENDATIONS

Based on the findings of this study, the following recommendations are proposed for the field of AI-assisted journalism and the use of deepfake-generated audio and video content:

- Increasing awareness of AI-assisted journalism and deepfake technologies is essential.
- Students in journalism and new media departments should receive structured education on AI and deepfake technologies and their applications.
- Students should be trained in digital literacy and new media literacy to critically engage with fake news content generated by AI and deepfakes.
- Students should develop fake news verification skill sets to address news credibility concerns arising from the use of AI-enabled journalism and deepfake technologies in journalism.

REFERENCES

AA teyithattı. (2023, March 27). *"Papa Francis'in beyaz mont giydiği" iddiası.* AA Teyit Hattı: https://www.aa.com.tr/tr/teyithatti/aktuel/papa-francisin-beyaz-mont-giydigi-iddiasi-/1815693

Aria, M., & Cuccurullo, C. (2017). Bibliometrix: An R-Tool For Comprehensive Science Mapping Analysis. *Journal of Informetrics, 11*(4), 959–975. DOI: 10.1016/j.joi.2017.08.007

Ay, A. (2022, October). Yapay Zeka Haberciliği ve Gazetecilik Tartışmalarına Dair Bir Değerlendirme. *The Turkish Online Journal of Design, Art and Communication - TOJDAC, 12*(4), s. 913-926

BBC. (2018, December 19). *Der Spiegel reporter Claas Relotius sacked over 'invented' stories.* BBC: https://www.bbc.com/news/world-europe-46624297

Beckett, C. (2019). *New powers, New Responsibilities- A global survey of journalism and artificial intelligence.* LSE.

Büyükafşar, M., & Yıldırım, O. (2022). Yapay Zeka Gazeteciliği. S. Özay, & S. Bayrakcı (Dü) içinde [Çizgi Kitabevi.]. *Dijital Çağda Uzman Gazetecilik, 2*, 311–332.

Camacho, M. M. (2019). *The era of post-truth, post-veracity and charlatanism.* Universidad de Navarra: https://www.unav.edu/web/ciencia-razon-y-fe/the-era-of-post-truth-post-veracity-and-charlatanismhttps://www.unav.edu/web/ciencia-razon-y-fe/the-era-of-post-truth-post-veracity-and-charlatanismss

Çavuş, G. (2017, June 27). *Emekli postacının bin 300 çocuğun babası olduğu iddiası.* Teyit.org: https://teyit.org/analiz/emekli-postacinin-bin-300-cocugun-babasi-oldugu-iddiasi

Değirmencioğlu, G. (2016). Temmuz 2). Dijitalleşme Çağında Gazeteciliğin Geleceği ve İnovasyon Haberciliği. *TRT Akademi, 1*(2), 590–606.

Dupré, M. H. (2023, May 18). *Trump Shares AI Voice-Cloned Fake Video of Anderson Cooper.* Futurism: https://futurism.com/trump-ai-voice-cloned-fake-video-anderson-cooper adresinden alındı

Durdak, A. (2024, Fabruary 11). *Anadolu Ajansı Medyada Yapay Zeka Etik Kullanım Rehber Hazırladı.* AA: https://www.aa.com.tr/tr/kurumsal-haberler/anadolu-ajansi-medyada-yapay-zeka-etik-kullanim-rehberi-hazirladi/3133162?utm_source=chatgpt.com#

Fitzgerald, L. (2024, October 7). *The Impact of Deepfakes on Journalism.* Pindrop: https://www.pindrop.com/article/impact-deepfakes-journalism/

Gökbel, H. (2024, November 30). Yapay Zekanın Gazetecilik Pratiklerindeki Yeri . *Tam Akademi Dergisi*, s. 135-162.

Kaplan, J. (2016). *Artificial Intelligence- What Everyone Needs to Know.* Oxford University Press. DOI: 10.1093/wentk/9780190602383.001.0001

Kılıç, B., & Kahraman, M. E. (2023, September). Current Usage Areas of Deepfake Applications with Artificial Intelligence Technology. *Journal CSS*, s. 301-332.

Kırık, A. M., Göksu, O., & Yegen, C. (2024, November 11). Yapay Zeka ve Gazetecilik: Türk Medyasında ChatGPT Kullanımı. *İletişim Kuram ve Araştırma Dergisi*, s. 90-109.

Knickrehm, M. (2020). Yapay Zeka İşi Nasıl Değiştirecek? *Yapay Zeka* (L. Göktem, Çev., s. 155-168). içinde Harvard Business Review Press.

Lundberg, E., & Mozelius, P. (2023, October 23). The potential effects of deepfakes on news media and entertainment. *AI & Society*, •••, 2159–2170.

Merkezi, B. H. (2023, November 13). *Gazetecilikte yapay zeka kullanımına karşı ilk etik ilkeler belirlendi.* Bianet: https://bianet.org/haber/gazetecilikte-yapay-zeka-kullanimina-karsi-ilk-etik-ilkeler-belirlendi-287811

Narin, B. (2017). *Uzman Görüşleri Bağlamında Haber Üretiminde Otomatikleştirme: Robot Gazetecilik.* Galatasaray Üniversitesi İleti-ş-im Dergisi.

Newman, N., Fletcher, R., Kueng, L., Nielsen, R. K., Selva, M., & Suarez, E. (2020). *Journalism, Media, and Technology Trends and Predictions 2020.* Reuters Institute for the Study of Jounalism.

Oksijen. (2025, February 20). *Trump'tan sonra oğlu da Zelenskiy'i hedef aldı.* Oksijen: https://gazeteoksijen.com/dunya/trumptan-sonra-oglu-da-zelenskiyi-hedef-aldi-235616 adresinden alındı

Oxford English Dictionary. (2025, May 19). *Deepfake.* Oxford English Dictionary: https://www.oed.com/dictionary/deepfake_n?tl=true adresinden alındı

Payne, L. (2025, March 14). *deepfake.* Britannica: https://www.britannica.com/technology/deepfake

Ruhanen, L., Weiler, B., Moyle, B. D., & McLennan, C. J. (2015). Trends and patterns in sustainable tourism research: A 25-year bibliometric analysis. *Journal of Sustainable Tourism, 23*(4), 517–535. DOI: 10.1080/09669582.2014.978790

Sample, I. (2020, January 13). *What are deepfakes – and how can you spot them?* The Guardian: https://www.theguardian.com/technology/2020/jan/13/what-are-deepfakes-and-how-can-you-spot-them

Şener, N. K. (2020). *Yapay Zekanın Habercilikte Kullanımı: Olanaklar ve Sakıncalar. F. Zengin, & B. Kapır (Dü) içinde, Yapay Zeka ve Medya.* Doruk Yayıncılık.

Stanford, H. A. I. (2025, January 15). *Artificial Intelligence (AI)- Information about AI: how to use, evaluate, and learn more.* Ball State University- University Libraries: https://bsu.libguides.com/c.php?g=1395427&p=10320854#:~:text=Artificial%20intelligence%20(AI)%2C%20is,like%20playing%20chess%2C%20but%20today%2C

Thormundsson, B. (2024, June 19). *Artificial intelligence (AI) worldwide - statistics & facts.* Statista: https://www.statista.com/topics/3104/artificial-intelligence-ai-worldwide/#topicOverview

Timur, T. (2017, May 22). *Suyun üzerinde yürümeye çalışan papazı timsahlar yedi iddiası.* Teyit.org: https://teyit.org/analiz/suyun-uzerinde-yurumeye-calisan-papazi-timsahlar-yedi-iddiasi

ULAKBİM. (2025). *Bibliyometrik Analiz.* https://cabim.ulakbim.gov.tr/bibliyometrik-analiz/

Yasar, K., Barney, N., & Wigmore, I. (n.d.). *What is deepfake technology?* WhatIs?: https://www.techtarget.com/whatis/definition/deepfake

Zinderen, İ. E. (2024). *Yapay Zeka Gazetecilik İlişkisi. Y. Bayram (Dü.) içinde, Temel Gazetecilik-Kavramlar, Teknikler, Yenilikler.* Akademisyen Kitabevi.

Chapter 6
The Political Economy of Artificial Intelligence: A Critical Assessment of DeepSeek

Cem Sefa Sütcü
https://orcid.org/0000-0002-9389-6832
Marmara Üniversitesi, Turkey

Elif Akçay
https://orcid.org/0000-0002-2566-7288
Maltepe Üniversitesi, Turkey

ABSTRACT

This study argues that AI technologies, as exemplified by DeepSeek, must be examined not only in terms of economic efficiency and cost advantages but also through the lenses of data ownership, surveillance, ethical responsibility, and global inequalities. Rather than adopting a merely critical perspective, the study embraces a critical stance to analyze the societal implications of DeepSeek and similar AI applications. It draws upon current academic research in critical theory, political economy, and communication studies to explore how the rapid adoption of AI is deeply intertwined with broader social, economic, and political dynamics. In this context, the future of AI is not merely a technological issue, but a normative one, the protection of data privacy, the design of systems for the public good, and the fair distribution of benefits must be safeguarded through democratic governance. The impacts of DeepSeek and similar systems will ultimately be shaped by how these fundamental questions are addressed.

DOI: 10.4018/979-8-3373-2960-4.ch006

INTRODUCTION

The emergence of DeepSeek, a Chinese artificial intelligence company offering low-cost, open-source large language models, marks a turning point in the global AI landscape. Following the release of its R1 model in January 2025, DeepSeek's mobile AI assistant quickly topped app store rankings within days, surpassing OpenAI's ChatGPT. This rapid success triggered stock selloffs among major U.S. tech companies as investors began to reassess the dominance of Western AI providers. Far from being a straightforward tale of technological triumph, the rise of DeepSeek brings urgent and critical questions to the forefront. Who controls the data and infrastructure that support such AI applications? What are the ethical implications in terms of privacy and surveillance? How might these systems transform democratic flows of information and the public knowledge sphere? And how do geopolitical asymmetries—such as China's advantage in AI development due to data-rich platforms like WeChat—shape this process?

This chapter addresses these issues through a political economy framework that foregrounds power, inequality, and governance, adopting a communication and information science perspective. Rather than merely adopting a critical viewpoint, the chapter takes a critical stance to analyze the social implications of AI applications such as DeepSeek. The main themes include: (1) ethical challenges such as data privacy, surveillance, and security vulnerabilities; (2) impacts on access to democratic information and the public sphere; and (3) competitive advantages shaped by geopolitical and infrastructural factors. Furthermore, the chapter draws on contemporary academic research from critical theory, political economy, and communication studies to understand how the rapid adoption of AI is interwoven with broader social, economic, and political dynamics.

Although AI applications are often portrayed as a technological "revolution" or a sudden leap forward, they are, in fact, products of a socio-technical transformation arising from the evolutionary deepening of digital infrastructures. A core misunderstanding lies in framing AI merely as a "tool" or a technical system. Technologies, however, are not just technical objects; they are also regulatory forces that shape social relations (Winner, 2020). In this context, AI constitutes the institutionalization of cybernetic rationalities—such as control, automation, and predictability—within the digital ecosystem. These systems evolve not only through increased computational power, advanced network infrastructures, or software architectures, but also through political-economic decisions, regulatory frameworks, cultural norms, and ethical concerns. Sheila Jasanoff's concept of "co-production" becomes crucial here: technologies like AI are shaped not only by scientific knowledge but also by social values and institutional power relations. Technologies are co-produced with society; and society is simultaneously reconfigured through technologies (Jasanoff, 2004).

This "co-evolutionary" nature of AI compels us to consider it not merely as an engineering product, but as an ideological and governance instrument. For instance, the training of large language models like GPT-4 or DeepSeek is not solely a matter of data and energy; it also involves questions of whose data is used, who controls it, and which social realities are reproduced. The algorithmic infrastructures of digital platforms not only shape user experience, but also determine what counts as truth, who gets to speak, and which regimes of visibility dominate. Thus, the emergence of AI applications is not the outcome of technological determinism, but rather of complex socio-technical configurations. Digitalization produces not only new tools but also new "ways of life." As Langdon Winner famously noted, "technologies are forms of life"—choosing certain technological systems entails choosing particular kinds of social relationships (Winner, 2020). Therefore, to understand the core dynamics of AI development, one must look not only at technological progress, but also at political power structures, market conditions, ethical standards, and mechanisms of public oversight.

1. WHAT IS DEEPSEEK?

The development of open-source large language models (LLMs) has been remarkable. LLMs undergo a self-supervised pre-training process on vast datasets by predicting the next word in a continuous stream of text. This enables them to perform a variety of tasks such as content generation, text summarization, and code completion, allowing them to serve multiple functions. Subsequently, techniques such as supervised fine-tuning and reward modeling have made LLMs increasingly capable of understanding and following user instructions more effectively. As a result, these models now offer more flexible and sophisticated conversational experiences, and their social impact has grown rapidly (Bi et al., 2024).

DeepSeek has recently emerged as a major actor in the field of artificial intelligence. Based on deep learning techniques, DeepSeek is a large language model (LLM) that employs advanced natural language processing (NLP) technologies. It is capable of performing a range of tasks including text generation, comprehension, translation, summarization, and question-answering. DeepSeek stands out among open-source and commercial models, finding applications in both academic and industrial domains (Zhao et al., 2023). Built on large-scale neural network architectures, DeepSeek demonstrates high performance especially in processing long texts and capturing contextual meaning (Vaswani et al., 2017). Under the leadership of its founder and CEO Liang Wenfeng, DeepSeek's innovative approaches to deep learning and data analytics make it a significant case for understanding the economic and political dimensions of AI.

DeepSeek's core features and functionalities can be summarized as follows:

- DeepSeek is equipped with a broad context window capable of processing long texts. This feature facilitates the analysis of lengthy documents and the generation of coherent output (DeepSeek, 2024).
- It provides high-performance text processing in multiple languages, including English, Chinese, and Turkish (Brown et al., 2020), and can generate academic article summaries and analyze technical documents by responding accurately to complex queries (Devlin et al., 2019).
- Researchers and developers can fine-tune the model with their own datasets (Liu et al., 2021).
- DeepSeek can integrate with internet search to retrieve real-time information, offering responses based on up-to-date data (Borgeaud et al., 2022).

One of DeepSeek's greatest advantages lies in its use of "sparsity" techniques, which allow it to perform more computations with significantly fewer parameters. With the release of its third version (V3 and R1), DeepSeek made a substantial impact by introducing a model that, in some areas, outperforms OpenAI's GPT models—while doing so at much lower cost and with significantly reduced resource consumption. Offering twice the speed at 90% less cost compared to OpenAI, DeepSeek rapidly became one of the most downloaded applications (Kuzuluoğlu, 2025).

2. TECHNOLOGICAL INFRASTRUCTURE AND INNOVATIONS

Today, the competition among large language models is driving rapid advancements in technological innovation. The future of deep learning-based language models depends on factors such as real-time data processing, multilingual support, and energy efficiency. While OpenAI's ChatGPT, Google's Gemini, and Meta's LLaMA stand out for their wide range of applications, DeepSeek differentiates itself through its extended context window, open-source flexibility, and high-performance data processing capabilities.

Although ChatGPT remains popular due to its user-friendly interface and extensive integration capabilities, DeepSeek's 128K-token[1] context window allows it to deliver more coherent results when processing technical or academic texts (Zhao et al., 2023). In the context of language models, a token refers to the smallest unit of text the model can process. A 128K-token window signifies the capacity to handle massive text blocks at once—an invaluable asset in domains such as law, academia, and data analytics.

When it comes to large-scale data analysis, DeepSeek's integrated search function and its high-accuracy text processing capabilities make it especially appealing for business applications. While ChatGPT performs strongly in general-purpose conversations, DeepSeek's optimized algorithms often yield more consistent results for tasks such as summarizing technical reports or conducting financial data analysis (Borgeaud et al., 2022). On the other hand, Google's Gemini excels in multimodal processing (handling text, image, and audio inputs), while DeepSeek currently specializes in text-based applications with a high degree of focus.

Thanks to its integration with Microsoft products (such as Copilot) and advanced APIs, ChatGPT has been widely adopted in corporate environments. DeepSeek, although not yet supported by such an expansive ecosystem, offers free access and high token efficiency, making it an attractive option particularly for academic and technical users. Moreover, in terms of localized language support—including Turkish—it demonstrates strong performance compared to its competitors (Brown et al., 2020).

Table 1. A comparison of DeepSeek, ChatGPT, and Gemini in terms of key features

Feature	**DeepSeek**	**ChatGPT (GPT-4-turbo)**	**Gemini (Gemini 1.5)**
Context Window	128K tokens	32K tokens	128K tokens
Open-Source Availability	Partial (some models)	No	No
Multimodal Support	Text-focused	Text + Image (GPT-4V)	Text + Image + Audio
Integrated Search	Yes	No (Plugins required)	Partial (via Google Search)
Turkish Language Performance	High	Medium to High	Medium

The table highlights DeepSeek's competitive strengths in handling extended text contexts and offering open-source adaptability, while also revealing its relative shortcomings in multimodal capabilities and ecosystem integration compared to its rivals.

3. A POLITICAL ECONOMY PERSPECTIVE

According to Yanis Varoufakis, the reason behind the United States launching a new Cold War against China lies in China's development of a digital payment system that poses a direct challenge to the hegemony of the U.S. dollar. Varoufakis argues that this situation is rooted in deep economic and political dynamics: China seeks to engage in global trade, while the U.S. has devised strategies to contain China's economic ascent. As he puts it: "*This is not about China growing, nor is it about Chinese espionage. It's not even about Taiwan. The problem is that China has created a cloud-based digital payments highway, which constitutes a clear and present danger to the monopoly of the dollar-based payment system—and that monopoly is the sole foundation of U.S. global hegemony*" (*Rise of Asia*, 2025).

Before 2020, one of the most debated issues in the context of technology and globalization was the emergence of social networking companies as "transnational organizations" that rivaled, and in some cases surpassed, the regulatory capacity of nation-states. Several theoretical approaches were employed to explain this transformation. For instance, in the "controlled hegemony" model, global digital networks were freely used but subject to strict state regulation. In the "compelled hegemony" model, the state lacked the infrastructure to build its own national platforms and was thus unable to effectively regulate foreign platforms due to excessive user demand—a form of regulatory impotence. The "alternative hegemony" model envisioned a hybrid approach in which both global and local platforms coexisted under defined legal constraints. At the extreme end of the spectrum were rigid state-centric hegemonic models, such as those seen in Russia and China, where only state-controlled networks were permitted.

This context gains further significance when we consider the role of Tim Cook, who took over Apple following Steve Jobs' death and expanded the company by 25 times in 14 years—eight of which coincided with one of the most intense trade wars of the modern era. Given Apple's heavy reliance on both Chinese manufacturing and Chinese consumers, one might have expected the company to be severely affected. Indeed, both the Trump administration and the Chinese government possessed considerable leverage over Apple. Nevertheless, Tim Cook managed to secure support from both sides. Historically, Apple had manufactured its Macintosh computers in California. Steve Jobs took pride in declaring, "This is a machine made in America." Cook, on the other hand, had previously worked at Compaq, a PC giant that had long embraced outsourcing. He convinced Foxconn to assemble the first iPhone at a loss, with the promise of future lucrative contracts. This gamble paid off, and many others followed suit (TechAltar, 2025).

Perhaps Cook's most notable strategic move was the partnership he forged with China—not merely accepting the country but fully embracing it, so much so that the phrase "Designed in California, Assembled in China" became inscribed on all Apple products. This partnership proved immensely profitable. In the early phases, much of the negotiation and relationship-building was facilitated by Foxconn's charismatic founder. A *New York Times* investigation revealed that the Chinese government effectively built an entire city for Apple. In addition to a $600 million production complex, $1 billion was spent on worker housing. The government provided extensive energy infrastructure, credit, recruitment and training support, tax exemptions, and bonuses—and even created a "bonded zone," a territory within China legally treated as foreign soil. "iPhone City" was one of several such production hubs built in China for Apple's benefit.

In February 2025, Apple announced it would invest over $500 billion in the United States over the next four years. This announcement included plans to open a new manufacturing facility in Houston, double the U.S. Advanced Manufacturing Fund from $5 billion to $10 billion, and create 20,000 new high-skilled jobs. Apple also declared its intention to open a new Manufacturing Academy in Detroit. The media and Trump administration greeted this announcement positively. However, this $500 billion figure represents an incremental increase, rather than a radical shift, given that Apple had already invested $350 billion in 2018 and $430 billion in 2021. The 20,000 jobs being created primarily reflect roles in AI engineering and software development—positions Apple already had in the U.S. Thus, while the numbers appear impressive, they do little to alter the structural status quo (TechAltar, 2025).

While Apple is one of the most visible examples, other tech giants also fully capitalized on the benefits of the Web2 era (up to around 2020), transforming into trillion-dollar corporations and subsequently pivoting toward investments in AI. For instance, Microsoft invested approximately $14 billion in OpenAI last year (Gairola, 2024). OpenAI announced that it spends $5 billion annually on developing ChatGPT (Ma, 2024). Google, in turn, has invested an estimated $50 billion in building and expanding its Gemini AI platform (Farooque, 2024).

Today, we are witnessing a clear shift in the global axis of power. Nation-states have begun to realize that tech companies can wield their extraordinary capabilities as instruments of geopolitical influence. Consequently, governments are paying increasing attention to the intersection of digital infrastructure and national security. For example, during his second term, Donald Trump announced the "Stargate" project, committing $500 billion in AI infrastructure investments. He established a Bureau of Government Efficiency and appointed Elon Musk—the world's richest man, founder of Tesla (the top-selling car brand globally), and developer of the Grok AI application—along with Vivek Ramaswamy to lead this effort. In effect, this move brought private tech corporations directly into the apparatus of state governance.

The United States has been implementing a trade embargo for six years to restrict China's access to high-tech products. The primary goal is to prevent China from surpassing the U.S. in technological innovation. For example, they have blocked Chinese mobile phone companies like Huawei, social media platforms like TikTok, and the sale of powerful GPUs—recently released by Nvidia and used for AI processing—to China. On the other hand, following a news announcement made by China on January 20, 2025, discussions began to emerge suggesting that China was not affected by these restrictions at all. In fact, it had reportedly developed an

AI application named DeepSeek (https://chat.deepseek.com/sign_in), accessible to everyone, that was more successful than ChatGPT, cost only $6 million, and operated at 30 times lower computational power and 100 times lower cost (Kerner, 2025).

Immediately afterward, the shares of tech companies investing in AI—particularly Nvidia—on U.S. stock markets experienced significant losses, as did cryptocurrencies such as Bitcoin. The total loss in the stock market amounted to $1 trillion (McDermott, J. & O'Brien, 2025). Moreover, since China's DeepSeek announcement coincided with the period when U.S. technology companies were preparing their annual financial reports, regulations prohibited these companies from making any statements that could influence the stock market, preventing them from intervening to stop the decline.

In another recent announcement by the U.S., it was stated that advanced technology products would only be shared with 18 countries classified as "allies," and that these restrictions would be implemented within the next few months. Turkey is not included among these allies (Freifeld, 2025). With this announcement, the U.S. effectively declared its intention to maintain technological monopoly. It is now widely acknowledged that dominance in AI technologies in the 21st century equates to the power to shape the new world order according to national interests.

The timing of the DeepSeek incident can thus be interpreted as a "counter move" against this vision of a global order. Interestingly, DeepSeek was built using older-generation Nvidia processors. In this sense, the restrictions did not stop China but instead pushed it to be more creative in innovation. China's development of cheaper AI applications with better performance using lower computational power suggests that U.S. hegemony in the field of innovation may soon shift in favor of China. It has now become evident that such technologies can be developed without massive expenditures. This also implies that future AI initiatives may struggle to attract the level of investment they have seen so far, and large-scale projects like Stargate are already being questioned (D'Cruze, 2025).

Many fear that AI is not just a tool, but also a force that could replace human labor. This concern can be expressed as the fear that economic power will become increasingly concentrated in the hands of a small elite that owns AI. As states and corporations become less dependent on human labor, it is anticipated that social inequality will deepen and that fundamental changes will occur in societal structures. The influence of AI may render public investments in people—such as education and infrastructure—obsolete, leading to a decrease in support for such areas. It is not difficult to foresee that this may negatively affect democracy and strengthen authoritarian tendencies (Lee, 2018).

One of the biggest problems encountered in AI development is the excessive energy consumption of AI systems, which poses a threat to ecological balance. Another is the need for vast amounts of data to train these systems. For example, training the earlier GPT-3 model of ChatGPT required as much energy as 100 households consume in a year, while training the latest version, GPT-4, required energy equivalent to the annual consumption of 5,000 households (Zewe, 2025; Cohen, 2024). It is also said that the supply of high-quality textual data available on the Internet to train AI will be exhausted by 2028. Additionally, media outlets like *The Wall Street Journal* have filed lawsuits against OpenAI for using their news articles as training data. In response to such data constraints, some AI companies are planning to turn to high-quality data sources such as textbooks and to generate "synthetic data" (Shanbhogue, 2024).

Issues such as the transformations DeepSeek brings to business, its contributions to increased efficiency and reduced costs, the role of data in economic value creation, debates on monopolization and data ownership, and the impact of these developments on class inequalities in the data economy are worthy of examination from informatics and communication perspectives. Experts suggest that DeepSeek, through its advanced AI models, can offer businesses faster and more cost-effective solutions, improve operational efficiency—especially by providing rapid responses to programming queries—and, thanks to its open-source approach, allow companies to customize models according to their specific needs (Unite.AI, 2023). This implies potential contributions to increased efficiency and cost reduction.

At this point, it is necessary to examine the role of data in economic value creation. In his article *The Protection of Personal Data from a Political Economy Perspective* (2013), Karlıdağ notes that when individual concerns conflict with capital interests, public authorities adopt different approaches depending on the society in question, defining and protecting privacy as a right. He emphasizes that this right can be defined through national laws and in the context of human rights. While privacy is considered a fundamental human right in the EU, in the U.S., the issue is largely left to corporate self-regulation. This divergence is one of the reasons the EU has lagged behind the U.S. and China in AI development over the past decade (Karlıdağ, 2013).

In his book *AI Superpowers: China, Silicon Valley, and the New World Order* (2018), Kai-Fu Lee underlines that China and the U.S. have made such rapid progress in AI that they are paving the way for a bipolar world order. Despite the presence of talented researchers and AI labs in countries like the UK, France, and Canada, he notes that the lack of large user bases and venture capital ecosystems hampers their ability to generate the massive datasets required for AI development (Lee, 2018).

The increasing monopolization of digital platforms has sparked significant debate around issues of data ownership and control. The collection and processing of user data by major tech companies has led to the centralization of economic power. This has triggered discussions around concepts like data sovereignty and global data imperialism (Güney, 2020). The data economy may serve not only to reproduce material inequalities but also to reinforce cognitive domination. The monopolization of data by major technology companies concentrates economic power in the hands of a few, effectively rendering users digital serfs. This highlights the need to raise social awareness and to develop alternative models (Kaymakçı, 2025).

4. DEEPSEEK AND ITS SOCIETAL IMPACTS

AI applications like DeepSeek are built on the collection and processing of vast amounts of data. This foundation raises significant ethical concerns around privacy and surveillance. Modern AI systems are often trained using personal, sensitive, or proprietary data, creating a tension between innovation and individuals' rights to privacy and data protection. For example, Geoffrey Hinton has expressed concern that AI-driven data analysis could amplify privacy-invading practices such as surveillance and identification, resulting in increased power and control for the watchers, thereby worsening income inequality and potentially leading to authoritarianism (Boulton, 2025). In other words, the very algorithms that enable beneficial AI services can also enhance the capabilities of those collecting and monitoring data—whether corporations or governments.

The case of DeepSeek illustrates these concerns. Security researchers discovered that DeepSeek's chatbot platform included hidden code linking user data to servers belonging to China Mobile, raising fears that user information might be leaked to government authorities. DeepSeek's own privacy policy confirms that user data is stored on servers located within the People's Republic of China (Tau, 2025). All of this heightens fears surrounding government surveillance and data sovereignty, especially considering China's track record with state monitoring of digital platforms. It recalls similar data privacy concerns that have been raised with other Chinese applications like TikTok, which has been debated as a national security threat (Yuko, 2024; Hutchinson, 2025). The political economy of data is becoming a key area of focus. AI firms hold vast amounts of user data as a new form of capital, and in certain jurisdictions—such as China—this capital is strictly regulated or even directly utilized by the state (Schmalz, 2024).

Not only authoritarian regimes, but also democratic societies must grapple with AI's surveillance capacities. From facial recognition cameras to algorithmic monitoring on social media, AI-enabled surveillance technologies are now deployed globally. Yet, their implementation varies widely across different political systems. In democratic contexts, these surveillance activities are generally bound by legal frameworks, accountability mechanisms, and principles of civil liberty. At the very least, human rights-based approaches require that such interventions be limited and subject to oversight. In contrast, AI surveillance systems operate with far fewer constraints in authoritarian regimes. These systems are used not only for public order but also to “detect and suppress dissenting elements.” In the absence of strong transparency or accountability mechanisms, governments can use AI to monitor activists, censor speech, and suppress opposition with unprecedented efficiency. As Azgın and Kıralp (2024) point out, AI has become “an indispensable tool for surveillance” serving very different purposes in open societies versus authoritarian regimes. This dual use of AI surveillance dramatically intensifies ethical concerns. Globally, digital authoritarianism powered by AI is on the rise: The latest report from Freedom House highlights how repressive regimes use AI technologies for mass surveillance, online censorship, disinformation, and targeted repression, contributing to 13 consecutive years of decline in global internet freedom. From a political economy perspective, such developments are not accidental misuses of AI but rather deliberate strategies by those in power to consolidate control through digital tools (Azgın & Kıralp, 2024).

Beyond surveillance, data security and system vulnerabilities are other major ethical challenges posed by AI. AI applications may inadvertently disclose sensitive information or be manipulated into producing harmful outputs. For instance, it has been observed that large language model-based assistants have, under certain conditions, leaked private data. There have been documented incidents of data leaks involving generative AI tools like ChatGPT. In one example described by Ye and colleagues, ChatGPT exhibited a flaw that allowed users to see others’ chat data, revealing the potential inadequacies of such systems in protecting personal information. Serious data breaches have also occurred in China (Ye et al., 2024). Moreover, these models are often trained on vast datasets scraped from the web, including personal information obtained without consent, raising concerns over “centralized data control” and whether individuals have any say in how their data is used to train AI (Office of the Chief Information Officer, 2025).

AI’s complexity also introduces new security risks: Malicious actors may carry out “prompt injection” attacks to trick chatbots into revealing confidential information or producing prohibited content. Concerns persist about hidden “backdoors” in AI models that could be exploited (Humphreys et al., 2024). Furthermore, generative AI can be weaponized by bad actors to produce convincing phishing messages or automate the creation of malicious software, expanding the toolkit for cybercrime (Schmitt & Flechais, 2023). These vulnerabilities highlight the need for robust governance and technical safeguards for AI systems. However, regulatory frameworks continue to lag behind technological developments. A recent study by Chinese legal scholars argues that current personal data protection regimes—based on individual consent and control—are “ill-suited” for the data processing methods of generative AI and that achieving “trustworthy AI” will require urgent institutional innovations (Ye et al., 2024).

The widespread adoption of AI in communication platforms and information services has complex implications for democracy, particularly in relation to access to information and the public sphere—that is, a knowledge ecosystem where a society's various voices, perspectives, and ideas are freely expressed, accessed, and debated. While supporters often celebrate AI-driven systems (from social media algorithms to search engines and chatbots) as tools that improve access to information, personalize content, or even help prevent misinformation, research in communication and political science offers a more critical perspective—highlighting how AI may disrupt the democratic public sphere and undermine the quality of public knowledge.

One of the greatest concerns is that AI systems acting as gatekeepers may, often unknowingly, reinforce biases or suppress minority viewpoints. Machine-learning-powered content curation and moderation algorithms do not merely reflect a "neutral social wisdom"; they also carry their own implicit tendencies. In his work *Artificial Intelligence and Democracy: A Conceptual Framework* (2023), Jungherr suggests that AI-based moderation will tend to "lean toward the average" by learning from typical patterns in training data. This implies that when tasked with filtering or summarizing public discourse, AI will favor common or mainstream perspectives, while unconventional or dissenting views risk being marginalized. Unless corrective measures are taken in this "AI-shaped communication environment," Jungherr warns that marginal and minority voices may become "invisible and disappear." Ultimately, democratic systems may lose their capacity to process information effectively if the visible range of opinions narrows, reinforcing political status quos (Jungherr, 2023). If our online forums, news feeds, or AI assistants prioritize majority views or officially sanctioned narratives (as prevalent in training datasets), the public's ability to recognize and engage with the full diversity of viewpoints diminishes. This dynamic threatens the pluralism necessary for a healthy democracy. In line with concerns voiced by critical theorists, digital algorithms can function as gatekeepers that support dominant ideologies and marginalize dissenting groups—unless explicitly designed otherwise (Tosyalı, 2021).

Another threat AI poses to democracy is the risk of large-scale manipulation and misinformation. The sophistication of generative AI has made it easier than ever to produce "deepfakes" and synthetic media—automated texts that mimic human speech. These tools can be used to spread propaganda and misinformation with unprecedented speed and realism. Research by Goldstein and colleagues (2024) demonstrates that AI-generated propaganda can be as effective as traditional forms. Such capabilities allow malicious actors—from state-run disinformation campaigns to profit-driven clickbait farms—to flood the information ecosystem with fake or misleading content (Goldstein et al., 2024).

AI systems can also direct such content through micro-targeting. Leveraging big data, AI can predict individual vulnerabilities and craft personalized messages to influence their opinions or behavior. This raises the threat of "hyper-targeted" manipulation. Political advertisers or lobbying groups can use AI to identify the most susceptible segments of the population and reach them with tailored propaganda. Early cases like the Cambridge Analytica scandal have already shown how targeted political persuasion can be enabled by personal data (Akçay & Sütcü, 2024). AI takes this a step further. Jungherr (2023) argues that consultants can use AI to dynamically test and optimize messages, enabling a level of public opinion engineering far beyond what traditional mass communication could achieve. This presents a serious challenge to democratic processes. Elections and public debates may be manipulated through AI-curated information flows, where accuracy and deliberation are compromised. Scholars have begun referring to this as an "AI-mediated disinformation paradigm"—one in which it becomes increasingly difficult to distinguish real news from AI-generated falsehoods (De Nadal & Jančárik, 2024; Bontcheva et al., 2024). The concern is not only about the spread of misinformation, but also the erosion of public trust in information itself. A populace inundated with fake news may become deeply skeptical of all media, undermining the informed citizenry necessary for democracy.

From a geopolitical perspective, the development and deployment of AI do not occur in a vacuum. These processes are deeply embedded in global geopolitical and infrastructural contexts. A critical political economy perspective reveals that differences in data infrastructure, regulatory regimes, and market structures across countries create unequal competitive advantages in the AI field. China's rise as an AI power demonstrates how a state's political-economic model can accelerate AI development—though often at the cost of significant ethical compromises. As venture capitalist Kai-Fu Lee famously noted, success in modern AI depends on three key ingredients: vast data, computing power, and skilled engineers. Lee argued that, especially in terms of data, China holds a unique wealth of resources (Lee, 2018). Over the past decade, China has leveraged its massive population and deeply integrated digital platforms to generate "oceans of everyday data." For instance, applications like WeChat (Weixin), which has over a billion users, combine multiple functions—messaging, social media, payments, ride-hailing—within a single platform, thereby collecting an unmatched volume and variety of user data. Some analyses show that Chinese users generate digital data at rates several times higher than Western users, largely because of how pervasively platforms like WeChat infiltrate daily life. Combined with relatively flexible privacy norms and innovation-driven state policies, this data abundance provides Chinese AI firms with a powerful advantage in training their models. Access to large and diverse datasets is seen as a key factor behind China's edge in AI development. In areas ranging from speech recognition to recommendation systems, Chinese companies have the ability to train models on datasets of a magnitude that rivals often cannot match (Lee, 2018).

The U.S.-China AI rivalry is often framed as a race for supremacy, but it might be better understood as the emergence of "distinct digital spheres," each shaped by different governance values. Schmalz (2024) describes the rise of competing technological domains: the U.S.-led sphere is based on a liberal internationalist model, while the China-led sphere emphasizes state-driven technological advancement. In the U.S. and allied digital domain, AI development is largely led by globally expanding private tech companies, which integrate world markets into their own structures (e.g., Google, Microsoft, Amazon, and Meta's global dominance). As a result, much of the world's digital infrastructure now falls under the influence of a few American firms. By contrast, China's sphere was initially insular—due in part to the Great Firewall—but has increasingly begun exporting its technologies abroad (e.g., Huawei's AI-powered telecom equipment, TikTok's global reach, and Chinese surveillance systems sold internationally). Thus, geopolitical competition intersects with infrastructure: while the U.S. fears that Chinese applications like DeepSeek or TikTok may function as Trojan horses for data extraction, China is committed to reducing dependence on Western technologies and establishing its own standards. These tensions are evident in debates over 5G networks, semiconductor export controls, and AI research capabilities—all of which are elements of a broader power struggle. In the context of AI, political economy suggests that global power is, at least in part, determined by who controls data centers, chip manufacturing plants, dominant algorithms, and platforms with the most users (Schmalz, 2024).

In this light, China's integrated approach—combining population scale, data access, and state direction—has enabled rapid scaling advantages. This is evident in cases such as DeepSeek's rapid development and adoption, allowing it to overtake Western competitors. As Kai-Fu Lee has observed, China's technology culture also promotes iterative innovation and aggressive implementation (often at the expense of strict regulation), which can accelerate the deployment of AI applications (Lee, 2018). However, from a critical perspective, this should not be seen as a simple success story for China. The competitive advantage derived from lax privacy policies and state surveillance also comes with social costs. Chinese citizens are subject to intense monitoring; the very data used to train AI products is also used to assign social credit scores or identify protesters. The development model exemplified by WeChat—offering convenience in exchange for extensive data collection—may yield economic benefits and AI leadership but simultaneously entrenches a surveillance society. Moreover, other countries may find it increasingly difficult to compete without compromising democratic values. Liberal democracies face a pressing dilemma: how to foster AI innovation without reproducing the surveillance capitalism observed in major U.S. tech firms (Zuboff, 2019) or the state surveillance model seen in China.

CONCLUSION

DeepSeek stands out for its transformative effects in business, cost-efficiency, and productivity gains. However, issues such as data ownership, monopolization, and class-based inequalities in the data economy represent crucial areas of debate for the future. Thus, developments in AI and the data economy must be addressed not only from a technological standpoint but also through ethical and societal lenses. AI encompasses ethical challenges, privacy violations, advanced surveillance capacities, and security vulnerabilities—all of which stem from imbalances of power between those who develop or deploy AI and the public subjected to these technologies. A critical perspective emphasizes the need for accountability: without strong oversight, the deployment of AI often prioritizes corporate or state interests in data extraction and social control over individual rights and public safety.

The rise of DeepSeek and similar AI applications represents a double-edged sword for society, requiring a more nuanced and critical analysis beyond celebratory narratives of technological progress. On one hand, these innovations promise convenience, efficiency, and economic growth. On the other, they deepen inequality, threaten privacy, and pose new dangers to the public sphere. From the perspective of communication and information sciences, AI applications are actively reshaping power relations across various domains.

Ethically, AI intensifies surveillance capitalism and state control, raising fundamental questions such as "Who watches the watchers?" and how personal data is being exploited.

In the realm of knowledge and democracy, AI's role as a gatekeeper of information entails the risk of narrowing discursive diversity and enabling mass manipulation. Unless robust accountability and transparency mechanisms are established, these risks may become reality.

Geopolitically, the political economy of AI technologies is creating new winners and losers: those with access to vast datasets and infrastructural control (e.g., China's rapid ascent in AI) gain strategic advantages, while others fear losing digital sovereignty or being left behind. Yet these developments are not technological inevitabilities—they are shaped by political choices, institutional practices, and societal values.

A critical political economy approach reminds us that the trajectory of AI must not be left solely to dynamics of profit and power but should instead be guided by democratic debate and regulation. The societal impact of DeepSeek and similar applications ultimately depends on how we collectively respond to these emerging challenges.

Key questions remain:

- Will data privacy be treated as a fundamental right or as a commodified asset?
- Will AI systems be designed to support human judgment for the public good, or to automate control mechanisms and manufacture consent?
- As AI's benefits are distributed globally, will equity be ensured, or will those benefits be concentrated in the hands of a powerful few?

Answering these questions will require insights from disciplines such as critical theory and communication studies. Only then can we envision pathways for AI development that prioritize ethical safeguards, democratic governance, and fair infrastructures. In the end, the success of AI should not be measured solely by economic returns or algorithmic superiority, but by its ability to uphold and advance our shared social values. Achieving this goal requires a strong commitment to democratizing AI—ensuring that technologies like DeepSeek are embedded within accountability frameworks and used not to empower the few, but to uplift the many.

REFERENCES

Akçay, E., ve Sütcü, C. (2024). Bilişimsel Propaganda Farkındalık Ölçeği ve Kamuoyu Üzerindeki Etkisi. *Türkiye İletişim Araştırmaları Dergisi* (*46*), 45-74. DOI: 10.17829/turcom.1489518

Azgin, B., & Kiralp, S. (2024). Surveillance, disinformation, and legislative measures in the 21st century: AI, social media, and the future of democracies. *Social Sciences (Basel, Switzerland)*, *13*(10), 510. DOI: 10.3390/socsci13100510

Bontcheva, K., Papadopoulous, S., Tsalakanidou, F., ... (2024). Generative AI and Disinformation: Recent Advances, Challenges, and Opportunities. Whitepaper (Ed: Kalina Bontcheva), https://edmo.eu/wp-content/uploads/2023/12/Generative-AI-and-Disinformation_-White-Paper-v8.pdf

Borgeaud, S., Mensch, A., Hoffmann, J., Cai, T., Rutherford, E., Millican, K., van den Driessche, G., Lespiau, J.-B., Damoc, B., Clark, A., Casas, D. de L., Guy, A., Menick, J., Ring, R., Hennigan, T., Huang, S., Maggiore, L., Jones, C., Cassirer, A., . . . Sifre, L. (2022). *Improving language models by retrieving from trillions of tokens*. /arXiv.2112.04426DOI: 10.48550

Boulton, H. (2025). *'Godfather of AI' explains how 'scary' AI will increase the wealth gap and 'make society worse'*. UniladTech. https://www.uniladtech.com/news/ai/ai-godfather-explains-ai-will-increase-wealth-gap-318842-20250113

Brown, T. B., Mann, B., Ryder, N., Subbiah, M., Kaplan, J., Dhariwal, P., Neelakantan, A., Shyam, P., Sastry, G., Askell, A., Agarwal, S., Herbert-Voss, A., Krueger, G., Henighan, T., Child, R., Ramesh, A., Ziegler, D. M., Wu, J., Winter, C., . . . Amodei, D. (2020). *Language Models are Few-Shot Learners*. /arXiv.2005.14165DOI: 10.48550

Cohen, A. (2024, 20 Aralık). *2025's energy megatrends: Seeking energy security and reviving nuclear*. Forbes. https://www.forbes.com/sites/arielcohen/2024/12/20/2025s-energy-megatrends-seeking-energy-security-and-reviving-nuclear/

D'Cruze, D. (2025, 23 Ocak). *Elon Musk criticises $500 billion AI project announced by Trump; OpenAI CEO Sam Altman fires back*. Business Today. https://www.businesstoday.in/technology/news/story/elon-musk-criticises-500-billion-ai-project-announced-by-trump-openai-ceo-sam-altman-fires-back-461757-2025-01-23

De Nadal, L., & Jančárik, P. (2024). Beyond the deepfake hype: AI, democracy, and "the Slovak case". Harvard Kennedy School (HKS) Misinformation Review, 5(4).

DeepSeek-AI. Liu, A., Feng, B., Xue, B., Wang, B., Wu, B., Lu, C., Zhao, C., Deng, C., Zhang, C., Ruan, C., Dai, D., Guo, D., Yang, D., Chen, D., Ji, D., Li, E., Lin, F., Dai, F., … Pan, Z. (2025). *DeepSeek-V3 Technical Report.* /arXiv.2412.19437DOI: 10.48550

Devlin, J., Chang, M.-W., Lee, K., & Toutanova, K. (2019). BERT: Pre-training of Deep Bidirectional Transformers for Language Understanding. İçinde J. Burstein, C. Doran, & T. Solorio (Ed.), *Proceedings of the 2019 Conference of the North American Chapter of the Association for Computational Linguistics: Human Language Technologies,* Volume 1 *(Long and Short Papers)* (ss. 4171-4186). Association for Computational Linguistics. DOI: 10.18653/v1/N19-1423

Farooque, M. (2024, 11 Aralık). Alphabet Bets Big on AI with $50B Investment to Transform Google Search and Cloud Services. Yahoo Finance. https://finance.yahoo.com/news/alphabet-bets-big-ai-50b-151247722.html

Freifeld, K. (2025, 13 Ocak). *US tightens its grip on AI chip flows across the globe.* Reuters. https://www.reuters.com/technology/artificial-intelligence/us-tightens-its-grip-ai-chip-flows-across-globe-2025-01-13/

Gairola, A. (2024, 26 Aralık). *Microsoft Invested Nearly $14 Billion In OpenAI But Now Its Reducing Its Dependence On The ChatGPT-Parent: Report.* Yahoo Finance. https://finance.yahoo.com/news/microsoft-invested-nearly-14-billion-000512844.html

Goldstein, M. A., Kumar, N., & Thomas, D. (2024). Digital propaganda: The effectiveness of AI-generated persuasive messages. *Journal of Information Technology & Politics, 21*(1), 37–54. DOI: 10.1080/19331681.2023.2182965

Güney, C. (2020). *Dijital Dünyanın Ortaçağında Veri Egemenliği.* https://canerguney.medium.com/dijital-d%C3%BCnyan%C4%B1n-orta%C3%A7a%C4%9F%C4%B1nda-veri-egemenli%C4%9Fi-b7ea4ba2087

Humphreys, D., Koay, A., Desmond, D., & Mealy, E. (2024). AI hype as a cyber security risk: The moral responsibility of implementing generative AI in business. *AI and Ethics, 4*(3), 791–804. DOI: 10.1007/s43681-024-00443-4

Hutchinson, A. (2025, 9 Şubat). TikTok Looks To Alleviate Data Security Concerns in the US. *Social Media Today.* https://www.socialmediatoday.com/news/tiktok-outlines-us-data-security-measures/739631/

Jasanoff, S. (2004). *States of knowledge: The co-production of science and social order.* Routledge., DOI: 10.4324/9780203413845

Jungherr, A. (2023). Artificial intelligence and democracy: A conceptual framework. *Social Media + Society*, *9*(3), 1–14. DOI: 10.1177/20563051231186353

Karlıdağ, S. (2013). Ekonomi Politik Açıdan Kişisel Verilerin Korunması. *Amme İdaresi Dergisi*, 46(1), 127-152. Erişim adresi: https://ammeidaresi.hacibayram.edu.tr/documents/article/1/46/1/6_karlidag.pdf

Kaymakçı, Ö. B. (2025). *Veri Egemenliği: Yeni Bir Kolonyalizm mi?* https://www.ekoturk.com/yazi/veri-egemenligi-yeni-bir-kolonyalizm-mi/

Kerner, S. M. (2025, 20 Ocak). *DeepSeek explained: Everything you need to know*. TechTarget. https://www.techtarget.com/whatis/feature/DeepSeek-explained-Everything-you-need-to-know

Lee, K. (2018). Yapay Zekâ ve Yeni Dünya Düzeni: Çin, Silikon Vadisi, Optimist Yayın Grubu (MyTECHNIC), İstanbul, ISBN: 978-605-2202-49-4.

Liu, Y., Ott, M., Goyal, N., Du, J., Joshi, M., Chen, D., . . . Stoyanov, V. (2021). RoBERTa: A robustly optimized BERT pretraining approach. arXiv preprint arXiv:1907.11692.

Ma, J. (2024, 28 Eylül). *OpenAI sees $5 billion loss in 2024 and soaring sales as big ChatGPT fee hikes planned, report says*. Forbes. https://fortune.com/2024/09/28/openai-5-billion-loss-2024-revenue-forecasts-fundraising-chapgpt-fee-hikes/

McDermott, J. & O'Brien, M. (2025, 20 Ocak). *Chinese AI firm DeepSeek debuts low-cost language model*. AP News., https://apnews.com/article/00c594310b22afbf150559d08b43d3a5

Office of the Chief Information. (2025). *Privacy Considerations for Generative AI*. University of Illinois Urbana-Champain. https://www.cybersecurity.illinois.edu/policies-governance/privacy-considerations-for-generative-ai/

Schmalz, S. (2024). Varieties of digital capitalism and the US–China rivalry: The rise of competing technological spheres. *Critical Sociology*. Advance online publication. DOI: 10.1177/08969205241291645

Schmitt, M., & Flechais, I. (2023). Digital Deception: Generative Artificial Intelligence in Social Engineering and Phishing. SSRN Electronic Journal. DOI: 10.2139/ssrn.4602790

Shanbhogue, R. (2024, 15 Kasım). *Yapay zekâ için karar anı*. The Economist, The World Ahead 2025.

Tau. B. (2025). Researchers link DeepSeek's blockbuster chatbot to Chinese Telecom banned from doing business in US.

Tosyalı, H. (2021). Dijital Çağda Siyasal İletişim: Algoritmalar ve Botlar. Communication and Technology Congress – CTC 2021, 12-14 Nisan, 2021 – Turkiye, İstanbul. https://web.archive.org/web/20210616092152id_/https://ctc.aydin.edu.tr/wp-content/uploads/2021/06/10.17932CTC2021ctc21011.pdf

Vaswani, A., Shazeer, N., Parmar, N., Uszkoreit, J., Jones, L., Gomez, A. N., ... & Polosukhin, I. (2017). Attention is all you need. NeurIPS.

Winner, L. (2020). *The whale and the reactor: A search for limits in an age of high technology*. 2. Baskı. University of Chicago Press. DOI: 10.7208/chicago/9780226692685.001.0001

Ye, X., Yan, Y., Li, J., & Jiang, B. (2024). Privacy and personal data risk governance for generative artificial intelligence: A Chinese perspective. *Computer Law & Security Review*. Advance online publication. DOI: 10.1016/j.clsr.2023.105753

Zewe, A. (2025, 17 Ocak). *Explained: Generative AI's environmental impact*. MIT News. https://news.mit.edu/2025/explained-generative-ai-environmental-impact-0117

Zhao, W. X., Zhou, K., Li, J., Tang, T., Wang, X., Hou, Y., . . . Wen, J. R. (2023). A survey of large language models. arXiv preprint arXiv:2303.18223.

Zuboff, S. (2019). *The age of surveillance capitalism: The fight for a human future at the new frontier of power*. PublicAffairs.

ENDNOTES

1 A 128K-token context window refers to the maximum text length a large language model (LLM) can process at once. This feature enables the model to consistently analyze long documents, complex dialogues, or technical texts.

Chapter 7
Combating Fake News With Artificial Intelligence: A Hope or a Threat?

Sinem Yeles Karaman
https://orcid.org/0000-0003-4127-6970
Konya Technical University, Turkey

ABSTRACT

Recent technological advances have significantly transformed media, replacing traditional one-way communication with interactive digital structures. However, this shift has also accelerated the spread of fake news, posing serious social and political risks. Artificial intelligence (AI) technologies—such as machine learning and natural language processing—offer promising tools to detect and limit disinformation. Yet, these systems face limitations, including bias, ethical concerns, and misclassification risks. This chapter explores both the opportunities and threats of AI in combating fake news, emphasizing that effective solutions require not only technology but also enhanced media literacy to foster critical, informed news consumption.

INTRODUCTION

With the development of the digital world, profound changes have taken place in many areas of life, including the media. Unlike traditional media, new media environments, which stand out with their interactive nature, have also transformed the understanding of news. The phenomenon of fake news, which has existed for a long time, has become more visible and widespread with the impact of digitalization.

DOI: 10.4018/979-8-3373-2960-4.ch007

The main reason for this is that with the increase in the production and circulation of information, such content can reach hundreds or even thousands of people in a very short time.

However, the rapid spread of fake news and its dissemination to large audiences pose serious threats to individuals, societies, institutions, and the functioning of democracy. Information pollution not only misleads public opinion but also leads to a loss of trust and a deepening of social polarization. Therefore, in the digital age, media literacy, verification mechanisms, and journalism based on ethical principles are more important than ever before.

According to Allcott and Gentzkow, fake news is defined as news articles that are intentionally written, verifiable, and deliberately intended to mislead readers (Allcott & Gentzkow, 2017). In fact, although fake news has always existed, it has found more space for itself especially in digital environments such as social media. In addition to personal accounts and widely followed news channels, fake news also spreads through anonymous accounts, providing people with false information and manipulating them through misinformation.

Fake news has many dimensions; it may be produced deliberately, created under the assumption that it is true without verifying its accuracy, or designed as satire or parody. According to the definition by Tandoc et al., fake news is not a new term, and false news is a concept with a long history dating back centuries. They identified six types of fake news: (1) news satire, (2) news parody, (3) fabrication, (4) manipulation, (5) advertising, and (6) propaganda (Tandoc Jr et al., 2018).

Not only fake news, but also other types of information disorder such as misinformation and disinformation (Lazer et al., 2018) overlap with fake news. In general, the main intentions of publishers—such as deceiving the audience, causing harm, or pursuing personal interests like popularity or financial gain—are also taken into account in definitions of fake news. Some researchers emphasize that fake news does not necessarily consist solely of completely false or fabricated claims. Some statements may be considered "misleading" by containing "significant omissions" (Dang, 2021). All of these are evaluated as fake news and pose social problems.

It has been widely experienced that fake news increases during times such as pandemics, natural disasters, or elections. For instance, during election periods, there are examples of fake news ranging from reports produced with political concerns that ridicule the opposition and aim to embarrass them in the eyes of voters, to stories that damage the reputation of well-known brands (Yeles Sinem, 2024). A prominent example of the relationship between global crises and fake news is the COVID-19 pandemic. In this regard, Director-General of the World Health Organization (WHO), Tedros Adhanom Ghebreyesus, clearly described the situation by stating that fake news "spreads faster and more easily than this virus" and "we are not just fighting an epidemic; we are fighting an infodemic" (Dang, 2021).

Fake news, which has become significant enough to seriously affect countries, social life processes, and events, has also transformed journalism practices in various ways through new media environments that allow active user participation, thereby creating a participatory public sphere. For this reason, it is believed that a more democratic environment has also been enabled (Demirel, 2018). However, the biggest problem here is the uncertainty about the accuracy of information. In an environment where false content and fake news are highly prevalent, it seems quite difficult to claim that a truly democratic atmosphere is being formed.

Every day, thousands of pieces of information are produced either intentionally or unintentionally, without being verified for accuracy. These pieces of information are then shared and interpreted by individuals, and new information is generated from incorrect data and presented to other users. The journey of fake news in digital environments brings along different debates and causes serious problems. According to *The Telegraph*, fake news is now seen as one of the greatest threats to democracy, free debate, and the Western order (Aggarwal et al., 2020).

Numerous serious efforts are being made to prevent this highly significant and socially impactful problem of fake news. Artificial intelligence technologies are also stepping in as effective tools for detecting fake news and analyzing their accuracy. Widely used in many areas such as health, economy, agriculture, and communication, artificial intelligence is also playing an increasingly active role in the media sector. In addition to its use in processes such as news writing, content production, and image generation, AI technologies make significant contributions to verification and control stages by checking the accuracy of texts and visuals found in digital environments.

What is particularly striking at this point is that artificial intelligence, which is used in the fight against fake news, can also be used in the production of fake content. These types of content, generally defined as fake news, are now being analyzed and identified through AI-supported systems. However, this contradictory situation reveals that artificial intelligence has become both part of the solution and part of the problem. While AI technologies are being used to combat disinformation on one hand, the accuracy of the information produced by these technologies is also being questioned on the other. This situation leads not only to technical issues but also to ethical, legal, and epistemological debates. Evaluating the impact of artificial intelligence on media content should not be limited to criteria such as accuracy or speed; it must also encompass aspects such as information security, user awareness, and digital literacy. In order for artificial intelligence to be effective in combating fake news, it must be developed with a transparent, accountable, and multi-stakeholder approach.

Looking at the historical processes of technological developments, especially in the field of media, every new advancement has brought along numerous debates.

For instance, after the invention of television, discussions began about its effects on individuals. These debates continued for many years, and various scientific studies have identified its negative effects on individuals. However, on the other hand, media tools like television have also been used for the purpose of educating the masses. Despite criticisms that it may sometimes have negative effects on individuals, television has remained one of the most widespread and influential mass communication tools for decades. Television has gone beyond being merely a tool for entertainment; it plays a significant role in educating individuals, raising public awareness, and learning and transmitting cultural values. Additionally, by offering content in various areas such as sports, news, art, and science, it has contributed to social development and transformation, shaping the processes through which individuals acquire knowledge about the world. In this respect, television is a powerful media tool that supports learning, awareness, and socialization processes at both the individual and societal levels.

Artificial intelligence refers to computer-aided systems that have continuously evolved in various fields since the 20th century, particularly with developments in automation, mechanics and fluid dynamics, construction infrastructure, machine design, and especially computers and information and communication technologies (ICT) (Hussein & Hejase, 2022). However, like other technological advancements, artificial intelligence has also raised concerns among people due to its potential to cause negative consequences. While some of these concerns are unfounded, certain problems may indeed arise in ethical and legal processes. These systems, which are actively used during news production stages, have also become a subject of research regarding issues such as the use of illegal data and the proliferation of fake news.

In today's evolving artificial intelligence ecosystem, generative models enable the creation of hyper-realistic manipulations, which are highly plausible due to the sensitivity of audiovisual objects. These deepfakes are often undetectable due to their components, raising concerns about how the distortion of reality in the information ecosystem and the diminishing ability to distinguish between real and fake audiovisual content affect public trust and democratic systems (Sanchez-Acedo et al., 2024). On one hand, AI-based systems are used in the fight against such threats; on the other hand, the fake content generated by AI itself creates considerable confusion.

With AI-powered large language models and image generation systems, it is now possible to produce realistic text, audio, and visual content within seconds. This facilitates the spread of realistic yet entirely fabricated news, allowing for the creation of content that can damage the reputation of individuals and institutions through deepfake videos and fake audio recordings. Especially on social media platforms, algorithmic disinformation campaigns enable such fake content to circulate rapidly and widely. The use of AI in generating such content poses serious threats to public order and democratic processes, particularly during election periods, times of crisis, and periods of social unrest.

At the same time, artificial intelligence is not only a source of fake news but also one of the most effective tools in combating it. Advanced AI systems analyze large datasets and are much faster and more comprehensive than humans in detecting fake content. Thanks to automated fact-checking systems, news texts can be instantly compared with reliable sources, image manipulations can be detected, and disinformation networks can be identified through social media analyses. These applications are actively used by news agencies, social media platforms, and public institutions, contributing to ensuring information security and accurate public information.

The dual nature of artificial intelligence has brought the discussion of dual-use technology to the forefront in the digital media age. The same technology can be used for both beneficial and harmful purposes. In this context, the key determinant is who controls the technology. If in the hands of malicious actors, the scale and impact of disinformation dramatically increase; however, when used by institutions based on ethical principles, transparency, and social responsibility, artificial intelligence plays a transformative role in the fight against fake news.

Therefore, ethical principles, oversight mechanisms, open-source reliable models, and policies prioritizing the public interest are vital in the use of AI technologies. Effective combat against fake news requires not only technological tools but also a holistic approach grounded in ethics, legal frameworks, and social responsibilities. Although AI poses a potential threat in the production of fake news, when used properly, it can become one of the strongest defense mechanisms.

For individuals, it is also important to understand for what purpose they use AI and how well they can benefit from these tools. While AI facilitates the creation of content such as news, it has also brought about problems like the production of fake news. Therefore, it can be said that AI has both positive and negative impacts on people's lives (Ulaş, 2024).

As AI technologies in this field develop over time, more effective results can be achieved in the fight against fake news, or the debates may grow, continuing a vicious cycle where every positive development is followed by another negative one. It may become clearer in the coming years, but at present, it can be said that a dual perspective predominates.

1. THE RISE OF ARTIFICIAL INTELLIGENCE IN COMBATING DIGITAL DISINFORMATION

Following the Industrial Revolution, significant advancements have occurred in many fields; while these developments have made life easier in many ways, they have also paved the way for new problems to emerge. As individuals and societies continually strive to adapt to these changes, they are also faced with the challenges that accompany them.

Technological advancements are not limited to technical fields alone; they have a direct impact on many areas related to sociology, communication, and daily life. In this context, artificial intelligence (AI) offers practical solutions at both individual and societal levels. It is increasingly seen as an effective tool in the fight against one of the major issues of our time: fake news.

On the other hand, with the widespread use of the internet, billions of users are now simultaneously producing and sharing content on digital platforms. This has created a fertile environment for the rapid and unregulated spread of fake news. The uncontrolled dissemination of fake news leads to misinformation on an individual level, while on a societal scale, it can cause trust crises, polarization, and serious consequences that hinder the healthy formation of public opinion.

Various fields of study have proposed different solutions to combat fake news, and artificial intelligence has become one of the most prominent among them in recent years. Although the concept of artificial intelligence was first introduced in academia in the 1950s (Haenlein & Kaplan, 2019), today this technology plays a critical role in ensuring information security, particularly in digital media environments. In this regard, it is not only important to understand how fake news is produced, but also how it can be detected, how its spread can be prevented, and how its effects can be mitigated — all of which are areas where AI continues to offer innovative solutions.

News content today occupies a significant place not only in traditional media but also increasingly on the web, particularly on social media. In fact, the sharing and reading of news on social media have surpassed that of traditional media. However, while the quality of news on social media is generally lower than that of traditional news sources, social media is highly conducive to the spread of fake news. This dynamic contributes to a higher volume of fake news compared to traditional media. In digital environments where information is shared every moment, the proliferation of fake news leads to various forms of disinformation.

Due to the harmful effects of fake news on individuals and society, detecting fake news has become a prominent area of concern (Altunbey Özbay & Alataş, 2020). Especially in terms of information security, public opinion management, and social perception, this issue presents serious threats, making the detection and prevention of the spread of fake news an urgent necessity. In this context, the use of artificial intelligence-based technologies such as Natural Language Processing (NLP), machine learning, and deep learning is considered an essential requirement (Toğaçar et al., 2021).

In this regard, researchers have developed various algorithms and models to classify fake news. These models, which analyze both textual and visual content, have achieved success rates of over 90% in distinguishing between fake and real news (Altunbey Özbay & Alataş, 2020; Horne & Adali, 2017; Bock & Weiß, 2019). For instance, in his study, Chitic (2021) analyzed 6,335 news items and identified 3,171 as real and 3,164 as fake, thereby demonstrating the high accuracy rate of the model he developed.

A review of the literature reveals that artificial intelligence (AI)-based systems offer effective and reliable tools in the fight against fake news. These technologies go beyond mere content analysis by also examining user behavior and the dynamics of news dissemination, thereby adopting a more holistic approach. While these systems have the capacity to distinguish between real and fake news, the reliability of the data source being analyzed is of critical importance. If the data source is incorrect or fraudulent, AI systems cannot yield accurate results. This highlights certain risks associated with the role of AI in fake news detection.

It is well known that the majority of individuals today no longer follow news through traditional media but instead rely on digital and social media platforms. In an age where many print newspapers have ceased publication, a large number of users consume news directly via social media. While content published on official news websites is typically subject to stricter fact-checking procedures, content circulated on social media is often anonymous and therefore more likely to be false. The instantaneous and unfiltered spread of information on these platforms leads to the exponential dissemination of misinformation (Prachi et al., 2022)This represents one of the most significant drawbacks of social media.

At this point, AI technologies play a crucial role by automating fact-checking processes, reducing the need for human intervention, and enhancing both speed and efficiency. The fact-checking process involves verifying whether content that is suspected of being false or misleading is accurate, using a variety of methods. In this regard, many international and national organizations, institutions, and platforms operate to verify the accuracy of news content, both in traditional and digital media. On a global scale, organizations such as the International Fact-Checking Network (IFCN) have emerged. Numerous national and international fact-checking platforms support this organization and adopt its principles by signing its code of conduct. While these fact-checking platforms continue to evolve alongside technological advancements, the battle against fake news is increasingly being carried out through AI-based detection and verification systems (Ulaş, 2024). However, issues such as the ethical use of these systems, algorithmic neutrality, and data privacy must also be carefully considered. In this context, whether AI systems offer a promising solution in the fight against fake news—or whether they give rise to new threats—remains a subject of ongoing debate.

At this point, artificial intelligence technologies come into play by automating fact-checking processes, reducing the need for human intervention, and increasing both speed and efficiency. The fact-checking process is defined as the verification of whether content suspected to be false or misleading is actually true or false, using various methods. In this regard, numerous international and national centers, organizations, and platforms are engaged in verifying the accuracy of news content in both traditional and digital media. On a global scale, institutions such as the International Fact-Checking Network (IFCN) play a key role. Many national and international fact-checking platforms support this organization and adopt its principles by signing the code of conduct published by the IFCN. While fact-checking platforms are still evolving with advancing technology, the fight against fake news continues with the support of AI-powered systems (Ulaş, 2024).

The technological foundation of these verification processes is built on one of the most critical subfields of artificial intelligence: machine learning. Machine learning is an approach that enables computers to learn from data without being explicitly programmed, which allows algorithms used in fake news detection to improve continuously. Conceptualized in 1959 by Arthur Samuel, this technology is now positioned as a distinct discipline within computer science and enhances the flexibility and adaptability of AI systems. The combination of AI and machine learning makes it possible to develop more effective, rapid, and scalable solutions in dynamic and constantly changing information environments such as fact-checking.

Moreover, Deep Neural Networks (DNNs), which stand out with their ability to deeply analyze both the structural and semantic features of text, offer significant advantages in fake news detection. These multi-layered network structures mimic the learning process of the human brain and are capable of identifying complex patterns within input data, enabling high-level abstraction and meaning extraction from various types of data. Thanks to these features, DNNs are widely used in areas such as natural language processing (NLP), image analysis, speech recognition, and decision support systems (Jain et al., 2019). The advanced learning capacity of DNNs enhances the accuracy of AI-based news analysis systems, enabling more precise detection of fake news.

However, despite all these technological advancements, fundamental principles such as the ethical use of systems, algorithmic neutrality, data privacy, and accountability must not be overlooked. When the decision-making processes of these systems lack sufficient transparency or are trained on biased datasets, the reliability of fact-checking processes can become questionable. Therefore, establishing a balanced structure between technological advancement and ethical principles—as well as human oversight—is critically important to ensure the long-term sustainability of the fight against fake news using AI-based systems.

In conclusion, artificial intelligence technologies undeniably possess significant potential for driving societal change. Closely followed by scientists, businesses, politicians, media professionals, and the general public alike, these technologies also bring certain concerns. AI-based systems provide a powerful toolkit in the fight against fake news and play a vital role in ensuring information security and enhancing media literacy. The promising aspects of these systems, along with the potential risks they entail, must be evaluated as separate but equally important dimensions.

2. ADVANTAGES: PROMISING ASPECTS

One of the most pressing issues brought about by the digital age is the proliferation of misinformation, particularly the presence and rapid spread of fake news. With social media platforms becoming primary channels for communication and information acquisition, unverified content can reach large audiences in a very short time. This situation can lead to public misinformation, societal polarization, and harm to democratic processes. In response to this challenge, artificial intelligence-based systems have emerged as a promising alternative, particularly in the context of news verification processes.

The use of artificial intelligence technologies in the verification of news and content has recently gained prominence as a new and important trend. Today, AI-powered systems can analyze and monitor questionable content through various methods, enabling the detection of fake news and misleading information with the help of specific algorithms. Although the number of verification platforms and centers has increased, it remains nearly impossible to detect and control all fake content circulating in both traditional and digital media. Therefore, it is crucial for media users to develop individual awareness and make personal efforts to question the accuracy of the content they encounter (Ulaş, 2024).

In this context, the question of how artificial intelligence systems analyze content and detect fake news gains significant importance. Thanks to its subfields such as natural language processing (NLP), machine learning (ML), and deep learning (DL), AI can analyze large datasets to evaluate the meaning, context, and reliability of content. Machine learning refers to the development of algorithms and statistical models that enable computer systems to perform tasks by identifying patterns and relationships in data without being explicitly programmed. This approach forms the foundation for AI systems' decision-making and prediction capabilities. One of the important application areas of machine learning, Natural Language Processing (NLP), enables the processing of linguistic data such as text or speech into a format understandable by machines. Deep learning, a more advanced subfield of machine learning, utilizes multi-layered artificial neural networks to analyze complex patterns within data. While feature extraction in traditional machine learning often requires manual intervention, deep learning automates this process, offering higher levels of abstraction and learning capacity. In this respect, deep learning provides highly effective solutions, especially in data-intensive areas like natural language processing (Dayan & Yılmaz, 2022).

AI-based systems can classify the accuracy level of news by examining the linguistic structure and content coherence of texts with high success rates. These systems also contribute to the development of preventive algorithms by identifying specific linguistic patterns and cues commonly found in the spread of fake news. Particularly in the media sector, AI technologies verify the accuracy of news content and prevent the circulation of misinformation. AI techniques aim to enhance trustworthiness in the digital information ecosystem by effectively detecting fake news encountered on social media platforms (Hussein & Hejase, 2022).

One of the greatest advantages of AI-based systems is their ability to analyze large volumes of content rapidly without the need for human intervention. This not only saves time in verification processes but also minimizes human error. Considering the intensity of social media feeds and news websites, AI solutions play a decisive role in areas where manual review processes are insufficient.

Moreover, the continuous learning and evolving nature of artificial intelligence technologies provides flexibility to adapt to the increasing complexity of fake news. AI has become an effective tool not only in analyzing textual content but also in examining visual and video materials. AI-powered software is producing increasingly effective solutions in detecting complex forms of disinformation such as deepfake videos. Similarly, AI-generated content—both textual and visual—can create the impression of authenticity among media users. This especially affects individuals who do not read carefully or critically evaluate the text or visuals, leading them to believe what they see immediately.

When evaluated from all these perspectives, AI-based systems should be regarded not only as technical tools in the fight against fake news but also as strategic components contributing to information security in digital media environments. However, to enhance the effectiveness of these systems, it is crucial that they are designed and implemented in accordance with principles of ethics, transparency, and user privacy.

The fact that media is no longer limited to newspapers, radio, or a few television channels, but has become a digital resource such as the web and social media, makes the situation even more challenging. The solution to combating fake content is seen again at the source where the problem originates. In other words, it is believed that the problem can be solved through software capable of filtering billions of pieces of information in a short time across social and digital media platforms (Toğaçar et al., 2021). The most significant issue supporting this view is the sheer volume of data. When fake content is distributed simultaneously across different channels, it becomes increasingly difficult for individuals to find accurate information. This situation validates the advantages provided by AI capabilities.

All these developments indicate that solutions to problems encountered in digital media are possible through digital tools themselves. Thanks to its capacity to analyze large datasets and high processing power, AI has become a key actor not only in filtering fake content but also in reshaping journalistic practices.

With the advancement of AI technologies, the transformation in the field of journalism has become quite evident. Particularly, the advantages provided by AI in news production processes are listed by Zengin and Kapır as follows:

- Thanks to automated journalism applications used in routine news, content can be produced more rapidly. This accelerates the production processes of media professionals and enables them to be supported by AI tools.
- The production of often repetitive and monotonous news by machines allows journalists to devote more time to in-depth fields such as investigative journalism. Especially, the ease of processing data-driven and regular content with the help of AI reduces the workload of journalists.
- In disciplines like investigative journalism and data journalism, journalists can perform more comprehensive data analyses due to AI's capacity to process big data. This provides a significant time advantage.
- The use of AI in fact-checking reduces the workload of human editors and allows for faster and more systematic verification of content accuracy.
- Automated fact-checking has made it possible to verify a greater amount of content in real-time (Zengin & Kapır, 2021).

Artificial intelligence (AI) tools position themselves as supportive elements within journalistic practice; they enhance journalists' competencies, facilitate production processes, and elevate professional standards (Tejedor & Vila, 2021). With functions such as data provision and editorial support, AI can contribute to journalists producing more successful content. However, the ethical stance and independence of the journalist remain critically important. It is essential for journalists not to produce manipulative content financed by any interest group, in order to preserve professional credibility.

In newsrooms, AI-supported production of content based on continuously updated information allows reporters more time for creating exclusive stories (Van Dalen, 2012). This time gain facilitates journalists' focus on their work and strengthens their professional performance.

Automation of routine tasks offers various opportunities to improve the quality of journalism. Many news items that remain unaddressed due to lack of funding today can be automatically generated with AI. Freeing human journalists from routine duties enables them to engage in high-quality and in-depth reporting. In this context, the introduction of AI into the news industry marks one of the most radical transformations of the journalistic profession. Alongside the new technological media ecosystem, new narratives and forms of journalism are emerging in the digital society; a new intellectual framework is developing around the possibilities, production formats, and evolution offered by these technologies (Tejedor & Vila, 2021)

While AI can enhance journalists' capabilities by handling data-intensive tasks and providing analytical insights, it may also overshadow human values and critical decision-making with automated processes (Porlezza & Schapals, 2024). It is necessary to conduct studies that prevent such significant and risky situations.

In brief, AI's important advantages include time-saving, speed, data support, assistance, and editorial aid. Its benefits are expected to increase over time, with data becoming more accurate and reliable—developments that we will all likely witness. However, every advancement also brings new risks and topics for debate.

3. THREATS: BOUNDARIES AND RISKS

Just like other technological innovations that have previously entered our lives, artificial intelligence has also sparked various debates. Questions such as "Will cinema come to an end?" or "Will radio no longer be preferred?"—which emerged in the early years of television—have reemerged today in the context of artificial intelligence. Over time, television has come to be used both as a tool for entertainment and education; while the risks to children's psychological development were discussed, it also assumed a role as a teaching tool that could reach large audiences. This example is meaningful as it demonstrates how new technologies are often met with contradictory evaluations.

Today, a similar discussion is ongoing regarding the impact of artificial intelligence on journalism and the media. Contrary to the benefits discussed in the previous section, this part will focus on the threats, limitations, and ethical risks that AI technologies may pose.

Artificial intelligence, particularly in the area of automated content production, presents a serious challenge to journalists who perform basic and routine tasks, raising concerns about job security and competition. The integration of AI into news production processes has sparked an intense debate within the media world around the question of whether this could devalue journalistic labor. In this context, questions like "Will algorithms replace humans?" or "Can AI write better news than humans?" sometimes even make it to the headlines of newspapers themselves (Carlson, 2015).

As with the predictions about the relationship between television and cinema, the future of the relationship between artificial intelligence and journalism will become clearer over time. However, the main issue to focus on for now is that the threats brought by these technologies are not limited to the professional existence of journalists; rather, they create a multilayered area of risk extending to access to public information, ethical principles in journalism, and democratic values.

Despite claims that artificial intelligence may "challenge" human journalists, it is important to note that human labor is still required for its creation, implementation, and maintenance. However, it must be clarified to what extent this labor falls under the umbrella of "journalism," and it is seen as a point of contention within newsrooms as the use of technology increases (Moran & Shaikh, 2022).

When routine journalistic tasks can be automated, journalists are forced to deliver a better product in order to survive. At the heart of these reflections lies the idea that journalists should focus on their own strengths rather than competing with the strengths of automated content creation. Journalists must be more creative in their writing, offer more in-depth reporting and context, go beyond routine news coverage, and even perform at a higher level than they do today. Opinion pieces, breaking news, feature stories, and news analyses are seen as article types where humans remain unmatched. However, if machine-generated writing becomes more widespread in the future, it seems unlikely that journalists will be able to compete by continuing to perform routine tasks such as simple descriptive game reports. In other words, the competition brought on by machine-written news forces human journalists to excel even further in tasks where they can truly make a difference (Van Dalen, 2012). This situation presents a particular risk for journalists.

When AI-based systems are evaluated in terms of fake news, they reveal another area of risk. While AI systems offer significant advantages in the fight against fake news, these technologies should not be considered limitless or risk-free. Relying on automated decision-making mechanisms—especially in the processes of news verification—brings with it a number of ethical, technical, and societal issues. In this context, the limitations and potential threats of AI-based verification tools must be addressed in a multifaceted way.

Data-driven biases pose significant ethical risks in AI systems. Since these systems function largely based on the datasets they are fed, systematic errors or biases in the data can directly affect the model's outputs. This can lead to false positives or false negatives, especially in the classification of political or ideological content. Such errors may pave the way for practices that spark serious debates regarding freedom of expression.

AI not only raises direct ethical concerns such as generating unchecked information or violating privacy; it can also reinforce existing social inequalities by perpetuating biases present in its training data. If the training data contain biases based on race, gender, or other demographic factors, AI can learn and propagate these biases. This leads to a further decrease in the visibility of social diversity and minority groups. AI systems not only reflect the existing power dynamics in society but also have the potential to deepen them. The unequal distribution of information and the vast data divide may cause individuals to see reality only through the lens of institutions or dominant narratives. This results in technology functioning not as a neutral tool, but as a mechanism that reproduces existing structures (Kayıhan, 2024).

Secondly, when AI systems do not operate in accordance with the principles of transparency and accountability, the so-called "black box" nature of algorithmic processes makes it difficult to question them. The inability to clearly explain why a piece of content is classified as fake undermines user trust and raises issues of algorithmic justice. In this regard, it is of great importance that AI-based decisions are supported by human oversight and that systems are designed in accordance with explainable AI principles.

Another important limitation is the increasingly complex race between technological adaptation and disinformation. Producers of fake news are developing more sophisticated strategies to bypass AI-based detection methods. For example, by manipulating the linguistic patterns on which AI systems are based, they aim to deceive the algorithms or employ advanced fake content creation techniques such as deepfakes. This situation poses a serious threat to the sustainability of technological solutions. Deepfake technology enables the visual and auditory manipulation of reality to fabricate sequences of actions and events that are unlikely to occur in objective reality, thereby undermining the reliability of the virtual in our hybrid lives (Elitaş, 2022).

It should also be remembered that AI systems carry certain risks in terms of privacy and data security. The processing, monitoring, and analysis of user data may result in violations of personal rights and freedoms. Such ethical risks can lead to serious consequences, particularly in countries governed by legal frameworks such as the European Union's General Data Protection Regulation (GDPR).

Excessive trust in artificial intelligence may dull media literacy and critical thinking skills. Blind reliance on automated systems may cause individuals to delegate the responsibility of verifying information and become passive media consumers. Therefore, no matter how advanced technological solutions may be, the conscious and active participation of users must be encouraged.

Another problem is that it may deepen the already existing media distrust and biases. Studies show that individuals' trust in the media is negatively affected by the spread of fake news, disinformation, and manipulation. This mistrust exacerbates media-related prejudices, affecting individuals' relationship with media and harming democratic processes.

When we examine the news production process, it becomes evident that AI is used in many stages, including researching, gathering, organizing news, and even automatically writing texts. However, when used in fields like media and journalism, AI can also contribute to problems such as fake journalism. Fake journalism refers to the intentional publication of news containing false or misleading information (Özsalih, 2023)This content may result from journalists using incorrect data or from AI systems providing misleading information. The possibility of AI generating false data is real. Even though AI is employed to detect fake news, it can also absorb and reproduce fake data.

There are also areas where AI poses significant threats to democratic life and institutions. Particularly in processes of surveillance and manipulation, AI-based tools may be used to influence individuals' thoughts and behaviors. The deep integration of AI into social media and digital platforms opens up new possibilities for manipulating citizens' voting behaviors. One of the most powerful instruments of this manipulation is the media. Videos, news content, and social media posts generated by AI may erode public trust in information and constitute a threat capable of misleading public opinion (Kaplan, 2020).

In this context, artificial intelligence significantly affects not only individuals but also democratic institutions and the media industry. The use of AI technologies in newsrooms has reached a point where it prompts questions about the nature of journalism and the roles of journalists. Automated content creation and algorithmic news feeds create uncertainty in many areas, from job security to the accuracy of news—thus necessitating a comprehensive evaluation of both the benefits and risks of AI in media (Moran & Shaikh, 2022).

Considering all these threats, limitations, and potential benefits, **a** multilayered approach must be adopted for the ethical and effective use of AI-based systems in the fight against fake news. This approach should not only focus on technical competencies but also incorporate ethical standards, legal frameworks, and public awareness. In this regard, AI should be viewed not merely as a technological tool but as an intervention domain requiring responsibility and oversight.

Despite the growing importance of detecting fake news in politics, relatively limited research efforts have been made to develop suitable AI and machine learning (ML)-based FNaD (Fake News and Disinformation) detection models aimed at minimizing supply chain disruptions (SCDs).

Digital media, emerging as an alternative to traditional media with the advancement of communication technologies, has transformed access to information. While the flow of news in traditional media was bound to specific time slots (such as newspaper publication or scheduled TV news), in digital media environments, the news flow has become instant and continuous. This allows users to access information anytime and from anywhere, accelerating both information consumption and content production. Social media platforms, blogs, online news sites, and video-sharing networks have turned users into not only consumers of content but also producers.

4. ETHICAL AND LEGAL PERSPECTIVES

The use of artificial intelligence in combating fake news also raises serious ethical and legal concerns. While these tools can undertake crucial tasks such as information verification, content filtering, and misinformation detection, they also bring fundamental challenges related to freedom of expression, the risk of censorship, and algorithmic neutrality. Since AI systems cannot fully grasp abstract concepts such as intent, context, and emotion behind human communication, they lack the capacity to make ethical judgments. This constitutes one of the most significant ethical issues surrounding artificial intelligence.

Artificial intelligence, also referred to as machine intelligence, is a technology that enables machines to emulate human actions and behaviors. This means AI is capable of exhibiting uniquely human abilities such as planning, reasoning, creativity, and learning. However, these capabilities, while impressive, also come with various risks—foremost among them being data security and privacy concerns. AI applications can infringe on user privacy while collecting data; for example, many AI-driven applications are capable of tracking users' digital footprints. Personal data may be used by AI systems without the users' explicit consent, and in some cases, such data may even be shared with advertisers without user permission (Kayıhan, 2024).

As AI systems become more powerful each day, their ethical implications are also gaining momentum (Fast & Horvitz, 2017). Leslie describes AI ethics as a set of values, principles, and techniques applied in the development and deployment of AI technologies (Leslie, 2019)

In journalism, artificial intelligence can autonomously collect data and generate content without human intervention. It is used in automated news writing, fact-checking, news personalization, content recommendation, and audience analysis (Dhiman, n.d.).

Huang and colleagues, proposed eleven ethical principles for artificial intelligence. These principles broadly encompass the necessary ethical standards for the field (Huang et al., 2022). Adıyaman, adapted these principles to the context of journalism, emphasizing their relevance to the news industry (Adıyaman, 2023). Accordingly, the eleven ethical principles for AI are as follows:

1- **Transparency:** This principle concerns understanding how and why AI models operate. In journalism, transparency is reflected in the ability to explain how and why an AI system selects certain news stories over others.

2- **Fairness and Justice**: AI should be developed, distributed, and used in a fair and equitable manner. In journalism, this means that AI systems must not produce biased or discriminatory content against any particular group.

3- **Responsibility and Accountability**: AI systems must be auditable, meaning their designers, developers, owners, and operators are responsible and accountable for the system's decisions and behavior. In the news industry, this includes identifying editors or engineers accountable for AI-generated outputs.
4- **Non-Maleficence (Do No Harm)**: AI systems should avoid causing harm or increasing risks to individuals or society. This includes protecting mental and physical well-being, dignity, and integrity. News generated by AI should not result in material or moral harm to individuals or the public.
5- **Privacy:** AI systems should respect privacy and ensure data protection. This includes the secure management of all data used or generated throughout the AI system's lifecycle. Journalists must handle reader data ethically and avoid commodifying personal information without consent.
6- **Beneficence**: AI should promote human well-being and provide societal and environmental benefits. Journalism, beyond just informing the public, has a social responsibility. This principle aligns closely with journalism's public-interest mission.
7- **Freedom and Autonomy**: Freedom and autonomy relate to individuals' ability to make decisions that align with their goals and values—fundamental in democratic societies. AI-generated content in journalism should not manipulate or undermine users' decision-making processes.
8- **Solidarity**: This principle emphasizes that AI systems should be developed and deployed in a way that supports solidarity across communities and generations. AI should foster social cohesion and mutual support.
9- **Sustainability**: As climate change and environmental degradation become increasingly urgent, AI must be integrated into sustainable development goals. Journalism's use of AI should also consider its ecological footprint and support environmental responsibility.
10- **Trust and Trustworthiness**: Trust is a prerequisite for the adoption of AI by individuals and societies. It depends not only on the technology itself but also on the broader sociotechnical systems it operates within. In journalism—where public trust is already fragile—ensuring AI-generated content is reliable and verifiable is essential.
11- **Human Dignity**: This principle holds that all individuals have inherent value based on their humanity, regardless of class, race, gender, religion, or abilities. AI systems in journalism must not produce content that violates or diminishes human dignity.

These 11 ethical principles outline the core values that must be upheld both in the development and implementation of artificial intelligence (AI) systems and in journalistic practice. When the principles defined by Huang et al. are evaluated together with the adaptations made by Adıyaman specifically for journalism, it is emphasized that AI in news production processes must align with universal ethical values such as responsibility, transparency, fairness, privacy, and respect for human dignity. As the use of AI in journalism becomes more widespread, establishing an ethical framework guided by these principles—and ensuring that this framework is observed by all stakeholders—is critically important both for protecting the public interest and for restoring trust in the media sector.

At this point, the classification of content by AI systems as fake or reliable necessitates questioning the data, algorithms, and frameworks on which these decisions are based. If the decision-making processes of algorithms lack transparency, it can remain unclear to users and content creators why certain content is labeled as fake. This situation particularly increases ethical risks in the monitoring of politically or socially sensitive content. Algorithmic biases can cause the system to systematically disadvantage certain individuals, groups, or viewpoints, which constitutes a violation of the right to access information. All these developments have rendered the adequacy of AI against existing ethical norms questionable and brought the need for new ethical principles to the forefront (Porlezza & Schapals, 2024)

Moreover, the legal boundaries of AI-based content moderation systems remain unclear in many countries. Although various regulations exist globally and in Turkey concerning digital content control, disinformation laws, and platform accountability, the legal foundations for interventions carried out by AI remain ambiguous. Within this context, three main issues arise:

- Data protection and privacy, as AI systems' access to user data may cause serious violations;
- Freedom of expression, which can be indirectly harmed through the labeling of content as "fake";
- Responsibility, as legal ambiguity exists regarding who is accountable in cases of misclassification.

AI has become an increasingly effective tool in combating fake news. However, this effectiveness can only be sustainable if these technologies are designed and implemented in accordance with ethical principles and legal norms. In this regard, developing AI systems based on the principle of transparency is of paramount importance. Algorithmic transparency refers to providing clear and understandable information about how systems operate; the human-in-the-loop principle advocates for continuous human intervention in AI decision-making processes. Thus, decisions are ensured to be made not automatically but under the supervision of human judgment and responsibility.

Additionally, independent auditing mechanisms and user complaint rights create security layers against unethical or erroneous applications of AI. Particularly in the media sector, the use of AI-based systems ranges widely—from facial recognition technologies to machine learning algorithms. However, these technologies not only transform the production and dissemination of information but also bring serious ethical challenges and social consequences.

As highlighted by Fast and Horvitz, these digital technologies used in media give rise to multidimensional issues such as privacy violations, algorithmic biases, opaque decision-making mechanisms, unauthorized use of user data, lack of accountability, and occasional inefficiencies of the systems. This situation undermines not only individuals but also the general public's perception of security and the trust relationship with the media (Fast & Horvitz, 2017).

Therefore, to sustain the effectiveness of AI-based tools in combating fake news, it is essential that they be equipped not only with technical competence but also with ethical responsibility. In this context, it is necessary to question not only what AI systems do but also how and why they do it; the design, implementation, and supervision of these systems must be addressed within a multi-stakeholder, transparent, and human-rights-sensitive framework.

As AI increasingly influences the entire news cycle, the demand for transparency grows daily to ensure accountability, reduce algorithmic biases, and avoid the thematic bubbles created by personalized content. Transparency is not only a fundamental principle of journalism but also regarded as a critical safeguard for ensuring the accountability of AI's effects on media (Porlezza & Schapals, 2024). Indeed, Deuze and Beckett, emphasize that the core issue concerning AI is less about machines replacing journalists and more about ethics and transparency (Deuze & Beckett, 2022).

The rise of artificial intelligence in journalism not only transforms the modes of production and consumption but also reshapes digital rights and the understanding of ethical reporting. Experiences drawn from media history show that, as with every technological shift, AI brings with it both utopian hopes and dystopian anxieties. In this context, AI—with its power and influence—has the potential to shape all aspects of journalism; yet, due to its complex and often opaque nature, it also raises serious ethical and societal questions (Deuze & Beckett, 2022).

Accountability in journalism refers to news organizations and journalists being responsible for their content production processes, but the inclusion of AI technologies in these processes blurs the boundaries of this responsibility. Algorithms, often described as "black boxes," complicate the traceability of decisions and the identification of those accountable for errors. Therefore, it is imperative to establish mechanisms in AI-supported journalistic practices that guarantee editorial oversight, adherence to ethical principles, and transparent decision-making processes (Porlezza & Schapals, 2024).

Finally, the production of fake news is not only a technical issue but also a matter of conscience. While individuals may intentionally spread disinformation for political or economic gain, AI can assist in detecting such content or, conversely, inadvertently generate new fake material. However, it must be remembered that AI is, by definition, "artificial": it cannot feel, lacks conscience and value judgments, cannot think critically, nor understand socio-cultural contexts. Therefore, AI should be regarded solely as an aid, and the ultimate responsibility still lies with the individual and their media literacy. For now, using AI to the extent that it facilitates tasks is sufficient; what truly matters is how individuals use the technology and their ability to critically evaluate media content through a discerning lens.

CONCLUSION

In the digital age, where the fight against fake news is becoming increasingly complex, artificial intelligence (AI) technologies emerge as both a powerful ally and a potential threat in this struggle. Today, as the circulation of information is largely entrusted to algorithms, these technologies have made it possible to detect misleading content more quickly and stop it before it spreads. However, the same algorithms can also be manipulated by malicious actors to produce and disseminate fake news. This contradictory situation calls for a deeper examination of the nature of AI.

This duality shows that the role AI plays in combating fake news is not merely a technical issue but a complex matter that also involves ethical, social, and political dimensions. Therefore, AI should be seen both as a line of defense that prevents the spread of misinformation and as a tool that, if misused, can accelerate that spread.

This two-sided situation stems partly from AI sometimes being accused of spreading misinformation (Roszell, 2021) and, on the other hand, from AI being regarded by many researchers as an effective tool to ensure accuracy and detect fake news.

Artificial intelligence has become an indispensable component in combating misinformation, particularly within digital journalism. AI-based fact-checking tools are capable of processing vast amounts of data in real time, enabling the rapid detection of potentially deceptive or false narratives. These technologies not only streamline verification processes but also alleviate the burden on human fact-checkers by handling repetitive, large-scale tasks.

Despite these advantages, such systems are not foolproof. In some cases, they generate classification errors, leading to false positives—where accurate information is flagged as false—and false negatives—where misleading content is overlooked. Furthermore, when trained on biased or incomplete datasets, AI tools may unintentionally reproduce existing social or cultural prejudices, thereby compromising the integrity of news evaluation.

Another layer of concern relates to algorithmic opacity. Especially in complex machine learning models, it is often unclear how decisions are made, which presents a challenge for ensuring accountability and public trust. Without explainability, users and journalists alike may struggle to understand or contest AI-driven conclusions. Therefore, while AI can significantly enhance the accuracy and efficiency of fact-checking, its implementation must be accompanied by ethical safeguards, human oversight, and transparent practices to ensure responsible use in the media domain.

The platform where these technological gains are deployed also crucially shapes the risk. Social media platforms and search engines have become the new generation of "gatekeepers" in filtering and distributing information (Whittaker, 2019).This power dynamic creates opportunities for certain actors to exploit these structures to spread fake news (Paura, 2022: 23). In this context, algorithmic systems are seen to both undermine trust in the media and negatively impact democratic processes.

The so-called "black box" nature of AI further complicates accountability. At this point, especially in AI-supported journalism, editorial oversight, ethical frameworks, and transparency mechanisms become critically important (Porlezza & Schapals, 2024). Journalists, striving to balance normative values with economic and technological realities, see AI both as a tool and a challenge (Milosavljević & Vobič, 2019; Kim & Kim, 2018). This shows that the question "Threat or hope?" cannot be answered unilaterally; AI's potential in combating fake news is quite promising when used properly, but it can also create new risks if ethical, legal, and social responsibilities are ignored.

Ensuring the reliability of AI systems should be supported not only by ethical principles but also by technical frameworks. Here, control theory comes into play. It should be remembered that AI can carry human errors while processing data. Bias in algorithms is not only a technical issue but also an ethical matter that risks reproducing social inequalities (McCarthy, 2021). Therefore, the limitations of the datasets used must be clearly stated, decision-making processes must be transparent, and accountability mechanisms must be clarified.

Barfield, points out that control theory is an important tool for understanding feedback among system components and controlling the system. This approach is valuable not only for AI engineers but also for academics involved in AI governance. Automation control theory aims to control machines integrated with information technologies by reducing human intervention (Barfield, 2021). This research will base itself on automation control theory to detect fake news and ensure media verification, utilizing big data and analytic solutions accordingly.

In conclusion, while AI technologies offer significant opportunities in the fight against fake news, evaluating these opportunities in a reliable, fair, and transparent manner requires a multi-stakeholder, ethically grounded, and human-centered approach. In this struggle, not only technology but also human intellect, critical thinking, and ethical responsibility will be decisive. Whether AI is "hope or threat" will depend on how this balance is established.

A striking perspective on this uncertainty was also expressed by (Hawking, 2016). The rapid rise of AI could be the best or the worst thing to happen to humanity. Which it will be is not yet known. In a world full of contradictions, the most advanced versions of information and communication technology will shed light on the dark side of media, especially on the production and spread of fake news. AI can detect fake news or generate new ones. Although the balance may shift from time to time, it does not appear possible to definitively state whether AI is spreading fake news or preventing it by detection.

REFERENCES

Adıyaman, F. (2023). Yapay Zekâ Çağında Gazetecilik ve Etik: Güncel Tartışmalar Üzerinden Bir Değerlendirme. In Kenan, A. (Ed.), *Medya ve Habercilik Alanında Yapay Zekanın Yükselişi* (pp. 29–48). Eğitim Yayınevi.

Aggarwal, S., Sinha, T., Kukreti, Y., & Shikhar, S. (2020). Media bias detection and bias short term impact assessment. *Array (New York, N.Y.)*, *6*, 100025. https://doi.org/https://doi.org/10.1016/j.array.2020.100025. DOI: 10.1016/j.array.2020.100025

Allcott, H., & Gentzkow, M. (2017). Social media and fake news in the 2016 election. *The Journal of Economic Perspectives*, *31*(2), 211–236. DOI: 10.1257/jep.31.2.211

Altunbey Özbay, F., & Alataş, B. (2020). Çevrimiçi sosyal medyada sahte haber tespiti. *Dicle Üniversitesi Mühendislik Fakültesi Mühendislik Dergisi*, *11*(1), 91–103. DOI: 10.24012/dumf.629368

Barfield, W. (2021). A Systems and Control Theory Approach for Law and Artificial Intelligence: Demystifying the "Black-Box." *J*, *4*(4), 564–576. DOI: 10.3390/j4040041

Bock, S., & Weiß, M. (2019). A Proof of Local Convergence for the Adam Optimizer. *2019 International Joint Conference on Neural Networks (IJCNN)*, 1–8. DOI: 10.1109/IJCNN.2019.8852239

Carlson, M. (2015). The Robotic Reporter. *Digital Journalism (Abingdon, England)*, *3*(3), 416–431. DOI: 10.1080/21670811.2014.976412

Dang, H. L. (2021). Social media, fake news, and the COVID-19 pandemic: Sketching the case of Southeast Asia. *Advances in Southeast Asian Studies*, *14*(1), 37–58.

Dayan, A., & Yılmaz, A. (2022). Doğal dil işleme ve derin öğrenme algoritmaları ile makine dili modellemesi. *Dicle Üniversitesi Mühendislik Fakültesi Mühendislik Dergisi*, *13*(3), 467–475. DOI: 10.24012/dumf.1131565

Demirel, S. D. (2018). Dijital Medyada Haber Üretim Sürecinde Okuyucu Odaklılık. *Journal of International Social Research*, *11*(55), 824–831. DOI: 10.17719/jisr.20185537253

Deuze, M., & Beckett, C. (2022). Imagination, Algorithms and News: Developing AI Literacy for Journalism. *Digital Journalism (Abingdon, England)*, *10*(10), 1913–1918. DOI: 10.1080/21670811.2022.2119152

Dhiman, B. (n.d.). Does Artificial Intelligence help Journalists: A Boon or Bane? *Preprints 2023,* 2023030428.

Elitaş, T. (2022). Dijital Manipülasyon 'Deepfake'teknolojisi Ve Olmayanın İnandırıcılığı. *Hatay Mustafa Kemal Üniversitesi Sosyal Bilimler Enstitüsü Dergisi, 19*(49), 113–128.

Fast, E., & Horvitz, E. (2017). Long-term trends in the public perception of artificial intelligence. *Proceedings of the AAAI Conference on Artificial Intelligence, 31*(1). Advance online publication. DOI: 10.1609/aaai.v31i1.10635

Haenlein, M., & Kaplan, A. (2019). A Brief History of Artificial Intelligence: On the Past, Present, and Future of Artificial Intelligence. *California Management Review, 61*(4), 5–14. DOI: 10.1177/0008125619864925

Hawking, S. (2016, October 20). *Stephen Hawking warns of dangerous AI.*

Horne, B., & Adali, S. (2017). This just in: Fake news packs a lot in title, uses simpler, repetitive content in text body, more similar to satire than real news. *Proceedings of the International AAAI Conference on Web and Social Media, 11*(1), 759–766.

Huang, C., Zhang, Z., Mao, B., & Yao, X. (2022). An overview of artificial intelligence ethics. *IEEE Transactions on Artificial Intelligence, 4*(4), 799–819. DOI: 10.1109/TAI.2022.3194503

Hussein, F., & Hejase, H. J. (2022). Artificial Intelligence and Fake News. *Žurnalistikos Tyrimai, 16*, 39–71.

Jain, A., Shakya, A., Khatter, H., & Gupta, A. K. (2019). A smart System for Fake News Detection Using Machine Learning. *2019 International Conference on Issues and Challenges in Intelligent Computing Techniques (ICICT), 1*, 1–4. DOI: 10.1109/ICICT46931.2019.8977659

Kaplan, A. (2020). Digital Transformation. In Akkor Gül, A., Ertürk, Y. D., & Elmer, P. (Eds.), *Media & Society* (pp. 149–162). Istanbul University Press.

Kayıhan, B. (2024, December 8). *Yapay Zekâ ve Etik Sorunlar: İnsanlık, Teknolojinin Kontrolünü Kaybediyor Mu?* Kim, D., & Kim, S. (2018). Newspaper journalists' attitudes towards robot journalism. *Telematics and Informatics, 35*(2), 340–357.

Lazer, D. M. J., Baum, M. A., Benkler, Y., Berinsky, A. J., Greenhill, K. M., Menczer, F., Metzger, M. J., Nyhan, B., Pennycook, G., Rothschild, D., Schudson, M., Sloman, S. A., Sunstein, C. R., Thorson, E. A., Watts, D. J., & Zittrain, J. L. (2018). The science of fake news. *Science, 359*(6380), 1094–1096. DOI: 10.1126/science.aao2998 PMID: 29590025

Leslie, D. (2019). *Understanding artificial intelligence ethics and safety: A guide for the responsible design and implementation of AI systems in the public sector*. The Alan Turing Institute.

McCarthy, I. & K. M. (2021, May 26). *How artificial intelligence can help solve journalism's problems*.

Milosavljević, M., & Vobič, I. (2019). Human still in the loop: Editors reconsider the ideals of professional journalism through automation. *Digital Journalism (Abingdon, England)*, *7*(8), 1098–1116. DOI: 10.1080/21670811.2019.1601576

Moran, R. E., & Shaikh, S. J. (2022). Robots in the News and Newsrooms: Unpacking Meta-Journalistic Discourse on the Use of Artificial Intelligence in Journalism. *Digital Journalism (Abingdon, England)*, *10*(10), 1756–1774. DOI: 10.1080/21670811.2022.2085129

Özsalih, A. (2023). Yapay Zekâ Yoluyla Oluşturulan Sahte Haberlerin Medya Gündemini Belirlemesi. *Turkish Online Journal of Design Art and Communication*, *13*(3), 533–550. DOI: 10.7456/tojdac.1285554

Porlezza, C., & Schapals, A. K. (2024). AI Ethics in Journalism (Studies): An Evolving Field Between Research and Practice. *Emerging Media*, *2*(3), 356–370. DOI: 10.1177/27523543241288818

Prachi, N. N., Habibullah, M., Rafi, M. E. H., Alam, E., & Khan, R. (2022). Detection of fake news using machine learning and natural language processing algorithms. *Journal of Advances in Information Technology*, *13*(6). Advance online publication. DOI: 10.12720/jait.13.6.652-661

Roszell, O. A. (2021, November 8). *AI Learned How to Generate Fake News, and It's Terrifying Fake News, Deep Learning and Machine Learning Technology Changing the News*.

Sanchez-Acedo, A., Carbonell-Alcocer, A., Gertrudix, M., & Rubio-Tamayo, J. L. (2024). *The challenges of media and information literacy in the artificial intelligence ecology: deepfakes and misinformation*.

Tandoc, E. C.Jr, Lim, Z. W., & Ling, R. (2018). Defining "fake news" A typology of scholarly definitions. *Digital Journalism (Abingdon, England)*, *6*(2), 137–153. DOI: 10.1080/21670811.2017.1360143

Tejedor, S., & Vila, P. (2021). Exo Journalism: A Conceptual Approach to a Hybrid Formula between Journalism and Artificial Intelligence. *Journalism and Media*, *2*(4), 830–840. DOI: 10.3390/journalmedia2040048

Toğaçar, M., Eşidir, K. A., & Ergen, B. (2021). Yapay Zekâ Tabanlı Doğal Dil İşleme Yaklaşımını Kullanarak İnternet Ortamında Yayınlanmış Sahte Haberlerin Tespiti. *Journal of Intelligent Systems: Theory and Applications*, *5*(1), 1–8.

Ulaş, T. (2024). Yapay Zekâ Ve Haber Doğrulama Konusunda Yapılan Araştırmalar Üzerine Bibliyometrik Bir Analiz. *Pamukkale Üniversitesi İletişim Bilimleri Dergisi*, *3*(2), 247–267.

Van Dalen, A. (2012). The algorithms behind the headlines: How machine-written news redefines the core skills of human journalists. *Journalism Practice*, *6*(5–6), 648–658. DOI: 10.1080/17512786.2012.667268

Whittaker, J. P. (2019). *Tech giants, artificial intelligence and the future of journalism*. Taylor & Francis. DOI: 10.4324/9781351013758

Yeles Sinem, S. (2024). *Yalan Haber ve Medya Okuryazarlığı: Medya Okuryazarlığının Medya Önyargıları Üzerindeki Etkileri*. Graduate of Social Sciences.

Zengin, F., & Kapır, B. (2021). *Yapay Zeka ve Medya*. Doruk Yayımcılık.

Chapter 8
Evolution of Fake-News Detection:
Conventional, Automatic, and AI-Based Methods

Ahmet Çetinkaya
https://orcid.org/0000-0001-6272-5566
Faculty of Communication, Marmara University, Turkey

Huseyn Aghayev
Institute of Social Sciences, Istanbul, Turkey

ABSTRACT

The viral spread of fake news on social media platforms has become a significant concern. Detecting and mitigating the spread of fake news pose a major challenge, requiring extensive effort from fact-checkers, governments, and organizations. However, the speed and volume of disinformation on social media reach far beyond the capacity of manual efforts to prebunk it. In recent years, various automatic fake news detection mechanisms have been proposed, ranging from models focusing on linguistic cues to approaches analyzing network characteristics. While these methods produce successful results, ever-evolving techniques of deception often outpace them. AI-based approaches offer a new opportunity in the subject matter. Especially deep learning-based detection systems provide substantial new ways to understand the context while adapting well to the evolving patterns of fake news. In this study, we explore the evolution of fake news detection. We discuss conventional and automatic fake news detection methods and the state-of-the-art deep learning approaches.

DOI: 10.4018/979-8-3373-2960-4.ch008

INTRODUCTION

Fake news is a kind of information that has been intentionally shared to deceive people. It's contents are false in nature but purposefully designed to mimick the truth (Mahid et al., 2018, p. 2). Fake news is a serious threat. It can be weaponized by any motivated actor to cause fear, chaos, and destruction. It can be used by countries to weaken their rivals or can be used by malicious groups to cause distrust towards democratic governments. It is a proven threat against public health and democracy (Allcott & Gentzkow, 2017; Lin et al., 2022).

A series of new technologies and paradigm shifts contributed to the rise of fake news in the previous decade. Social media is the major enabler among them, followed by the decline of traditional journalism, the rise of bots, and clickbait. Recently, another brand-new technology has been added to the fake news arsenal, which is AI-generated content. These factors and paradigm shifts do not play out in isolation; in fact, the combination of them creates a fertile environment where fake news can thrive.

Being a constantly evolving problem, more effort and resources are required to overcome fake news as time passes. Manual fact-checking cannot keep up with the speed of social media. Traditional automated detection algorithms, on the other hand, struggle with the transformation and sophistication of fake news content. At this point, AI offers promising new ways to help address the old problem more effectively.

FAKE NEWS AND ITS CONSEQUENCES

Fake news is as old as human communication. However, the rise of mass communication means paved the way for fake news to be used as a tool. Partisan newspapers have been using propaganda and defamation of the opponent for centuries. Even in the 19th century, Americans were discussing the integrity of the press as a balance mechanism in democracy because of fake news (Allcott & Gentzkow, 2017, p. 1).

Screen media brought a new dimension to the propaganda and fake news field. Infamous Propaganda Minister of Nazi Germany Joseph Goebbels effectively used and perfected this tool (Geltzer, 2017, p. 306). Cinema screens and TV have proven to be more effective in spreading fear and anger among the population. Manipulated and purposefully cherry-picked visuals paired with inflammatory speech have proven to be capable of deceiving a whole nation.

However, no other media provided such a fertile environment for fake news as social media. The incentive mechanism in social media encourages inflammatory and sensational language, as that type of content gets more clicks, thus more profit. Personalization algorithms are helping to create filter bubbles, strengthening the biases and existing beliefs towards conspiracies and fake news. Bots are another tactic in information warfare, being used to accelerate the spread of fake news to make it more far-reaching and effective.

Types of Fake News

Fake news is not a uniform concept. It can manifest itself in various forms and intentions. First Draft (n.d.) coins an umbrella term of "Information Disorder" for all types of fake news and creates seven categories:

1. Satire or parody means no harm but can be misunderstood.
2. Misleading content uses pieces of information to prove a favourable point.
3. Imposter content is a message that mimics a person or an organization to gain credibility.
4. Fabricated content is a lie, intended to deceive and harm.
5. False connection is a statement with a conflicting visual or headline.
6. False context is a fact framed in an irrelevant context.
7. Manipulated content consists of genuine pieces, arranged in a way to deceive.

Another classification of fake news belongs to the European Association for Viewers' Interests. The organization designates 10 types of fake news based on intention and potential harm (European Association for Viewers Interests, 2017). Only one of those types is specified as neutral impact, which is propaganda. Low-impact types include clickbait, sponsored content, satire and hoax, and error. Partisan content belongs to a medium impact group. Conspiracy theory, pseudoscience, misinformation, and bogus belong to the high-impact group.

In this work, we will focus on the content that is intended to deceive and do harm, and we will use the term "fake news" for simplicity.

Cost of Fake News

Fake news is a threat to democracy, public health, and the overall unity and cohesion of society. It also leads to polarization and public distrust. In this chapter, we will analyze the consequences of fake news with recent examples.

A U.S. Senate Report, published in 2018, stated that Russia was heavily involved in disinformation activities on social media to interfere with the 2016 U.S. elections (*Russia "meddled in all big social media" around US election*, 2018). During the election campaign period, fake news was not only coming from the Russian side. Many hoaxes and manipulated images circulating on social media originated from various sources. While the effectiveness of this disinformation on the election result is debatable, a study by Allcott and Gentzkow (2017) estimates that an average voter has encountered and memorized at least one fake news content, if not many, and mostly pro-Trump content (Allcott & Gentzkow, 2017, p. 22).

Another example is the COVID-19 period, which was an intense few years filled with fear and uncertainty. These were the perfect combinations for the spread of fake news, considering the country-wide lockdowns, when people were spending more time on social media than ever. The fake news on social media has worsened the global health crisis by increasing depression and anxiety among the population who are exposed to large amounts of disinformation (Rocha et al., 2021, p. 7). In this crisis, governments and political interests played an especially critical role in the dissemination of fake news. Lin et al. (2022) conclude that government-backed disinformation considerably contributed to the spread of the disease (p. 9).

Global climate change has become a constant target of conspiracies and fake news on social media in recent years. Al-Rawi et al. (2021) conducted an experiment on Twitter by choosing the 500 most retweeted posts related to climate change discussion. More than half of those tweets were found to be suggesting either that climate change is not real or that it is not related to human actions (p. 6). Research also emphasizes the influence of politics and statements of high-ranking politicians in the dissemination of climate-related disinformation (Al-Rawi et al., 2021, p. 6). Brown (2017) suggests that the systemic disinformation campaign around climate change delayed global response to the issue by 50 years (p. 137).

TRADITIONAL METHODS OF FAKE NEWS DETECTION

It is important to understand traditional fake news detection methods as they are the pillars of the modern AI-based approaches. The traditional detection approaches can be grouped into two broad categories: manual fact-checking and automatic detection algorithms. In this section, we will explore the legacy approaches to combat fake news, starting with manual fact-checking.

Manual Fact-Checking

Manual fact-checking mostly depends on the expertise and know-how of the fact-checkers, the motivation and incentive of the fact-checking organizations, and the collaboration and leadership of the platforms and institutions. The institutions include, but are not limited to, government bodies, social media platforms, and international organizations. For many years, this symbiotic relationship created a safe and predictable environment for the fact-checking organizations to blossom, increasing their coverage and reaching wider audiences.

While fact-checking was the inextricable part of classic journalism, modern fact-checking practice started with the emergence of the dedicated fact-checking organizations. FactCheck.org and PolitiFact were the pioneers of the field in the U.S. ("Fact-Checking," 2025). In Turkey, Dogrulukpayi and Teyit lead the way in forming the fact-checking service for content in the Turkish language. While relying on similar methods of journalism, this new kind of fact-checking had a major difference from the fact-checking that traditional newsrooms did. Since fact-checking is a practice done by journalists to verify their research before publication, inaccurate or false news was usually not published. Fact-checking organizations, on the other hand, focus on working on an already published material and apply similar techniques as journalists did.

Manual fact-checking employs a few common processes shared among many fact-checking organizations. The typical manual fact-checking process consists of the following phases:

1. Finding the content
2. Prioritization
3. Evidence gathering
4. Writing
5. Publishing

Each organization may employ a different approach for each of these steps according to their methodology, but overall, the fact-checking study should be actual, transparent, and reproducible. For example, FactCheck.org specializes in political topics, and its content selection process is adapted to this specialization ("Our Process," n.d.). Teyit.org, on the other hand, depends on their community to gather the topics to be fact-checked (Metodoloji - Teyit, n.d.). This specialization among the organizations itself creates a unique opportunity for the readers to choose their go-to fact-checking service, based on the topics they cover.

Manual fact-checking has its advantages. Since each report is prepared by an expert, it has top-level accuracy. Fact-checkers not just provide a reproducible analysis, with a strict methodology, but at the same time, they provide the context and background information about the topic. Also, it gives an opportunity to form a bond between a reader and a fact-checker, which journalists enjoy.

In 2015 Poynter Institute announced the International Fact-Checking Network (IFCN). IFCN created a set of commitments for the fact-checking organizations to be part of ("Poynter Institute," 2025). These commitments, called the Code of Principles and include five core principles:

1. A commitment to Non-partisanship and Fairness
2. A commitment to Standards and Transparency of Sources
3. A commitment to Transparency of Funding & Organization
4. A commitment to Standards and Transparency of Methodology
5. A commitment to an Open & Honest Corrections Policy (IFCN, n.d.)

Fact-checking organizations passing the assessment of IFCN can be a signatory to the Code of Principles. Being a signatory provides credibility to the fact-checking organization, which could be beneficial, especially for new organizations. Once Meta started its external fact-checking program, IFCN signatory organizations also gained a pathway to partner with Meta to verify the suspicious content on the social media platform Facebook (Calma, 2025). This partnership provided extra funding to the fact-checking organizations, turning the mostly volunteer endeavor into a professionalized industry.

However, the political developments of the recent months created a new set of challenges for all the parties involved. With the U.S. government deciding to cut the support towards NGOs and social initiatives, social media companies followed suit. With Facebook announcing to halt its fact-checking program, many fact-checking organizations around the world lost their main funding source instantly.

Funding is not the only challenge fact-checkers are facing. While analyzing the spread of false and true rumors on the internet, Vosoughi et al. discovered that the fake news spread six times faster than the truth (Vosoughi et al., 2018, p. 1148). This forces the fact-checkers to enter a race whose rules are not fair.

With social media becoming a new medium for journalism and amateur news sharing, fake news acquired new sophisticated characteristics. Social media allows anybody to share the information they have, whether it's true or false, verified or out of context. It could've started with conspiracies, hoaxes, and rumors, but once the potential for manipulation came to light, malicious actors started to use fake news on social media as a tool to achieve their goals. All these new developments posed a substantial challenge to fact-checkers.

Ideologically motivated crowd poses another challenge to the manual fact-checking endeavor and to fact-checkers personally. Fake news on topics like war, religion, or politics can create a significant backlash toward the fact-checkers. A study by Nyhan and Reifler (2010) demonstrated that fact-checking not only reduces misperception among the ideologically committed people, on the contrary it strengthens their beliefs (p. 23). In some cases, fact-checks even cause personal attacks and lynching campaigns towards the fact-checkers and the organizations they belong to (Funke, 2018).

Automated Fact-Checking

The challenges of manual fact-checking raise the necessity for new solutions. As the social media adoption expands and the amount of social media posts increases exponentially, time-consuming fact-checking practices quickly become obsolete. The concern is not only the amount of the content to be verified, but also the appetite for the malicious use of fake news. A study by Bradshaw and Howard (2019) discovered that there has been a 150 percent increase in the number of countries using social media manipulation campaigns over a two-year period (p. 2).

To overcome these challenges, various automated fact-checking methods have been introduced over the past decades. Automatic fact-checking techniques rely on Information Retrieval (IR), Machine Learning (ML) techniques, Natural Language Processing (NLP), and graph theory (Zhou & Zafarani, 2021, p. 10).

Automated fact-checking can solve the capacity issue and the velocity issue. There is another major problem with the manual fact-checking that automated fact-checking can solve effortlessly. Manual fact-checking is being achieved by analyzing the content, and for that, language and background information about the topic are required. Some topics are underserved because of the lack of specialization. Also, some languages do not enjoy the fact-checking coverage as much as English. According to the statistics gathered by Stencel et al. (2020), North America and Europe have a disproportionately high amount of fact-checking coverage compared to the rest of the world. This is a perfect problem set for the automated fact-checking, because automated detection methods do not solely rely on the semantics. Some methods just employ linguistic patterns, while others use social context parameters to detect fake news, without evaluating the content itself.

Content-Based Fact-Checking

Content-based automated fact-checking methods focus on the distinctive features of the message. Fake news usually contains strong emotions and sentiments and can be expressive or aggressive to catch the attention (Hamed et al., 2023, p. 9). These characteristics are being reflected in the choice of words, capitalization, and punctuation. Finding these cues is the first step to creating an automated fact-checking algorithm. Depending on the type of the cue, content-based methods usually utilize a linguistic or style-based approach. While they both explore the structure and elements of the content, each technique looks for a different feature in the content.

Linguistic Approach

Linguistic approaches look for the syntactic features at the word, sentence, or document level (Mahid et al., 2018, p. 3). One common linguistic approach is called the Bag of Words, where each word is treated and analyzed independently for the signs of falsehood. However, this approach has a major downside. Separating the words from each other leads to the loss of the context (Conroy et al., 2015, p. 2). Zhou and Zafarani mention two more approaches that are being applied on the syntax level. Shallow syntax technique uses Part-Of-Speech (POS) tagging and analyzes the frequencies of the parts of the text. Deep syntax, on the other hand, uses Probabilistic Context-Free Grammar (PCFG) to analyze the grammatical patterns (Zhou & Zafarani, 2021, p. 14).

Another branch of the linguistic approach is the style-based technique. Style-based techniques focus on the intention behind the message to assess if the message is intended to deceive a wider audience or not (Zhou & Zafarani, 2021, p. 14). This intention may reproduce a distinct writing style that can be used as a cue to detect the falsehood. A study by Horne and Adali (2017) discovered a set of features that are helpful to detect fake news:

- Longer titles
- Simple words and less technicality
- All capitalized words are being used frequently
- Fewer nouns and fewer stop words (p. 6)

In order to define the style-based rules, researchers often analyze the features of satirical news content. As the satirical content has the same motivation to deceive the audience, it features many useful cues, which can be used to detect the actual fake news (Mahid et al., 2018, p. 3). The research specifically focused on satire, irony, and humor detection by Rubin et al. (2016) established an impressive precision rate of 90 percent (p. 10).

Visual-Based Approach

In the last decade, social media platforms became more visual oriented. New, specialized social media platforms appeared to offer only multimedia-based content, and existing platforms started to adopt multimedia formats in their user experience. There is a reason for these developments. Visual-based content attracts more attention, gets more engagement, and keeps users on the platform. Tweets with visual content are getting “18% more clicks, 89% more likes, and 150% more retweets” (Cao et al., 2020, p. 2). From the deceiver’s perspective, visuals are the perfect medium to achieve the goal. With today's technology, it is easy to edit an image or convincingly combine multiple images to convey a deceptive message. Guo et al. (2021) describe three major types of visual content on social media that are being used to spread fake news: image tampering through malicious modification, image mismatching in which authentic images are coupled with deceptive text, and image mixing that repurposes visuals from prior content (p. 12).

Verifying the visuals gives a valuable context about the authenticity of the content. Combined with the linguistic methods, it can boost the success rate of the verification process. Various solutions suggested in this regard both involve the image binary data and metadata. Some major approaches involve isolating physical cues, detecting misaligned blocks, color filtering array discrepancies, and detecting the cues related to the camera itself (Huh et al., 2018, p. 3).

A study by Jin et al. (2017) analyzes the images based on statistical features. The research establishes five features in the image to provide a score, to be used in the evaluation process. These features include visual clarity, visual coherence, visual similarity distribution histogram, visual diversity, and visual clustering (p. 602).

Social Context-Based Fact-Checking

Social context-based automatic fact-checking methods focus on the features that are related to the content without involving the content itself. Since content-based methods isolate the content to apply linguistic or visual-based analysis to it, external variables often get overlooked. Context-based analysis, on the other hand, brings all the ignored information back to the equation. These variables could include the user's engagement data, network data, and the characteristic features of the post itself (Mahid et al., 2018, p. 4). Context-based methods could be grouped under two major headings: Propagation-based and User-based analysis (Guo et al., 2021, p. 7; Hamed et al., 2023, p. 6).

Propagation-based methods depend on the dissemination path of the message. Fake news tends to show distinctive features while being propagated on social networks, especially when it is an orchestrated campaign. Zhou et al. propose two different approaches to propagation analysis: representing the propagation path in a direct way, or a news cascade, including extra data in the propagation path representation, and forming a custom graph. These graphs represent the characteristics of the dissemination from the initial message posting toward the subsequent shares and reposts (Zhou & Zafarani, 2021, p. 20).

Propagation-based analysis is helpful to detect fake news at an early stage, once it shows the common cues. A study by Liu and Wu focusing on the propagation-based early detection with 85% and 92% accuracy, depending on the social media platform. Their approach involves the characteristics of the users who share the news along with the propagation sequence. The resulting model detects fake news within the five minutes it starts to be shared (Y. Liu & Wu, 2018, p. 1).

Another study by Jin et al. (2017) uses a three-layer propagation approach by connecting the related posts and events to the main content. Each layer then contributes to forming the credibility value of the message. The model increases the precision of the detection by 16% over a baseline method.

User-based methods rely on the network activity of the user. From the profile information to the actions and reactions on the platform can help determine the credibility of the user. As the fake news gets more attention and interaction, focusing on the engagement metrics is also a tried and tested option (Guo et al., 2021, p. 7).

Hamed et al. discuss three major focus areas in user-based fake news detection:

- Credibility of the user: Overall reputation of the user as a part of the network. Follower friend ratio is an important metric in this regard.
- Conduct of the user: Users spreading fake news tend to have suspicious activity patterns. Time-bound activity metrics are often used as a criterion.
- Profile information of the user: From the profile photo to the personal details, many characteristics can shed light on the user's motivation (Hamed et al., 2023, p. 6).

ARTIFICIAL INTELLIGENCE IN FAKE NEWS DETECTION

The emergence of artificial intelligence (AI) transformed the automated fact-checking field drastically. Utilizing machine learning and deep learning algorithms, and NLP presented a whole new horizon to the old problem. Instead of focusing on the high-level patterns and rule-based analysis, these systems are providing a powerful solution at the many stages of the fact-checking process: detecting the fake news based on both content and context cues, finding the evidence to debunk the claims, and assisting humans to take appropriate actions.

In the past decade, many different AI approaches have been tried and tested to tackle the fake news problem. Some of those focus on text-based fake news, the others focus on multimedia content. Another type of approach called multimodal detection combines both text and multimedia to increase effectiveness (Gulzar Hussain et al., 2025, p. 16). Depending on the content type and intended outcome, detection systems may use various AI models, including Convolutional Neural Network (CNN), Graph Neural Network (GNN), Bidirectional Encoder Representations from Transformers (BERT), or Generative Pre-trained Transformers (GPT). These advanced capabilities in AI technology are achieved through a set of breakthrough technologies, which include deep learning and NLP. In this chapter, we will first explore the major enabling technologies, followed by the AI models that are foundational in the AI-based fact-checking literature.

Deep Learning

Deep learning is a specific branch of machine learning that builds hierarchical knowledge representations through multiple processing layers. Each layer in the hierarchy transforms the features from the previous layer into increasingly abstract representations. This method involves multiple levels of data representation and abstraction, which enables the understanding of various kinds of media, such as image, text, or audio (T. Liu et al., 2015, p. 1). The difference between deep learning from other machine learning models is that traditional models tend to have one or two layers, while a deep learning model can have thousands of layers (What Is Deep Learning?, 2024).

Deep learning has some advantages, such as better detecting patterns and better understanding the context, depending on the model. These advantages lead to the widespread use of this model in automatic fake news detection applications. Mridha et al. (2021) discuss three major advantages for deep learning models compared to traditional machine learning models: 1. They allow feature extraction, 2. their data preprocessing reliance is low, and 3. they can learn high-dimensional patterns (p. 2). These advantages, combined with the benefits of newer, transformer-based models, drastically advanced the NLP-based applications. These models can understand subtle context, nuance, and intention in the text, which makes them highly suitable for automatic fact checking.

Natural Language Processing (NLP)

NLP is a branch of computer science, especially connected to AI, to process, understand, and replicate human language. NLP lies at the intersection of various fields, such as linguistics, computer science, statistics, psychology, and others (Chowdhury, 2003, p. 1). The ultimate goal of NLP is to enable computers to actively use human language, to automate tasks depending on this ability.

There are various applications of NLP, such as rule-based, statistical, and deep learning based NLP. Rule-based NLP uses basic conditional decision trees. It relies upon the patterns that are preprogrammed to achieve a specific task (IBM, 2021). Statistical NLP uses mathematical models to predict the meaning based on the colocation of the words. Statistical NLP gets better results when supplied with a greater dataset (Nadkarni et al., 2011, p. 2). Deep learning based NLP, on the other hand, achieves even higher precision. Using models like Convolutional Neural Networks (CNN) in the context of text processing was highly successful. However, the real breakthrough came from Transformer models, in terms of understanding the context (*Natural Language Processing (NLP) - A Complete Guide*, 2023).

Convolutional Neural Network

CNN is a feedforward deep learning model. As a powerful pattern detector, it has been used in image classification, language detection, speech recognition, and facial point detection applications (T. Liu et al., 2015, p. 3).

In fact-checking applications CNN being used to achieve text classification. Provided with the one-dimensional text data, it can extract the features of the n-gram patterns (Mridha et al., 2021, p. 8). Apart from text-only approaches, CNN is also used in visual and multi-modal verification processes. Since CNN excels in image analysis tasks, it is a crucial tool to detect manipulations on the visuals (Vishnupriya et al., 2024, p. 3).

CNN consists of many hidden layers between the input and output layers. These layers include a convolutional layer, a pooling layer, a fully connected layer, and regularization. The role of the convolutional layer is to extract the features from the input, using the kernel. The amount of the feature being captured is based on the kernel size. Pooling layer helps to reduce the extracted features into the most distinct patterns, reducing the noise. For the fake news detection, the most common function is max pooling (Alsaeedi & Al-Sarem, 2020, p. 11). Regularization is a solution to the overfitting issue, where the training data specializes the model and makes it hard to catch the novel patterns that are not covered in the training. There are multiple approaches for the regularization, but for the fake news detection, dropout regularization is the most widely used method (Mridha et al., 2021, p. 9).

A study conducted by Yu et al. (2017) uses a CNN-based model to detect misinformation (p. 1). It uses a two-dimensional CNN model with k-max polling. While the model performs well compared to the baseline approaches, it falls short against some of them in terms of accuracy (Alsaeedi & Al-Sarem, 2020, p. 7).

Another research by Santhoshkumar and Babu (2020) uses a Dual CNN approach (p. 1). It uses propagation features along with the content as input. To reach a conclusion, the model uses the output of both CNNs and combines them. The approach shows an increased success rate in early detection (Alsaeedi & Al-Sarem, 2020, p. 10).

Bidirectional Encoder Representations for Transformers (BERT)

The introduction of the BERT by Google in 2018 was a turning point in the NLP (Szczepański et al., 2021, p. 3). It outperformed its predecessors by a margin and ousted the early NLP approaches thanks to its bidirectional approach and the capacity of maintaining the context in a text (Kula et al., 2021, p. 252).

BERT uses the Masked Language Model (MLM), which allows it to approach the text in a bidirectional manner (Kaliyar et al., 2021, p. 8). Being bidirectional, it can process the tokens both from left to right and from right to left, allowing it to better preserve the context (Kula et al., 2021, p. 253). To further strengthen the contextuality, BERT applies MLM, where a random portion of the tokens from the input is masked. Then the model predicts those tokens based on the neighboring tokens and the overall context. With the repetition throughout the pre-training process, BERT gains the ability to understand the context and the predict missing parts (Jwa et al., 2019, p. 3). It allows the model to recognize the detailed linguistic features, which is a useful asset in fact-checking applications (Vishnupriya et al., 2024, p. 3).

A notable study conducted by Jwa et al. (2019) uses improved BERT with extra unlabeled data provided at the pre-training stage. The model, called exBAKE, analyzes the relationship of content with the title and outperforms the baseline models by 0.14 F-score (p. 6). Another research by Kaliyar et al. (2021) proposes a model, called FakeBERT, which uses BERT with three CNN blocks with variable-sized kernels. The model classifies the fake news with 98.90% accuracy (p. 21). Kula et al. (2021) propose a hybrid architecture where BERT is used for the word embeddings along with RNN for document embeddings (p. 247). The model labels the fake news with 90% accuracy (p. 245).

BERT and similar deep learning approaches are being criticized for having an opaque decision-making process. Also being called the "black boxes," their decision-making is not transparent or explainable. This leads to an erosion of trust towards these models and their outputs (Szczepański et al., 2021, p. 3). Szczepański et al. (2021) focus on this problem and propose an explainable fake news detection system based on BERT. The approach enables the integration with LIME and Anchors to the BERT-based verification systems, allowing for the implementation of explainability without altering the underlying model (p. 4).

Generative Pre-trained Transformers (GPT)

GPT marks the new era in AI. This remarkable technology has started a new kind of revolution in recent years across multiple domains. It started to automate not just mundane repetitive tasks, but the most creative processes that humans enjoyed an absolute hegemony from the inception. For the fake news frontier, however, this new technology means both the good news and the bad news.

GPT, like BERT, is a Large Language Model (LLM), pre-trained on a massive text corpus. However, unlike BERT, which uses MLM to predict the masked tokens, it uses Causal Language Modeling (CLM) to predict the following token in the sequence (Hugging Face, n.d.). GPT uses a unidirectional transformer model and a self-attention mechanism. This allows the model to preserve the whole context for the sentence, while generating the following tokens (Yenduri et al., 2024, p. 2). Therefore, this model is also able to generate natural language texts. It has two training phases. In the first phase, the model is being pre-trained on a large text corpus to gain the ability to understand and generate natural language. To specialize it for the unique tasks, fine-tuning is applied as a second phase.

The advent of the GPT raised concerns in terms of synthetic content. It became an efficient tool to craft and spread custom-made and goal-oriented fake news, even for inexperienced people. Computer-generated text is not just convincing, but usually more sophisticated than the human-made false claims. Spitale et al. (2023) discovered that the respondents believed GPT generated deception even more than organically made deception. Moreover, it takes less time to deceive them with the synthetic content (p. 3). The study also finds that humans tend to lose confidence in their judgment once they become aware that they were deceived by the computer-generated text. This partly happens because they underestimate the new technology (Spitale et al., 2023, p. 5). GPT is also capable of deceiving seasoned journalists. In a recent incident, a The Guardian journalist was contacted about an article they supposedly wrote, but after searching their website, they discovered the article never existed. The article generated with ChatGPT by a researcher who was studying the about articles on the same topic (Moran, 2023).

While this new technology is set to open the floodgates of fake news towards social media, new preventative measures and detection methods are being developed. OpenAI restricts the usage of its application (ChatGPT) for misleading and fraud by terms of use and enforces it by banning the wrongdoers (Usage Policies, n.d.). Also, ChatGPT has an internal mechanism preventing it from fulfilling fake news generation requests; however, only 20 times out of 102 requests (Spitale et al., 2023, p. 3).

In recent years number of studies have proposed GPT-based fake news detection systems or measured the performance of the state-of-the-art GPT tools in detecting deception. Anjos et al. (2023) experimented to test the classification capabilities of ChatGPT-3.5, developed by OpenAI (p. 3). Research uses the API endpoints of ChatGPT and the ISOT Fake News Dataset. The experiment achieves a 56% recall score and a 66.6% F1-score with 72% accuracy (Anjos et al., 2023, p. 5).

A study by Choi and Ferrara (2024) measures the effectiveness of GPT-3.5-Turbo and Llama-2-7b LLMs in fact-checking tasks (p. 1). The experiment compares pre-trained models with fine-tuned models. For the fine-tuning, it uses GPT-4-generated fake news content. Findings show that fine-tuning affects the accuracy and overall performance notably (Choi & Ferrara, 2024).

Advantages of AI-based Fake News Detection

Disinformation tactics change rapidly. Emerging social media platforms, new content types, and formats contribute to this change. Social media content started with text-based posts, then evolved into image-heavy platforms, and after short-video formats. Now, computer-generated images are starting to gain a foothold. Just like any other social media post, a disinformation post from five years ago is not the same as today. This rapid change requires equally adaptable and resilient methods of detection.

AI, compared to rule-based systems and pattern-detecting algorithms, has much greater flexibility and adaptability to meet this challenge. Especially LLMs with massive parameters, thanks to pre-training data, show a strong sign of adaptability. Gondwe (2025) mentions the flexibility and the adaptability of BERT in the U.S. Presidential Debate, where the model was able to distinguish facts and opinions, and lies (p. 5). However, to achieve such adaptability, AI systems should undergo frequent training and updates, which requires human involvement (Saeidnia et al., 2025, p. 7).

Traditional rule-based detection models require humans to detect the patterns of fake news and shape the algorithms accordingly. Moreover, their work mechanism often ignores the context, which can be essential to distinguish the intention. The content may have all the features of fake news, but it could be a joke or irony. AI models, on the other hand, like CNN are excellent tools to discover patterns in the content, and models like BERT or GPT are effective in context recognition, because of their self-attention mechanism (Yenduri et al., 2024, p. 2).

Challenges of AI-based Fake News Detection

AI presents new horizons and opportunities to solve the problems that have existed for many generations, one of them being fake news. However, AI has its own set of challenges, both as a stand-alone technology and as a tool of automatic fake news detection.

Training Data

One of the most prominent challenges in AI is finding a quality dataset for training. Many AI models, especially LLMs, require an immense amount of data to be trained. There are many open data sources on the internet, like Wikipedia, Project Gutenberg, etc. However, the list shrinks over time. In recent years, many social media platforms implemented restrictions on their API services to be able to charge a fee. Most recently, Reddit decided to sell its data, which was once free

(Goswami, 2023). Acquiring the dataset could also cause ethical concerns. In one of the recent incidents disclosed court documents revealed that Meta, the parent company of Facebook, used millions of pirated books from the torrent network to train their AI (Brittain & Brittain, 2025).

Finding the data is the first prong of the challenge. The data must have specific qualities, such as accuracy and objectivity. Social media data contains conversations with highly biased opinions. Training the AI with biased data would make the output partial and inaccurate, perpetuating and worsening the existing biases (Vishnupriya et al., 2024, p. 4).

Black Box Problem

AI models consist of many layers between the input and output. These layers process the input with the available training bias to form an output. Since it is impractical to trace the output through all the complicated layers, the decision-making process of the AI often remains a puzzle. This has been called the "black-box problem" (Castelvecchi, 2016).

The black box problem makes the AI-generated outputs unexplainable to humans. A regular algorithm, when followed from top to bottom, reveals the whole process of decision-making. AI, on the other hand, depending on the model, can create its algorithms in the hidden layers. The black-box problem makes it impossible to assume or guarantee that the AI output is free from biases and impartialities (Szczepański et al., 2021, p. 3). This leads to distrust among the public and the users towards AI-based solutions (Vishnupriya et al., 2024, p. 4).

High Computational Requirements

Training an AI model is a computationally demanding process. Modern AI models, particularly LLMs, have billions of parameters, necessitating supercomputers and graphical processing units (GPUs) specifically designed for these tasks. Training a BERT model takes approximately 79 hours for NVIDIA (Strubell et al., 2019, p. 3).

The total cost of the AI training is not just financial. The computation process requires a high amount of electricity, which contributes to carbon emissions. A single GPT-4 query can consume ten times more power compared to a search engine request (Carroll, 2025). A study by Strubell et al. estimates that the energy requirements to train a BERT model generate 652 kilogram CO_2 emissions (Strubell et al., 2019, p. 4).

Adversarial Attacks

AI-based fake news detection has the potential to disrupt the work of the actors who profit from spreading fake news. Therefore, these actors are constantly developing new tactics to avoid detection. Adversarial attacks are one of those tactics where the wrongdoers intentionally tweak their content to confuse the detection systems and evade them (Vishnupriya et al., 2024, p. 4).

Qiu et al. categorize three different types of adversarial attacks, involving the different stages of AI mode: the attacks targeting the training stage, testing stage attacks, and deployment stage attacks (Qiu et al., 2019, p. 1). To conduct the training-side adversarial attack, training data could be corrupted, or malicious data could be inserted into the data. For the testing and deployment stage, they can predict the detection patterns by providing malignant samples and measuring the results. Or even worse, they could be well informed about the particular model and its decision-making mechanism (Qiu et al., 2019, p. 7). Increasing the resilience of the AI model is the key to avoiding such attacks (Vishnupriya et al., 2024, p. 4).

CONCLUSION

In this new era of advanced technology, humanity is closer than ever to overcoming ignorance, with the knowledge that has become abundant and accessible with the internet. There is, however, a growing threat, looming on the horizon, threatening to damage all the progress that has been made. Fake news is challenging the world as never before. Whether it's vaccines, which are proven to save millions of lives, or human rights or democracy, every bit of progress is endangered by the actors weaponizing fake news to project low-cost soft power.

Now the tested and proven tactics of disinformation are accessible to everyone, and the AI-based tools effortlessly mimic human language. This gives an unprecedented opportunity to anyone to use fake news to achieve goals. Decades ago, fake news may have been a tool reserved for a few to manipulate masses, influence elections, and shape public opinion. But today, it's available to be used for micro gains by anyone who has the motivation.

This new challenge puts pressure on the old institutions, fact-checking organizations, and fact-checkers who apply the practice manually, with old methods. However, reaching the speed of social media and AI with manual fact-checking is impossible. To solve this problem, many automated fake news detection systems have been proposed. These systems vary significantly based on the features they focus on. One group of models is focused on the content itself, analyzing linguistic or style-based features of the content. Another group solely focuses on visual cues.

The third group analyzes the propagation path and social parameters of the content and the user who shares it. These models constitute a significant breakthrough in terms of automatic fake news detection. They shape our approaches to the new tools and technologies, and act as a baseline to evaluate new methods.

The next step in the evolution of automated fake news detection is AI. In recent years, AI has gained strong momentum with the advent of LLMs like BERT and GPT. While generative AI models pose a new challenge in terms of the dissemination of fake news, they also provide greater opportunities to tackle the fake news problem. In this work, we've explored different kinds of AI models that have been used in fake news detection systems, their challenges, and benefits. AI seems to be the centerpiece of coming inventions and technological breakthroughs in the coming decades. It is important to understand and harness its potential to stay prepared against the next wave of fake news, the old problem, evolving faster than ever.

REFERENCES

Al-Rawi, A., O'Keefe, D., Kane, O., & Bizimana, A.-J. (2021). Twitter's Fake News Discourses Around Climate Change and Global Warming. *Frontiers in Communication, 6*. Advance online publication. DOI: 10.3389/fcomm.2021.729818

Allcott, H., & Gentzkow, M. (2017). Social Media and Fake News in the 2016 Election. *The Journal of Economic Perspectives, 31*(2), 211–236. DOI: 10.1257/jep.31.2.211

Alsaeedi, A., & Al-Sarem, M. (2020). Detecting Rumors on Social Media Based on a CNN Deep Learning Technique. *Arabian Journal for Science and Engineering, 45*(12), 10813–10844. DOI: 10.1007/s13369-020-04839-2

Anjos, L. S., Quincozes, S. E., Kazienko, J. F., & Quincozes, V. E. (2023). Investigating the Performance of the GPT-3.5 Model in Fake News Detection: An Experimental Analysis. *Anais Do XXIII Simpósio Brasileiro de Segurança Da Informação e de Sistemas Computacionais (SBSeg 2023)*, 552–557. https://doi.org/DOI: 10.5753/sbseg.2023.233647

Bradshaw, S., & Howard, P. (2019). The Global Disinformation Order: 2019 Global Inventory of Organised Social Media Manipulation. *Copyright, Fair Use, Scholarly Communication, Etc.* https://digitalcommons.unl.edu/scholcom/207

Brittain, B., & Brittain, B. (2025, January 9). Meta knew it used pirated books to train AI, authors say. *Reuters*. https://www.reuters.com/technology/artificial-intelligence/meta-knew-it-used-pirated-books-train-ai-authors-say-2025-01-09/

Brown, D. A. (2017). The Enormity of the Damage Done by the Climate Change Disinformation Campaign as the World Struggles to Implement the Paris Agreement. In *The Role of Integrity in the Governance of the Commons* (pp. 125–139). Springer., DOI: 10.1007/978-3-319-54392-5_8

Calma, J. (2025, January 7). *Meta is leaving its users to wade through hate and disinformation*. The Verge. https://www.theverge.com/2025/1/7/24338127/meta-end-fact-checking-misinformation-zuckerberg

Cao, J., Qi, P., Sheng, Q., Yang, T., Guo, J., & Li, J. (2020). *Exploring the Role of Visual Content in Fake News Detection*. https://doi.org/DOI: 10.1007/978-3-030-42699-6

Carroll, S. (2025, April 21). *Saying "please" and "thank you" to ChatGPT costs OpenAI millions, Sam Altman says*. Quartz. https://qz.com/open-ai-sam-altman-chatgpt-gpt4-please-thank-you-1851777047

Castelvecchi, D. (2016). Can we open the black box of AI? *NATNews*, *538*(7623), 20. DOI: 10.1038/538020a PMID: 27708329

Choi, E. C., & Ferrara, E. (2024). FACT-GPT: Fact-Checking Augmentation via Claim Matching with LLMs. *Companion Proceedings of the ACM Web Conference 2024*, 883–886. https://doi.org/DOI: 10.1145/3589335.3651504

Chowdhury, G. G. (2003). *Natural Language Processing.*

Conroy, N. K., Rubin, V. L., & Chen, Y. (2015). Automatic deception detection: Methods for finding fake news. *Proceedings of the Association for Information Science and Technology*, *52*(1), 1–4. DOI: 10.1002/pra2.2015.145052010082

Environment, U. N. (2018, October 29). *About Montreal Protocol.* https://www.unep.org/ozonaction/who-we-are/about-montreal-protocol

Fact-checking. (2025). In *Wikipedia.* https://en.wikipedia.org/w/index.php?title=Fact-checking&oldid=1289589114

Funke, D. (2018, September 10). These fact-checkers were attacked online after partnering with Facebook. *Poynter.* https://www.poynter.org/fact-checking/2018/these-fact-checkers-were-attacked-online-after-partnering-with-facebook/

Geltzer, J. (2017). *FAKE NEWS & FILM: HOW ALTERNATIVE FACTS INFLUENCE THE NATIONAL DISCOURSE. 47.*

Gondwe, G. (2025). Can AI Outsmart Fake News? Detecting Misinformation With AI Models in Real-Time. *Emerging Media, 27523543251325902.* Advance online publication. DOI: 10.1177/27523543251325902

Goswami, R. (2023, June 1). *Reddit will charge hefty fees to the many third-party apps that access its data.* CNBC. https://www.cnbc.com/2023/06/01/reddit-eyeing-ipo-charge-millions-in-fees-for-third-party-api-access.html

Gulzar Hussain, F., Wasim, M., Hameed, S., Rehman, A., Nabeel Asim, M., & Dengel, A. (2025). Fake News Detection Landscape: Datasets, Data Modalities, AI Approaches, Their Challenges, and Future Perspectives. *IEEE Access : Practical Innovations, Open Solutions*, *13*, 54757–54778. DOI: 10.1109/ACCESS.2025.3553909

Guo, B., Ding, Y., Yao, L., Liang, Y., & Yu, Z. (2021). The Future of False Information Detection on Social Media: New Perspectives and Trends. *ACM Computing Surveys*, *53*(4), 1–36. DOI: 10.1145/3393880

Hamed, S. K., Ab Aziz, M. J., & Yaakub, M. R. (2023). A review of fake news detection approaches: A critical analysis of relevant studies and highlighting key challenges associated with the dataset, feature representation, and data fusion. *Heliyon*, *9*(10), e20382. DOI: 10.1016/j.heliyon.2023.e20382 PMID: 37780751

Horne, B. D., & Adali, S. (2017). *This Just In: Fake News Packs a Lot in Title, Uses Simpler, Repetitive Content in Text Body, More Similar to Satire than Real News* (arXiv:1703.09398). arXiv. https://doi.org//arXiv.1703.09398DOI: 10.48550

Hugging Face. (n.d.). *OpenAI GPT*. Retrieved May 20, 2025, from https://huggingface.co/docs/transformers/v4.34.0/en/model_doc/openai-gpt

Huh, M., Liu, A., Owens, A., & Efros, A. A. (2018). Fighting Fake News: Image Splice Detection via Learned Self-Consistency. In Ferrari, V., Hebert, M., Sminchisescu, C., & Weiss, Y. (Eds.), *Computer Vision – ECCV 2018* (Vol. 11215, pp. 106–124). Springer International Publishing., DOI: 10.1007/978-3-030-01252-6_7

IBM. (2021, September 23). *What Is NLP (Natural Language Processing)? | IBM*. https://www.ibm.com/think/topics/natural-language-processing

IFCN. (n.d.). *The commitments of the Code of Principles*. Retrieved May 11, 2025, from https://www.ifcncodeofprinciples.poynter.org/the-commitments

Jin, Z., Cao, J., Zhang, Y., Zhou, J., & Tian, Q. (2017). Novel Visual and Statistical Image Features for Microblogs News Verification. *IEEE Transactions on Multimedia*, *19*(3), 598–608. DOI: 10.1109/TMM.2016.2617078

Jwa, H., Oh, D., Park, K., Kang, J., & Lim, H. (2019). exBAKE: Automatic Fake News Detection Model Based on Bidirectional Encoder Representations from Transformers (BERT). *Applied Sciences (Basel, Switzerland)*, *9*(19), 4062. DOI: 10.3390/app9194062

Kaliyar, R. K., Goswami, A., & Narang, P. (2021). FakeBERT: Fake news detection in social media with a BERT-based deep learning approach. *Multimedia Tools and Applications*, *80*(8), 11765–11788. DOI: 10.1007/s11042-020-10183-2 PMID: 33432264

Kula, S., Choraś, M., & Kozik, R. (2021). Application of the BERT-Based Architecture in Fake News Detection. In Herrero, Á., Cambra, C., Urda, D., Sedano, J., Quintián, H., & Corchado, E. (Eds.), *13th International Conference on Computational Intelligence in Security for Information Systems (CISIS 2020)* (pp. 239–249). Springer International Publishing. https://doi.org/DOI: 10.1007/978-3-030-57805-3_23

Lin, T.-H., Chang, M.-C., Chang, C.-C., & Chou, Y.-H. (2022). Government-sponsored disinformation and the severity of respiratory infection epidemics including COVID-19: A global analysis, 2001–2020. *Social Science & Medicine*, *296*, 114744. DOI: 10.1016/j.socscimed.2022.114744 PMID: 35124544

Liu, T., Fang, S., Zhao, Y., Wang, P., & Zhang, J. (2015). *Implementation of Training Convolutional Neural Networks.*

Liu, Y., & Wu, Y.-F. (2018). Early Detection of Fake News on Social Media Through Propagation Path Classification with Recurrent and Convolutional Networks. *Proceedings of the AAAI Conference on Artificial Intelligence*, *32*(1), 1. Advance online publication. DOI: 10.1609/aaai.v32i1.11268

Mahid, Z. I., Manickam, S., & Karuppayah, S. (2018). Fake News on Social Media: Brief Review on Detection Techniques. *2018 Fourth International Conference on Advances in Computing, Communication & Automation (ICACCA)*, 1–5. https://doi.org/DOI: 10.1109/ICACCAF.2018.8776689

Metodoloji—Teyit. (n.d.). Retrieved May 11, 2025, from https://teyit.org/metodoloji

Moran, C. (2023, April 6). ChatGPT is making up fake Guardian articles. Here's how we're responding. *The Guardian*. https://www.theguardian.com/commentisfree/2023/apr/06/ai-chatgpt-guardian-technology-risks-fake-article

Mridha, M. F., Keya, A. J., & Hamid, Md. A., Monowar, M. M., & Rahman, Md. S. (2021). A Comprehensive Review on Fake News Detection With Deep Learning. *IEEE Access : Practical Innovations, Open Solutions*, *9*, 156151–156170. DOI: 10.1109/ACCESS.2021.3129329

Nadkarni, P. M., Ohno-Machado, L., & Chapman, W. W. (2011). Natural language processing: An introduction. *Journal of the American Medical Informatics Association : JAMIA*, *18*(5), 544–551. DOI: 10.1136/amiajnl-2011-000464 PMID: 21846786

Natural Language Processing (NLP)—A Complete Guide. (2023, January 11). https://www.deeplearning.ai/resources/natural-language-processing/

Nyhan, B., & Reifler, J. (2010). When Corrections Fail: The Persistence of Political Misperceptions. *Political Behavior*, *32*(2), 303–330. DOI: 10.1007/s11109-010-9112-2

Our Process. (n.d.). *FactCheck.Org*. Retrieved May 11, 2025, from https://www.factcheck.org/our-process/

Poynter Institute. (2025). In *Wikipedia*. https://en.wikipedia.org/w/index.php?title=Poynter_Institute&oldid=1286699137

Qiu, S., Liu, Q., Zhou, S., & Wu, C. (2019). Review of Artificial Intelligence Adversarial Attack and Defense Technologies. *Applied Sciences (Basel, Switzerland)*, *9*(5), 909. DOI: 10.3390/app9050909

Rocha, Y. M., de Moura, G. A., Desidério, G. A., de Oliveira, C. H., Lourenço, F. D., & de Figueiredo Nicolete, L. D. (2021). The impact of fake news on social media and its influence on health during the COVID-19 pandemic: A systematic review. *Journal of Public Health*. Advance online publication. DOI: 10.1007/s10389-021-01658-z PMID: 34660175

Rubin, V., Conroy, N., Chen, Y., & Cornwell, S. (2016). Fake News or Truth? Using Satirical Cues to Detect Potentially Misleading News. *Proceedings of the Second Workshop on Computational Approaches to Deception Detection*, 7–17. https://doi.org/DOI: 10.18653/v1/W16-0802

Russia "meddled in all big social media" around US election. (2018, December 17). https://www.bbc.com/news/technology-46590890

Saeidnia, H. R., Hosseini, E., Lund, B., Tehrani, M. A., Zaker, S., & Molaei, S. (2025). Artificial intelligence in the battle against disinformation and misinformation: A systematic review of challenges and approaches. *Knowledge and Information Systems*, *67*(4), 3139–3158. DOI: 10.1007/s10115-024-02337-7

Spitale, G., Biller-Andorno, N., & Germani, F. (2023). *AI model GPT-3 (dis) informs us better than humans* (arXiv:2301.11924). arXiv. https://doi.org//arXiv.2301.11924DOI: 10.48550

Stencel, M., Luther, J., & Luther, M. S. and J. (2020, April 3). Update: 237 fact-checkers in nearly 80 countries ... and counting. *Reporters' Lab*. https://reporterslab.org/2020/04/03/update-237-fact-checkers-in-nearly-80-countries-and-counting/

Strubell, E., Ganesh, A., & McCallum, A. (2019). *Energy and Policy Considerations for Deep Learning in NLP* (arXiv:1906.02243). arXiv. https://doi.org//arXiv.1906.02243DOI: 10.48550

Szczepański, M., Pawlicki, M., Kozik, R., & Choraś, M. (2021). New explainability method for BERT-based model in fake news detection. *Scientific Reports*, *11*(1), 23705. DOI: 10.1038/s41598-021-03100-6 PMID: 34880354

Understanding Information disorder. (n.d.). First Draft. Retrieved May 25, 2025, from https://firstdraftnews.org/long-form-article/understanding-information-disorder/

Usage policies. (n.d.). Retrieved May 21, 2025, from https://openai.com/policies/usage-policies/

Vishnupriya, G., & Jeriel, K. A., RNS, A., Ajay, G., & J, A. G. (2024). Combating Fake News in the Digital Age: A Review of AI-Based Approaches. *2024 IEEE 9th International Conference for Convergence in Technology (I2CT)*, 1–6. https://doi .org/DOI: 10.1109/I2CT61223.2024.10544008

Vosoughi, S., Roy, D., & Aral, S. (2018). The spread of true and false news online. *Science*, *359*(6380), 1146–1151. DOI: 10.1126/science.aap9559 PMID: 29590045

What Is Deep Learning? | IBM. (2024, June 17). https://www.ibm.com/think/topics/ deep-learning

Yenduri, G., Ramalingam, M., Selvi, G. C., Supriya, Y., Srivastava, G., Maddikunta, P. K. R., Raj, G. D., Jhaveri, R. H., Prabadevi, B., Wang, W., Vasilakos, A. V., & Gadekallu, T. R. (2024). GPT (Generative Pre-Trained Transformer)—A Comprehensive Review on Enabling Technologies, Potential Applications, Emerging Challenges, and Future Directions. *IEEE Access : Practical Innovations, Open Solutions*, *12*, 54608–54649. DOI: 10.1109/ACCESS.2024.3389497

Yu, F., Liu, Q., Wu, S., Wang, L., & Tan, T. (2017). A convolutional approach for misinformation identification. *Proceedings of the 26th International Joint Conference on Artificial Intelligence*, 3901–3907.

Zhou, X., & Zafarani, R. (2021). A Survey of Fake News: Fundamental Theories, Detection Methods, and Opportunities. *ACM Computing Surveys*, *53*(5), 1–40. DOI: 10.1145/3395046

Chapter 9
Deepfakes:
Ethical and Legal Implications Across Business, Politics, and Society

Krishna Khanal
https://orcid.org/0009-0003-1369-0952
Westcliff University, USA

Ashutosh Koirala
https://orcid.org/0009-0004-5983-5894
Westcliff University, USA

ABSTRACT

This chapter explores deepfake technology's ethical and legal implications across business, politics, and society. Deepfakes, utilizing advanced AI techniques, pose significant threats, including the erosion of trust, manipulation of public opinion, privacy violations, and legal challenges such as defamation and intellectual property infringement. This work examines the technology's potential for misuse in creating deceptive content, impacting areas from financial fraud to political disinformation. It analyzes existing legal frameworks, including those in China, the EU, and the USA. It proposes mitigation strategies, such as AI-driven detection tools, blockchain verification, and educational initiatives to foster media literacy. The analysis underscores the need for collaborative efforts between businesses, regulators, and technology developers to navigate the complexities of deepfakes and safeguard the authenticity of digital information, emphasizing the balance between technological innovation and ethical responsibility.

DOI: 10.4018/979-8-3373-2960-4.ch009

INTRODUCTION

Machine learning models have recently been able to generate photorealistic fake images, clone voices, alter lip movements, and, by using text prompts, create synthetic videos (Groh et al., 2024). In this age of artificial intelligence (AI), the occurrence of technology like deepfakes has marked a major stage. Deepfakes leverage deep learning techniques to create hyper-realistic digital content, particularly video and audio, that can convincingly imitate real individuals (Chesney & Citron, 2019; Mustak et al., 2023). They are vivid, persuasive, and credible, and are more likely to be shared, making it very difficult for a person to differentiate them from authentic media (Hwang et al., 2021; Gosse & Burkell, 2020; Li & Wan, 2023). The rise of deepfakes has led to "Impostor Bias," where people increasingly doubt whether digital content is real, making it harder to trust online interactions. An example of deepfakes is the face of celebrities being swapped with the faces in pornographic videos. For instance, in 2019, deepfake technology was used to create a fake pornographic video featuring Taylor Swift's face superimposed onto the body of an adult film actress. This video circulated widely on the internet, causing distress and damaging her reputation. The majority of explicit deepfake videos circulating online predominantly involve women (Adjer et al., 2019). Deepfakes represent a significant form of harassment toward women due to their explicit and often non-consensual nature. These digitally manipulated videos and images can falsely depict women in compromising situations, leading to severe emotional distress and reputational damage. The impact is multifaceted, including emotional and psychological trauma, strain on personal relationships, and professional repercussions such as job loss or damaged career prospects. Additionally, deepfakes violate women's privacy and dignity, creating legal and social challenges in seeking justice. Deepfakes can highly impact the justice system as they are able to create fake evidence, which might lead to confusion in deciding what is real and what is fake. Due to this, people can even doubt evidence that is real; this phenomenon is known as "Liar's Dividend," where individuals evade accountability by dismissing genuine evidence as deepfakes (Lundberg & Mozelius, 2025).

Even though deepfakes have huge applications and benefits for businesses in terms of creating content and maintaining engagement (Etienne, 2021), their misuse has raised substantial ethical and legal concerns. Some of the most concerning issues where AI is being used are fake audio and fake video content; they can further lead to crime or terrorism as deepfakes can create very realistic and convincing audios or videos that can be used to manipulate public opinion, spread disinformation, blackmail individuals, or incite violence, thereby posing significant risks to security and societal stability (Caldwell et al., 2020). Groups that do not belong to any government, like terrorists or insurgents, can create deepfakes to make it look like some government leaders said something, which they never did, and this makes people upset and even go against their own state or country. For example, in late 2020, some deepfake videos were made by a US-based anti-corruption group that showed Vladimir Putin and Kim Jong-Un supporting U.S. politicians for weakening democracy. Likewise, in 2022, another deepfake video was made, which showed Ukrainian President Volodymyr Zelenskyy telling his soldiers to surrender to Russia even though he never said that (Cavedon-Taylor, 2024).

Deepfakes pose significant threats to business. According to a Private Industry Notification by the F.B.I. in March 2021, deepfakes can be used to impersonate company staff for financial crimes. For instance, attackers can create realistic deepfakes of executives' audio or video to authorize fraudulent transactions or gain access to sensitive information. The old data security frameworks will not be able to cope with the emerging deepfakes threats, and for this, we need better and advanced solutions (Kaur et al., 2024). Multiple high-profile cases have shown how deepfakes can seriously harm businesses. For example, in 2019, a criminal used deepfake audio and pretended to be the CEO of an energy company based in the UK, tricking an employee of the company into sending €220,000. This shows how financial and security risks can be created by using deepfakes. Deepfakes have been created in such a way that art and reality can be mixed together, creating confusion, which raises multiple questions about technology, artificial creativity, and authorship (Cejudo, 2023). In the business context, these challenges are particularly pronounced, given the potential for deepfakes to disrupt operations, cause reputational damage, spread deception, and foster distrust among stakeholders. Deepfakes are leading us toward an "infopocalypse," where distinguishing between real and fake content becomes nearly impossible (Toews, 2020). Deepfake technology is changing marketing by helping brands connect better with customers using realistic fake videos of celebrities to build trust and interest. Using deepfakes in business and marketing requires careful consideration, as if people find out the content is bogus, they may feel misled, which can hurt the brand. Companies should be honest, raise awareness, and help people understand how to identify fake content to avoid problems such as false information or negative reviews (Pramod et al., 2025).

Deepfakes can negatively impact politics because they can create disturbance in elections, damage relations that exist between countries, and lead to people losing their trust in leaders and news media (Jacobsen & Simpson, 2023). Deepfakes will undermine democracy by impeding citizens' inclusion in debates and decisions, hampering the accountability of political representatives, marginalizing societal groups, degrading the quality of deliberation and mutual empathy, and fostering fears of election manipulation, ultimately threatening the legitimacy of collective decisions (Pawelec, 2022). They have the power to threaten weak democracies in Asia and Africa. On April 11, 2023, a fake video was seen on the internet in which

Hillary Clinton was supporting Republican Florida Governor Ron DeSantis for the presidency, even though she never said so. The video went viral on social media platforms when the Florida Governor was preparing for his 2024 campaign (Momeni, 2024). Deepfakes can incite armed conflict, posing threats to both national and global security, as demonstrated by the 2019 fake video of Gabon's President Ali Bongo Ondimba, which sparked concerns about his health and triggered an attempted coup (Chuming et al., 2022; Langa, 2021). Restricting deepfake technology could infringe on individual rights, yet a lack of regulation exposes the country to risks such as election interference and political destabilization.

Even if we try to remove deepfakes, they spread very quickly and appear highly realistic, making it harder to control them. This highlights the seriousness of the problem of deepfakes, especially when they are created without someone's consent.

Despite efforts to remove such content, the rapid dissemination and the convincing nature of deepfakes make it challenging to control and mitigate their harmful effects, highlighting the serious consequences of nonconsensual AI-generated images. When people start seeing edited or fake videos, even the fake event starts to feel familiar, and it becomes very easy to imagine events. That familiarity makes it seem more believable, and people actually start thinking the event happened. Due to this, some researchers also state that deepfakes can strongly twist our past events' memories (Murphy et al., 2023; Nash & Wade, 2009; Liv & Greenbaum, 2020).

This chapter delves into the ethical and legal ramifications of deepfakes in the modern world, exploring their impact, regulatory responses, and the strategies companies can adopt to mitigate associated risks.

UNDERSTANDING DEEPFAKES

In today's time, where people's psychology is highly manipulated by images and fake news is everywhere, a new technology called deepfake is emerging. Deepfakes represent a novel and distinctive type of visual disinformation created through video (Bhandari & Bhandari, 2025; Vaccari & Chadwick, 2020). Disinformation can play a huge role in making people divided, become doubtful, and grow negative, which further creates distrust and confusion among the public (Freelon & Wells, 2020; Hameleers et al., 2022). It was the year 2017 in which Deepfakes became very popular when a Reddit user shared a video in which celebrities were seen in explicit and embarrassing pornographic scenarios, even though it was not real. Deepfake technology relies on machine learning, typically deep learning techniques, to create or modify videos, making it appear as though events occurred that did not. Previously, generating fake videos was a costly endeavor, demanding substantial skill, time, and money. Using open-source AI, it has been very easy for anyone to create realistic videos and images that are fake. Deepfakes can just be created using a gaming laptop, the internet, and basic knowledge about neural networks.

Some apps allow you can swap faces in videos with just one click (Thaware & Agnihotri, 2018). Making technology easy to use for everyone has many positive aspects, but it has some big negative effects as well. If anyone can create and share fake media, then it will get harder to tell which is real and what is not. This can further impact media, entertainment, politics, cybersecurity, etc., as deepfakes can be used for both fun and harmful purposes.

AI now facilitates the large-scale production of "deepfakes": artificial videos that closely mimic real ones. Deepfake technologies specially use AI algorithms called GANs (Generative Adversarial Networks) to create synthetic media. This algorithm studies large amounts of real images, videos, and audio, and, after that, it produces new content that mimics those appearances and voices, which is very close to those media fed to it. Graph Neural Networks (GNNs) facilitate the mass synthesis of manipulated digital content by encoding and replicating human features in images and videos (Doss et al., 2023). These networks can fabricate images by learning and replicating human characteristics, manipulate existing images by replacing specific components, and animate still images using the traits of a source video. By leveraging these capabilities, GNNs can produce digital content that is indistinguishable from reality, making them powerful tools for both innovation and potential misuse. GNNs can mix and create new content, which brings up ethical concerns and makes it necessary for us to reflect on why we need strong tools to detect fake media. The word "deepfake" comes from two words: "deep learning" and "fake," which describe the technology perfectly.

ETHICAL CHALLENGES OF MISREPRESENTATION AND DECEPTION

Deepfakes pose a growing threat to decision integrity, increasing business risks, eroding confidence, and undermining certainty in decision-making processes (Vecchietti et al., 2025). The major issue with deepfakes is that they can easily trick people and spread false information. Previously, there was no such technology that was able to make realistic fake videos or audio of people doing things or saying things they never did. But now, with the arrival of deepfakes, it has been possible, which gives deepfakes a very strong power to deceive people. Deception breaches norms of honesty, cultivates false beliefs, is regarded as a moral failing, and is detrimental to social relationships and trust (de Ruiter, 2021). Deepfakes can fool our eyes, ears, etc., making them very powerful for spreading false information (Brown et al., 2023). In business, deepfakes can be used to create and send fake messages from company executives, trick investors, and harm competitors' brand image. If we create convincing fake content, it can break trust and cause serious financial and reputation harm. Even though some recent studies say that deepfakes are not that misleading in comparison to written lies (Hameleers et al., 2022), the biggest worry is that they may destroy trust in all types of visuals. If that happens, the statement "seeing is believing" may get outdated for people (Weikmann et al., 2024; Barnes & Barraclough, 2020). This could happen because people might generalize their experiences with isolated false visuals to all visual content or because the lifelike nature of deepfakes could deceive even those skilled at detecting fakes, thus reducing their confidence in identifying manipulations and undermining their self-efficacy (Zhang et al., 2023; York et al., 2020).

In the marketplace today, deception has been very common. It can include: using fake numbers or resource findings, trying to distract customers with too much information, showing false emotions, copying brands, and lying about features and results of products to gain illegal or unethical advantages (Taylor, 2021; Mustak et al., 2023; Xie et al., 2020). Businesses are often seen creating and sharing fake product reviews, written by people or generated by a computer, in order to mislead customers and competitors for financial gain, and this portrays taking advantage of how buyers depend on reviews when shopping online (Muastak et al., 2023).

It is very likely for people to accept deepfake content if they find it enjoyable, and if the content is entertaining, then it has a higher chance of sparking curiosity and pleasure, which further increases its social acceptance (Li & Wan, 2023). Such easy acceptance can hide ethical concerns because having fun or entertaining deepfakes can still mislead people. They can be widely acceptable even if they are not ethically acceptable, and this portrays why people don't worry or worry very little about deepfakes in the field of entertainment (Cochran & Napshin, 2021).

HUMAN IDENTITY AND PRIVACY INVASION

Human identity is a significant target of deepfake cloning (Thies et al., 2016), as it is expressed through unique visual and acoustic features (Roswandowitz et al., 2024). Each individual possesses a distinct voice profile that is used by both other humans (Perrodin et al., 2015) and automated systems (Bai & Zhang, 2021) to identify them. This uniqueness in voice characteristics, such as pitch, tone, and cadence, plays a crucial role in personal identification. With advances in technology, voice synthesis algorithms have become incredibly sophisticated, which has further allowed the creation of deepfakes voice clones that sound almost the same as the real speakers (Sisman et al., 2021). These advancements not only replicate the sound but also the subtle nuances that make each person's voice unique, blurring the lines between authentic and synthetic voices. Since our face and voice reflect who we are, it is very necessary to protect their digital versions from manipulation, and it should be seen as a basic moral right, especially in this age of deepfakes (de Ruiter, 2021). Non-consensual deepfakes violate people's right to control how they are digitally represented. While people can't wholly control their online portrayals, others shouldn't manipulate their image or voice in realistic footage that they would disagree with.

Deepfakes create a very serious risk to the privacy of individuals. Unauthorized creation and distribution of deepfake content involving employees or executives can lead to severe personal and professional harm. Deepfakes have the potential to take away people's control over their own images, invading their own privacy and further impacting their dignity, independence, and sense of identity (Kugler & Pace, 2021). By manipulating and misrepresenting personal images and videos, deepfakes can cause harm and mislead others, ultimately compromising the authenticity and integrity of one's individual identity. Businesses must navigate the ethical implications of protecting their personnel from such privacy invasions. AI development depends heavily on large datasets, often sourced unknowingly from users through activities like CAPTCHA. This practice creates serious ethical and legal issues involving consent, privacy, and data rights because it involves the use of people's data without their explicit permission or compensation. Ensuring that companies provide clear notices and opt-out options is crucial to maintaining trust and respecting user privacy in AI development. Protecting privacy is essential, both ethically and legally, because deepfake platforms and users can reuse personal data without any permission, and the fear of such leaks of privacy makes the public more resistant towards deepfake technologies (Hong & Thong, 2013).

EROSION OF TRUST

The threat posed by untrustworthy AI reaches its peak with deepfakes, which are often seen as the ultimate destroyers of online trust (Etienne, 2021). The proliferation of deepfakes erodes public trust in digital content (Rana et al., 2022). Despite the rise of image-editing technology that has eroded trust in photography over recent decades, photographic evidence remains highly valued. This deep-seated trust extends to videos, which we inherently believe to be truthful representations of reality. However, this trust can be exploited through deepfakes, which leverage advanced technology to create videos that appear convincingly real. Our brains are wired to trust visual information, making us susceptible to misperceptions. Just as optical illusions or magic tricks can fool us, deepfakes target this same vulnerability, manipulating what we see and hear, which makes it harder for us to tell what is real and what is fake (Kietzmann et al., 2020; Granot et al., 2018). In a business environment, this erosion can have far-reaching consequences, affecting everything from marketing efforts to internal communications. Considering all this, The European Commission formed an expert group to create 'ethics guidelines for trustworthy AI' (HLEGAI, 2019), aiming to create a foundational framework for regulating AI development within the EU. The ability to easily manipulate content using generative AI makes deepfakes a serious risk to the accuracy of information and overall trust in public communication (Romero Moreno, 2024). Deepfake technology undermines trust in recordings' reliability, as the real harm lies not just in fabricating actions or speech but also in eroding confidence in visual and auditory evidence (Fletcher, 2018; Vaccari & Chadwick, 2020). The inability to distinguish between real and fake content can lead to skepticism and hesitancy among consumers, investors, and employees. While online disinformation is not new, AI tools have greatly intensified its impact. AI-driven deepfakes have influenced elections globally, including in Bangladesh and Moldova, causing widespread distrust in essential democratic information. As of late 2023, 85% of internet users were concerned about spotting fake content online, a critical issue ahead of the major 2024 elections. We must acknowledge that disinformation will be challenging to eradicate and, depending on the region, may even increase in volume and deceptiveness due to the growing sophistication of AI-aided deepfakes.

LEGAL CHALLENGES OF INTELLECTUAL PROPERTY VIOLATIONS

Deepfakes are often created using someone's image or identity without their permission, which breaks their ownership rights. Especially celebrities and other famous people are at risk of being victims of such exploitation. Businesses must be vigilant in protecting their brand and likeness from being co-opted by deepfake technology. Copyright law is likely ineffective in curbing malicious deepfakes because these are often made for non-commercial purposes and are considered transformative (Chawki, 2023). Copyright law protects specific expressions, not ideas or facts, raising the question of whether a person's face or voice can be copyrighted. Courts have held that while song lyrics are copyrightable, the voice itself is not. Additionally, deepfakes may be considered derivative works, but copyright does not extend to a person's inherent qualities.

Deepfakes present complex challenges that go beyond copyright law, involving significant issues of personal rights such as privacy, defamation, and harassment. In jurisdictions like the United States, where the fair use doctrine often limits copyright claims, it is more effective for victims to address malicious deepfakes through data protection and privacy laws. The evolving landscape demands proactive legal reforms, including new legislation that defines rights and protections for individuals' likenesses, as well as international cooperation to enforce these standards globally. Additionally, ethical considerations, such as transparency and consent, must be addressed, requiring a multifaceted approach from lawmakers, platforms, and technology providers.

Unlike copyright, which protects the original works of authors and creators, performers' rights specifically safeguard performers' personal and economic interests (Pavis, 2021). While performers' rights seem like an effective solution for regulating deepfakes, the technology challenges their scope because it uses content protected by these rights in ways that intellectual property policymakers did not anticipate when these laws were established. Consequently, there is a growing need to revisit and expand performers' rights to ensure they can maintain control over their likenesses and performances in the digital age.

DEFAMATION AND LIBEL

The use of deepfakes to create defamatory content poses significant legal challenges. Fabricated videos or audio recordings depicting business leaders or employees engaging in unethical or illegal activities can lead to defamation and libel lawsuits. Companies must be prepared to address such threats through legal channels.

The legal standards for defamation vary based on whether the subject is a public figure or a private individual. Public figures have to prove that the person who made the deep fake knew it was fake or that they did not care whether it was true or not, as established in New York Times Co. v. Sullivan. For ordinary individuals, the standard is generally negligence. The technical complexity of creating convincing deepfakes, which requires advanced skills and substantial effort, further complicates these cases. Creators often claim their works are parodies, protected under the First Amendment. However, the emotional and reputational damage inflicted by deepfakes, particularly those depicting nonconsensual explicit content, underscores the need for robust legal recourse. States have started to enact laws addressing nonconsensual pornography, including deepfake pornography, recognizing its severe impact. Balancing free speech rights with protections against false and harmful information is essential in the evolving legal landscape surrounding deepfakes.

In June 2021, Mr. Kwon sued for defamation after a deepfake photo was posted showing him in a compromising position, illustrating the legal challenges private individuals face compared to high-profile individuals. The decision of the Supreme Court in Gertz v. Robert Welch allows states to set their liability standards for defamatory statements against private individuals, provided they don't impose strict liability. Therefore, in defamation cases involving deepfakes, private individuals like Mr. Kwon must meticulously demonstrate the content's malicious intent and falsity under state law (Chawki, 2024).

Closely related to deception risks are the threats to user agency - the ability to make free and informed decisions about technology use (Ananny & Crawford, 2018). When deepfakes are seamlessly integrated into user interfaces without providing explicit consent or opt-out options, they can significantly compromise this autonomy. For instance, a personal assistant AI might use deepfake technology to mimic the voices and appearances of users' deceased loved ones without their permission. This appropriation not only breaches ethical boundaries but also manipulates users' emotional responses, making it difficult for them to disengage or critically assess the technology's influence on their decision-making.

Moreover, marketing strategies that leverage hyper-personalized deepfakes can further erode user autonomy (Taddeo & Floridi, 2018). By dynamically altering content to suit individual preferences and psychological triggers in real time, these manipulations can exert an overwhelming influence on consumer behavior (Reddy, 2023). Users might find themselves swayed by hyper-realistic advertisements that speak directly to their desires and fears, crafted through advanced deepfake techniques. This level of personalization can cross the line from tailored experiences to intrusive manipulations, stripping users of their ability to make independent choices free from covert technological influence.

Defamation laws already impose liability for reputational damage caused by false statements. However, these laws vary by state, require false statements to be presented as facts, and may not fully address the emotional distress caused by deepfakes.

REGULATORY COMPLIANCE

Navigating the regulatory landscape surrounding deepfakes is complex. While some jurisdictions have begun implementing laws targeting deepfake technology, the global nature of business means companies must be aware of and comply with a myriad of regulations. There can be legal penalties and reputational damage if the regulations are not followed properly. The rapid evolution of technology quickly renders legal norms outdated, necessitating a clear definition of proper technology usage. Additionally, the cross-border nature of technologies complicates rule identification and enforcement, often leading to registration in lenient jurisdictions, partial responsibilities of interested parties, and easy circumvention of jurisdictional rules (van der Sloot et al. 2021).

The European AI Act has put deepfakes in a 'low-risk' category, and it requires only providing basic transparency. But in the United States and China, some forms of deepfakes have been made illegal, and some worry that such laws could be used to restrict free speech as well as control what information people can share (Hine & Floridi, 2022; Birrer & Just, 2024). In the UK in 2020, a groundbreaking legal event happened when a deepfake was used as evidence in a case of child custody. The mother submitted an audio recording of the father making threats, and at first, it sounded very convincing (The Telegraph, 2020). However, the father's legal team challenged its authenticity, leading to a forensic examination that revealed the recording had been tampered with using deepfake technology to insert fabricated dialogue. This discovery prompted the court to dismiss the evidence, highlighting significant concerns about the misuse of advanced digital technologies in legal contexts (Durães et al., 2024). This case showed how easily digital evidence can be faked, the crucial role of forensic experts, and highlighted the need for legal systems to update their rules to deal with such emerging threats.

EXISTING LAWS

One method to combat malicious deepfakes is to use privacy law to address the appropriation of an individual's likeness, though this may be ineffective for non-commercial deepfakes. But as technology becomes more widespread, companies might use deepfakes to issue false celebrity or political endorsements to gain a competitive advantage.

China was one of the first countries to make rules about deepfakes through a law that started on January 10, 2023, covering all kinds of fake media. The rules ban content that breaks the law or harms the country, and they ask apps and platforms to label fake content and remove false or harmful information clearly. In 2021, China implemented a data protection law that set strict guidelines requiring user consent for data collection. This law aims to enhance user privacy and control over personal information in the digital age. Recently, China also introduced a pioneering policy specifically targeting "deep synthesis technologies" used to create "deepfakes." This regulation is designed so that problems caused by AI that can fake voices, videos, or messages can be handled, and it makes sure that people use this technology honestly. By doing this, China wants to stop deepfakes from being used in harmful ways and keep people safe from fake information and privacy breaches.

The Artificial Intelligence Act (AIA) of the EU has created some important rules for deepfakes, but these rules have a chance of limiting some freedoms or rights of people and companies who create, use, and work with AI (Romero Moreno, 2024). The EU already has different online safety laws, and harmful deepfakes are treated as part of dangerous or illegal online content that those laws are supposed to control. These include the General Data Protection Regulation (GDPR), the AI

Act, the Digital Services Act (DSA), and national laws (Karaboga, 2023). This has the chance of clashing with the rights of privacy and free expression stated in the European Convention on Human Rights (Article 8 and 10), as well as the EU's GDPR rule 016/679.

In the USA, defamation statutes provide a legal framework to hold those using deepfake technology to spread false information accountable, allowing targeted individuals or institutions to sue creators for defamation and seek damages. This approach offers a means of deterrence and can help reduce the prevalence of deepfakes in political campaigns and media. However, it is crucial to balance free speech protection with the need to prevent the spread of false information. Several rules aim to counter deepfakes' threats. One of them is the 2019 Deepfake Report Act, which requires the U.S. Department of Homeland Security to release a yearly report about deepfake technology and how it might affect national security. Additionally, to help detect and fight fake media, the National Institute of Standards and Technology has also started a program to develop standards.

In contrast, platforms like Twitter and Facebook have implemented algorithms and fact-checking measures to flag and remove deepfake content. Texas was one of the first states to criminalize the creation of deepfake videos. In 2019, the state passed a law making it illegal to create or distribute deepfakes intended to harm or defraud another person. The Federal Election Commission and the U.S. "Protect Elections from Deceptive AI Act" both try to stop the use of misleading deepfake content in political advertisements.

MITIGATION STRATEGIES: TECHNOLOGICAL SOLUTIONS

Businesses can employ several technological solutions to combat the threat of deepfakes. By finding out little hints of editing in digital content, AI tools can figure out when something is a deepfake. If digital watermarks or signatures are used on content, then it gets easier to trace where it came from and also find out if it is real or not (Wazid et al., 2024). There are different types of watermarks we can use - like fragile, public, visible, and hidden types and we can also use different types of digital signature methods, like RSA, ECDSA, and DSA. In the U.S., universities, research groups, and tech companies are developing tools to detect deepfakes using machine learning and datasets of fake videos. Projects like Princeton's DeepTrace, the Deepfake Detection Challenge, Google's FaceForensics, and Truepic's blockchain-based Foresight are helping improve deepfake detection and reduce the risk of misinformation (Chawki, 2024). Blockchain, which is still an emerging technology, can be used to make the results more reliable (Patil & Chouragade, 2021). Blockchain can help confirm whether a digital media is real by keeping a secure record that cannot be altered, and it can show the source of the media, i.e., where it came from, and verify it has not been tampered with. Different powerful forensic tools like Wireshark, Volatility, and Nmap can check digital files for strange patterns, tampering, or hidden changes in audio, images, or video, which provides solid evidence in court that further helps in serving serious consequences for people who intentionally misuse digital content (Quershi et al., 2021). To ensure the content comes from a trustworthy source, systems have to check the identity of the creator, verify where it originated, and confirm that it has not been tampered with (Zhang et al., 2023).

DISCUSSIONS

It is very necessary to create rules that are able to deal with legal and ethical challenges caused by deepfakes. These policies should include guidelines for creating, distributing, and verifying digital content, as well as protocols for responding to incidents involving deepfakes. Employee training and awareness programs can also play a key role in mitigating risks. Schoolchildren should be educated in creative and rational thinking and should acquire computer literacy skills to effectively identify false information and engage in respectful online communication with one another. Governments should implement strict regulations to ban deepfakes, ensuring accountability at every stage of their creation and distribution (Fabuyi et al., 2024). This involves establishing legal liability for developers, distributors, and platforms that host or promote deepfake content to curb their spread and potential misuse. The future of deepfakes in business is fraught with both challenges and opportunities. Collaboration among companies, regulators, and technology developers will be crucial to shaping a future in which the benefits of deepfakes can be harnessed while minimizing their risks. For businesses, deepfakes can bring new possibilities, but they also come with massive challenges. On one hand, deepfakes offer innovative ways to enhance marketing and customer engagement. Companies can create hyper-realistic and personalized content, such as virtual spokespeople or dynamic advertisements tailored to individual preferences. This level of personalization can lead to more effective marketing campaigns and stronger customer relationships. Additionally, deepfakes can be used for training and development, creating realistic simulations for employee training without the need for expensive and logistically challenging setups. Using this, corporate training programs can be made much more efficient as well as effective, leading to better prepared employees and improved business outcomes

At the same time, if deepfakes are used in business, it brings a big concern related to security and ethics. If the technology is misused in order to create fraudulent or deceptive content, then it can harm brand integrity and consumer trust (Vecchietti et al., 2025; Mustak et al., 2023). Businesses must make sure that they are using this technology for good purposes and make sure that it is not being used for harmful things, like spreading misinformation or stealing identities. Regulatory frameworks and robust ethical guidelines will be essential for governing the use of deepfakes in business, ensuring that the benefits are maximized while minimizing risks. Companies will need to invest in advanced security measures and establish clear policies to mitigate the potential negative impacts, ensuring that deepfakes are used responsibly and transparently. Despite the challenges, deepfake technology also holds potential for positive applications in business. For example, deepfakes can be used for personalized marketing, creating realistic and engaging customer interactions. They can also facilitate remote work and virtual meetings by generating realistic avatars for participants. Exploring these positive uses while mitigating risks will be key to leveraging deepfakes effectively. Positive uses of deepfakes span a wide range of applications, significantly enhancing entertainment, education, and accessibility. In the field of entertainment, deepfakes have been able to allowed filmmakers to make historical figures appear on screen or make the actors look younger, which further gives the audience a very smooth and realistic experience. This technology can also be used to dub films and TV shows into multiple languages with the actors' lip movements perfectly synced, making content more accessible and enjoyable for global audiences.

Additionally, deepfakes offer artists and content creators a creative tool for experimenting with new forms of storytelling and visual effects, pushing the boundaries of what is possible in digital media. In the education sector, deepfakes can revolutionize the way knowledge is delivered and absorbed. Educational institutions can use deepfake technology to create lifelike simulations of historical events, allowing students to interact with digital representations of historical figures or witness pivotal moments as if they were there (Murillo-Ligorred et al., 2023). This immersive learning experience can make complex subjects more engaging and easier to understand. Deepfakes can also help in creating personalized lessons and explanations for individual students, which makes learning very effective and fit for individual needs. By using this technology, students can practice languages in realistic and hands-on situations, which makes their learning very practical and engaging.

CONCLUSIONS

Deepfake technology poses complex ethical and legal challenges for businesses. The risks of misrepresentation, privacy invasion, and trust erosion highlight why we need proactive measures to reduce the harm deepfakes can cause. Legal frameworks, technological solutions, and comprehensive policies are essential tools in this effort. By staying informed and adapting to the evolving landscape, businesses can handle challenges created by deepfakes while also using their potential for positive impact.

While the challenges posed by deepfakes are undeniable, this chapter has also revealed the potential for proactive solutions. By actively fostering media literacy programs, educating schoolchildren in critical thinking and digital literacy, developing robust AI-powered detection technologies, including digital watermarking, blockchain verification, and advanced forensic tools, and implementing responsible, adaptive legal frameworks, we can effectively mitigate the risks and harness the innovation potential. The path forward demands a collaborative effort between businesses, regulators, and technology developers, one that prioritizes ethical considerations and transparency and empowers individuals to evaluate the information they consume critically. Ultimately, our collective ability to adapt, innovate, and educate will determine whether deepfakes become a tool of widespread manipulation or a catalyst for a more transparent and accountable digital age, where truth, trust, and the integrity of digital content remain cornerstones of our society (Al-kfairy et al., 2024). By implementing strong regulations and accountability measures, we can ensure that deepfakes are used for good rather than nefarious purposes.

As deepfake technology continues to advance, its implications for the business world will become increasingly significant. By understanding and addressing the ethical and legal challenges it presents, businesses can protect themselves and their stakeholders from the potential harms of this powerful technology.

REFERENCES

Al-kfairy, M., Mustafa, D., Kshetri, N., Insiew, M., & Alfandi, O. (2024). Ethical challenges and solutions of generative AI: An interdisciplinary perspective. *Informatics (MDPI)*, *11*(3), 58. DOI: 10.3390/informatics11030058

Ananny, M., & Crawford, K. (2018). Seeing without knowing: Limitations of the transparency ideal and its application to algorithmic accountability. *New Media & Society*, *20*(3), 973–989. DOI: 10.1177/1461444816676645

Barnes, C., & Barraclough, T. (2020). Deepfakes and synthetic media. In Steff, R., Burton, J., & Soare, S. R. (Eds.), *Emerging technologies and international security* (1st ed., pp. 206–220). Routledge. DOI: 10.4324/9780367808846-16

Bhandari, R., & Bhandari, S. (2025). Artificial intelligence: understanding deepfakes. *EDPACS,* 1–11. DOI: 10.1080/07366981.2025.2484863

Birrer, A., & Just, N. (2024). What we know and don't know about deepfakes: An investigation into the state of the research and regulatory landscape. *New Media & Society*. Advance online publication. DOI: 10.1177/14614448241253138

Brown, J. G., Bailenson, J. N., & Hancock, J. (2023). Misinformation in virtual reality. *Journal of Online Trust & Safety*, *1*(1), 1–31.

Caldwell, J., Delaye, A., Esposito, T., Petti, T., Black, T., Fallon, B., & Trocmé, N. (2020). "Essential" services, risk, and child protection in the time of COVID-19: An opportunity to prioritize chronic need. *Developmental Child Welfare*, *2*(3), 208–223. DOI: 10.1177/2516103220968842

Cavedon-Taylor, D. (2024). Deepfakes: *A survey and introduction to the topical collection. Synthese*, *204*(14), 14. Advance online publication. DOI: 10.1007/s11229-024-04634-8

Cejudo, R. (2023). Ethical problems of the use of deepfakes in the arts and culture. In Lara, F., & Deckers, J. (Eds.), *Ethics of artificial intelligence. The International Library of Ethics, Law and Technology* (Vol. 41). Springer., DOI: 10.1007/978-3-031-48135-2_7

Chawki, M. (2024). Navigating legal challenges of deepfakes in the American context: A call to action. *Cogent Engineering*, *11*(1), 2320971. DOI: 10.1080/23311916.2024.2320971

Chuming, Y. A., Wu, D. J., & Hong, K. (2022*). Practical deepfake detection: vulnerabilities in global contexts* [arXiv preprint]. https://doi.org//arXiv.2206.09842DOI: 10.48550

Cochran, J. D., & Napshin, S. A. (2021). Deepfakes: Awareness, concerns, and platform accountability. *Cyberpsychology, Behavior, and Social Networking*, *24*(3), 164–172. DOI: 10.1089/cyber.2020.0100 PMID: 33760667

de Ruiter, A. (2021). The distinct wrong of deepfakes. *Philosophy & Technology*, *34*(4), 1311–1332. DOI: 10.1007/s13347-021-00459-2

Doss, C., Mondschein, J., Shu, D., Wolfson, T., Kopecky, D., Fitton-Kane, V. A., Bush, L., & Tucker, C. (2023). Deepfakes and scientific knowledge dissemination. *Scientific Reports*, *13*(1), 13429. DOI: 10.1038/s41598-023-39944-3 PMID: 37596384

Durães, D., Freitas, P. M., & Novais, P. (2024). The relevance of deepfakes in the administration of criminal justice. In H. Sousa Antunes, P.M. Freitas, A.L. Oliveira, C. Martins Pereira, E. Vaz de Sequeira, & L. Barreto Xavier (Eds.), *Multidisciplinary Perspectives on Artificial Intelligence and the Law* (Law, Governance and Technology Series, Vol. 58). Springer, Cham. DOI: 10.1007/978-3-031-41264-6_19

Etienne, H. (2021). The future of online trust (and why Deepfake is advancing it). *AI and Ethics*, *1*(4), 553–562. DOI: 10.1007/s43681-021-00072-1 PMID: 34790952

Fabuyi, J. A., Olaniyi, O. O., Olateju, O. O., Aideyan, N. T., Selesi-Aina, O., & Olaniyi, F. G. (2024). Deepfake Regulations and Their Impact on Content Creation in the Entertainment Industry. *Archives of Current Research International*, *24*(12), 52–74. DOI: 10.9734/acri/2024/v24i12997

Fletcher, J. (2018). Deepfakes, artificial intelligence, and some kind of dystopia: The new faces of online post-fact performance. *Theatre Journal*, *70*(4), 455–471. DOI: 10.1353/tj.2018.0097

Freelon, D., & Wells, C. (2020). Disinformation as political communication. *Political Communication*, *37*(2), 145–156. DOI: 10.1080/10584609.2020.1723755

Gosse, C., & Burkell, J. (2020). Politics and porn: How news media characterizes problems presented by deepfakes. *Critical Studies in Media Communication*, *37*(5), 497–511. DOI: 10.1080/15295036.2020.1832697

Hameleers, M., van der Meer, T. G. L. A., & Dobber, T. (2022). You won't believe what they just said! The effects of political deepfakes embedded as vox populi on social media. *Social Media + Society*, *8*(3), 205630512211163. DOI: 10.1177/20563051221116346

High-Level Expert Group on AI (HLEGAI). (2019). *Ethics guidelines for trustworthy artificial intelligence*. European Commission.

Hong, W., & Thong, J. Y. L. (2013). Internet privacy concerns: An integrated conceptualization and four empirical studies. *Management Information Systems Quarterly*, *37*(1), 275–298. DOI: 10.25300/MISQ/2013/37.1.12

Hwang, Y., Ryu, J. Y., & Jeong, S. H. (2021). Effects of disinformation using deepfake: The protective effect of media literacy education. *Cyberpsychology, Behavior, and Social Networking*, *24*(3), 188–193. DOI: 10.1089/cyber.2020.0174 PMID: 33646021

Jacobsen, B. N., & Simpson, J. (2023). The tensions of deepfakes. *Information Communication and Society*, *27*(6), 1095–1109. DOI: 10.1080/1369118X.2023.2234980

Karaboga, M. (2023). Die Regulierung von Deepfakes auf EU-Ebene: *Überblick eines Flickenteppichs und Einordnung des Digital Services Act- und KI-Regulierungsvorschlags*. In Jaki, S., & Steiger, S. (Eds.), *Digitale Hate Speech: Interdisziplinäre Perspektiven auf Erkennung, Beschreibung und Regulation* (pp. 197–220). Springer. DOI: 10.1007/978-3-662-65964-9_10

Kaur, A., Hoshyar, A. N., Saikrishna, V., Firmin, S., & Xia, F. (2024). Deepfake video detection: Challenges and opportunities. *Artificial Intelligence Review*, *57*(6), 1–47. DOI: 10.1007/s10462-024-10810-6

Langa, J. (2021). Deepfakes, real consequences: Crafting legislation to combat threats posed by deepfakes. *Boston University Law Review. Boston University. School of Law*, *101*, 761.

Li, M., & Wan, Y. (2023). Norms or fun? The influence of ethical concerns and perceived enjoyment on the regulation of deepfake information. *Internet Research*, *33*(5), 1750–1773. DOI: 10.1108/INTR-07-2022-0561

Liv, N., & Greenbaum, D. (2020). Deepfakes and memory malleability: False memories in the service of fake news. *AJOB Neuroscience*, *11*(2), 96–104. DOI: 10.1080/21507740.2020.1740351 PMID: 32228386

Lundberg, E., & Mozelius, P. (2025). The potential effects of deepfakes on news media and entertainment. *AI & Society*, *40*(4), 2159–2170. DOI: 10.1007/s00146-024-02072-1

Momeni, M. (2024). Artificial Intelligence and Political Deepfakes: Shaping Citizen Perceptions Through Misinformation. *Journal of Creative Communications*, *20*(1), 41–56. DOI: 10.1177/09732586241277335

Murillo-Ligorred, V., Ramos-Vallecillo, N., Covaleda, I., & Fayos, L. (2023). Knowledge, Integration and Scope of Deepfakes in Arts Education: The Development of Critical Thinking in Postgraduate Students in Primary Education and Master's Degree in Secondary Education. *Education Sciences*, *13*(11), 1073. DOI: 10.3390/educsci13111073

Murphy, G., Ching, D., Twomey, J., & Linehan, C. (2023). Face/Off: Changing the face of movies with deepfakes. *PLoS One*, *18*(7), e0287503. DOI: 10.1371/journal.pone.0287503 PMID: 37410765

Mustak, M., Salminen, J., Mäntymäki, M., Rahman, A., & Dwivedi, Y. K. (2023). Deepfakes: Deceptions, mitigations, and opportunities. *Journal of Business Research*, *154*, 2023. DOI: 10.1016/j.jbusres.2022.113368

Nash, R. A., & Wade, K. A. (2009). Innocent but proven guilty: Eliciting internalized false confessions using doctored-video evidence. *Applied Cognitive Psychology*, *23*(5), 624–637. DOI: 10.1002/acp.1500

Patil, U., & Chouragade, P. (2021). Deepfake video authentication based on blockchain. In *IEEE Second International Conference on Electronics and Sustainable Communication Systems (ICESC)* (pp. 1110–1113). Coimbatore, India.

Pavis, M. (2021). Rebalancing our regulatory response to Deepfakes with performers' rights. *Convergence (London)*, *27*(4), 974–998. DOI: 10.1177/13548565211033418

Pawelec, M. (2022). Deepfakes and democracy (theory): How synthetic audio-visual media for disinformation and hate speech threaten core democratic functions. *Digital Society : Ethics, Socio-Legal and Governance of Digital Technology*, *1*(2), 19. DOI: 10.1007/s44206-022-00010-6 PMID: 36097613

Pramod, D., Patil, K. P., & Bharathi, S. V. (2025). Is it really unreal? A two-theory approach on the impact of deepfakes technology on the protection motivation of consumers. *Cogent Business & Management*, *12*(1), 2461239. Advance online publication. DOI: 10.1080/23311975.2025.2461239

Rana, M. S., Nobi, M. N., Murali, B., & Sung, A. H. (2022). Deepfake detection: A systematic literature review. *IEEE Access : Practical Innovations, Open Solutions*, *10*, 25494–25513. DOI: 10.1109/ACCESS.2022.3154404

Reddy Sure, T. A. (2023). Ethical implications of deepfake technology in user interfaces. *International Journal of Computers and Technology*, *10*(2).

Romero Moreno, F. (2024). Generative AI and deepfakes: A human rights approach to tackling harmful content. *International Review of Law Computers & Technology*, *38*(3), 1–30. DOI: 10.1080/13600869.2024.2324540

Sisman, B., Yamagishi, J., King, S., & Li, H. (2021). An overview of voice conversion and its challenges: From statistical modeling to deep learning. *IEEE/ACM Transactions on Audio, Speech, and Language Processing*, *29*, 132–157. DOI: 10.1109/TASLP.2020.3038524

Thaware, N., & Agnihotri, N. (2018). AI gone rogue: Exterminating deep fakes before they cause menace. *Blackhat. com/eu-18/Thu-Dec-6/eu-18 Disponible en.*

The Telegraph. (2020) Doctor Audio Evidence used to damn Father in Custody Battle. In: The Telegraph Newspaper. https://www.telegraph.co.uk/news/2020/01/31/deepfake-audio-used-custody-battle-lawyer-reveals-doctored-evidence/. Accessed 14 July 2024

Vaccari, C., & Chadwick, A. (2020). Deepfakes and disinformation: Exploring the impact of synthetic political video on deception, uncertainty, and trust in news. *Social Media + Society*, *6*(1), 1–13. DOI: 10.1177/2056305120903408

van der Sloot, B., Wagensveld, Y., & Koops, B. J. (2021). *Summary Deepfakes: The legal challenges of a synthetic society. In the Tilburg Institute for Law, Technology, and Society*. Tilburg University.

Vecchietti, G., Liyanaarachchi, G., & Viglia, G. (2025). Managing deepfakes with artificial intelligence: Introducing the business privacy calculus. *Journal of Business Research*, *186*, 115010. DOI: 10.1016/j.jbusres.2024.115010

Wazid, M., Mishra, A. K., Mohd, N., & Das, A. K. (2024). A secure deepfake mitigation framework: Architecture, issues, challenges, and societal impact. *Cyber Security and Applications, 2.*

Weikmann, T., Greber, H., & Nikolaou, A. (2024). After deception: How falling for a deepfake affects the way we see, hear, and experience media. *The International Journal of Press/Politics.*

York, C., Ponder, J. D., Humphries, Z., Goodall, C., Beam, M., & Winters, C. (2020). Effects of fact-checking political misinformation on perceptual accuracy and epistemic political efficacy. *Journalism & Mass Communication Quarterly*, *97*(4), 958–980. DOI: 10.1177/1077699019890119

Zhang, L., Qiao, T., Xu, M., Zheng, N., & Xie, S. (2023). Unsupervised learning-based framework for deepfake video detection. *IEEE Transactions on Multimedia*, *25*, 4785–4799. DOI: 10.1109/TMM.2022.3182509

Chapter 10
Artificial Intelligence, Digital Media, and the Future of Journalism

Faik Tanrikulu
https://orcid.org/0000-0002-0654-3140
Political Science and Public Administration, Turkey

ABSTRACT

AI-powered digital media tools have emerged as indicators of a new era, particularly in the field of journalism. As the ways in which information is produced, disseminated and verified continue to evolve, the function, responsibility and ethical boundaries of journalism in democratic societies have become subjects of renewed debate. This study aims to examine the societal impacts of the accelerated digitalization process in the post-COVID-19 era, with a specific focus on how AI and emerging media technologies are shaping the future of journalism. The rise of algorithmically generated news, personalized information flows, and automated editorial decisions has accelerated the transformation of traditional journalism into a hybrid model. Drawing on theoretical insights from Zuboff, Castells, and McLuhan, this study examines how AI challenges the public responsibility of journalism, particularly in the aftermath of the COVID-19 pandemic. It argues that the future of journalism depends on a delicate balance between technological innovation and ethical accountability.

INTRODUCTION

Since the early 21st century, rapid developments in communication technologies have brought a new dimension to both social life and public services. As a result of these technological advancements, social habits, ways of accessing information,

DOI: 10.4018/979-8-3373-2960-4.ch010

and news channels have changed significantly. Throughout history, the interaction between technology and social events has played an important role in triggering social change. Although social transformations cannot be reduced to a single factor, the influence of technological innovations has been both evident and transformative. During the COVID-19 pandemic, lockdown measures forced individuals and institutions to turn to internet-based digital services to maintain communication, social interaction, and professional responsibilities. As a result, practices such as online meetings, remote working models, and digital education systems became part of the so-called new normal. Office work shifted to home environments, and hybrid or remote working models gained traction, laying the foundation for long-term changes in work culture.

Digital transformation has led to comprehensive changes in many areas, from daily routines to professional skills. Before the pandemic, the use of digital tools was mostly limited to certain age and socioeconomic groups. However, during the pandemic, the range of users and fields of use expanded significantly. Extended periods of isolation increased the time spent on digital devices, and many activities including access to education, healthcare, social interaction, and public services moved to digital platforms. The global process of digitalization has also caused structural transformations in the fields of media and journalism. Traditional media institutions have been forced to adapt to new technologies. Especially in the first quarter of the 21st century, digital transformation has created significant changes in every stage of news production, distribution, consumption, and analysis. Artificial intelligence (AI), algorithms, and big data technologies have become key components of news production, rather than being just tools.

AI systems are actively used in news writing, headline generation, content personalization, audience segmentation, and even fake news detection. (Marconi, 2020). Marconi argues that the rise of algorithmically generated content, data-driven news production, and automation is reshaping the field of journalism. According to him, the source of news is no longer limited to the reporter alone but also includes lines of code and datasets. These technologies enable media organizations to accelerate content production while also developing more targeted publishing strategies based on reader behavior. However, with the integration of AI-supported algorithms, the traditional journalism model based on the "human touch" in news production has undergone a significant transformation. Journalism has evolved from merely transmitting information to becoming a content architecture grounded in data analytics and algorithmic processes. In this context, the digital media environment redefines classical journalism norms through parameters such as speed, accessibility, personalization, and data orientation. Fundamental principles of journalism, such as objectivity, editorial independence, and public interest, have been reopened for discussion in light of the dynamics of digitalization. With the increasing use of AI-based applications, issues such as ethical responsibility, algorithmic transparency, and the fight against disinformation have become key priorities in contemporary media studies.

THE TRANSFORMATION OF MASS COMMUNICATION IN HISTORICAL CONTEXT: FROM THE INDUSTRIAL REVOLUTION TO DIGITAL MEDIA

With the invention of key technologies such as James Watt's double-acting steam engines and mechanical looms, profound transformations occurred in various fields including agriculture, production, transportation, and mining. These developments also had a deep impact on societal habits and ways of life. The production model based on natural resources gave way to a machine-based production process. Accompanied by the Scientific Renaissance that began in Europe, technological, communicational, and scientific innovations accelerated across all fields. In particular, the invention of the telegraph in the mid-19th century is considered a turning point in the history of communication. Thanks to this innovation, the time required for long-distance communication was significantly reduced, and communication across geographic boundaries increasingly relied on the telegraph. Thompson (Thompson, 2008)., It is argued that the telegraph initiated the process of transforming local markets into a single, larger market. According to this view, the establishment of submarine cable networks in the late 19th century marked the beginning of a de facto global communication network. Although this communication infrastructure was initially developed for military purposes, it gradually became an indispensable tool for social and economic activities as well. The historical trajectory of social and political developments has directly influenced the evolution of communication technologies and paved the way for the emergence of new communication platforms. In particular, the global upheavals experienced in the first half of the 20th century, most notably the Great Depression of 1929 and the Second World War, led to increased interest in communication tools. During this period, print media played a leading role in informing and guiding public opinion, resulting in a significant rise in newspaper readership. For instance, between 1920 and 1950, the number of newspaper readers in the United States nearly doubled. It is reported that during this period, there were approximately 300 to 350 newspapers for every 100 people. Similarly, in European countries such as Austria and the United Kingdom, there was also a marked interest in print media. These figures indicate that the political and economic climate of the time heightened the public's need for access to information and shaped media consumption habits (Hobsbawm, 2006). One of the alternative ways of receiving news during this period was through short news films shown in cinemas. These films were widely used in the 1920s and 1930s to reach large audiences and inform the public. However, with the advancement of communication technologies, this method was gradually replaced by radio broadcasting. In the 1930s in particular, radio broadcasts in public spaces within Japanese-occupied territories were used as an effective tool of propaganda, a practice that continued until the end of World War II. By the early 21st century, radio had become a widely used means of communication by individuals, states, and political actors. Nevertheless, due to its high cost and technical challenges, radio usage during this period remained largely limited to developed countries. Despite this, the capacity of radio broadcasts to reach wider audiences compared to cinema and print media made it one of the most influential mass communication tools of the time. Indeed, advertising and political propaganda efforts that had previously been conducted through cinema and newspapers gradually shifted to radio, which assumed a central role in shaping public opinion. (Hobsbawm, 2006). Giddens states that during the periods when radio and television were dominant, societies could be more easily directed, and public information was systematically disseminated through these mass communication tools. In this context, it is known that mass communication played a significant role during the dissolution of the Soviet Union. Although Eastern European countries under the Soviet regime attempted to block access to Western radio and television broadcasts, these efforts were largely unsuccessful. The alternative flow of information and ideas from the West gradually contributed to shaping public opinion and strengthening dissident discourse. As a result of these developments, street protests became widespread, and with the influence of mass communication tools, social opposition to the regime became more visible. For this reason, the anti-regime movements that took place in Eastern Europe in 1989 are frequently referred to in the literature as "television revolutions." (Giddens, 2000). Until the 1980s, a large portion of television broadcasts in the United States was carried out under state supervision, and content was generally determined by bureaucratic structures. Through these broadcasts produced by central authorities, it became possible to deliver messages to millions of viewers simultaneously. Castells, in his assessment of this situation, notes that with the eventual emergence of private television channels, communication platforms began to diversify. However, he emphasizes that for a long time, state-controlled broadcasts maintained a dominant position in the media landscape (Castells, 2005).

Giddens states that the processes transforming individuals' lifestyles have progressed in parallel with technological developments. In particular, the global spread of the internet has led to the gradual decline of traditional mass communication tools such as radio and television, giving way to digital platforms. These developments mark the beginning of a new era of communication. Indeed, with the discovery and rapid expansion of the internet in the 1990s, a new period referred to as the "information age" began. During this process, information ceased to be monopolized by a specific class and became accessible to all segments of society. (Giddens, 2000). This evolutionary process entered an entirely new phase in the early 21st century with the rise of artificial intelligence-powered digital platforms. Journalism is no longer limited to news produced solely by humans; algorithms, big data, and AI systems now play an active role in the creation, distribution, and delivery of news content to target audiences. (Carlson, 2015). Journalism is no longer limited to news produced solely by humans; algorithms, big data, and AI systems now play an active role in the creation, distribution, and delivery of news content to target audiences. This development has not only transformed the content production processes in journalism but has also reopened discussions about core principles such as ethics, accuracy, credibility, and editorial oversight. This new practice, known as automated journalism, brings significant transformations in terms of the objectivity of news, the reliability of sources, and the relationship established with readers. The integration of data-driven algorithms into editorial decision-making processes influences not only the format but also the content of news, necessitating a redefinition of traditional journalism norms in the digital age (Diakopoulos, 2019).

THEORETICAL BACKGROUND: AUTONOMY AND AUTOMATION IN THE MEDIA ECOSYSTEM

Understanding the rise of AI-assisted journalism requires addressing today's media ecosystem not only from a technological perspective but also within a sociological and philosophical framework. In this context, the media is not merely a channel for conveying news; it has become an institutional domain that shapes the structural forms of information production, redefines political power relations, and transforms societal perception. The media ecosystem represents a multi-layered structure that extends beyond traditional print outlets: conventional media organizations, social media platforms, data providers, algorithms, content creators, and users all constitute its components. The ecosystem approach allows for an analysis of the interaction and transformation among these elements. In this context, McLuhan's thesis that "the medium is the extension of man" becomes particularly relevant (McLuhan, 1964).

To understand the transformative impact of AI on media production processes, Manuel Castells' concept of the "network society" (2000) is particularly illuminating. According to Castells, information and power no longer stem from centralized structures but emerge from decentralized digital networks. Network society does not represent a communication model based on a single center of dissemination; instead, it embodies a flexible, dynamic, and complex structure shaped through the interactions between nodes. Within this structure, algorithms act as "actors" in their own right. In this context, AI is not merely a tool for selecting content it functions as a digital gatekeeper that determines which content becomes visible, who gains access to what, and what is considered "important." Algorithmic gatekeeping is replacing traditional editorial decisions, ushering in an era of "autonomous automation" in the media. In this context, decision-making processes are no longer solely based on the ethical standards and newsworthiness criteria of human editors but are increasingly shaped by data-driven models such as click-through rates, reading time, and engagement scores. This shift contributes to the commodification of media content and places the economic attention at the core of contemporary journalism (Zuboff, 2019). The presence of AI in the media field also necessitates a reconsideration of the concepts of "autonomy" and "independence." What is at stake is not only technological autonomy but also an epistemological rupture. The nature of content, how it is produced, and the way it is presented are no longer solely the result of human judgment. AI-powered systems increasingly make decisions about when, where, and under what headline a news story will be published, based on data analytics.

Gilles Deleuze's (1992) concept of the "society of control" provides a critical lens through which to understand this process. According to Deleuze, modern surveillance is no longer enforced through fixed boundaries such as prisons or schools, but rather through continuous data production and monitoring. Today's media algorithms perform similar functions by constantly analyzing viewer behavior, click patterns, and modes of engagement, thereby enabling predictability and behavioral steering. As a result, media content not only serves to provide information but also becomes a structure that shapes user behavior, filters social reality, and potentially fuels societal polarization .Automation in journalism does not merely imply the mechanization of content production; it also signals a transformation in which algorithms gain editorial authority. Carlson (2015) describes this phenomenon as "robot journalism redefining authority." In traditional journalism, editorial control rested with human agents, but with artificial intelligence, that authority has become distributed, encoded, and commercialized. The media ecosystem is being reshaped in the digital age along the axes of automation and autonomy. AI is not just a technical innovation; it is a force that transforms the societal regime of knowledge and redefines epistemic authority. This transformation must be evaluated not only in terms of efficiency and speed but also through the lenses of ethics, transparency, and democratic balance.

CONTENT PRODUCTION WITH ARTIFICIAL INTELLIGENCE: THE LIMITS OF AUTOMATION

The integration of AI technologies into content production processes has brought about a profound paradigm shift in the fields of media and communication. This new mode of production, often referred to as "automated journalism" or "robot journalism," enables the creation of text, visual, audio, and video content with minimal or no human intervention. However, this technological advancement also introduces both ethical and structural limitations. Therefore, to fully grasp AI-supported content production, it is essential to consider not only its technical achievements but also the cognitive, ethical, and societal boundaries of these systems. One of the earliest applications of AI-based content production in media was Associated Press's use of Narrative Science's Quill software in 2014 to automate sports and financial news (Carlson, 2015). Today, generative AI systems such as GPT models, DALL·E, and Midjourney are being used not only for text generation but also for producing artwork, audio, scripts, news bulletins, and even music. These developments are transforming the media production process in ways that both complement and, at times, substitute for human labor (Diakopoulos, 2019). The main advantages of AI in content creation include speed, scalability, and data-driven personalization. For example, a news agency can generate different versions of the same story tailored to various geographic, demographic, or political preferences within seconds. This capability has given rise to a model of "hyper-personalized journalism" (Thurman et al., 2019). AI systems rely heavily on statistical prediction and language modeling in content production. As a result, the content they generate can face limitations in terms of semantic coherence, contextual accuracy, and creative originality (Floridi & Chiriatti, 2020). Particularly in topics requiring political, cultural, or ethical sensitivity, AI may fail to interpret context appropriately, thereby jeopardizing content quality and reliability. Moreover, the tendency of AI systems to generate false or fabricated information referred to as "hallucination"poses a serious issue for news accuracy (Maynez et al., 2020). Another key limitation of automation lies in its inability to sufficiently replicate the human elements of journalism, such as narrative construction and interpretative analysis.

ETHICAL ISSUES IN AI-DRIVEN CONTENT PRODUCTION

Ethical issues in AI-driven content production are multidimensional. One primary concern is the question of authorship whether the creator is a machine or a human—which blurs the boundaries of ethical responsibility. Furthermore, risks related to copyright infringement, plagiarism, data manipulation, and disinformation have significantly increased in AI-mediated media (Zuboff, 2019). The European Commission's proposed AI Act (2021) identifies media and news production as high-risk areas and emphasizes the principle of transparency. Principles requiring that the role of AI in automated content be explicitly disclosed are included in both the European Commission's framework and UNESCO's *Recommendation on the*

Ethics of AI(UNESCO, 2021). According to these guidelines, informing users that content has been generated by AI is a democratic ethical obligation in journalism. In this context, a prominent emerging trend is the adoption of hybrid content production models rather than fully automated systems. In these models, human journalists use data analysis, linguistic suggestions, and content drafts provided by AI to produce the final text (Graefe, 2016). This not only enhances the efficiency of the production process but also preserves the interpretative and creative role of journalism. For instance, *The Washington Post* has used its AI system Heliograf to generate real-time, data-driven reports on events such as the Olympics and elections, while leaving commentary and analysis to human journalists (Latar, 2018). Such systems integrate AI's generative capabilities with the contextual and supervisory roles of human journalism.

While the capabilities of AI in content production are promising, they are equally fraught with risk. Automation accelerates and diversifies content generation, but essential journalistic values such as meaning, context, and ethical oversight still require human intervention. The future media landscape should not only be shaped by technological superiority but also grounded in ethical accountability, the principle of accuracy, and the power of creative interpretation.

DISINFORMATION AND ARTIFICIAL REALITIES: A NEW GENERATION THREAT

In the digital age, the processes of producing, circulating, and verifying information have undergone a profound transformation through AI-powered systems. One of the most critical outcomes of this transformation is the emergence of disinformation, the deliberate creation of misleading content which can now be generated not only by humans but also by automated systems. As AI's capabilities in generating text, audio, and visual content continue to grow, the speed and persuasiveness of fake content increase, blurring the boundaries between reality and fiction. AI's role in producing disinformation is not only technical; it also has deep political implications. Especially during periods of critical democratic legitimacy such as election processes AI-generated content has the potential to influence public opinion. For instance, during the 2024 U.S. Presidential election, fake audio recordings of Joe Biden and Donald Trump, generated using AI, reached millions of users on social media. These recordings portrayed the candidates saying things they had never said, aiming to manipulate voter behavior. Following a strong public reaction, the election commission questioned the authenticity of such content and implemented a new regulation mandating clear labeling of AI-generated materials (Thompson, 2024). This example demonstrates how AI can impact not only individual perception but also collective decision-making mechanisms. AI's ability to produce content through natural language processing (NLP), deep learning, and generative adversarial networks (GANs) enables the automation of disinformation across a wide spectrum from fake news to manipulative videos (West, 2019). Systems like OpenAI's GPT models or Meta's LLaMA models can generate highly convincing but unfounded content, which can be used for political manipulation, economic speculation, and beyond (Weidinger et al., 2021). One of the most dangerous forms of such content is deepfake technology. Deepfakes enable the synthetic reproduction of a person's image or voice in a different context or entirely fabricated scenario. With this technology, it has become remarkably easy to produce fake videos involving politicians, journalists, or public figures. Deepfake technology can be used without individuals' consent to discredit them and has increasingly become a tool that threatens election processes, public trust, and social stability (Chesney & Citron, 2019).

The impact of disinformation is not only technical but also deeply psychological and sociopolitical. People construct their "sense of reality" through the information they are continually exposed to. In this regard, Jean Baudrillard's concept of "hyperreality" is highly relevant. According to Baudrillard, media produces such intense simulations that they begin to replace reality eventually blurring the distinction between what is real and what is a simulation (Baudrillard, 1994). Today, AI-generated content similarly creates hyperrealities, crafting digital parallel worlds that manipulate public perceptions of reality. The main engine driving the spread of these artificial realities is social media algorithms. Platforms such as Facebook, X, YouTube, and TikTok operate on algorithmic models that tailor content based on user interest. As a result, sensational and emotionally charged fake content often spreads faster than factual information (Vosoughi, Roy & Aral, 2018). This system not only makes disinformation possible but structurally incentivizes it. These developments raise serious concerns in terms of journalism and media ethics. While traditional journalism is based on principles such as accuracy, objectivity, and source verification, AI-driven disinformation content follows a logic of production that disregards these norms entirely. Furthermore, many users lack the critical skills to question the source of the news, which contributes to the rapid normalization of fake content within society. The global effects of disinformation are becoming increasingly pronounced. During the 2020 U.S. presidential election, the Brexit process, and the COVID-19 pandemic, the spread of false information not only influenced individual behavior but also shaped societal polarization, election outcomes, and public health policies. International organizations have begun to recognize the scale of this threat and are developing legal, technical, and ethical frameworks in response. The European Commission's "Code of Practice on Disinformation" emphasizes the need for platforms to be more transparent and accountable in combating AI-driven disinformation (European Commission, 2022).In this context, solutions must go beyond just technological filtering systems. They must also involve enhancing digital media literacy, designing ethical algorithms, and strengthening legal regulations through multi-layered interventions. Otherwise, rather than empowering the information society, digital technologies risk becoming tools of manipulation in a post-truth order built on engineered realities.

JOURNALISTIC ETHICS AND ARTIFICIAL INTELLIGENCE: NEW NORMS AND LEGAL FRAMEWORK

The integration of AI into journalism is transforming the entire structural framework from the way news is produced and distributed to content verification and professional responsibilities. This transformation is not only technological but also ethical and legal, necessitating a redefinition of the universal values of the journalistic profession. With the use of AI in news processes, the human-centered structure of professional norms has given way to new debates, such as the oversight of algorithmic production methods and the determination of accountability (Diakopoulos, 2019).

The use of AI in content production necessitates a reexamination of core journalistic ethics principles such as accuracy, transparency, public interest, and accountability. Automated content generation systems can produce news stories without human intervention, recommend content based on users' behavioral data, and even influence public discourse through social media algorithms. This increasingly complicates the evaluation of content from an ethical perspective and raises uncertainties about how fundamental journalistic values like "accuracy" should be defined in the context of AI systems (Marconi, 2020). This emerging practice in journalism is often referred to as algorithmic journalism. While it accelerates content creation and optimizes resource use, it also introduces ethical grey areas due to the shift of professional responsibilities to non-human systems. In particular, the lack of transparency in many algorithmic decision-making processes, known as black-box systems, contributes to the spread of embedded biases in content recommendation and ranking mechanisms (Pasquale, 2015). In parallel with these developments, the European Commission's AI Act, drafted in 2021 and expected to enter into force in 2025, outlines legal norms for the use of AI systems in media and information environments. According to the regulation, AI-based tools for content creation and recommendation that fall under the high-risk systems category must comply with principles of transparency, traceability, and human oversight (European Commission, 2024). Specifically in the media domain, it is required that AI-generated content be clearly disclosed to users, with mandatory labels indicating machine-generated content. This regulation aims to ensure both ethical accountability and the user's right to informed awareness. AI-assisted journalism practices are also producing numerous situations that may conflict with legal frameworks. For instance, in the case of a news article containing false information generated by AI, the question of legal liability remains unresolved. Is the developer of the algorithm responsible, the media organization deploying the system, or the publisher that disseminated the content without verification? Existing legal frameworks often fall short in addressing such scenarios, prompting many countries to review and update their media law regulations accordingly (Gillespie, 2018).

The integration of AI technologies into journalism is bringing about profound changes in the processes of content creation, distribution, and verification. However, instead of fully automating the profession, these technological advancements highlight a hybrid journalism model that merges the creative, ethical, and contextual strengths of human journalists with the technical capabilities of AI (Marconi, 2020). This emerging model aims to combine AI's ability to process data and generate content with interpretive insight, investigative rigor, and public interest consciousness of human journalists.

The fundamental principles of traditional journalism such as accuracy, transparency, and public accountability are increasingly being shaped by algorithmic structures in the digital media environment. Particularly, the personalized algorithms of social media platforms tend to deliver content based on users' interests, which often diminishes the visibility of content with high public value (Helberger, 2019). Secondly, media organizations must institutionalize the principles of algorithmic transparency and neutrality as part of their corporate policies. Transparent explanations should be provided regarding how news recommendation systems, content-ranking algorithms, and user data analytics operate. Such disclosures will allow users to critically evaluate media content (Pasquale, 2015).

Thirdly, the function of public service broadcasting must be redefined. In the digital age, public broadcasting should not be confined to radio and television but must also extend to social media, digital platforms, and data journalism. In this regard, public content production that is not bound by algorithms and that prioritizes diversity, and informational equity should be supported (UNESCO, 2021). The calls made by the European Broadcasting Union (EBU) in this direction highlight the need to reposition public service broadcasting within the digital environment (Ebu, 2023). Finally, the establishment of independent AI ethics committees is recommended. These committees should be responsible for auditing the AI systems used in the media sector, monitoring the compliance of content with ethical principles, and mitigating algorithmic biases. These bodies should include not only technical experts but also ethicists, and their oversight functions over platforms should be integrated into a democratic accountability mechanism (Floridi et al., 2018).The hybrid journalism model enables a vision of journalism in which technology and human ethical judgment can coexist. For this vision to become institutionalized, professional training, media policies, and public media literacy must all be transformed. Otherwise, the opportunities offered by AI may evolve into serious threats to media ethics.

AI AND THE DISRUPTION OF JOURNALISM: CHALLENGES OF TRUTH, TRUST, AND TECHNOLOGY

The intersection of AI and digital media has led to profound changes in journalism, transforming not only how news is produced and disseminated but also how it is consumed, verified, and monetized. The COVID-19 pandemic accelerated the widespread adoption of digital technologies in everyday life, and the media sector was significantly influenced by this digital wave. In this new media ecosystem, algorithms, machine learning, and data analytics have become not just complementary tools, but core components of journalistic processes (Carlson, 2015). As of today, many news organizations use AI-powered tools in areas such as automated journalism, fake news detection, personalized news feeds, and multimedia content creation. Media outlets such as The Washington Post, Reuters, and Bloomberg have developed systems like Heliograf and Cyborg to produce real-time, data-driven content with minimal human intervention (Marconi, 2020). While these developments increase speed and efficiency in content production, they also raise new concerns about accuracy, ethical responsibility, and the role of human journalists. Furthermore, the use of AI in audience analytics enables media platforms to better understand their target demographics, allowing for the delivery of personalized content. However, although these practices enhance user experience, they can also lead to issues such as "filter bubbles" and "echo chambers," ultimately weakening the shared public sphere (Pariser, 2011). As journalism becomes increasingly dependent on AI, issues such as algorithmic accountability and editorial autonomy gain greater significance. Unregulated algorithms can reproduce biases, suppress minority voices, or amplify specific ideologies. Therefore, it is crucial that the algorithms used in news production are designed in accordance with ethical standards, ensuring transparency and openness to human oversight (Zuboff, 2019). Journalism education is also being reshaped by this transformation. Data literacy, algorithmic accountability, and interdisciplinary skills are now among the essential qualifications for the next generation of journalists. The journalist of the future must be capable of combining storytelling skills with the effective use of technological tools (Schiffrin, 2021).

CONCLUSION

Technological developments categorized under "new media" such as the internet, social media, and AI have led to significant changes and transformations in our lives. From shopping habits to payment methods, from education to the business world and working conditions, profound changes have pushed people into this process either voluntarily or involuntarily. Throughout history, societies have often been hesitant in the face of innovation and have experienced difficulties in adoption. Especially the widespread use of mass media tools has created concerns in some societies about losing their traditions. Therefore, many initially resisted adapting to these changes. Although the spread of innovations varied by region, it generally took time. It is known that it took 38 years for radio broadcasts and 13 years for television to become widespread worldwide. However, the internet became widespread in a much shorter time, and its broad adoption is assumed to have taken only 4 years. Until now, governments were primarily interested in knowing what you clicked on when you touched your smartphone or connected to a website. However, with the pandemic, the focus began to shift. After this process, governments now want to know your body temperature and even the blood pressure beneath your skin. Although governments initially showed a tendency to impose restrictions or limitations, over time especially in free societies they began to demonstrate a willingness to use these tools effectively. Decision-makers and governments are striving to manage this crisis. Authorities are required not only to manage public health systems but also to govern matters related to the economy, politics, and digitalization. With the increased use of smartphones across different age groups beyond just computers, the masses have started to spend a large part of their day on the internet. Traditional media tools such as printed publications and television channels are witnessing a decline in viewership, while societies are increasingly following news streams via social media. Parallel to these developments, social issues have also been affected. In the 21st century, particularly in the context of global events, digital media platforms have played an active role throughout these processes.

Beyond computers, the increasing use of smartphones across different age groups has led people to spend a significant portion of their day online. Traditional media tools such as print publications and television channels are witnessing a relative decline in viewership, while societies increasingly follow news streams through social media. In parallel with these developments, societal issues have also been affected. In the 21st century, particularly when global events are analyzed, digital media platforms have played an active role throughout these processes.

AI is transforming 21st-century journalism not only at a formal level but also normatively and structurally. This transformation reshapes all processes from production to the dissemination, verification, and interpretation of news. Automated content generation, personalized news feeds, algorithmic editorial decisions, and deep learning-based analysis techniques have turned the media environment into a space capable of producing at unprecedented speed and scale. However, when this technological transformation strays from journalism's core function of serving the public interest, the resulting media order can be neither democratic nor trustworthy.

The algorithmizing of information production often does not facilitate public access to truth but instead confines users to specific tendencies, epistemically isolating individuals through digital echo chambers and filter bubbles (Pariser, 2011; Sunstein, 2017). This not only threatens individual knowledge acquisition but also undermines social consensus and the foundations of public debate. Journalism, however, must be built on the principles of transparency, accountability, and plurality—values indispensable for the functioning of democracy (Schudson, 2008). In this context, the understanding of journalism in the digital age should see AI not merely as a technical tool but should build upon a normative framework that evaluates ultimate responsibility on the basis of ethics, human rights, and information justice. Expanding the technological capabilities of journalism should not replace its public function; rather, it should be reinforced with structures that strengthen that function. The transparency, auditability, and accountability of AI-based systems are prerequisites for a trustworthy media ecosystem (Floridi et al., 2018). Therefore, the future of journalism must evolve in a hybrid structure where the critical thinking, ethical responsibility, and contextual interpretation of human journalists are balanced with the data-processing and content-creation capabilities of AI. In this hybrid model, the goal should not only be efficiency or speed but ensuring equitable, trustworthy, and multi-dimensional access to information for society. In particular, public broadcasting should offer content produced with a sense of public responsibility, free from commercial pressures and algorithmic manipulation; and digital media literacy programs should be expanded to strengthen the public's critical awareness. AI-driven digitalization is fundamentally transforming both the production techniques and ethical responsibilities of journalism. In this context, the key question that must be addressed is: How can journalism's public responsibility be preserved in the age of artificial intelligence? Journalism must be reconstructed not only through the lens of speed and efficiency brought by technological innovations but also in accordance with principles of ethics, social legitimacy, and democratic oversight. In this regard, the algorithms used in media organizations must be transparent and subject to regular audits. These technological systems, which directly affect the public's right to information, should be reviewed periodically by independent committees for ethical compliance. Furthermore, national level legal frameworks must be established regarding the use of AI in journalism, and these frameworks should align with international ethical standards. To encourage public interest content production, digital media initiatives that operate within ethical boundaries should be supported through public funding and incentive programs. To cultivate a critically aware public, digital media literacy education should be expanded particularly among younger generations to raise awareness about the influence of algorithms. At the same time, it must be recognized that no automated system can replace human judgment and ethical responsibility in journalism. Therefore, hybrid and supervised models—where AI collaborates with human journalists should be promoted.

In conclusion, the restructuring of journalism in the age of AI is not merely a technical necessity but an ethical and societal obligation. Accuracy of information, preservation of meaning, and prioritization of public interest must be considered non-negotiable principles in shaping the future media landscape. Otherwise, we risk facing a media environment where the volume of content increases, but trust declines and meaning is lost.

REFERENCES

Baudrillard, J. (1994). *Simulacra and simulation*. University of Michigan Press.

Carlson, M. (2015). The robotic reporter: Automated journalism and the redefinition of labor, compositional forms, and journalistic authority. *Digital Journalism (Abingdon, England)*, *3*(3), 416–431. DOI: 10.1080/21670811.2014.976412

Castells, M. (2000). *The rise of the network society* (2nd ed.). Blackwell.

Castells, M. (2005). *Enformasyon çağı: Ekonomi, toplum ve kültür – Ağ toplumunun yükselişi*. İstanbul Bilgi Üniversitesi Yayınları.

Chesney, R., & Citron, D. (2019). Deep fakes: A looming challenge for privacy, democracy, and national security. *SSRN*, *107*(6), 1753–1819. DOI: 10.2139/ssrn.3213954

Deleuze, G. (1992). Postscript on the societies of control. *October*, 59, 3–7.

Diakopoulos, N. (2019). *Automating the news: How algorithms are rewriting the media*. Harvard University Press. DOI: 10.4159/9780674239302

European Broadcasting Union (EBU). (2023). *Public service media in the age of artificial intelligence*. https://www.ebu.ch/publications

European Commission. (2022). *Code of practice on disinformation*. https://digital-strategy.ec.europa.eu/en/policies/code-practice-disinformation

European Commission. (2024). *Proposal for a regulation of the European Parliament and of the Council laying down harmonised rules on AI(AIAct)*. Brussels: European Commission. https://digital-strategy.ec.europa.eu/en/policies/european-approach-artificial-intelligence

Floridi, L., & Chiriatti, M. (2020). GPT-3: Its nature, scope, limits, and consequences. *Philosophy & Technology*, *33*(4), 669–678. DOI: 10.1007/s13347-020-00473-1

Floridi, L., Cowls, J., Beltrametti, M., Chatila, R., Chazerand, P., Dignum, V., Luetge, C., Madelin, R., Pagallo, U., Rossi, F., Schafer, B., Valcke, P., & Vayena, E. (2018). AI4People—An ethical framework for a good AI society: Opportunities, risks, principles, and recommendations. *Minds and Machines*, *28*(4), 689–707. DOI: 10.1007/s11023-018-9482-5 PMID: 30930541

Giddens, A. (2000). *Sosyoloji*. Phoenix Yayınevi.

Gillespie, T. (2018). *Custodians of the internet: Platforms, content moderation, and the hidden decisions that shape social media*. Yale University Press.

Graefe, A. (2016). *Guide to automated journalism*. Columbia University Tow Center for Digital Journalism.

Helberger, N. (2019). On the democratic role of news recommenders. *Digital Journalism (Abingdon, England)*, *7*(8), 993–1012. DOI: 10.1080/21670811.2019.1623700

Hobsbawm, E. (2006). *Kısa 20. yüzyıl: Aşırılıklar çağı, 1914–1991* (Çev. Yavuz Alogan). İstanbul: Everest Yayınları.

Latar, N. L. (2018). AI in journalism: AIand the reshaping of news publishing. In Latar, N. L. (Ed.), *The robot journalism* (pp. 65–86). Springer. DOI: 10.1142/10913

Marconi, F. (2020). *Newsmakers: AIand the future of journalism*. Columbia University Press. DOI: 10.7312/marc19136

Maynez, J., Narayan, S., Bohnet, B., & McDonald, R. (2020). On faithfulness and factuality in abstractive summarization. In *Proceedings of the 58th Annual Meeting of the Association for Computational Linguistics* (pp. 1906–1919). DOI: 10.18653/v1/2020.acl-main.173

McLuhan, M. (1964). *Understanding media: The extensions of man*. McGraw-Hill.

Pariser, E. (2011). *The filter bubble: What the internet is hiding from you*. Penguin Press.

Pasquale, F. (2015). *The black box society: The secret algorithms that control money and information*. Harvard University Press. DOI: 10.4159/harvard.9780674736061

Schiffrin, A. (2021). AI, automation, and the future of journalism: Report. *Center for International Media Assistance*. https://www.cima.ned.org/

Schudson, M. (2008). *Why democracies need an unlovable press*. Polity Press.

Sunstein, C. R. (2017). *Republic: Divided democracy in the age of social media*. Princeton University Press. DOI: 10.1515/9781400884711

Thompson, J. B. (2008). *İletişimin küreselleşmesi*. Phoenix Yayınları.

Thompson, S. A. (2024, September 17). *California passes election 'deepfake' laws, forcing social media companies to take action*. The New York Times. https://www.nytimes.com/2024/09/17/technology/california-deepfakes-law-social-media-newsom.html

UNESCO. (2021). *Recommendation on the ethics of artificial intelligence*. https://unesdoc.unesco.org/ark:/48223/pf0000379939

Vosoughi, S., Roy, D., & Aral, S. (2018). The spread of true and false news online. *Science*, *359*(6380), 1146–1151. DOI: 10.1126/science.aap9559 PMID: 29590045

Weidinger, L., Mellor, J., Rauh, M., Griffin, C., & Uesato, J. (2021). Ethical and social risks of harm from language models. *arXiv preprint*. https://arxiv.org/abs/2112.04359

West, D. M. (2019). *The future of work: Robots, AI, and automation*. Brookings Institution Press.

Zuboff, S. (2019). *The age of surveillance capitalism: The fight for a human future at the new frontier of power*. PublicAffairs.

Chapter 11

Exploring Transparency in Data Journalism in the United Kingdom Through Ethical Tensions, Practical Challenges, and Organizational Influences

Sana Ali

https://orcid.org/0000-0003-3474-000X

Birmingham City University, UK & Allama Iqbal Open University, Pakistan

ABSTRACT

Transparency is one of the primary ethical practices in journalism. From traditional to modern journalism, maintaining transparency is a core consideration for journalists to sustain objectivity and audience trust as a social responsibility of journalism. This study also explores the transparency practices among data journalists in the United Kingdom (UK) under the social responsibility theory. Data acquired from data journalists indicated that UK-based data journalists recognize transparency as crucial, aiming to disclose methods, sources, and processes despite challenges like time constraints, data privacy, and audience engagement. Organizational support for transparency remained prominent but also emphasized a need for clear policies and better resources. Participants recommended ongoing professional development and training in data handling, visualization tools, and ethical practices to improve the credibility and transparency of the news reports. Participants also emphasized working collaboratively to enhance the transparency and credibility of the final news product.

DOI: 10.4018/979-8-3373-2960-4.ch011

1. INTRODUCTION

Transparency in journalism, where news media organizations openly share how news is created, has been a crucial topic of debate among researchers and key stakeholders (Uth et al., 2021). Especially, the rise of digital journalism has further highlighted transparency as a crisis journalistic practice. The fast-paced approach of digital publishing usually leads to accuracy concerns, emphasizing the need for transparency. Besides, digital platforms enable strong public attention and scrutiny, further providing ample space for explaining editorial decisions, public engagement, and corrections (Prochazka & Obermaier, 2022). The rise of digital journalism has further amplified the notion of transparency obligating news media organizations to share how news story is created openly. According to Prochazka and Obermaier (2022), transparency has become a core principle in ethical and professional standards. For academics, transparency works as a means to counteract growing skepticism about today's news media and rebuild public trust. The general public also considers transparency as a critical factor in sustaining trust in news media organizations. Notably, today, journalism practices use computational tools and machine learning to collect, verify, and produce news, extending the capacities of traditional reporting. While ethical principles, i.e., accuracy, fairness, and transparency, are emphasized, ensuring high-quality data is critical, as errors in datasets can compromise automated reporting. Combining ethical journalism with data-centric AI practices helps maintain accountability and reliability in news production. News media also shape public understanding of data-driven technologies by covering both opportunities and risks. Stories about innovations (Kevin-Alerechi et al., 2025) inform audiences, while reporting on scandals like Cambridge Analytica or algorithmic bias (Piasecki et al., 2024) highlights threats to privacy, fairness, and inclusion (Dierickx et al., 2024). Through such coverage, data journalism fosters public trust, promotes scrutiny of algorithmic systems, and supports the democratic mission of the press (Verma, 2024).

The narrative around the purpose of transparency in journalism is based on certain assumptions and expectations that further scrutiny. One key assumption is that enhancing journalism practices can positively affect public trust. By altering the way news reports are created and represented, perceived public attitudes can change since behaviors impact trust (Uth et al., 2021). Another assertion is that both journalistic transparency and the public are uniform concepts, leading to predictions that transparency as a single idea can improve public trust and reliability in journalism. An alternative theoretical perspective indicates that different types of transparency may have different effects on different people. Evidence from relevant fields, such as transparency in political journalism, implies that views on transparency are diverse. Besides, existing research on news media shows that different demographic factors, i.e., age, gender, race, education, and media consumption patterns, shape perceptions about news media (Magaña & Perdomo, 2024).

The notion of transparency as a pathway to enhance journalism and form a robust relationship with the public has been a core consideration for journalists and news media organizations (Zamith, 2019a). Talking especially about digital journalism practices today, data journalism is one of the leading journalistic practices, focusing on transparency as "openness" of data (Parasie, 2019b). A rapid yet subtle shift from traditional to modern journalism further liberated professional practices to the concept of "open journalism." Consequently, today, data journalists not just consider readers as passive consumers of information but rather as active producers and contributors (Gehrke, 2024). This indicates the role and effect of data journalists in providing transparent and open resources and platforms for public participation and engagement. Considering the current attitudes and practices regarding transparency in data journalism (Ramsälv et al., 2024), current research focuses on exploring data journalists' perceptions of transparency in their everyday professional practices. The primary focus is on analyzing the participants' basic perceptions about transparency in journalism, particularly data journalism. Second, the aim is also to probe about approaches to ensure transparency and the potential challenges they confront. Finally, potential external and internal factors affecting transparency practices are explored. Thus, this study addresses the following questions.

Q1. How do data journalists describe transparency, and what specific steps do they take to ensure it in their reporting practices?
RQ2. How do data journalists communicate their data sources and approaches to their audience, and what challenges do they face in maintaining transparency?
RQ3. How do organizational factors influence data journalists' ability to practice transparency?

1.1 Conceptualizing Social Responsibility in Data Journalism

Considering the current research, social responsibility theory is an important theoretical framework for examining transparency among data journalists in the United Kingdom. It is assumed that the theory is strongly relevant to data journalism practices, as it shapes public discourse through visualization and data analysis techniques (Loosen et al., 2020). Transparency is considered an integral aspect of data journalism practices to fulfill the social responsibility of media (Merwe, 2022). By sharing open and accessible data sources, approaches, and possible biases, data journalists improve the trustworthiness and credibility of their work. The theory highlights that media should not only provide truthful and accurate information but also explain from what sources this information is obtained (Tsukamoto, 2006).

This idea is consistent with the principles of transparency and accountability, where data journalists reveal their decisions and procedures, enabling the public to comprehend and analyze the information presented. As the selected theory also supports the media 's role in shaping and encouraging public discourse and understanding, transparency in data journalism remains consistent by making large and complex data understandable to the public (Phillips, 2010). It is asserted that when data journalists are transparent about their sources and approaches, they not only educate their audiences but also invite their participation in journalism practices. This interactive relationship between the public and journalists can lead to a more subtle public discourse consistent with the core propositions of the social responsibility theory (Craft & Vos, 2021). Accordingly, Appelgren et al. (2019) stated that data has brought both disruptive changes and promise transformations to societies, leading to complicating the relationship between transparency and accountability. Although data journalism is practiced along with the contradictory rules of data protection and privacy, it is assumed that the rules of transparency are indispensable to follow in data journalism.

Consequently, Zamith (2019) argued that journalism has radically transformed in the past twenty years, especially openness, indicating the availability of data for public consideration. One of the basic reasons behind disruption in classic journalism is the generalization of citizen journalism. This change in perceptions and practices led to the development of a unique journalism paradigm that exceeds the notions that all facts of newsrooms are restricted to journalists only. For example, the emergence of crowdsourcing as an open call for users to partake in several online activities, including gathering information, also indicates the transparency and active engagement of the audience in journalism practices (Aitamurto, 2016). Data journalism emerged unevenly both within and across different media systems, indicating news media organizations may not consent to offer the required resources concerning money and time to develop sufficient data literacy or sustain a specialized team. It implies that openness and transparency in data journalism rely on both journalists and their organizations, suggesting that the social responsibility of the press is an equal responsibility for journalists and their organizations (Porlezza & Splendor, 2019).

To further investigate the transparency in data journalism practices, (Arias-Robles & López López, 2021) conducted a study on Spanish news media. Data gathered from 62 qualitative and quantitative content news articles revealed the infrequent and unusual use of elements, i.e., the possibility of data download and explanation of the research process. However, a greater consideration of transparency was found in small, specialized news projects and native online media. However, along with certain exceptions, an overall reluctance of some media organizations to execute transparency practices was found in the relevant study. Finally, a strong effect of

COVID-19 is found on these practices, implying a crucial transformation of data journalism and a greater emphasis on transparency. In their study, (Kashyap et al., 2020) also examined the perceptions of Indian journalists regarding interactivity and transparency in their data journalism practices. Data were collected by conducting qualitative interviews and content analysis to examine transparency practices in the relevant news stories. Results show that data journalists in India greatly acknowledge the significance of interactivity and transparency in their practices. However, they adopt a cautious approach to using them. These results show a contradiction between the data journalists and traditional journalists in the same media organizations.

1.2 Transparency, Audience Perception, and Emerging Technologies in Data Journalism

Data journalism has increasingly shaped news production since the late 2000s, as journalists use databases, algorithms, and computational tools to collect, analyze, and present information (Coddington, 2015; Parasie, 2019a). This approach allows newsrooms to produce not only conventional articles but also interactive visualizations and applications, making news processes more structured and data-driven. By integrating digital technologies, journalists aim to reduce reliance on traditional sources and enhance objectivity, with the promise of more robust and accountable reporting. Researchers argue that data journalism can address challenges, including reduced investigative resources, declining public trust, and financial pressures on news organizations, while simultaneously increasing the scope and reach of reporting (Chang, 2010). However, these promises are contingent on how newsrooms adopt computational methods, as technology alone does not guarantee transparency (Anderson, 2014).

Emerging research highlights the centrality of transparency in building audience trust, particularly when using data visualizations (Engebretsen et al., 2018). Transparency in this context goes beyond simply presenting data; it involves communicating the underlying processes, i.e., data sourcing, cleaning, assumptions, and analytical methods, many of which are not directly visible to audiences. Being explicit about these processes helps to reinforce credibility in an environment where trust in media is increasingly fragile. Kennedy et al. (year) note that even though audiences may not always perceive these transparency practices, they play a crucial role in fostering engagement and confidence in journalistic outputs. This aligns with broader arguments that participatory openness and clarity in methodology are essential for enhancing audience understanding and trust (Coddington, 2018).

The adoption of computational tools has also led to a reconfiguration of newsroom labor, with journalists collaborating more closely with programmers, data scientists, and other technical professionals (Gillespie, Boczkowski & Foot, 2014; Lewis &

Usher, 2014). While these collaborations enable the production of more rigorous and reproducible investigations, they also raise questions regarding algorithmic accountability, professional norms, and the balance of editorial control (Kashyap et al., 2020; Parasie, 2019). In addition, journalists must navigate ethical and practical challenges, such as managing privacy concerns, interpreting complex datasets for audiences with varying data literacy, and addressing potential misuse of data (Denis & Goëta, 2017). The effective practice of transparency requires not only technical competence but also careful attention to audience engagement, ethical responsibility, and organizational policies that support openness without compromising privacy or journalistic integrity (Lewis, 2015).

1.3 Impact of Journalistic Transparency on Democratic Process

Journalistic transparency plays a critical role in promoting democratic accountability by enabling citizens to monitor government actions and hold elected officials responsible. In representative democracies, decision-making is delegated from voters (principals) to elected officials (agents), who are expected to act in the public interest. However, hidden actions and information asymmetries create opportunities for agents to pursue agendas that may diverge from those of the principals (Bowles & David, 2013). Open government data and freedom of information policies, as transparency mechanisms, help reduce these asymmetries by making governmental decisions and processes more observable, thereby lowering the transaction costs for both journalists and citizens who seek to monitor public officials (Garland, 2015) Journalism organizations serve as intermediaries in this process, translating complex government data into accessible information for the public. Investigative journalism, through systematic research and exposure of wrongdoing, strengthens the accountability function by uncovering corruption, policy failures, or systemic inequities that might otherwise remain hidden (Houston, 2009). Journalists increase the responsiveness of agents to the preferences and interests of principals by reporting these findings, strengthening democratic oversight. The transparency of journalistic processes further reinforces trust, as audiences are better able to evaluate the credibility of the information provided (Engebretsen et al., 2018).

The digital era has both amplified and complicated this dynamic. Access to digital government datasets, coupled with computational tools and data visualization techniques, allows journalists to scrutinize vast quantities of information efficiently and present findings in ways that are more understandable for the public (Bowles & David, 2013; Engebretsen & Kennedy, 2025). However, challenges persist: declining traditional revenue models have limited the resources available for investigative reporting, while algorithmically-driven platforms can fragment audiences and amplify misinformation, potentially undermining public trust (Bowles et al., 2025). Despite these challenges, transparency in journalistic practices remains essential not only as an instrumental good, improving monitoring and accountability, but also as an intrinsic good, reflecting citizens' fundamental right to know how public power is exercised (Hollyer, 2011).

2. RESEARCH METHODOLOGY

2.1 Research Design

This research employed a qualitative design. Data are gathered by conducting online, face-to-face, semi-structured interviews. The relevant design focuses on asking questions based on "Why" and "How," lacking a linear nature like quantitative design. One notable strength of the qualitative design is its capability to explain patterns and processes of human behavior that can be hard to quantify (Akinyode & Khan, 2018). Further, data is gathered by conducting online, face-to-face interviews and emailing interview questionnaires to some of the participants (due to time restrictions and unavailability. Each online interview took approximately 25 to 35 minutes. According to Adams and Cox (2008), semi-structured interviews are used as interviewing formats both with an individual or with a group of participants. Thus, before conducting the interviews, the researcher informed the participants about the research process and aims. Also, the interviewees were asked to introduce themselves. Once the initial phase of interviews was performed, the researcher asked each question one by one. Notably, each question was based on further root questions to ensure that responses were enriched and provided in-depth insights. The interviews were recorded using Zoom and Microsoft Teams applications. The researcher also took notes of the responses in a notebook for further analysis. As data is gathered by employing a semi-structured interview comprised of some open-ended questions, a formal interview questionnaire was designed, based on a total of six root questions consistent with each research question (Table 1).

Table 1. Data gathering instrument

Main questions	Root Questions
RQ1. How do data journalist perceive transparency in their professional work?	How do you describe transparency in the context of your work as a data journalist?
RQ2. How do data journalists practice in their professional work?	What specific steps do you take to ensure transparency in your reporting practices?
	How do you communicate your data sources and methodologies to your audience?

continued on following page

Table 1. Continued

Main questions	Root Questions
RQ3. What are the factors affecting transparency in data journalism practices?	What challenges do you face when trying to maintain transparency in your work?
	How do organizational policies influence your ability to practice transparency?
	Being a data journalist, what do you recommend or suggest to improve transparency in daily journalism practices?

2.2 Population and Sampling

The population of current research involves data journalists in the United Kingdom. Further, this study applies a convenience sampling approach for the data gathering. It is notable that despite the convenience sampling has received much criticism due to a chance of researchers' own bias in sample selection, it is considered one of the most preferred approaches in social sciences research (Emerson, 2015). Furthermore, considering the current evidence on the suitable sample size in qualitative studies, this research selected a sample size of 5 data journalists for data-gathering purposes consistent with the study (Bekele & Ago, 2022). According to Hu and Chang (2017), a sample size of 10 to 50 participants can be considered suitable for a qualitative study. While Bekele and Ago (2022) argued that a sample size of 5 to 25 interviews can be suitable for a qualitative study. Accordingly, Mocăna u (2020) argued that there is no consensus on the exact sample size, further indicating the abundance of data as a main factor in determining the sample size in qualitative research. This research is conducted from June 2024 to August 2024, while data is gathered from July 2024 to March 2025.

2.3 Data Analysis Methods

This research included thematic analysis as suggested by Braun and Clarke (2006), considering thematic analysis as a foundational approach in qualitative analysis. The researcher followed a step-by-step process to conduct the relevant analysis (Braun & Clarke, 2006). First, the researcher followed data familiarization by reading and re-reading the gathered data. However, the second step, "transcription of data," was skipped as the researcher had already noted down all the responses during the interview process. In the third step, the researcher generated initial codes by assigning numerical codes to each response. After assigning initial codes, the researcher re-read the whole data to identify themes. Once themes were identified, the researcher reviewed the themes, matching them with the rough data. Further, each theme was given a name/title based on the determined dominant answers. Finally, all the themes with the responses are reported after identifying the themes and coding them as C1, C2, and C3.

2.4 Research Ethics

Some primary ethics are also obligated in current research. For example, it is ensured that all study participants provide their informed consent to participate in the current research. Also, the researcher ensured them their responses would be used solely for the current research, and she would refrain from sharing them with anyone, especially for commercial purposes. Another important consideration is confidentiality and anonymity. All the participants are ensured that their basic identity will be kept confidential, and results will be represented without mentioning their names. Finally, this research is ethically approved by ----------, United Kingdom.

3. ANALYSIS AND RESULTS

This section represents data analysis and results. First, participants' demographics are briefly explained. Then, thematic analysis results are reported in detail, accompanied by their relevance to the current literature.

3.1 Participants' Demographics

Table 1 summarizes the details of each participant along with their gender, age, qualification, work experience (in years), and organization. However, keeping the primary ethics under consideration, the names of the participants are not revealed. Rather, codes are assigned to each participant, i.e., P1, P2, P3, etc., to ensure that their identity is not disclosed. Table 2 provides the demographics of study participants.

Table 2. Study participants' details

Codes	Age	Qualification	Location	Work Experience	Organization Name
P1	49	MPhil	Birmingham	28 years	British Broadcasting Corporation
P2	33	Masters	London	More than 5 years	Financial Times
P3	37	Masters	Birmingham	4 years	British Broadcasting Corporation, Google News

continued on following page

Table 2. Continued

Codes	Age	Qualification	Location	Work Experience	Organization Name
P4	28	Masters	London	1.5 years	Guardian
P5	27	Masters	Birmingham	3 years	The Asterisk

3.2 Themes and Coding Process

Table 3 represents the themes generated from the gathered data. Further, codes are assigned during data analysis to identify the responses relevant to each theme. Notably, data indicated 2-3 themes related to each questionnaire item relevant to the participants' responses.

Table 3. Root questions (questionnaire items), themes, and codes

Serial #	Root Questions	Themes	Codes
1.	How do you describe transparency in the context of your work as a data journalist?	Open-source culture and methodology sharing	C1
		Clarity and trust building with the audience	C2
2.	What specific steps do you take to ensure transparency in your reporting practices?	Open sharing of data, methodologies, and tools.	C1
		Addressing limitations and encouraging critical engagement	C2
3.	How do you communicate your data sources and methodologies to your audience?	Providing detailed annotations and direct links to data sources and methodologies	C1
		Engaging the audience and addressing literacy challenges	C2
4.	What challenges do you face when trying to maintain transparency in your work?	Technical challenges and time constraints	C1
		Challenges related to privacy	C2
5.	How do organizational policies influence your ability to practice transparency?	Supportive or neutral organizational policies	C1
		Organizational policies as barriers to transparency	C2
6.	Being a data journalist, what do you recommend or suggest to improve transparency in daily journalism practices?	Establish clear policies and encourage a culture of transparency	C1
		Improve practical tools and practices for transparency	C2

3.3 Results

This section discusses the gathered data and results. The responses are quotes that highlight the participants' opinions precisely.

Question 1. How Do You Describe Transparency in the Context of Your Work as a Data Journalist?

The first root question explored the participants' general perceptions of transparency in their daily professional practice. Notably, this question aimed to analyze their own opinions that may affect or shape their transparency practices. The relevant question further led to the generalization of three primary themes: open-source culture and methodology sharing, clarity and trust building with the audience, and citing sources and ethical considerations. According to Koliska (2021), professional journalists aim to ensure transparency as much as they can. Their primary aim is to reform this field from top to bottom. These efforts have also encouraged newsrooms to talk about transparency in diverse journalism traditions, leading the journalists to practice it in their everyday tasks and responsibilities.

Theme 1. Open-Source Culture and Methodology Sharing

According to Porlezza and Splendor (2019), the evolution of journalism led to the rise of an early version of "open journalism." This model relies on collective participation and sharing acknowledgment, proposing public and journalists actively engage with one another. Despite this mainstream notion, journalism remained reluctant, and participatory journalism remained practiced only in ways that supported traditional journalism practices. Comparing data journalism with modern practices, the first theme focused on the notion that transparency in data journalism is rooted in the open-source culture, where sharing data, tools, and methodology openly is critical. For example, participant 4 from the Guardian argued that:

"Well, for the transparency, I have some personal rules, and my organization also provides a code of ethics. Especially, my organization usually obligates us to mention the methodology in the article. For example, regarding an article on riots, we wrote. The Guardian has scrutinized data that provides insights into the lives of those accused of taking part in the unrest. Using court filings, we have tracked the cases of almost 500 alleged rioters and cross-referenced their details with other publicly available data". This is the best way. At least I consider it quite useful, ensuring transparency".

Participant 3 of the study further added that.

"Transparency is considered as simply talking about your practice. Bare minimum, we can provide a link to the source and use code on GitHub to share and

ensure transparency. We often provide details of the methodology we use, provide notebooks and other relevant things".

Theme 2. Clarity and Trust Building With the Audience

Curry and Stroud (2021) further investigated the relationship between journalistic transparency and the perceived credibility of news organizations in the United States. Experimental findings revealed that when news consumers are given more information, i.e., the reasoning behind a story, production details, and journalists' background, credibility perceptions and engagement with the news increase, leading to greater trust in news organizations.

The second theme acquired from the first question revolved around making the journalistic process clearer to the audience to build trust and demonstrate the work's credibility. According to Participant 1, working at BBC Birmingham as a senior data journalist,

"In the context of my work, transparency is about making it as easy and clear as possible for audiences. Of my work to understand how I arrived at the facts that I'm presenting to them. So, in a data journalism story, how did I arrive at the figures in that story? What data did I use? First of all, what calculations did I perform on that? What actions did I perform with that, and also, were there any checks that I made regarding contacting experts or conducting interviews? It helps the audience understand the process behind my journalism, which allows them to arrive at a judgment in terms of its quality, trustworthiness, accuracy, and objectivity."

As noted by Bloebaum (2017, p. 22), similar to other social institutions, journalism depends much on public trust. However, it is distinguished in the aspect that it is accountable for fostering in itself, but in other sectors of society as a whole. Building credibility for itself and other institutions is a critical responsibility of today's journalism. Indeed, journalists are accountable for behaving in a way that audiences' trust in journalism practices is not compromised (p.31). Thus, participant 5, on the other hand, emphasized the importance of transparency in addressing skepticism and building trust with the audience. As opined,

"Since I run my own publication, I have made sure that transparency is one of the pillars of my work. The audience should also have access to sources (exceptions: anonymity, protection) to have the ability to verify further any information that I have published and make up their minds.

Question 2. What specific steps do you take to ensure transparency in your reporting practices?

Analyzing the data gathered as a result of the second root question generated two primary themes, indicating the participants' own methods of transparency in their everyday professional practices. These themes involved open sharing of data, methodologies, and tools, Addressing limitations, and encouraging critical engagement.

Theme 1. Open Sharing of Data, Methodologies, and Tools.

According to Rodrigues (2023, p. 2), the rise of open data movement and increasing trend of datafication in society have developed transparency portals in different countries. These developments are closely associated with the data-driven culture shaping the practice of Open Data Journalism (ODL). Popular investigations, including Panama Papers and WikiLeaks, provided access to vast amounts of open data and played a critical role in strengthening this journalistic approach to promote a collaborative and transparent journalistic model. Consistent with the relevant argumentation, the first theme of the second root question highlighted the use of platforms and practices that may facilitate the open sharing of data, methodologies, and codes to ensure transparency in their professional practices. Participants indicated different methods to ensure transparency, preferring platforms like GitHub and sharing URLs. For example, participant 2 revealed that.

> *"Uhhhh..... well, the biggest is that I maintain a GitHub account. I'm and get Hope is a website that makes it easy for programmers mainly to share code. So, I use that, too. For every story I work on or every story that the data team works on, some aren't necessarily stories. Still, I've worked on each of our stories; I will create a GitHub repository, and in that repository, I will put any data sets we've used. Such as Python scripts, which we've used, and the spreadsheets that will include analysis. It is the only analysis that we've done. So, are there any FOI requests we've written, as well as a description of the methodology? Is there any material to help people understand and recreate what we have done? In the same way, in science, you want other researchers to be able to recreate what you have done and arrive at the same results. The GitHub report is intended to tell the story behind the story. That's one thing I do, and other things that I do include blogging about my work. I might write blog posts explaining how and why I took specific steps on a story I will use. I used to use Twitter quite a lot to do this. I use LinkedIn and other social media platforms to do it. Yes, it may, and often news. And let us engage in communities of practice and talk with other journalists about what we have done.*

Consistent with Participant 1, Participant 2, who works as a data journalist in the Financial Times, UK, further added that.

"As I mentioned earlier, URLs, sources, and sharing GitHub codes all fall under what I practice as transparency in my journalistic practices. For larger datasets, I normally create a box containing all the data, sources, article copies, and others for the readers. My purpose is to provide direct details of what procedures and sources are used and how they are employed to create a story."

Theme 2. Addressing Limitations and Encouraging Critical Engagement

The second theme generated from the second route questions focused on discussing uncertainties, assumptions, and limitations in data reporting to set realistic expectations for the audience and encourage critical engagement with the content. Study participants emphasized addressing the concerns regarding clarity of this story and accurate data interpretation. Accordingly, participant 5 argued that.

"To ensure transparency in my reporting practices, I focus on the collaborative aspect of discussing uncertainties and limitations of the sources I use. When the uncertainties are significant, I acknowledge that they may hinder the clarity of the story. However, when these challenges are worth tackling, I openly address them, helping to set realistic expectations for what the data can and cannot show. This approach ensures that my audience is fully aware of the strengths and limitations of the data, fostering trust and transparency in my reporting."

Appelgren (2018), on the other hand, links this transparency to newsroom culture, where data sharing is prevalent with peers, leading to the consideration of audience engagement as an equally critical factor. In line with Appelgren's argument (2018), participant 4 mentioned their organization as an influential factor in providing access to their potential audience.

"Usually, as I mentioned earlier, my organization ensures that we explain the methodology used in an article and will always state the sources of data. Stating data sources is the main thing here. Readers can access and make sure that it is accurate and reliable."

Question 3. How do You Communicate Your Data Sources and Methodologies To Your Audience?

Based on the third research question about communicating data sources and methodologies to audiences, two themes were generated. These themes mainly involved providing detailed annotations and direct links to data sources and methodologies, engaging the audience, and addressing literacy challenges.

Theme 1. Providing Detailed Annotations and Direct Links to Data Sources and Methodologies

The first team focuses on communicating data sources and methodologies by providing detailed notes, direct links, footnotes, and other in-depth explanations to make the data and methods accessible to the audiences. For example, Participant 3 argued that.

"I think one of the better ways is to provide footnotes, explaining difficult terms in a simple manner, and telling how datasets are used and calculations are made. In my opinion, methodology boxes are important elements to provide all the details about the data for the audience to understand and interpret accordingly."

Participant 5 further backed Participant 4's responses by arguing that.

"I explicitly state the source with a link or simply hyperlink words that direct the audience to the source. As for methodologies, either include them in a paragraph of a story or the form of notes in the case of a data visualization. This is, at least, what I do to ensure that my audience knows about the data and methodology I have used in my news reports."

Theme 2. Engaging the Audience and Addressing Literacy Challenges

The second team revolved around actively engaging with the audience to make complex data more understandable and handling challenges related to the audience's changing levels of data literacy. Accordingly, a study by Martin et al. (2024) in the United States indicated several strategies used by data journalists to uphold audience engagement in journalism. From crowdsourcing to other different approaches, i.e., interactivity, data disclosure, and news sharing, journalists indicated a strong emphasis on audience engagement. The current study also participants emphasized audience engagement from the lens of the audience's understanding as the central factor to be taken into consideration while providing details about data sources, methodologies, and other information. According to Participant 4, a data journalist currently working with Publicis Groupe, revealed that.

Participant 4, a journalist from the Guardian, further added that.

"Despite, methodology and data sources might not always be mentioned, it depends on the scope of the article. It is important that readers can see the methodology if they wish to check themselves. If they have doubts about the methodology and the findings they can contact us. It increases trust in the reporting. Our audience is aware of the data and sources to evaluate them, if needed, carefully.

Participant 2 further emphasized addressing the challenge of audience literacy by recognizing that not all people can understand complex data formats like Python scripts or spreadsheets. The journalist communicates methodologies and data on different platforms, understanding that this serves a niche audience. Besides, they provide information that includes full codes, tables, charts, and methodological descriptions to make the data more accessible to their audience. The relevant participant also discussed the challenges of possible data misuse and the need to be cautious about how much information to disclose to avoid reinforcing biases. As argued.

"So, first of all, there is always a challenge regarding audience literacy. So, the vast majority of your audience will not be able to understand Python, Think, or even spreadsheets? When I put stuff on GitHub, I am conscious that the audience is relatively small. What's important is that I am opening myself up, you know. I am making myself vulnerable to a certain extent. I am giving away a little bit of power, which changes the power relationship to an extent, and there is only so much of it. You can change that power relationship. In terms of the stories, generally, what the what? The data team does, so I do not do this. Someone else on the team does this, but for every story, we do a pack, and that pack is a document. It includes the full quotes from all the people that we have interviewed. It has a description of the methodology. It will have tables and charts and other such things, like a background document, and we will usually link to that at the end of the story. If you like, that is for a wider audience, and it will allow more people to read about the story behind the story. Moreover, now we did have an experience where that was misused by our, by people who wanted to misrepresent what we were doing...."

Question 4. What Challenges Do You Face When Trying to Maintain Transparency in Your Work?

The fourth root question aimed to explore the challenges participants confront when trying to maintain transparency in their professional responsibilities. Data gathered for this question helped generate two primary themes: technical challenges and time constraints and challenges related to privacy, audience engagement, data sensitivity, and others.

Theme 1. Technical Challenges and Time Constraints

The first theme highlighted challenges related to time limitations, technical barriers, professional policies, and other structural obstacles that impede the ability to maintain transparency in their daily practices. For instance, participant 4 of the study argued that.

"I think methodology can be quite complicated and technical, so it is difficult to explain in depth to readers without going off the point of the article. You have to explain it in a concise way that does not lose readers' interest. Readers are also always free to contact reporters to find out more about the methodology. If there is something they disagree with, they can write in, and it will be picked

up. Good journalism is interactive, comprising a two-way dialogue between audiences and journalists."

According to participant 1,

"One of the main obstacles to transparency in journalism is time; journalists often have to prioritize their workload, and transparency usually is not high on the list. There are also technical limitations; for example, I do not write or edit the stories, so I cannot add links or additional context. To me, time and technical limitations are preceding barriers at the moment."

Theme 2. Challenges Related to Privacy

The second theme covers challenges related to privacy concerns, appreciation of transparency efforts, audience engagement, and sensitivity of data sources. These different perspectives from the study participants provided in-depth details about the challenges hindering transparency in data journalism practices. For example, participant 2 revealed that.

"Well, sources themselves are transparent. However, sometimes, the source providers prefer to remain private. You know, sometimes, it is a matter of personal privacy and concerns for the subjects. So, this is the primary challenge and nothing else.

As noted by Martins (2014, p. 186), emerging situations that raise ethical concerns usually challenge the line between private and public spheres in journalism. Issues like family life, security, health, property, religious beliefs, political convictions, and others are deemed private and do not fall within the Publix right to know. Reporting on these issues needs strong justification and ethical compliance. Journalists should carefully evaluate whether the public's right to know outweighs the individual's right to privacy, both fundamental values in democratic societies. Accordingly, participant 5 further added that.

"Unless the information comes from a source that has requested anonymity, it is normally a straightforward process. However, I take into consideration the information that has been provided and check if it could harm either the source itself or another organization.

Participants 3 opined that,

"One of the main ways I ensure transparency in my work is by sharing sources and links where people can find more information. While I have not faced major challenges with this approach, working on sensitive topics, like a story on domestic abuse faced by men in the UK, highlighted specific difficulties. In that case, I had to be very careful with data, especially local datasets, to avoid unintentionally exposing victims through "jigsaw identification." Due to safety and safeguarding concerns, it is crucial to protect the anonymity of vulnerable

individuals, and journalists must provide a safe space for interviewees, especially when covering such delicate issues."

Question 5. How Do Organizational Policies Influence Your Ability to Practice Transparency?

The fifth root question focused on exploring the participants' opinions about potential organizational policies affecting the ability to practice transparency. The relevant question further generated two primary themes, including supportive or neutral organizational policies and organizational policies as barriers to transparency.

Theme 1. Supportive or Neutral Organizational Policies

The first theme revealed that study participants indicated that their organization does not restrict but rather encourages transparency in their journalism practices. For example, participant 4 argued that.

"Well, I believe that my organization is a very transparent entity, so I feel encouraged to practice transparency. As I mentioned earlier, we are provided with a code of ethics. They make us follow the primary rules, which is quite ethical. Besides, I also follow these rules, ensuring that we mention the sources and methods we apply while obtaining, preparing, and representing a news story.

Participant 2 further added that.

"Well, my organization is in support of transparency in our journalism practices. If being a journalist, I do not want to provide the details or copy of my dataset, it is my own choice. However, also, organizational policies are in line with the readers' interests. They are supportive and this can be seen in cases of data protection, sensitive and private data."

Theme 2. Organizational Policies and Resources as Barriers to Transparency

Theme 2 of the fifth study question indicated participants' responses indicating challenges due to organizational policies or lack of any specific policies promoting transparency. For example, Participant 2 revealed that.

"I need to find out about organizations with a proactive policy regarding transparency. I was going to say specifically in terms of things like sharing data, but actually, even basic things like linking. Some organizations must say, "You should be transparent in linking and things like that," but umm, yeah, that's it. That does make me quite curious about how proactive organizations have been. You know, I am certainly aware that many organizations have a policy of saying do not link outside of our website. So that scenario where news organizations could

be much better, especially given that audience Trust is such a big issue and, you know, news organizations are conscious. That said, the research on transparency suggests that it only sometimes improves Trust anyway. They do not have little influence on the BBC's policies, and I am not aware of anything. Apart from the fact that it is the past, I need to be made aware of any policy that specifically encourages it. So, I have had to create that space myself. An established practice and. Yeah, I mean, to an extent, the fact that the shared data unit is. A brief to serve and support local news organizations that encourages transparency in a way that does not often happen in data teams."

Participant 3, on the contrary, revealed that.

"The level of transparency a journalist can achieve often depends on the organization they work for, its policies, available resources, and the structure of the newsroom. In smaller, regional, or nonprofit newsrooms with limited budgets and small teams, often including part-time or freelance staff, everyone has to be mindful of each other's time and workload, which can limit the depth of engagement and transparency. In contrast, larger organizations like the BBC or The Guardian have more resources and dedicated roles, such as engagement editors, to interact with audiences and provide detailed responses. However, even within big organizations, not all projects get the same level of support. While these differences do not necessarily affect a journalist's ethics or commitment, they impact how much detail and interaction they can offer, finally shaping how transparent they can be in practice."

Question 6. Being a Data Journalist, What Do You Recommend or Suggest to Improve Transparency in Daily Journalism Practices?

Finally, the last study question aimed to explore and acquire practical recommendations to improve the prevalent transparency practices in current data journalism. Data collected from the relevant question further generated two prominent themes, including establishing clear policies, encouraging a culture of transparency, and improving practical tools and practices for transparency. As noted by Allen (2008), news organizations prefer ensuring transparency in their everyday practices to distinguish themselves from those disseminating misinformation and disinformation. Consequently, these organizations use different systems and approaches, especially in digital journalism practices.

Theme 1. Establish Clear Policies and Encourage a Culture of Transparency

News organisations have greatly engaged audiences through interactive web tools that present data on different issues, public safety, politics, the environment, and the economy. These platforms enable users to explore these issues in more in-depth detail. However, many news media organizations have been cautious about engaging the public in investigative journalism practices. This is partly due to the concerns of journalistic authorities and the difficulty in sustaining public engagement due to different reasons (Parasie, 2019, p. 16). The first themes generated from the gathered data indicated that study participants recommended and emphasized the need to establish clear policies and promote a culture of transparency to improve the current data journalism practices. According to participant 1,

"Organizations should encourage journalists to be transparent and provide policies about data sharing. Journalists should also make sure that their professional practices are according to the rules of transparency and ethics. Facts should be provided and followed because journalism is a responsible field and social, political, cultural, and other responsibilities should never be overlooked."

Participant 5 further suggested that.

"We should be more open in practicing transparency to ensure trust with our audience. Data journalists should make efforts to share more information about the sources and methods. They should make all the information understandable for the readers as well."

The study participants also emphasized encouraging a culture of transparency. For instance, participants underlined the role and importance of promoting a culture of transparency as an important consideration. Participant 2 argued that.

"I think having explicit policies will be relevant. Having a way of sharing data which as easy as possible. GitHub is not easy to use, and Google Sheets and Drive are also hard. Having clear workflow and framework for documenting what you are doing. Using project management tools data project management tool etc., can be used. Initially, it was more transparency because the culture of data journalists was form informalized, so data journalists did not have the job title of data journalist. Now, more people are hired as data journalists; they are more junior and less independent to be transparent and traditional, and so the culture in the early days was easy to link around many aspects. So, culturally there is much encouragement to be transparent that is not like today."

Theme 2. Improve Practical Tools and Practices for Transparency

According to Parasie and Dagiral (2013), one of the most prominent examples of transparency in data journalism is the availability of datasets to the public. These datasets are available on the database upon which the report is based, using hyperlinks or other methods. Readers can search, assess, replicate, and acquire information from the data used in the investigation. If datasets are not publicly available, this means the primary norms of journalism are violated (Porlezza & Splendor, 2019). Theme 2 also revealed that study participants emphasized more user-friendly tools for sharing data and reporting. Study participants also suggested accuracy in referencing sources, retaining transparency, and credibility in their work. For example, participant 3 argued that.

"Overall, good parameters are strongly required to ensure transparency in data journalism practices. Exemplifying my practices, data journalists should make notes of the work and save the sources, and note-keeping should be widely preferred. One more important thing is accuracy. Ensuring the accuracy of the source, and appropriately providing them is very important to improve data journalism and transparency practices.

According to participant 4,

"I've noticed that, in journalism, people sometimes gather information and then take credit for the work without properly attributing their sources. Occasionally, they claim it's to protect the anonymity or identity of the source. However, in some cases, it is more about taking credit without acknowledging who did the original work or where the information came from. I want to encourage my fellow journalists to be as transparent as possible while still safeguarding their sources and their safety. I am in touch with colleagues around the world, and I know many journalists have been threatened, injured, or even killed because of the sensitive information they handle. So yes, safety is a priority, but here, in this country, I hope to see more openness and accountability in the profession.

4. DISCUSSION

The results of this study highlighted in-depth insights into the current privacy practices of data journalists in the United Kingdom their perceptions, challenges, and recommendations about ensuring privacy in enduring data journalism practices. Focusing on transparency, as a crucial aspect, is relevant because transparency and openness are core ethical principles of the social responsibility of journalists. The results highlighted that journalists view transparency as a critical factor in their professional work, emphasizing the need to openly share data, tools, and methodologies with the audience. Consistent with the current study findings, existing research has shown open data accessibility being practised in many data journalism projects (Gehrke, 2020; Parasie, 2019; Zamith, 2019). Along with access to datasets, transparency also exists in other practices, i.e., updating and showing the publication dates, giving explanations of the reporting process, and describing the possible reporting errors. However, some studies also indicated that transparency is not very common, yet some consider them as consolidated actions (Loosen et al., 2020). The current study also indicated that reliance on platforms like GitHub is prominent, along with providing methodology noted to ensure the clarity and reproducibility of journalistic works. These findings also highlighted that transparency involves building an engaging audience and gaining their trust by clarifying the journalistic process, i.e., explaining how data are sourced and analyzed. These responses align well with the core principles of social responsibility theory, proposing educating and empowering citizens as a critical responsibility of journalism practices (Topsümer et al., 2023). The transparency practices in the current study indicate the "Participatory Openness" concept (Coddington, 2015), which may involve public participation in different parts of the journalism process. Open journalism, on the other hand, is another major approach, suggesting that journalistic procedures are more transparent (Porlezza & Splendore, 2019).

The study results also identified key barriers to transparency in data journalism, including time pressures, technical limitations, and privacy concerns. Journalists often struggle to explain complex methods clearly under tight deadlines and face editorial restrictions that hinder lining or adding context. It is further found that ethical challenges arise when reporting on sensitive topics, where protecting vulnerable sources takes precedence, needing careful anonymization to avoid harm. Accordingly, a study by Pinto (2009) further examined how Mexican news media organizations practice transparency in their journalism practices. Using an institutional perspective, data was collected from media professionals, media, and legal analysts. Findings showed that key pressures on the press coverage were political opposition on news organizations in Mexico.

Furthermore, it is found that organizational policies played mixed roles. Some journalists reported supportive environments with ethical guidelines. In contrast, others noted a lack of formal policies or restrictive practices that limit transparency, especially in under-resourced newsrooms. A study by Bhuiyan et al. (2021) further highlighted the effect of organizational policies regarding transparency practices in journalism and audience trust in the United States. Data gathered by using semi-structured interviews revealed that audiences emphasized that transparency is best demonstrated through evidence-based indicators in four key areas, i.e., the use of anonymous resources, the inclusion of source material, corrections of inaccurate reporting, and source verification approaches. While journalists agreed on the importance of evidence indicators, they also highlighted the need for additional transparency measures, including insights into the reporting process and disclosures of personal and organizational conflicts of interest. Hence, the current study participants recommended a need for clearer institutional policies, a culture of openness, and practical tools for data sharing and workflow management to improve transparency. Besides, there is an emphasis on accurate sourcing, ethical responsibility, and balancing transparency with source protection and journalists' safety.

5. IMPLICATIONS

Considering the study results, some practical implications are proposed as follows.

1. There is a need for an increased emphasis on open-source practices in data journalism. Motivating journalists to share tools, data, and methodologies can improve transparency and promote a culture of openness, accountability, and collaboration. This highlights the role of digital platforms and data management systems in supporting transparent journalistic practices.
2. Transparency in journalism is closely associated with building trust with the target audience. Journalists who are open about their methodologies, limitations, biases, and data sources can improve the credibility of their work and address audience mistrust. These implications further emphasize the significance of structured information handling and knowledge-sharing practices within media organizations.
3. Results also suggest that journalists prefer accessible and transparent communication of their data sources and methodologies. Providing links, detailed information, and explanations in understandable formats can improve the journalistic process for readers with different levels of data literacy. These practices contribute directly to knowledge dissemination and the efficient use of information systems.
4. Better tools and organizational support are needed to help journalists communicate their methodologies and data more transparently. Addressing technical, time, and organizational challenges can make transparency a more accessible goal in daily journalism practices, implying a need for integrated organizational systems and workflows that facilitate secure data sharing and methodological clarity.
5. Organizations must establish precise policies and guidelines that promote transparency. This may involve supporting journalists in their efforts to share methodologies and data, providing resources, and promoting an environment that values openness. Hence, strong data structures and clear data governance policies are critical to sustaining these transparency practices.

6. CONCLUSION

This research explored and discussed the importance of transparency as an important consideration for modern journalists. Notably, data journalism is a relatively new field that needs more in-depth analysis of its different aspects. Results highlighted their distinct understanding regarding data journalism as a core practice in modern journalism today. Study participants mutually highlighted the significance of transparency as a crucial phenomenon. The participants further indicated that they make possible efforts to ensure transparency by sharing and communicating details about the methods, sources, and other details they employ while preparing the news stories. It is also found that data privacy, audience engagement, and potential challenges regarding time restraints are some prevailing challenges participants face while maintaining transparency in their professional practices. Concerning the organizational policies, study participants revealed that their organizations are supportive of the practice of transparency, yet resources and clear policies are required. Finally, the study participants provided practical recommendations to improve the transparency practices in current data journalism practices. Overall, these results indicated transparency as a core consideration for data journalists in the United Kingdom, emphasizing the need to practice, especially under the established rules designed by respective organizations in the best possible manner.

7. LIMITATIONS

This research has primary limitations. First, this research is based on a single method (qualitative) that limits its scope. Future researchers can overcome this issue by integrating different methodologies, i.e., mixed methods. Second, this research involves journalists only from the United Kingdom, questioning the generalizability of results in other regions. More studies can replicate the current study design and approach to explore the relevant phenomenon in other regions. The third limitation involves the use of a non-probability sampling method, which may involve the researcher's bias in participants' selection. Using probability sampling approaches can delimit bias by providing equal chances of selection to the participants. Finally, the fourth limitation involves using a relatively small sample size, which is common in qualitative studies. However, despite the small sample size, this research is based on an exploratory study of transparency in data journalism that future researchers can expand.

REFERENCES

Adams, A., & Cox, A. L. (2008). Questionnaires, in-depth interviews and focus groups. In P. Cairns & A. L. Cox (Eds), *Research Methods for Human-Computer Interaction* (1st edn, pp. 17–34). Cambridge University Press. DOI: 10.1017/CBO9780511814570.003

Aitamurto, T. (2016). Crowdsourcing in Open Journalism: Benefits, challenges, and valu. In *The Routledge Companion to Digital Journalism Studies*. Routledge., https://www.taylorfrancis.com/chapters/edit/10.4324/9781315713793-19/crowdsourcing-open-journalism-tanja-aitamurto DOI: 10.4324/9781315713793-19

Akinyode, B. F., & Khan, T. H. (2018). Step by step approach for qualitative data analysis. *International Journal of Built Environment and Sustainability*, *5*(3), 3. Advance online publication. DOI: 10.11113/ijbes.v5.n3.267

Allen, D. S. (2008). *THE TROUBLE WITH TRANSPARENCY: The challenge of doing journalism ethics in a surveillance society. 9*(3). https://www.tandfonline.com/doi/abs/10.1080/14616700801997224

Anderson, T. L. (2014). *Understanding Deviance: Connecting Classical and Contemporary Perspectives*. Routledge. DOI: 10.4324/9781315879635

Appelgren, E. (2018). An Illusion of Interactivity. *Journalism Practice*, *12*(3), 308–325. DOI: 10.1080/17512786.2017.1299032

Appelgren, E., Lindén, C.-G., & van Dalen, A. (2019). Data Journalism Research: Studying a Maturing Field across Journalistic Cultures, Media Markets and Political Environments. *Digital Journalism (Abingdon, England)*, *7*(9), 1191–1199. DOI: 10.1080/21670811.2019.1685899

Arias-Robles, F., & López López, P. J. (2021). Driving the Closest Information. Local Data Journalism in the UK. *Journalism Practice*, *15*(5), 638–650. DOI: 10.1080/17512786.2020.1749109

Bekele, W. B., & Ago, F. Y. (2022). Sample Size for Interview in Qualitative Research in Social Sciences: A Guide to Novice Researchers. *Research in Educational Policy and Management*, *4*(1), 1. Advance online publication. DOI: 10.46303/repam.2022.3

Bhuiyan, M. M., Whitley, H., Horning, M., Lee, S. W., & Mitra, T. (2021). Designing Transparency Cues in Online News Platforms to Promote Trust: Journalists' & Consumers' Perspectives. *Proceedings of the ACM on Human-Computer Interaction*, *5*(CSCW2), 1–31. DOI: 10.1145/3479539

Bloebaum, B. (2017). *Trust and Journalism in a Digital Environment.* Reuters Institute for the Study of Journalism.

Bowles, N., & David, L. (2013). *Transparency in Politics and the Media.* https://www.torrossa.com/it/resources/an/5216033

Braun, V., & Clarke, V. (2006). *Using thematic analysis in psychology. 3*(2), 77–101. DOI: 10.1191/1478088706qp063oa

Chang, L. A., & Massey, B. L. (2010). Work motivation and journalists in Taiwan and the US: An integration of theory and culture. *Asian Journal of Communication, 20*(1), 51–68. https://www.tandfonline.com/doi/abs/10.1080/01292980903440814. DOI: 10.1080/01292980903440814

Coddington, M. (2015). Clarifying Journalism's Quantitative Turn. *Digital Journalism (Abingdon, England), 3*(3), 331–348. DOI: 10.1080/21670811.2014.976400

Coddington, M. (2018). In *Defining and Mapping Data Journalism and Computational Journalism | 18.* https://www.taylorfrancis.com/chapters/edit/10.4324/9781315270449-18/defining-mapping-data-journalism-computational-journalism-mark-coddington

Craft, S., & Vos, T. P. (2021). The ethics of transparency | 24. In *The Routledge Companion to Journalis.* https://www.taylorfrancis.com/chapters/edit/10.4324/9780429262708-24/ethics-transparency-stephanie-craft-tim-vos

Curry, A. L., & Stroud, N. J. (2021). The effects of journalistic transparency on credibility assessments and engagement intentions. *Journalism, 22*(4), 901–918. DOI: 10.1177/1464884919850387

Denis, J., & Goëta, S. (2017). Rawification and the careful generation of open government data. *Social Studies of Science, 47*(5), 604–629. DOI: 10.1177/0306312717712473

Dierickx, L., Opdahl, A. L., Khan, S. A., Lindén, C.-G., & Guerrero Rojas, D. C. (2024). A data-centric approach for ethical and trustworthy AI in journalism. *Ethics and Information Technology, 26*(4), 64. DOI: 10.1007/s10676-024-09801-6

Emerson, R. W. (2015). Convenience Sampling, Random Sampling, and Snowball Sampling: How Does Sampling Affect the Validity of Research? *Journal of Visual Impairment & Blindness, 109*(2), 164–168. DOI: 10.1177/0145482X1510900215

Engebretsen, M., & Kennedy, H. (2025). *Data Visualization in Society* (1st ed.). Routledge., DOI: 10.5117/9789463722902

Engebretsen, M., Kennedy, H., & Weber, W. (2018). Data Visualization in Scandinavian Newsrooms: Emerging Trends in Journalistic Visualization Practices. *Nordicom Review*, *39*(2), 3–18. DOI: 10.2478/nor-2018-0007

Garland, R. (2015). Transparency in politics and the media: Accountability and open government. *Journal of Media Practice*, *16*(1), 94–96. DOI: 10.1080/14682753.2015.1015804

Gehrke, M. (2020). *Transparency as a key element of data journalism.*

Gehrke, M. (2024). Revisiting the Origin and the Meaning of Transparency in Data Journalism | SpringerLink. In *The Palgrave Handbook of Global Digital Journalism*. Palgrave Macmillan, Cham. https://link.springer.com/chapter/10.1007/978-3-031-59379-6_24

Hollyer, J. R. (2011). *Democracy and Transparency. 73*(4). https://www.journals.uchicago.edu/doi/abs/10.1017/S0022381611000880

Houston, B. (2009). *Global Media Ethics—Google Books.* https://www.google.co.uk/books/edition/Global_Media_Ethics/sX7wUC5F-g8C?hl=en&gbpv=1&dq=transparency+in+journalism+Houston+%26+IRE,+2009.&pg=PA69&printsec=frontcover

Hu, C.-P., & Chang, Y.-Y. (2017). John W. Creswell, Research Design: Qualitative, Quantitative, and Mixed Methods Approaches. *Journal of Social and Administrative Sciences*, *4*(2), 205–207.

Kashyap, G., Bhaskaran, H., & Mishra, H. (2020). "We need to find a revenue model": Data journalists' perceptions on the challenges of practicing data journalism in India. *Observatorio (OBS*)*, *14*(2). DOI: 10.15847/obsOBS14220201552

Kevin-Alerechi, E., Abutu, I., Oladunni, O., Osanyinro, E., Ojumah, O., & Ogundele, R. (2025). AI and the Newsroom: Transforming Journalism with Intelligent Systems. *Journal of Artificial Intelligence. Machine Learning and Data Science*, *3*(1), 1629–1633. DOI: 10.51219/JAIMLD/Elfredah-Kevin-Alerechi/426

Koliska, M. (2021). Transparency in Journalism. In *Oxford Research Encyclopedia of Communication*. Oxford University Press., DOI: 10.1093/acrefore/9780190228613.013.883

Lewis, S. C. (2015). Journalism In An Era Of Big Data: Cases, concepts, and critiques. *Digital Journalism (Abingdon, England)*, *3*(3), 321–330. DOI: 10.1080/21670811.2014.976399

Loosen, W., Reimer, J., & De Silva-Schmidt, F. (2020). Data-driven reporting: An on-going (r)evolution? An analysis of projects nominated for the Data Journalism Awards 2013–2016. *Journalism, 21*(9), 1246–1263. DOI: 10.1177/1464884917735691

Magaña, M. I., & Perdomo, V. G. (2024). *Cracking the data journalism code in Latin America: Activism, transparency and democracy fuel the adoption of technology | Intellect*. https://intellectdiscover.com/content/journals/10.1386/ajms_00152_1

Martin, J. A., Camaj, L., & Lanosga, G. (2024). Audience engagement in data-driven journalism: Patterns in participatory practices across 34 countries. *Journalism, 25*(7), 1578–1596. DOI: 10.1177/14648849241230414

Martins, P. (2014). Respect for privacy begins when gathering information. *Comunicação e Sociedade, 25*, 186–201. DOI: 10.17231/comsoc.25(2014).1868

Merwe, J. V. D. (2022). *Data responsibility, corporate social responsibility, and corporate digital responsibility, 4*. https://www.cambridge.org/core/journals/data-and-policy/article/data-responsibility-corporate-social-responsibility-and-corporate-digital-responsibility/B7749EC986BFF98EF32D3192E8D4F9D7

Parasie, S. (2019a). Data journalism and the promise of transparency. In *The Routledge Companion to Media and Scandal*. Routledge., https://www.taylorfrancis.com/chapters/edit/10.4324/9781351173001-27/data-journalism-promise-transparency-sylvain-parasie?utm_source=researchgate.net&utm_medium=article DOI: 10.4324/9781351173001-27

Parasie, S. (2019b). *Data journalism and the promise of transparency | 27 | The Routledge C*. The Routledge Companion to Media and Scandal. https://www.taylorfrancis.com/chapters/edit/10.4324/9781351173001-27/data-journalism-promise-transparency-sylvain-parasie

Parasie, S., & Dagiral, E. (2013). *Data-driven journalism and the public good: "Computer-assisted-reporters" and "programmer-journalists" in Chicago. 15*(6). https://journals.sagepub.com/doi/abs/10.1177/1461444812463345

Phillips, A. (2010). Transparency And The New Ethics Of Journalism. *Journalism Practice, 4*(3), 373–382. DOI: 10.1080/17512781003642972

Piasecki, S., Morosoli, S., Helberger, N., & Naudts, L. (2024). AI-generated journalism: Do the transparency provisions in the AI Act give news readers what they hope for? *Internet Policy Review, 13*(4), 1–28. DOI: 10.14763/2024.4.1810

Pinto, J. G. (2009). *TRANSPARENCY POLICY INITIATIVES IN LATIN AMERICA: UNDERSTANDING POLICY OUTCOMES FROM AN INSTITUTIONAL PERSPECTIVE. 14*(1). https://www.tandfonline.com/doi/abs/10.1080/10811680802577665

Porlezza, C., & Splendore, S. (2019). From Open Journalism to Closed Data: Data Journalism in Italy. *Digital Journalism (Abingdon, England)*, *7*(9), 1230–1252. DOI: 10.1080/21670811.2019.1657778

Prochazka, F., & Obermaier, M. (2022). Trust through Transparency? How Jour nalistic Reactions to Media-Critical User Comments Affect Quality Perceptions and Behavior Intentions. *Digital Journalism (Abingdon, England)*, *10*(3), 452–472. DOI: 10.1080/21670811.2021.2017316

Ramsälv, A., Ekström, M., & Westlund, O. (2024). The epistemologies of data journalism. *New Media & Society*, *26*(11), 6307–6324. DOI: 10.1177/14614448221150439

Rodrigues, C. (2023). Evidence and transparency in Open Data Journalism: A case study on British and Brazilian news agencies [PDF]. DOI: 10.7275/CPO.1880

Rusu Mocăna u, D. (2020). DETERMINING THE SAMPLE SIZE IN QUALITATIVE RESEARCH. *International Multidisciplinary Scientific Conference on the Dialogue between Sciences & Arts. Religious Education (Chicago, Ill.)*, *4*(1), 181–187. DOI: 10.26520/mcdsare.2020.4.181-187

Topsümer, F., Durmuş, Y., & Yılmaz, B. A. (Eds.). (2023). *Media and Communication in the Digital Age: Changes and Dynamics*. Özgür Yayınları., DOI: 10.58830/ozgur.pub234

Tsukamoto, S. (2006). Social Responsibility Theory and the Study of Journalism Ethics in Japan. *Journal of Mass Media Ethics*, *20*(1), 55–69. Advance online publication. DOI: 10.1207/s15327728jmme2101_4

Uth, B., Badura, L., & Blöbaum, B. (2021). Perceptions of Trustworthiness and Risk: How Transparency Can Influence Trust in Journalism. In Blöbaum, B. (Ed.), *Trust and Communication: Findings and Implications of Trust Research* (pp. 61–81). Springer International Publishing., DOI: 10.1007/978-3-030-72945-5_3

Verma, D. (2024). Impact of Artificial Intelligence on Journalism: A Comprehensive Review of AI in Journalism. *Journal of Communication Management (London)*, *3*(02), 150–156. DOI: 10.58966/JCM20243212

Zamith, R. (2019a). Transparency, Interactivity, Diversity, and Information Provenance in Everyday Data Journalism. *Digital Journalism (Abingdon, England)*, *7*(4), 470–489. DOI: 10.1080/21670811.2018.1554409

Compilation of References

AA teyithattı. (2023, March 27). *"Papa Francis'in beyaz mont giydiği" iddiası*. AA Teyit Hattı: https://www.aa.com.tr/tr/teyithatti/aktuel/papa-francisin-beyaz-mont-giydigi-iddiasi-/1815693

Adams, A., & Cox, A. L. (2008). Questionnaires, in-depth interviews and focus groups. In P. Cairns & A. L. Cox (Eds), *Research Methods for Human-Computer Interaction* (1st edn, pp. 17–34). Cambridge University Press. DOI: 10.1017/CBO9780511814570.003

Adıyaman, F. (2023). Yapay Zekâ Çağında Gazetecilik ve Etik: Güncel Tartışmalar Üzerinden Bir Değerlendirme. In Kenan, A. (Ed.), *Medya ve Habercilik Alanında Yapay Zekanın Yükselişi* (pp. 29–48). Eğitim Yayınevi.

Afsar, M. M., Crump, T., & Far, B. (2022). Reinforcement learning based recommender systems: A survey. *ACM Computing Surveys*, *55*(7), 1–38. DOI: 10.1145/3543846

Aggarwal, S., Sinha, T., Kukreti, Y., & Shikhar, S. (2020). Media bias detection and bias short term impact assessment. *Array (New York, N.Y.)*, *6*, 100025. https://doi.org/https://doi.org/10.1016/j.array.2020.100025. DOI: 10.1016/j.array.2020.100025

Agner, L., Necyk, B., & Renzi, A. (2020). Recommendation systems and machine learning: Mapping the user experience. In A. Marcus & E. Rosenzweig (Eds.), *Design, user experience, and usability: Design for contemporary interactive environments* (LNCS, vol. 12201). Springer. DOI: 10.1007/978-3-030-49760-6_1

AI HLEG. (2019). Ethics guidelines for trustworthy AI. Temmuz 2025 tarihinde https://digital-strategy.ec.europa.eu/en/library/ethics-guidelines-trustworthy-ai adresinden alındı

Aitamurto, T. (2016). Crowdsourcing in Open Journalism: Benefits, challenges, and valu. In *The Routledge Companion to Digital Journalism Studies*. Routledge., https://www.taylorfrancis.com/chapters/edit/10.4324/9781315713793-19/crowdsourcing-open-journalism-tanja-aitamurto DOI: 10.4324/9781315713793-19

Akçay, E., ve Sütcü, C. (2024). Bilişimsel Propaganda Farkındalık Ölçeği ve Kamuoyu Üzerindeki Etkisi. *Türkiye İletişim Araştırmaları Dergisi* (*46*), 45-74. DOI: 10.17829/turcom.1489518

Akinyode, B. F., & Khan, T. H. (2018). Step by step approach for qualitative data analysis. *International Journal of Built Environment and Sustainability*, *5*(3), 3. Advance online publication. DOI: 10.11113/ijbes.v5.n3.267

Al-kfairy, M., Mustafa, D., Kshetri, N., Insiew, M., & Alfandi, O. (2024). Ethical challenges and solutions of generative AI: An interdisciplinary perspective. *Informatics (MDPI)*, *11*(3), 58. DOI: 10.3390/informatics11030058

Allcott, H., & Gentzkow, M. (2017). Social media and fake news in the 2016 election. *The Journal of Economic Perspectives*, *31*(2), 211–236. DOI: 10.1257/jep.31.2.211

Allen, D. S. (2008). *THE TROUBLE WITH TRANSPARENCY: The challenge of doing journalism ethics in a surveillance society*. *9*(3). https://www.tandfonline.com/doi/abs/10.1080/14616700801997224

Al-Rawi, A., O'Keefe, D., Kane, O., & Bizimana, A.-J. (2021). Twitter's Fake News Discourses Around Climate Change and Global Warming. *Frontiers in Communication*, *6*. Advance online publication. DOI: 10.3389/fcomm.2021.729818

Alsaeedi, A., & Al-Sarem, M. (2020). Detecting Rumors on Social Media Based on a CNN Deep Learning Technique. *Arabian Journal for Science and Engineering*, *45*(12), 10813–10844. DOI: 10.1007/s13369-020-04839-2

Altunbey Özbay, F., & Alataş, B. (2020). Çevrimiçi sosyal medyada sahte haber tespiti. *Dicle Üniversitesi Mühendislik Fakültesi Mühendislik Dergisi*, *11*(1), 91–103. DOI: 10.24012/dumf.629368

Amazon Web Services. (2023). Makine Öğrenimi ve Derin Öğrenme Arasındaki Fark Nedir? Şubat 2025 tarihinde https://aws.amazon.com/tr/compare/the-difference-between-machine-learning-and-deep-learning/ adresinden alındı

Amazon Web Services. (2023). Veri Bilimi ve Yapay Zeka arasındaki fark nedir? Şubat 2025 tarihinde https://aws.amazon.com/tr/compare/the-difference-between-data-science-and-ai/ adresinden alındı

Ananny, M., & Crawford, K. (2018). Seeing without knowing: Limitations of the transparency ideal and its application to algorithmic accountability. *New Media & Society*, *20*(3), 973–989. DOI: 10.1177/1461444816676645

Anderson, T. L. (2014). *Understanding Deviance: Connecting Classical and Contemporary Perspectives*. Routledge. DOI: 10.4324/9781315879635

Andrejevic, M. (2014). Big data, big questions| The big data divide. *International Journal of Communication, 8*, 1673–1689. https://ijoc.org/index.php/ijoc/article/view/2161/1163

Anjos, L. S., Quincozes, S. E., Kazienko, J. F., & Quincozes, V. E. (2023). Investigating the Performance of the GPT-3.5 Model in Fake News Detection: An Experimental Analysis. *Anais Do XXIII Simpósio Brasileiro de Segurança Da Informação e de Sistemas Computacionais (SBSeg 2023)*, 552–557. https://doi.org/DOI: 10.5753/sbseg.2023.233647

Appelgren, E. (2018). An Illusion of Interactivity. *Journalism Practice, 12*(3), 308–325. DOI: 10.1080/17512786.2017.1299032

Appelgren, E., Lindén, C.-G., & van Dalen, A. (2019). Data Journalism Research: Studying a Maturing Field across Journalistic Cultures, Media Markets and Political Environments. *Digital Journalism (Abingdon, England), 7*(9), 1191–1199. DOI: 10.1080/21670811.2019.1685899

Aria, M., & Cuccurullo, C. (2017). Bibliometrix: An R-Tool For Comprehensive Science Mapping Analysis. *Journal of Informetrics, 11*(4), 959–975. DOI: 10.1016/j.joi.2017.08.007

Arias-Robles, F., & López López, P. J. (2021). Driving the Closest Information. Local Data Journalism in the UK. *Journalism Practice, 15*(5), 638–650. DOI: 10.1080/17512786.2020.1749109

Asıl, S. (2025). Yapay Zekâ Etiği: Temel İlkeler, Sorunlar ve Disiplinlerarası Yaklaşımlar. *İNİF E- Dergi, 10*(1), 152-175.

Athens Technology Center. (2025, February 26). World Press Trends Outlook 2024–2025: How News Publishers Are Adapting to Change and Embracing AI-Driven Growth. Retrieved September 1, 2025, from https://www.atc.gr/wan-ifras-latest-world-press-trends-2024-2025-report/

Ay, A. (2022, October). Yapay Zeka Haberciliği ve Gazetecilik Tartışmalarına Dair Bir Değerlendirme. *The Turkish Online Journal of Design, Art and Communication - TOJDAC, 12*(4), s. 913-926

Ay, A. (2023). Gazetecilik 4.0: Yapay Zekâ Haberciliğinin Güncel Örneklerine Yönelik Bir İnceleme. *Süleyman Demirel Üniversitesi Vizyoner Dergisi, 14*(38), 412–435. DOI: 10.21076/vizyoner.1141093

Azgin, B., & Kiralp, S. (2024). Surveillance, disinformation, and legislative measures in the 21st century: AI, social media, and the future of democracies. *Social Sciences (Basel, Switzerland), 13*(10), 510. DOI: 10.3390/socsci13100510

Aziz, A. (2003). *Araştırma yöntemleri teknikleri ve iletişim. Ankara*. Turhan Kitabevi.

Barfield, W. (2021). A Systems and Control Theory Approach for Law and Artificial Intelligence: Demystifying the "Black-Box." *J, 4*(4), 564–576. DOI: 10.3390/j4040041

Barnes, C., & Barraclough, T. (2020). Deepfakes and synthetic media. In Steff, R., Burton, J., & Soare, S. R. (Eds.), *Emerging technologies and international security* (1st ed., pp. 206–220). Routledge. DOI: 10.4324/9780367808846-16

Baudrillard, J. (1994). *Simulacra and simulation.* University of Michigan Press.

Bazlutckaia, M., & Sytnik, A. (2023, June 28-July 1). Frame analysis in Russian with ChatGPT. Science Media International Forum, Saint-Petersburg, Russia.

BBC. (2018, December 19). *Der Spiegel reporter Claas Relotius sacked over 'invented' stories.* BBC: https://www.bbc.com/news/world-europe-46624297

Beckett, C., & Yaseen, M. (2023). Generating Change: A global survey of what news organisations are doing with artificial intelligence. JournalismAI, London School of Economics and Political Science.

Beckett, C. (2019). *New powers, New Responsibilities- A global survey of journalism and artificial intelligence.* LSE.

Beer, D. (2009). Power through the algorithm? Participatory web cultures and the technological unconscious. *New Media & Society, 11*(6), 985–1002. DOI: 10.1177/1461444809336551

Bekar, S. (2024). Yeni Medyada Yapay Zekâ Aracılığıyla Dezenformasyon Oluşturulması: Trump Örneği. *Uluslararası Batı Karadeniz Sosyal ve Beşeri Bilimler Dergisi, 8*(1), 40–66. DOI: 10.46452/baksoder.1448805

Bekele, W. B., & Ago, F. Y. (2022). Sample Size for Interview in Qualitative Research in Social Sciences: A Guide to Novice Researchers. *Research in Educational Policy and Management, 4*(1), 1. Advance online publication. DOI: 10.46303/repam.2022.3

Bhandari, R., & Bhandari, S. (2025). Artificial intelligence: understanding deepfakes. *EDPACS,* 1–11. DOI: 10.1080/07366981.2025.2484863

Bhargava, V. R., & Velasquez, M. (2021). Ethics of the attention economy: The problem of social media addiction. *Business Ethics Quarterly, 31*(3), 321–359. DOI: 10.1017/beq.2020.32

Bhuiyan, M. M., Whitley, H., Horning, M., Lee, S. W., & Mitra, T. (2021). Designing Transparency Cues in Online News Platforms to Promote Trust: Journalists' & Consumers' Perspectives. *Proceedings of the ACM on Human-Computer Interaction, 5*(CSCW2), 1–31. DOI: 10.1145/3479539

Bilgici, C. (2023). Yapay Zekâ ve Algoritmik Kültür Bağlaminda Sosyal Medya Deneyiminin Geleceği Üzerine Bir Değerlendirme. *Yeni Medya Elektronik Dergisi, 7*(3), 216–237. DOI: 10.17932/IAU.EJNM.25480200.2023/ejnm_v7i3003

Binbir, S. (2021). Pazarlama Çalışmalarında Yapay Zeka Kullanımı Üzerine Betimleyici Bir Çalışma. *e-Journal of New Media, 5*(3), 314-328.

Birrer, A., & Just, N. (2024). What we know and don't know about deepfakes: An investigation into the state of the research and regulatory landscape. *New Media & Society*. Advance online publication. DOI: 10.1177/14614448241253138

Bloebaum, B. (2017). *Trust and Journalism in a Digital Environment*. Reuters Institute for the Study of Journalism.

Bock, S., & Weiß, M. (2019). A Proof of Local Convergence for the Adam Optimizer. *2019 International Joint Conference on Neural Networks (IJCNN)*, 1–8. DOI: 10.1109/IJCNN.2019.8852239

Bojić, L., Zagovora, O., Zelenkauskaite, A., Veseljević Jerković, S., Vuković, V., Čabarkapa, M., & Jovančević, A. (2025). Comparing large language models and human annotators in latent content analysis of sentiment, political leaning, emotional intensity and sarcasm. *Scientific Reports*, *15*, 11477.

Bontcheva, K., Papadopoulous, S., Tsalakanidou, F., ... (2024). Generative AI and Disinformation: Recent Advances, Challenges, and Opportunities. Whitepaper (Ed: Kalina Bontcheva), https://edmo.eu/wp-content/uploads/2023/12/Generative-AI-and-Disinformation_-White-Paper-v8.pdf

Boulton, H. (2025). *'Godfather of AI' explains how 'scary' AI will increase the wealth gap and 'make society worse'*. UniladTech. https://www.uniladtech.com/news/ai/ai-godfather-explains-ai-will-increase-wealth-gap-318842-20250113

Bowles, N., & David, L. (2013). *Transparency in Politics and the Media*. https://www.torrossa.com/it/resources/an/5216033

Boydstun, A. E., Gross, J. H., Resnik, P., & Smith, N. A. (2013, September 16). Identifying media frames and frame dynamics within and across policy issues [Conference paper]. New Directions in Analyzing Text as Data Workshop, London, United Kingdom.

Böyük, M. (2024). Dijital Çağda Haber: İnsan ve Yapay Zeka Üretimi Haber İçeriklerinin Karşılaştırmalı Analizi. *Akdeniz İletişim*, (46), 44–72.

Bradshaw, S., & Howard, P. (2019). The Global Disinformation Order: 2019 Global Inventory of Organised Social Media Manipulation. *Copyright, Fair Use, Scholarly Communication, Etc.* https://digitalcommons.unl.edu/scholcom/207

Braun, V., & Clarke, V. (2006). *Using thematic analysis in psychology. 3*(2), 77–101. DOI: 10.1191/1478088706qp063oa

Breidbach, C. F., & Maglio, P. (2020). Accountable algorithms? The ethical implications of data-driven business models. *Journal of Service Management, 31*(2), 163–185. DOI: 10.1108/JOSM-03-2019-0073

Brittain, B., & Brittain, B. (2025, January 9). Meta knew it used pirated books to train AI, authors say. *Reuters*. https://www.reuters.com/technology/artificial-intelligence/meta-knew-it-used-pirated-books-train-ai-authors-say-2025-01-09/

Brown, D. A. (2017). The Enormity of the Damage Done by the Climate Change Disinformation Campaign as the World Struggles to Implement the Paris Agreement. In *The Role of Integrity in the Governance of the Commons* (pp. 125–139). Springer., DOI: 10.1007/978-3-319-54392-5_8

Brown, J. G., Bailenson, J. N., & Hancock, J. (2023). Misinformation in virtual reality. *Journal of Online Trust & Safety, 1*(1), 1–31.

Brüns, J. D., & Meißner, M. (2024). Do you create your content yourself? Using generative artificial intelligence for social media content creation diminishes perceived brand authenticity. *Journal of Retailing and Consumer Services, 79*, 103790. DOI: 10.1016/j.jretconser.2024.103790

Bucher, T. (2018). *If...then: Algorithmic power and politics*. Oxford University Press. DOI: 10.1093/oso/9780190493028.001.0001

Burrus, O., Curtis, A., & Herman, L. (2024). Unmasking AI: Informing authenticity decisions by labeling AI-generated content. *Interactions (New York, N.Y.), 31*(4), 38–42. https://interactions.acm.org/archive/view/july-august-2024/unmasking-ai-informing-authenticity-decisions-by-labeling-ai-generated-content. DOI: 10.1145/3665321

Büyükafşar, M., & Yıldırım, O. (2022). Yapay Zeka Gazeteciliği. S. Özay, & S. Bayrakcı (Dü) içinde [Çizgi Kitabevi.]. *Dijital Çağda Uzman Gazetecilik, 2*, 311–332.

Çağıltay, K. (2018). *İnsan Bilgisayar Etkileşimi ve Kullanılabilirlik Mühendisliği*. Seçkin.

Caldwell, J., Delaye, A., Esposito, T., Petti, T., Black, T., Fallon, B., & Trocmé, N. (2020). “Essential” services, risk, and child protection in the time of COVID-19: An opportunity to prioritize chronic need. *Developmental Child Welfare*, *2*(3), 208–223. DOI: 10.1177/2516103220968842

Calma, J. (2025, January 7). *Meta is leaving its users to wade through hate and disinformation.* The Verge. https://www.theverge.com/2025/1/7/24338127/meta-end-fact-checking-misinformation-zuckerberg

Camacho, M. M. (2019). *The era of post-truth, post-veracity and charlatanism.* Universidad de Navarra: https://www.unav.edu/web/ciencia-razon-y-fe/the-era-of-post-truth-post-veracity-and-charlatanismhttps://www.unav.edu/web/ciencia-razon-y-fe/the-era-of-post-truth-post-veracity-and-charlatanismss

Can, Ö., & Sezgin, M. (2024). Yapay Zeka Teknolojilerinin Kurumsal İletişimdeki Rolünün Değerlendirilmesi. *Uluslararası Sosyal Bilimler Akademik Araştırmalar Dergisi*, *8*(15), 103–114. DOI: 10.58201/utsobilder.1497333

Cao, J., Qi, P., Sheng, Q., Yang, T., Guo, J., & Li, J. (2020). *Exploring the Role of Visual Content in Fake News Detection.* https://doi.org/DOI: 10.1007/978-3-030-42699-6

Card, D., Boydstun, A. E., Gross, J. H., Resnik, P., & Smith, N. A. (2015). The Media Frames Corpus: Annotations of frames across issues. In *Proceedings of the 53rd Annual Meeting of the Association for Computational Linguistics and the 7th International Joint Conference on Natural Language Processing* (Vol. 2, pp. 438-444). Association for Computational Linguistics.

Carlson, M. (2015). The Robotic Reporter. *Digital Journalism (Abingdon, England)*, *3*(3), 416–431. DOI: 10.1080/21670811.2014.976412

Carroll, S. (2025, April 21). *Saying “please” and “thank you” to ChatGPT costs OpenAI millions, Sam Altman says.* Quartz. https://qz.com/open-ai-sam-altman-chatgpt-gpt4-please-thank-you-1851777047

Castells, M. (2000). *The rise of the network society* (2nd ed.). Blackwell.

Castells, M. (2005). *Enformasyon çağı: Ekonomi, toplum ve kültür – Ağ toplumunun yükselişi.* İstanbul Bilgi Üniversitesi Yayınları.

Castelvecchi, D. (2016). Can we open the black box of AI? *NATNews*, *538*(7623), 20. DOI: 10.1038/538020a PMID: 27708329

Cavedon-Taylor, D. (2024). Deepfakes: *A survey and introduction to the topical collection. Synthese, 204*(14), 14. Advance online publication. DOI: 10.1007/s11229-024-04634-8

Çavuş, G. (2017, June 27). *Emekli postacının bin 300 çocuğun babası olduğu iddiası*. Teyit.org: https://teyit.org/analiz/emekli-postacinin-bin-300-cocugun-babasi-oldugu-iddiasi

Çeber, B. (2024). Haziran). Yapay Zekâ Etiği Bağlamında Reklamcılık Sektörü Üzerine Uygulamalı Bir Araştırma. *Intermedia. International Journal (Toronto, Ont.), 11*(20), 63–84.

Çeber, B. (2024). *Yapay Zekayı Sorgulamak: Veri Etiği ve Dijital Reklamcılığın Kesişimi. B. Çeber içinde, Yapay Zekâ Etiği ve İletişim: Sorunlar, Sınırlar ve Zorluklar*. Nobel Akademik Yayıncılık.

Cejudo, R. (2023). Ethical problems of the use of deepfakes in the arts and culture. In Lara, F., & Deckers, J. (Eds.), *Ethics of artificial intelligence. The International Library of Ethics, Law and Technology* (Vol. 41). Springer., DOI: 10.1007/978-3-031-48135-2_7

Chakraborty, S., Hoque, M. S., Rahman Jeem, N., Biswas, M. C., Bardhan, D., & Lobaton, E. (2021). Fashion recommendation systems, models and methods: A review. *Informatics (MDPI), 8*(3), 49. DOI: 10.3390/informatics8030049

Chang, L. A., & Massey, B. L. (2010). Work motivation and journalists in Taiwan and the US: An integration of theory and culture. *Asian Journal of Communication, 20*(1), 51–68. https://www.tandfonline.com/doi/abs/10.1080/01292980903440814. DOI: 10.1080/01292980903440814

Chawki, M. (2024). Navigating legal challenges of deepfakes in the American context: A call to action. *Cogent Engineering, 11*(1), 2320971. DOI: 10.1080/23311916.2024.2320971

Chesney, R., & Citron, D. (2019). Deep fakes: A looming challenge for privacy, democracy, and national security. *SSRN, 107*(6), 1753–1819. DOI: 10.2139/ssrn.3213954

Cheung, J. C., & Ho, S. S. (2025a). Explainable AI and trust: How news media shapes public support for AI-powered autonomous passenger drones. *Public Understanding of Science (Bristol, England), 34*(3), 344–362. DOI: 10.1177/09636625241291192

Cheung, J. C., & Ho, S. S. (2025b). The effectiveness of explainable AI on human factors in trust models. *Scientific Reports, 15*(1), 23337. DOI: 10.1038/s41598-025-04189-9

Chitra, U., & Musco, C. (2020, January). Analyzing the impact of filter bubbles on social network polarization. In *Proceedings of the 13th international conference on web search and data mining* (pp. 115–123). Association for Computing Machinery. DOI: 10.1145/3336191.3371825

Choi, E. C., & Ferrara, E. (2024). FACT-GPT: Fact-Checking Augmentation via Claim Matching with LLMs. *Companion Proceedings of the ACM Web Conference 2024*, 883–886. https://doi.org/DOI: 10.1145/3589335.3651504

Chowdhury, G. G. (2003). *Natural Language Processing.*

Cochran, J. D., & Napshin, S. A. (2021). Deepfakes: Awareness, concerns, and platform accountability. *Cyberpsychology, Behavior, and Social Networking*, *24*(3), 164–172. DOI: 10.1089/cyber.2020.0100 PMID: 33760667

Coddington, M. (2018). In *Defining and Mapping Data Journalism and Computational Journalism | 18.* https://www.taylorfrancis.com/chapters/edit/10.4324/9781315270449-18/defining-mapping-data-journalism-computational-journalism-mark-coddington

Coddington, M. (2015). Clarifying Journalism's Quantitative Turn. *Digital Journalism (Abingdon, England)*, *3*(3), 331–348. DOI: 10.1080/21670811.2014.976400

Coderspace. (2024, Temmuz 8). *Derin Öğrenme Nedir? - Deep Learning Nasıl Çalışır?* Şubat 2025 tarihinde https://coderspace.io/blog/derin-ogrenme-nedir-deep-learning-nasil-calisir/ adresinden alındı

Cohen, A. (2024, 20 Aralık). *2025's energy megatrends: Seeking energy security and reviving nuclear.* Forbes. https://www.forbes.com/sites/arielcohen/2024/12/20/2025s-energy-megatrends-seeking-energy-security-and-reviving-nuclear/

Cohen, J. (1960). A coefficient of agreement for nominal scales. *Educational and Psychological Measurement*, *20*(1), 37–46.

Cole, M. D., Etteldorf, C., Schmitz, S., & Ukrow, J. (2023). Algorithmic transparency and accountability of digital services. *IRIS Special 2023-2*. European Audiovisual Observatory. Retrieved July 01, 2025, from https://rm.coe.int/iris-special-2023-02en/1680aeda48

Conroy, N. K., Rubin, V. L., & Chen, Y. (2015). Automatic deception detection: Methods for finding fake news. *Proceedings of the Association for Information Science and Technology*, *52*(1), 1–4. DOI: 10.1002/pra2.2015.145052010082

Cotter, K. (2019). Playing the visibility game: How digital influencers and algorithms negotiate influence on Instagram. *New Media & Society, 21*(4), 895–913. DOI: 10.1177/1461444818815684

Couldry, N., & Mejias, U. A. (2019). *The costs of connection: How data is colonizing human life and appropriating it for capitalism.* Stanford University Press.

Craft, S., & Vos, T. P. (2021). The ethics of transparency | 24. In *The Routledge Companion to Journalis.* https://www.taylorfrancis.com/chapters/edit/10.4324/9780429262708-24/ethics-transparency-stephanie-craft-tim-vos

Curry, A. L., & Stroud, N. J. (2021). The effects of journalistic transparency on credibility assessments and engagement intentions. *Journalism, 22*(4), 901–918. DOI: 10.1177/1464884919850387

D'Cruze, D. (2025, 23 Ocak). *Elon Musk criticises $500 billion AI project announced by Trump; OpenAI CEO Sam Altman fires back.* Business Today. https://www.businesstoday.in/technology/news/story/elon-musk-criticises-500-billion-ai-project-announced-by-trump-openai-ceo-sam-altman-fires-back-461757-2025-01-23

Dang, H. L. (2021). Social media, fake news, and the COVID-19 pandemic: Sketching the case of Southeast Asia. *Advances in Southeast Asian Studies, 14*(1), 37–58.

Darı, A. B., & Koçyiğit, A. (2024). Yapay Zekâ ve Etik: Yeni Medyanın Dönüşümünde Sorumluluk ve Sınırlar. *İletişim ve Toplum Araştırmaları Dergisi, 4*(2), 246-261.

Dayan, A., & Yılmaz, A. (2022). Doğal dil işleme ve derin öğrenme algoritmaları ile makine dili modellemesi. *Dicle Üniversitesi Mühendislik Fakültesi Mühendislik Dergisi, 13*(3), 467–475. DOI: 10.24012/dumf.1131565

De Nadal, L., & Jančárik, P. (2024). Beyond the deepfake hype: AI, democracy, and "the Slovak case". Harvard Kennedy School (HKS) Misinformation Review, 5(4).

de Ruiter, A. (2021). The distinct wrong of deepfakes. *Philosophy & Technology, 34*(4), 1311–1332. DOI: 10.1007/s13347-021-00459-2

Değirmencioğlu, G. (2016). Temmuz 2). Dijitalleşme Çağında Gazeteciliğin Geleceği ve İnovasyon Haberciliği. *TRT Akademi, 1*(2), 590–606.

Deleuze, G. (1992). Postscript on the societies of control. *October*, 59, 3–7.

Demirel, E. S. (2023). İletişim Alanında Yapay Zekâ: İletişim Fakültelerinde Yapay Zekâ. *International Social Sciences Studies Journal, 9*(118), 9842–9852. DOI: 10.29228/sssj.74032

Demirel, S. D. (2018). Dijital Medyada Haber Üretim Sürecinde Okuyucu Odaklılık. *Journal of International Social Research, 11*(55), 824–831. DOI: 10.17719/jisr.20185537253

Denis, J., & Goëta, S. (2017). Rawification and the careful generation of open government data. *Social Studies of Science, 47*(5), 604–629. DOI: 10.1177/0306312717712473

Deuze, M., & Beckett, C. (2022). Imagination, Algorithms and News: Developing AI Literacy for Journalism. *Digital Journalism (Abingdon, England), 10*(10), 1913–1918. DOI: 10.1080/21670811.2022.2119152

Devlin, J., Chang, M.-W., Lee, K., & Toutanova, K. (2019). BERT: Pre-training of Deep Bidirectional Transformers for Language Understanding. İçinde J. Burstein, C. Doran, & T. Solorio (Ed.), *Proceedings of the 2019 Conference of the North American Chapter of the Association for Computational Linguistics: Human Language Technologies,* Volume 1 *(Long and Short Papers)* (ss. 4171-4186). Association for Computational Linguistics. DOI: 10.18653/v1/N19-1423

Devlin, J., Chang, M.-W., Lee, K., & Toutanova, K. (2019). BERT: Pre-training of deep bidirectional transformers for language understanding. *NAACL-HLT, 2019*, 4171–4186.

Dhiman, B. (n.d.). Does Artificial Intelligence help Journalists: A Boon or Bane? *Preprints 2023,* 2023030428.

Diakopoulos, N. (2014, Haziran 12). *The Anatomy of a Robot Journalist.* Haziran 2025 tarihinde https://medium.com/tow-center/the-anatomy-of-a-robot-journalist-1aa879bc6769 adresinden alındı

Diakopoulos, N. (2019). *Automating the news: How algorithms are rewriting the media.* Harvard University Press. DOI: 10.4159/9780674239302

Dierickx, L., Opdahl, A. L., Khan, S. A., Lindén, C.-G., & Guerrero Rojas, D. C. (2024). A data-centric approach for ethical and trustworthy AI in journalism. *Ethics and Information Technology, 26*(4), 64. DOI: 10.1007/s10676-024-09801-6

Dogruel, L., Facciorusso, D., & Stark, B. (2020). 'I'm still the master of the machine.' Internet users' awareness of algorithmic decision-making and their perception of its effect on their autonomy. *Information Communication and Society, 25*(9), 1311–1332. DOI: 10.1080/1369118X.2020.1863999

DOMO. (2024). *Data Never Sleeps 12.0.* Şubat 2025 tarihinde https://www.domo.com/learn/infographic/data-never-sleeps-12 adresinden alındı

Doss, C., Mondschein, J., Shu, D., Wolfson, T., Kopecky, D., Fitton-Kane, V. A., Bush, L., & Tucker, C. (2023). Deepfakes and scientific knowledge dissemination. *Scientific Reports, 13*(1), 13429. DOI: 10.1038/s41598-023-39944-3 PMID: 37596384

Dupré, M. H. (2023, May 18). *Trump Shares AI Voice-Cloned Fake Video of Anderson Cooper.* Futurism: https://futurism.com/trump-ai-voice-cloned-fake-video-anderson-cooper adresinden alındı

Durães, D., Freitas, P. M., & Novais, P. (2024). The relevance of deepfakes in the administration of criminal justice. In H. Sousa Antunes, P.M. Freitas, A.L. Oliveira, C. Martins Pereira, E. Vaz de Sequeira, & L. Barreto Xavier (Eds.), *Multidisciplinary Perspectives on Artificial Intelligence and the Law* (Law, Governance and Technology Series, Vol. 58). Springer, Cham. DOI: 10.1007/978-3-031-41264-6_19

Durdak, A. (2024, Fabruary 11). *Anadolu Ajansı Medyada Yapay Zeka Etik Kullanım Rehber Hazırladı.* AA: https://www.aa.com.tr/tr/kurumsal-haberler/anadolu-ajansi-medyada-yapay-zeka-etik-kullanim-rehberi-hazirladi/3133162?utm_source=chatgpt.com#

Elitaş, T. (2022). Dijital Manipülasyon 'Deepfake'teknolojisi Ve Olmayanın İnandırıcılığı. *Hatay Mustafa Kemal Üniversitesi Sosyal Bilimler Enstitüsü Dergisi, 19*(49), 113–128.

Emerson, R. W. (2015). Convenience Sampling, Random Sampling, and Snowball Sampling: How Does Sampling Affect the Validity of Research? *Journal of Visual Impairment & Blindness, 109*(2), 164–168. DOI: 10.1177/0145482X1510900215

Emre, İ. E., & Erol, Ç. S. (2017). Veri Analizinde İstatistik mi Veri Madenciliği mi? *Bilişim Teknolojileri Dergisi, 10*(2), 161–167. DOI: 10.17671/gazibtd.309297

Engebretsen, M., & Kennedy, H. (2025). *Data Visualization in Society* (1st ed.). Routledge., DOI: 10.5117/9789463722902

Engebretsen, M., Kennedy, H., & Weber, W. (2018). Data Visualization in Scandinavian Newsrooms: Emerging Trends in Journalistic Visualization Practices. *Nordicom Review, 39*(2), 3–18. DOI: 10.2478/nor-2018-0007

Entman, R. M. (1993). Framing: Toward clarification of a fractured paradigm. *Journal of Communication, 43*(4), 51–58.

Environment, U. N. (2018, October 29). *About Montreal Protocol.* https://www.unep.org/ozonaction/who-we-are/about-montreal-protocol

Espinoza-Rojas, J., Siles, I., & Castelain, T. (2022). How using various platforms shapes awareness of algorithms. *Behaviour & Information Technology*. Advance online publication. DOI: 10.1080/0144929X.2022.2078224

Etienne, H. (2021). The future of online trust (and why Deepfake is advancing it). *AI and Ethics*, *1*(4), 553–562. DOI: 10.1007/s43681-021-00072-1 PMID: 34790952

European Broadcasting Union (EBU). (2023). *Public service media in the age of artificial intelligence*. https://www.ebu.ch/publications

European Commission. (2022). *Code of practice on disinformation*. https://digital-strategy.ec.europa.eu/en/policies/code-practice-disinformation

European Commission. (2024). *Proposal for a regulation of the European Parliament and of the Council laying down harmonised rules on AI(AIAct)*. Brussels: European Commission. https://digital-strategy.ec.europa.eu/en/policies/european-approach-artificial-intelligence

Ewert, B. (2020). Moving beyond the obsession with nudging individual behaviour: Towards a broader understanding of behavioural public policy. *Public Policy and Administration*, *35*(3), 337–360. DOI: 10.1177/0952076719889090

Fabuyi, J. A., Olaniyi, O. O., Olateju, O. O., Aideyan, N. T., Selesi-Aina, O., & Olaniyi, F. G. (2024). Deepfake Regulations and Their Impact on Content Creation in the Entertainment Industry. *Archives of Current Research International*, *24*(12), 52–74. DOI: 10.9734/acri/2024/v24i12997

Fact-checking. (2025). In *Wikipedia*. https://en.wikipedia.org/w/index.php?title=Fact-checking&oldid=1289589114

Farooque, M. (2024, 11 Aralık). Alphabet Bets Big on AI with $50B Investment to Transform Google Search and Cloud Services. Yahoo Finance. https://finance.yahoo.com/news/alphabet-bets-big-ai-50b-151247722.html

Fast, E., & Horvitz, E. (2017). Long-term trends in the public perception of artificial intelligence. *Proceedings of the AAAI Conference on Artificial Intelligence*, *31*(1). Advance online publication. DOI: 10.1609/aaai.v31i1.10635

Fayyad, U., Piatetsky-Shapiro, G., & Smyth, P. (1996). The KDD Process for Extracting Useful Knowledge from Volumes of Data. *Communications of the ACM*, *39*(11), 27–34. DOI: 10.1145/240455.240464

Feher, K., Vicsek, L., & Deuze, M. (2024). Modeling AI trust for 2050: Perspectives from media and info-communication experts. *AI & Society*, *39*(6), 2933–2946. DOI: 10.1007/s00146-023-01827-6

Fitzgerald, L. (2024, October 7). *The Impact of Deepfakes on Journalism.* Pindrop: https://www.pindrop.com/article/impact-deepfakes-journalism/

Fletcher, J. (2018). Deepfakes, artificial intelligence, and some kind of dystopia: The new faces of online post-fact performance. *Theatre Journal, 70*(4), 455–471. DOI: 10.1353/tj.2018.0097

Floridi, L., & Chiriatti, M. (2020). GPT-3: Its nature, scope, limits, and consequences. *Philosophy & Technology, 33*(4), 669–678. DOI: 10.1007/s13347-020-00473-1

Floridi, L., Cowls, J., Beltrametti, M., Chatila, R., Chazerand, P., Dignum, V., Luetge, C., Madelin, R., Pagallo, U., Rossi, F., Schafer, B., Valcke, P., & Vayena, E. (2018). AI4People—An ethical framework for a good AI society: Opportunities, risks, principles, and recommendations. *Minds and Machines, 28*(4), 689–707. DOI: 10.1007/s11023-018-9482-5 PMID: 30930541

Fogg, B. J. (2003). *Persuasive technology: Using computers to change what we think and do.* Morgan Kaufmann., DOI: 10.1016/B978-155860643-2/50011-1

Freelon, D., & Wells, C. (2020). Disinformation as political communication. *Political Communication, 37*(2), 145–156. DOI: 10.1080/10584609.2020.1723755

Freifeld, K. (2025, 13 Ocak). *US tightens its grip on AI chip flows across the globe.* Reuters. https://www.reuters.com/technology/artificial-intelligence/us-tightens-its-grip-ai-chip-flows-across-globe-2025-01-13/

Funke, D. (2018, September 10). These fact-checkers were attacked online after partnering with Facebook. *Poynter.* https://www.poynter.org/fact-checking/2018/these-fact-checkers-were-attacked-online-after-partnering-with-facebook/

Gairola, A. (2024, 26 Aralık). *Microsoft Invested Nearly $14 Billion In OpenAI But Now Its Reducing Its Dependence On The ChatGPT-Parent: Report.* Yahoo Finance. https://finance.yahoo.com/news/microsoft-invested-nearly-14-billion-000512844.html

Garland, R. (2015). Transparency in politics and the media: Accountability and open government. *Journal of Media Practice, 16*(1), 94–96. DOI: 10.1080/14682753.2015.1015804

Gehrke, M. (2020). *Transparency as a key element of data journalism.*

Gehrke, M. (2024). Revisiting the Origin and the Meaning of Transparency in Data Journalism | SpringerLink. In *The Palgrave Handbook of Global Digital Journalism.* Palgrave Macmillan, Cham. https://link.springer.com/chapter/10.1007/978-3-031-59379-6_24

Geltzer, J. (2017). *FAKE NEWS & FILM: HOW ALTERNATIVE FACTS INFLUENCE THE NATIONAL DISCOURSE. 47.*

Genovesi, S., Kaesling, K., & Robbins, S. (2023). Introduction: Understanding and regulating AI-powered recommender systems. In Genovesi, S., Kaesling, K., & Robbins, S. (Eds.), *Recommender systems: Legal and ethical issues* (Vol. 40, pp. 1–18). Springer., DOI: 10.1007/978-3-031-34804-4_1

Giddens, A. (2000). *Sosyoloji*. Phoenix Yayınevi.

Gillespie, T. (2014). The relevance of algorithms. In Gillespie, T., Boczkowski, P. J., & Foot, K. A. (Eds.), *Media technologies: Essays on communication, materiality, and society* (pp. 167–194). MIT Press., DOI: 10.7551/mitpress/9042.003.0013

Gillespie, T. (2018). *Custodians of the internet: Platforms, content moderation, and the hidden decisions that shape social media*. Yale University Press.

Glikson, E., & Woolley, A. W. (2020). Human trust in artificial intelligence: Review of empirical research. *The Academy of Management Annals*, *14*(2), 627–660. DOI: 10.5465/annals.2018.0057

Gökbel, H. (2024, November 30). Yapay Zekanın Gazetecilik Pratiklerindeki Yeri . *Tam Akademi Dergisi*, s. 135-162.

Goldstein, M. A., Kumar, N., & Thomas, D. (2024). Digital propaganda: The effectiveness of AI-generated persuasive messages. *Journal of Information Technology & Politics*, *21*(1), 37–54. DOI: 10.1080/19331681.2023.2182965

Gondwe, G. (2025). Can AI Outsmart Fake News? Detecting Misinformation With AI Models in Real-Time. *Emerging Media*, *27523543251325902*. Advance online publication. DOI: 10.1177/27523543251325902

Google. (2025). Embeddings (Machine Learning Crash Course). Retrieved September 1, 2025, from https://developers.google.com/machine-learning/crash-course/embeddings

Gosse, C., & Burkell, J. (2020). Politics and porn: How news media characterizes problems presented by deepfakes. *Critical Studies in Media Communication*, *37*(5), 497–511. DOI: 10.1080/15295036.2020.1832697

Goswami, R. (2023, June 1). *Reddit will charge hefty fees to the many third-party apps that access its data*. CNBC. https://www.cnbc.com/2023/06/01/reddit-eyeing-ipo-charge-millions-in-fees-for-third-party-api-access.html

Graefe, A. (2016). *Guide to automated journalism*. Columbia University Tow Center for Digital Journalism.

Gülleb, O. (2022). *Algoritmaların Haber Alma Biçimlerine Etkileri: Veri Gazeteciliği ve Algoritmalar. N. E. Dilmen, & C. T. Şahoğlu içinde, Sosyal Medya ve Algoritmalar.* Kriter Yayınevi.

Gulzar Hussain, F., Wasim, M., Hameed, S., Rehman, A., Nabeel Asim, M., & Dengel, A. (2025). Fake News Detection Landscape: Datasets, Data Modalities, AI Approaches, Their Challenges, and Future Perspectives. *IEEE Access : Practical Innovations, Open Solutions, 13*, 54757–54778. DOI: 10.1109/ACCESS.2025.3553909

Güney, C. (2020). *Dijital Dünyanın Ortaçağında Veri Egemenliği.* https://canerguney.medium.com/dijital-d%C3%BCnyan%C4%B1n-orta%C3%A7a%C4%9F%C4%B1nda-veri-egemenli%C4%9Fi-b7ea4ba2087

Guo, B., Ding, Y., Yao, L., Liang, Y., & Yu, Z. (2021). The Future of False Information Detection on Social Media: New Perspectives and Trends. *ACM Computing Surveys, 53*(4), 1–36. DOI: 10.1145/3393880

Guzman, A. L., & Lewis, S. C. (2019). Artificial intelligence and communication: A Human– Machine Communication research agenda. *New Media & Society, 22*(1), 70–86. DOI: 10.1177/1461444819858691

Haenlein, M., & Kaplan, A. (2019). A Brief History of Artificial Intelligence: On the Past, Present, and Future of Artificial Intelligence. *California Management Review, 61*(4), 5–14. DOI: 10.1177/0008125619864925

Haleem, A., Javaid, M., Qadri, M. A., Singh, R. P., & Suman, R. (2022). Artificial intelligence (AI) applications for marketing: A literature-based study. *International Journal of Intelligent Networks, 3*, 119–132. DOI: 10.1016/j.ijin.2022.08.005

Hamed, S. K., Ab Aziz, M. J., & Yaakub, M. R. (2023). A review of fake news detection approaches: A critical analysis of relevant studies and highlighting key challenges associated with the dataset, feature representation, and data fusion. *Heliyon, 9*(10), e20382. DOI: 10.1016/j.heliyon.2023.e20382 PMID: 37780751

Hameleers, M., van der Meer, T. G. L. A., & Dobber, T. (2022). You won't believe what they just said! The effects of political deepfakes embedded as vox populi on social media. *Social Media + Society, 8*(3), 205630512211163. DOI: 10.1177/20563051221116346

Han, H., Liang, Y., Bella, G., Giunchiglia, F., & Li, D. (2023). LFDNN: A novel hybrid recommendation model based on DeepFM and LightGBM. *Entropy (Basel, Switzerland), 25*(4), 638. DOI: 10.3390/e25040638

Harari, Y. N. (2018). *21. Yüzyıl İçin 21 Ders.* Kolektif Kitap.

Hawking, S. (2016, October 20). *Stephen Hawking warns of dangerous AI.*

Helberger, N. (2019). On the democratic role of news recommenders. *Digital Journalism (Abingdon, England), 7*(8), 993–1012. DOI: 10.1080/21670811.2019.1623700

Heseltine, M., & Clemm von Hohenberg, B. (2024). Large language models as a substitute for human experts in annotating political text. *Research and Politics, 11*(1), 1–10.

High-Level Expert Group on AI (HLEGAI). (2019). *Ethics guidelines for trustworthy artificial intelligence*. European Commission.

Hobsbawm, E. (2006). *Kısa 20. yüzyıl: Aşırılıklar çağı, 1914–1991* (Çev. Yavuz Alogan). İstanbul: Everest Yayınları.

Hohenstein, J., Kizilcec, R. F., DiFranzo, D., Aghajari, Z., Mieczkowski, H., Levy, K., Naaman, M., Hancock, J., & Jung, M. F. (2023). Artificial intelligence in communication impacts language and social relationships. *Scientific Reports, 13*(5487), 5487. DOI: 10.1038/s41598-023-30938-9

Hollyer, J. R. (2011). *Democracy and Transparency. 73*(4). https://www.journals.uchicago.edu/doi/abs/10.1017/S0022381611000880

Hong, W., & Thong, J. Y. L. (2013). Internet privacy concerns: An integrated conceptualization and four empirical studies. *Management Information Systems Quarterly, 37*(1), 275–298. DOI: 10.25300/MISQ/2013/37.1.12

Horne, B., & Adali, S. (2017). This just in: Fake news packs a lot in title, uses simpler, repetitive content in text body, more similar to satire than real news. *Proceedings of the International AAAI Conference on Web and Social Media, 11*(1), 759–766.

Houston, B. (2009). *Global Media Ethics—Google Books*. https://www.google.co.uk/books/edition/Global_Media_Ethics/sX7wUC5F-g8C?hl=en&gbpv=1&dq=transparency+in+journalism+Houston+%26+IRE,+2009.&pg=PA69&printsec=frontcover

Huang, C., Zhang, Z., Mao, B., & Yao, X. (2022). An overview of artificial intelligence ethics. *IEEE Transactions on Artificial Intelligence, 4*(4), 799–819. DOI: 10.1109/TAI.2022.3194503

Huang, Y., Jiao, J., & Zhu, D. (2025). Empowering the traveler: The impact of algorithm transparency and customer control on customer experience. *Asia Pacific Journal of Tourism Research*, •••, 1–19. DOI: 10.1080/10941665.2025.2523339

Hu, C.-P., & Chang, Y.-Y. (2017). John W. Creswell, Research Design: Qualitative, Quantitative, and Mixed Methods Approaches. *Journal of Social and Administrative Sciences*, *4*(2), 205–207.

Hugging Face. (n.d.). *OpenAI GPT*. Retrieved May 20, 2025, from https://huggingface.co/docs/transformers/v4.34.0/en/model_doc/openai-gpt

Huh, M., Liu, A., Owens, A., & Efros, A. A. (2018). Fighting Fake News: Image Splice Detection via Learned Self-Consistency. In Ferrari, V., Hebert, M., Sminchisescu, C., & Weiss, Y. (Eds.), *Computer Vision – ECCV 2018* (Vol. 11215, pp. 106–124). Springer International Publishing., DOI: 10.1007/978-3-030-01252-6_7

Humphreys, D., Koay, A., Desmond, D., & Mealy, E. (2024). AI hype as a cyber security risk: The moral responsibility of implementing generative AI in business. *AI and Ethics*, *4*(3), 791–804. DOI: 10.1007/s43681-024-00443-4

Hussein, F., & Hejase, H. J. (2022). Artificial Intelligence and Fake News. *Žurnalistikos Tyrimai, 16*, 39–71.

Hutchinson, A. (2025, 9 Şubat). TikTok Looks To Alleviate Data Security Concerns in the US. *Social Media Today*. https://www.socialmediatoday.com/news/tiktok-outlines-us-data-security-measures/739631/

Hwang, Y., Ryu, J. Y., & Jeong, S. H. (2021). Effects of disinformation using deepfake: The protective effect of media literacy education. *Cyberpsychology, Behavior, and Social Networking*, *24*(3), 188–193. DOI: 10.1089/cyber.2020.0174 PMID: 33646021

IBM. (2021, September 23). *What Is NLP (Natural Language Processing)? | IBM*. https://www.ibm.com/think/topics/natural-language-processing

IFCN. (n.d.). *The commitments of the Code of Principles*. Retrieved May 11, 2025, from https://www.ifcncodeofprinciples.poynter.org/the-commitments

Interian, R., Marzo, R. G., Mendoza, I., & Ribeiro, C. C. (2023). Network polarization, filter bubbles, and echo chambers: An annotated review of measures and reduction methods. *International Transactions in Operational Research, 30*(6), 3122–3158. DOI: 10.1111/itor.13224

Inverse. (2018, Temmuz 15). *How 'Knowhere' Uses Artificial Intelligence to Eliminate News Bias*. Haziran 2025 tarihinde https://www.inverse.com/article/46286-how-knowhere-uses-artificial-intelligence-to-eliminate-news-bias adresinden alındı

Işık, U., Ölçekçi, H., & Koz, K. A. (2022). Eylül). Yapay Zeka ve Algoritma Ekseninde Gazeteciliğin Geleceği ve Toplum İçin Anlamı. *Gümüşhane Üniversitesi İletişim Fakültesi Elektronik Dergisi, 10*(2), 1248–1275.

Jacobsen, B. N., & Simpson, J. (2023). The tensions of deepfakes. *Information Communication and Society, 27*(6), 1095–1109. DOI: 10.1080/1369118X.2023.2234980

Jain, A., Shakya, A., Khatter, H., & Gupta, A. K. (2019). A smart System for Fake News Detection Using Machine Learning. *2019 International Conference on Issues and Challenges in Intelligent Computing Techniques (ICICT), 1*, 1–4. DOI: 10.1109/ICICT46931.2019.8977659

Jasanoff, S. (2004). *States of knowledge: The co-production of science and social order*. Routledge., DOI: 10.4324/9780203413845

Jiang, C., & Qin, F. (2025, February). Research on algorithm of intelligent recommendation system in the era of big data. In *Proceedings of the 2025 international conference on digital analysis and processing, intelligent computation (DAPIC)* (pp. 358–362). IEEE. DOI: 10.1109/DAPIC66097.2025.00072

Jin, Z., Cao, J., Zhang, Y., Zhou, J., & Tian, Q. (2017). Novel Visual and Statistical Image Features for Microblogs News Verification. *IEEE Transactions on Multimedia, 19*(3), 598–608. DOI: 10.1109/TMM.2016.2617078

Jungherr, A. (2023). Artificial intelligence and democracy: A conceptual framework. *Social Media + Society, 9*(3), 1–14. DOI: 10.1177/20563051231186353

Jwa, H., Oh, D., Park, K., Kang, J., & Lim, H. (2019). exBAKE: Automatic Fake News Detection Model Based on Bidirectional Encoder Representations from Transformers (BERT). *Applied Sciences (Basel, Switzerland), 9*(19), 4062. DOI: 10.3390/app9194062

Kahneman, D. (2011). *Thinking, fast and slow*. Farrar, Straus and Giroux.

Kaliyar, R. K., Goswami, A., & Narang, P. (2021). FakeBERT: Fake news detection in social media with a BERT-based deep learning approach. *Multimedia Tools and Applications, 80*(8), 11765–11788. DOI: 10.1007/s11042-020-10183-2 PMID: 33432264

Kang, H., & Lou, C. (2022). AI agency vs. human agency: Understanding human-AI interactions on TikTok and their implications for user engagement. *Journal of Computer-Mediated Communication, 27*(5), zmac014. Advance online publication. DOI: 10.1093/jcmc/zmac014

Kaplan, A. (2020). Digital Transformation. In Akkor Gül, A., Ertürk, Y. D., & Elmer, P. (Eds.), *Media & Society* (pp. 149–162). Istanbul University Press.

Kaplan, A. B., & Kaplan, F. (2020). Haziran). Yeni İletişim Teknolojileri ve Yapay Zekâ Uygulamaları Bağlamında İhtiyaç Olgusunun Değişimi ve Toplumsal Dönüşüm. *Akademik Sosyal Araştırmalar Dergisi*, (46), 178–193.

Kaplan, A. M., & Haenlein, M. (2019). Siri, Siri, in my hand: Who's the fairest in the land? On the interpretations, illustrations, and implications of artificial intelligence. *Business Horizons*, *62*(1), 15–25. DOI: 10.1016/j.bushor.2018.08.004

Kaplan, J. (2016). *Artificial Intelligence- What Everyone Needs to Know*. Oxford University Press. DOI: 10.1093/wentk/9780190602383.001.0001

Karaboga, M. (2023). Die Regulierung von Deepfakes auf EU-Ebene: *Überblick eines Flickenteppichs und Einordnung des Digital Services Act- und KI-Regulierungsvorschlags*. In Jaki, S., & Steiger, S. (Eds.), *Digitale Hate Speech: Interdisziplinäre Perspektiven auf Erkennung, Beschreibung und Regulation* (pp. 197–220). Springer. DOI: 10.1007/978-3-662-65964-9_10

Karaman, Ö. (2021). Yapay Zeka Destekli Kişiselleştirme Algoritmalarının Tüketici Zihninde Filtre Balonu Yaratma Etkisinin İncelenmesi. *Vizyoner Dergisi*, *12*(32), 1339–1351. DOI: 10.21076/vizyoner.896059

Karlıdağ, S. (2013). Ekonomi Politik Açıdan Kişisel Verilerin Korunması. *Amme İdaresi Dergisi*, 46(1), 127-152. Erişim adresi: https://ammeidaresi.hacibayram.edu .tr/documents/article/1/46/1/6_karlidag.pdf

Karnouskos, S. (2020). Artificial intelligence in digital media: The era of deepfakes. *IEEE Transactions on Technology and Society*, *1*(3), 138–147. DOI: 10.1109/ TTS.2020.3001312

Kashyap, G., Bhaskaran, H., & Mishra, H. (2020). "We need to find a revenue model": Data journalists' perceptions on the challenges of practicing data journalism in India. *Observatorio (OBS*), 14*(2). DOI: 10.15847/obsOBS14220201552

Kaur, A., Hoshyar, A. N., Saikrishna, V., Firmin, S., & Xia, F. (2024). Deepfake video detection: Challenges and opportunities. *Artificial Intelligence Review*, *57*(6), 1–47. DOI: 10.1007/s10462-024-10810-6

Kavut, S. (2022). Yapay Zekâ Pazarlaması ve Yapay Zekâ Algoritmaları: Domino's Pizza Yapay Zekâ Uygulamaları. *9.Uluslararası İletişim Günleri Dijital Çağda İletişim Çalışmaları Sempozyumu*, (s. 537-552). İstanbul.

Kayıhan, B. (2024, December 8). *Yapay Zekâ ve Etik Sorunlar: İnsanlık, Teknolojinin Kontrolünü Kaybediyor Mu?* Kim, D., & Kim, S. (2018). Newspaper journalists' attitudes towards robot journalism. *Telematics and Informatics*, *35*(2), 340–357.

Kaymakçı, Ö. B. (2025). *Veri Egemenliği: Yeni Bir Kolonyalizm mi?* https://www.ekoturk.com/yazi/veri-egemenligi-yeni-bir-kolonyalizm-mi/

Kerner, S. M. (2025, 20 Ocak). *DeepSeek explained: Everything you need to know*. TechTarget. https://www.techtarget.com/whatis/feature/DeepSeek-explained-Everything-you-need-to-know

Kevin-Alerechi, E., Abutu, I., Oladunni, O., Osanyinro, E., Ojumah, O., & Ogundele, R. (2025). AI and the Newsroom: Transforming Journalism with Intelligent Systems. *Journal of Artificial Intelligence. Machine Learning and Data Science*, *3*(1), 1629–1633. DOI: 10.51219/JAIMLD/Elfredah-Kevin-Alerechi/426

Kılıç, B., & Kahraman, M. E. (2023, September). Current Usage Areas of Deepfake Applications with Artificial Intelligence Technology. *Journal CSS*, s. 301-332.

Kılınç, D., & Başeğmez, N. (2022). *Uygulamalarla Veri Bilimi*. Abaküs Yayınları.

Kim, J., Giroux, M., & Lee, J. C. (2021). When do you trust AI? The effect of number presentation detail on consumer trust and acceptance of AI recommendations. *Psychology and Marketing*, *38*(7), 1140–1155. DOI: 10.1002/mar.21498

Kırık, A. M., Göksu, O., & Yegen, C. (2024, November 11). Yapay Zeka ve Gazetecilik: Türk Medyasında ChatGPT Kullanımı. *İletişim Kuram ve Araştırma Dergisi*, s. 90-109.

Kırık, A. M., & Özkoçak, V. (2023). Medya ve İletişim Bağlamında Yapay Zeka Tarihi ve Teknolojisi: ChatGPT ve Deepfake ile Gelen Dijital Dönüşüm. *Karadeniz Uluslararası Bilimsel Dergi*, (58), 73–99. DOI: 10.17498/kdeniz.1308471

Kirk, C. P., & Givi, J. (2025). The AI-authorship effect: Understanding authenticity, moral disgust, and consumer responses to AI-generated marketing communications. *Journal of Business Research*, *186*, 114984. DOI: 10.1016/j.jbusres.2024.114984

Knickrehm, M. (2020). Yapay Zeka İşi Nasıl Değiştirecek? *Yapay Zeka* (L. Göktem, Çev., s. 155-168). içinde Harvard Business Review Press.

Koçyiğit, A., & Darı, A. B. (2023). Temmuz). Yapay Zekâ İletişiminde ChatGPT: İnsanlaşan Dijitalleşmenin Geleceği. *Stratejik ve Sosyal Araştırmalar Dergisi*, *7*(2), 427–438.

Koçyiğit, A., & Koçyiğit, M. (2024). Yapay Zekâ ve Yeni Medya: Fırsatlar, Tehditler ve Gelecek Perspektifi. *5.* [Akdeniz Üniversitesi.]. *Uluslarası Medya Çalışmaları Sempozyumu IMS, 2024*, 26–31.

Koene, A., Clifton, C., Hatada, Y., Webb, H., Patel, M., Machado, C., LaViolette, J., Richardson, R., & Reisman, D. (2019). *A governance framework for algorithmic accountability and transparency.* European Parliamentary Research Service, Panel for the Future of Science and Technology (STOA). Retrieved July 01, 2025, from https://www.europarl.europa.eu/RegData/etudes/STUD/2019/624262/EPRS_STU(2019)624262_EN.pdf

Koliska, M. (2021). Transparency in Journalism. In *Oxford Research Encyclopedia of Communication.* Oxford University Press., DOI: 10.1093/acrefore/9780190228613.013.883

Kolo, C., Mütterlein, J., & Schmid, S. A. (2022, January). Believing journalists, AI, or fake news: The role of trust in media. In *Proceedings of the 55th Hawaii international conference on system sciences* (pp. 3202–3211). Retrieved July 01, 2025, from https://hdl.handle.net/10125/79727

Kreps, S., McCain, R. M., & Brundage, M. (2022). All the news that's fit to fabricate: AI-generated text as a tool of media misinformation. *Journal of Experimental Political Science*, *9*(1), 104–117. DOI: 10.1017/XPS.2020.37

Krippendorff, K. (2004). *Content Analysis: An Introduction to Its Methodology* (2nd ed.). Sage Publications.

Küçükvardar, M., Aslan, A., & Bayrakcı, S. (2020). Yapay Zekâ Ve Etik Üzerine Bir Araştırma. *Atras Journal*, *6*(36), 1065–1077.

Kula, S., Choraś, M., & Kozik, R. (2021). Application of the BERT-Based Architecture in Fake News Detection. In Herrero, Á., Cambra, C., Urda, D., Sedano, J., Quintián, H., & Corchado, E. (Eds.), *13th International Conference on Computational Intelligence in Security for Information Systems (CISIS 2020)* (pp. 239–249). Springer International Publishing. https://doi.org/DOI: 10.1007/978-3-030-57805-3_23

Kümbetoğlu, B. (2008). *Sosyolojide ve antropolojide niteliksel yöntem ve araştırma. İstanbul.* Bağlam Yayınevi.

KVKK. (2025, Nisan 27). *Yapay Zeka Alanında Kişisel Verilerin Korunmasına Daire Tavsiyeler.* Haziran 2025 tarihinde http://www.kvkk.gov.tr/Icerik/7048/Yapay-Zeka-Alaninda-Kisisel-Verilerin-Korunmasina-Dair-Tavsiyeler adresinden alındı

Landis, J. R., & Koch, G. G. (1977). The measurement of observer agreement for categorical data. *Biometrics*, *33*(1), 159–174.

Langa, J. (2021). Deepfakes, real consequences: Crafting legislation to combat threats posed by deepfakes. *Boston University Law Review. Boston University. School of Law*, *101*, 761.

Larrondo, E., & Grandi, N. (2021). Artificial Intelligence, algorithms and freedom of expression. *Universitas (Accra)*, *34*(2), 169–186. DOI: 10.54517/met.v2i2.1790

Latar, N. L. (2018). AI in journalism: AIand the reshaping of news publishing. In Latar, N. L. (Ed.), *The robot journalism* (pp. 65–86). Springer. DOI: 10.1142/10913

Lazer, D. M. J., Baum, M. A., Benkler, Y., Berinsky, A. J., Greenhill, K. M., Menczer, F., Metzger, M. J., Nyhan, B., Pennycook, G., Rothschild, D., Schudson, M., Sloman, S. A., Sunstein, C. R., Thorson, E. A., Watts, D. J., & Zittrain, J. L. (2018). The science of fake news. *Science*, *359*(6380), 1094–1096. DOI: 10.1126/science.aao2998 PMID: 29590025

Lee, K. (2018). Yapay Zekâ ve Yeni Dünya Düzeni: Çin, Silikon Vadisi, Optimist Yayın Grubu (MyTECHNIC), İstanbul, ISBN: 978-605-2202-49-4.

Leslie, D. (2019). *Understanding artificial intelligence ethics and safety: A guide for the responsible design and implementation of AI systems in the public sector*. The Alan Turing Institute.

Lewis, P., Perez, E., Piktus, A., Petroni, F., Karpukhin, V., Goyal, N., Küttler, H., Lewis, M., Yih, W.-T., Rocktäschel, T., Riedel, S., & Kiela, D. (2020). Retrieval-augmented generation for knowledge-intensive NLP tasks. Advances in Neural Information Processing Systems, 33, 9459–9474. Retrieved September 3, 2025, from https://proceedings.neurips.cc/paper/2020/file/6b493230205f780e1bc26945df7481e5-Paper.pdf

Lewis, S. C. (2015). Journalism In An Era Of Big Data: Cases, concepts, and critiques. *Digital Journalism (Abingdon, England)*, *3*(3), 321–330. DOI: 10.1080/21670811.2014.976399

Liang, M. (2022). The end of social media? How data attraction model in the algorithmic media reshapes the attention economy. *Media Culture & Society*, *44*(6), 1110–1131. DOI: 10.1177/01634437221077168

Li, M., & Wan, Y. (2023). Norms or fun? The influence of ethical concerns and perceived enjoyment on the regulation of deepfake information. *Internet Research*, *33*(5), 1750–1773. DOI: 10.1108/INTR-07-2022-0561

Lin, T.-H., Chang, M.-C., Chang, C.-C., & Chou, Y.-H. (2022). Government-sponsored disinformation and the severity of respiratory infection epidemics including COVID-19: A global analysis, 2001–2020. *Social Science & Medicine*, *296*, 114744. DOI: 10.1016/j.socscimed.2022.114744 PMID: 35124544

Lipka, M. (2025, April 28). Americans largely foresee AI having negative effects on news, journalists. Pew Research Center. Retrieved September 1, 2025, from https://www.pewresearch.org/short-reads/2025/04/28/americans-largely-foresee-ai-having-negative-effects-on-news-journalists/

Liu, T., Fang, S., Zhao, Y., Wang, P., & Zhang, J. (2015). *Implementation of Training Convolutional Neural Networks.*

Liu, Y., Ott, M., Goyal, N., Du, J., Joshi, M., Chen, D., . . . Stoyanov, V. (2021). RoBERTa: A robustly optimized BERT pretraining approach. arXiv preprint arXiv:1907.11692.

Liu, Z. (2024). Fine-tuning technologies for reducing the FER bias across various distributions. In Y. Wang (Ed.), Proceedings of the 2024 2nd International Conference on Image, Algorithms and Artificial Intelligence (ICIAAI 2024) (Advances in Computer Science Research, Vol. 115). Atlantis Press.

Liu, B. (2021). In AI we trust? Effects of agency locus and transparency on uncertainty reduction in human-AI interaction. *Journal of Computer-Mediated Communication*, *26*(6), 384–402. DOI: 10.1093/jcmc/zmab013

Liu-Thompkins, Y., Okazaki, S., & Li, H. (2022). Artificial empathy in marketing interactions: Bridging the human-AI gap in affective and social customer experience. *Journal of the Academy of Marketing Science*, *50*(6), 1198–1218. DOI: 10.1007/s11747-022-00892-5

Liu, Y., & Wu, Y.-F. (2018). Early Detection of Fake News on Social Media Through Propagation Path Classification with Recurrent and Convolutional Networks. *Proceedings of the AAAI Conference on Artificial Intelligence*, *32*(1), 1. Advance online publication. DOI: 10.1609/aaai.v32i1.11268

Liv, N., & Greenbaum, D. (2020). Deepfakes and memory malleability: False memories in the service of fake news. *AJOB Neuroscience*, *11*(2), 96–104. DOI: 10.1080/21507740.2020.1740351 PMID: 32228386

Li, Y., & Cao, J. (2025). The role of recommendation algorithm in online social platforms. *Procedia Computer Science*, *261*, 674–681. DOI: 10.1016/j.procs.2025.04.320

Loosen, W., Reimer, J., & De Silva-Schmidt, F. (2020). Data-driven reporting: An ongoing (r)evolution? An analysis of projects nominated for the Data Journalism Awards 2013–2016. *Journalism, 21*(9), 1246–1263. DOI: 10.1177/1464884917735691

Lopezosa, C., Codina, L., Pont-Sorribes, C., & Vállez, M. (2023). Use of generative artificial intelligence in the training of journalists: Challenges, uses and training proposal. *El Profesional de la Información, 32*(4), e320408. DOI: 10.3145/epi.2023.jul.08

Luitse, D., & Denkena, W. (2021). The great transformer: Examining the role of large language models in the political economy of AI. *Big Data & Society, 8*(2), 1–14. DOI: 10.1177/20539517211047734

Lundberg, E., & Mozelius, P. (2023, October 23). The potential effects of deepfakes on news media and entertainment. *AI & Society*, •••, 2159–2170.

Lupano, E. (2025). Of Pride and Patriotism. The Representation of Artificial Intelligence in Chinese Official and Media Discourse. In Lupano, E., & Orrù, P. (Eds.), *Artificial Intelligenceand Human Perception Media Discourse and Public Opinion* (pp. 83–109).

Lv, X., Li, J., & Wang, Q. (2024). The dark side of recommendation algorithms in Chinese mass short video apps: Effect of perceived over-recommendation on users' cognitive dissonance and discontinuance intention. *International Journal of Human-Computer Interaction, 41*(11), 6701–6715. DOI: 10.1080/10447318.2024.2383038

Ma, J. (2024, 28 Eylül). *OpenAI sees $5 billion loss in 2024 and soaring sales as big ChatGPT fee hikes planned, report says*. Forbes. https://fortune.com/2024/09/28/openai-5-billion-loss-2024-revenue-forecasts-fundraising-chapgpt-fee-hikes/

Magaña, M. I., & Perdomo, V. G. (2024). *Cracking the data journalism code in Latin America: Activism, transparency and democracy fuel the adoption of technology | Intellect*. https://intellectdiscover.com/content/journals/10.1386/ajms_00152_1

Mahid, Z. I., Manickam, S., & Karuppayah, S. (2018). Fake News on Social Media: Brief Review on Detection Techniques. *2018 Fourth International Conference on Advances in Computing, Communication & Automation (ICACCA)*, 1–5. https://doi.org/DOI: 10.1109/ICACCAF.2018.8776689

Ma, L., & Sun, B. (2020, September). Machine learning and AI in marketing – Connecting computing power to human insights. *International Journal of Research in Marketing, 37*(3), 481–504. DOI: 10.1016/j.ijresmar.2020.04.005

Marconi, F. (2020). *Newsmakers: AIand the future of journalism*. Columbia University Press. DOI: 10.7312/marc19136

Martin, J. A., Camaj, L., & Lanosga, G. (2024). Audience engagement in data-driven journalism: Patterns in participatory practices across 34 countries. *Journalism, 25*(7), 1578–1596. DOI: 10.1177/14648849241230414

Martins, P. (2014). Respect for privacy begins when gathering information. *Comunicação e Sociedade, 25*, 186–201. DOI: 10.17231/comsoc.25(2014).1868

Maynez, J., Narayan, S., Bohnet, B., & McDonald, R. (2020). On faithfulness and factuality in abstractive summarization. In *Proceedings of the 58th Annual Meeting of the Association for Computational Linguistics* (pp. 1906–1919). DOI: 10.18653/v1/2020.acl-main.173

McCarthy, I. & K. M. (2021, May 26). *How artificial intelligence can help solve journalism's problems.*

McDermott, J. & O'Brien, M. (2025, 20 Ocak). *Chinese AI firm DeepSeek debuts low-cost language model.* AP News., https://apnews.com/article/00c594310b22afbf150559d08b43d3a5

McLuhan, M. (1964). *Understanding media: The extensions of man*. McGraw-Hill.

McStay, A. (2018). Emotional AI: The rise of empathic media. *Sage (Atlanta, Ga.)*. Advance online publication. DOI: 10.4135/9781526451293

Merkezi, B. H. (2023, November 13). *Gazetecilikte yapay zeka kullanımına karşı ilk etik ilkeler belirlendi.* Bianet: https://bianet.org/haber/gazetecilikte-yapay-zeka-kullanimina-karsi-ilk-etik-ilkeler-belirlendi-287811

Merritt, R. (2025, January 31). What is retrieval-augmented generation, aka RAG? NVIDIA Blog. Retrieved September 1, 2025, from https://blogs.nvidia.com/blog/what-is-retrieval-augmented-generation/

Merwe, J. V. D. (2022). *Data responsibility, corporate social responsibility, and corporate digital responsibility. 4.* https://www.cambridge.org/core/journals/data-and-policy/article/data-responsibility-corporate-social-responsibility-and-corporate-digital-responsibility/B7749EC986BFF98EF32D3192E8D4F9D7

Metodoloji—Teyit. (n.d.). Retrieved May 11, 2025, from https://teyit.org/metodoloji

Michiels, L., Vannieuwenhuyze, J., Leysen, J., Verachtert, R., Smets, A., & Goethals, B. (2023, September). How should we measure filter bubbles? A regression model and evidence for online news. In *Proceedings of the 17th ACM conference on recommender systems* (pp. 640–651). ACM. DOI: 10.1145/3604915.3608805

Mikolov, T., Chen, K., Corrado, G., & Dean, J. (2013). Efficient estimation of word representations in vector space. arXiv. Retrieved September 1, 2025, from https://arxiv.org/abs/1301.3781

Milosavljević, M., & Vobič, I. (2019). Human still in the loop: Editors reconsider the ideals of professional journalism through automation. *Digital Journalism (Abingdon, England)*, *7*(8), 1098–1116. DOI: 10.1080/21670811.2019.1601576

Mohsin, S. (2024). The influence of AI-driven personalization on consumer decision-making in e-commerce platforms. *Al-Rafidain Journal of Engineering Sciences*, *2*(2), 249–261. DOI: 10.61268/ajs54s12

Momeni, M. (2024). Artificial Intelligence and Political Deepfakes: Shaping Citizen Perceptions Through Misinformation. *Journal of Creative Communications*, *20*(1), 41–56. DOI: 10.1177/09732586241277335

Moran, C. (2023, April 6). ChatGPT is making up fake Guardian articles. Here's how we're responding. *The Guardian*. https://www.theguardian.com/commentisfree/2023/apr/06/ai-chatgpt-guardian-technology-risks-fake-article

Moran, R. E., & Shaikh, S. J. (2022). Robots in the News and Newsrooms: Unpacking Meta-Journalistic Discourse on the Use of Artificial Intelligence in Journalism. *Digital Journalism (Abingdon, England)*, *10*(10), 1756–1774. DOI: 10.1080/21670811.2022.2085129

Mridha, M. F., Keya, A. J., & Hamid, Md. A., Monowar, M. M., & Rahman, Md. S. (2021). A Comprehensive Review on Fake News Detection With Deep Learning. *IEEE Access : Practical Innovations, Open Solutions*, *9*, 156151–156170. DOI: 10.1109/ACCESS.2021.3129329

Muller, B. (2022, March 2). BERT 101, State Of The Art NLP Model Explained. Hugging Face, Retrieved September 3, 2025, from https://huggingface.co/blog/bert-101

Murillo-Ligorred, V., Ramos-Vallecillo, N., Covaleda, I., & Fayos, L. (2023). Knowledge, Integration and Scope of Deepfakes in Arts Education: The Development of Critical Thinking in Postgraduate Students in Primary Education and Master's Degree in Secondary Education. *Education Sciences*, *13*(11), 1073. DOI: 10.3390/educsci13111073

Murphy, G., Ching, D., Twomey, J., & Linehan, C. (2023). Face/Off: Changing the face of movies with deepfakes. *PLoS One*, *18*(7), e0287503. DOI: 10.1371/journal.pone.0287503 PMID: 37410765

Mustak, M., Salminen, J., Mäntymäki, M., Rahman, A., & Dwivedi, Y. K. (2023). Deepfakes: Deceptions, mitigations, and opportunities. *Journal of Business Research, 154*, 2023. DOI: 10.1016/j.jbusres.2022.113368

Mutlu, E. (2024). Yaratıcılığın Sınırları: Yapay Zeka Yaratıcılığına Bir Bakış. *Hacettepe Üniversitesi İletişin Fakültesi Kültürel Çalışmalar Dergisi, 11*(2), 422–446.

Nadkarni, P. M., Ohno-Machado, L., & Chapman, W. W. (2011). Natural language processing: An introduction. *Journal of the American Medical Informatics Association : JAMIA, 18*(5), 544–551. DOI: 10.1136/amiajnl-2011-000464 PMID: 21846786

Najafi, A., & Varol, O. (2024). TurkishBERTweet: Fast and reliable large language model for social media analysis. *Expert Systems with Applications, 255*(Part C), 124737.

Napoli, P. M. (2011). *Audience evolution: New technologies and the transformation of media audiences*. Columbia University Press.

Narin, B. (2017). *Uzman Görüşleri Bağlamında Haber Üretiminde Otomatikleştirme: Robot Gazetecilik*. Galatasaray Üniversitesi İleti-ş-im Dergisi.

Nash, R. A., & Wade, K. A. (2009). Innocent but proven guilty: Eliciting internalized false confessions using doctored-video evidence. *Applied Cognitive Psychology, 23*(5), 624–637. DOI: 10.1002/acp.1500

Natural Language Processing (NLP)—A Complete Guide. (2023, January 11). https://www.deeplearning.ai/resources/natural-language-processing/

Necula, S. C., & Păvăloaia, V. D. (2023). AI-driven recommendations: A systematic review of the state of the art in e-commerce. *Applied Sciences (Basel, Switzerland), 13*(9), 5531. DOI: 10.3390/app13095531

Newman, N., Ross Arguedas, A., Robertson, C. T., Fletcher, R., & Nielsen, R. K. (2025). Digital News Report 2025. Reuters Institute for the Study of Journalism, University of Oxford. Retrieved September 1, 2025, from https://reutersinstitute.politics.ox.ac.uk/digital-news-report/2025

Newman, N., Fletcher, R., Kueng, L., Nielsen, R. K., Selva, M., & Suarez, E. (2020). *Journalism, Media, and Technology Trends and Predictions 2020*. Reuters Institute for the Study of Jounalism.

Nguyen, D., & Hekman, E. (2022). The news framing of artificial intelligence: A critical exploration of how media discourses make sense of automation. *AI & Society, 39*(2), 437–451. Advance online publication. DOI: 10.1007/s00146-022-01511-1

Nguyen, M. H., Bol, N., & King, A. J. (2020). Customisation versus personalisation of digital health information: Effects of mode tailoring on information processing outcomes. *European Journal of Health Communication*, *1*(1), 30–54. DOI: 10.47368/ejhc.2020.003

Noble, S. U. (2018). *Algorithms of oppression: How search engines reinforce racism*. NYU Press. DOI: 10.18574/nyu/9781479833641.001.0001

Nurzhanov, A., & Sharipbay, A. (2025). Modern AI models for text analysis: A comparison of ChatGPT and RAG. *Journal of Data Analytics and Artificial Intelligence Applications*, *1*(1), 1–13.

Nyhan, B., & Reifler, J. (2010). When Corrections Fail: The Persistence of Political Misperceptions. *Political Behavior*, *32*(2), 303–330. DOI: 10.1007/s11109-010-9112-2

Nyrhinen, J., Sirola, A., Koskelainen, T., Munnukka, J., & Wilska, T. A. (2024). Online antecedents for young consumers' impulse buying behavior. *Computers in Human Behavior*, *153*, 108129. DOI: 10.1016/j.chb.2023.108129

Office of the Chief Information. (2025). *Privacy Considerations for Generative AI*. University of Illinois Urbana-Champain. https://www.cybersecurity.illinois.edu/policies-governance/privacy-considerations-for-generative-ai/

Oksijen. (2025, February 20). *Trump'tan sonra oğlu da Zelenskiy'i hedef aldı*. Oksijen: https://gazeteoksijen.com/dunya/trumptan-sonra-oglu-da-zelenskiyi-hedef-aldi-235616 adresinden alındı

Our Process. (n.d.). *FactCheck.Org*. Retrieved May 11, 2025, from https://www.factcheck.org/our-process/

Oxford English Dictionary. (2025, May 19). *Deepfake*. Oxford English Dictionary: https://www.oed.com/dictionary/deepfake_n?tl=true adresinden alındı

Oyekunle, D., Matthew, U. O., Preston, D., & Boohene, D. (2024). Trust beyond technology algorithms: A theoretical exploration of consumer trust and behavior in technological consumption and AI projects. *Journal of Computer and Communications*, *12*(6), 72–102. DOI: 10.4236/jcc.2024.126006

Özbay, F., & Alataş, B. (2019). Fake news detection within online social media using supervisedartificial intelligence algorithms. *Physica A*, *540*, 123174. DOI: 10.1016/j.physa.2019.123174

Özkeçeci, Z. (2019). Citizen journalism-opportunities and challenges. Asya Studies-Academic Social Studies/Akademik Sosyal Araştırmalar, (8), 33-39.

Özkececi, Z. (2018). Die Perspektiven des türkischen Journalismus: Ein Drahtseilakt zwischen eingeschränkter Pressefreiheit und begrenzten Alternativen. *SWS-Rundschau, 58*(3), 349–371.

Özkeçeci, Z. (2019). Citizen Journalism-Opportunities And Challenges. *Asya Studies-Academic Social Studies, 2*(8), 33–39. DOI: 10.31455/asya.565973

Özsalih, A. (2023). Yapay Zekâ Yoluyla Oluşturulan Sahte Haberlerin Medya Gündemini Belirlemesi. *Turkish Online Journal of Design Art and Communication, 13*(3), 533–550. DOI: 10.7456/tojdac.1285554

Öztemel, E. (2020). *Yapay Zekâ ve İnsanlığın Geleceği. M. Şeker, Y. Bulduklu, C. Korkut, & M. Doğrul içinde, Bilişim Teknolojileri ve iletişim: Birey ve Toplum Güvenliği*. Türkiye Bilimler Akademisi.

Parasie, S. (2019b). *Data journalism and the promise of transparency | 27 | The Routledge C.* The Routledge Companion to Media and Scandal. https://www.taylorfrancis.com/chapters/edit/10.4324/9781351173001-27/data-journalism-promise-transparency-sylvain-parasie

Parasie, S., & Dagiral, E. (2013). *Data-driven journalism and the public good: "Computer-assisted-reporters" and "programmer-journalists" in Chicago. 15*(6). https://journals.sagepub.com/doi/abs/10.1177/1461444812463345

Parasie, S. (2019a). Data journalism and the promise of transparency. In *The Routledge Companion to Media and Scandal*. Routledge., https://www.taylorfrancis.com/chapters/edit/10.4324/9781351173001-27/data-journalism-promise-transparency-sylvain-parasie?utm_source=researchgate.net&utm_medium=article DOI: 10.4324/9781351173001-27

Pariser, E. (2011). *The filter bubble: What the internet is hiding from you*. Penguin Press.

Pariser, E. (2011). *The filter bubble: What the Internet is hiding from you*. Penguin Press.

Pasquale, F. (2015). *The black box society: The secret algorithms that control money and information*. Harvard University Press. DOI: 10.4159/harvard.9780674736061

Patil, U., & Chouragade, P. (2021). Deepfake video authentication based on blockchain. In *IEEE Second International Conference on Electronics and Sustainable Communication Systems (ICESC)* (pp. 1110–1113). Coimbatore, India.

Pavis, M. (2021). Rebalancing our regulatory response to Deepfakes with performers' rights. *Convergence (London), 27*(4), 974–998. DOI: 10.1177/13548565211033418

Pawelec, M. (2022). Deepfakes and democracy (theory): How synthetic audio-visual media for disinformation and hate speech threaten core democratic functions. *Digital Society : Ethics, Socio-Legal and Governance of Digital Technology*, *1*(2), 19. DOI: 10.1007/s44206-022-00010-6 PMID: 36097613

Payne, L. (2025, March 14). *deepfake*. Britannica: https://www.britannica.com/technology/deepfake

Phillips, A. (2010). Transparency And The New Ethics Of Journalism. *Journalism Practice*, *4*(3), 373–382. DOI: 10.1080/17512781003642972

Piasecki, S., Morosoli, S., Helberger, N., & Naudts, L. (2024). AI-generated journalism: Do the transparency provisions in the AI Act give news readers what they hope for? *Internet Policy Review*, *13*(4), 1–28. DOI: 10.14763/2024.4.1810

Pinto, J. G. (2009). *TRANSPARENCY POLICY INITIATIVES IN LATIN AMERICA: UNDERSTANDING POLICY OUTCOMES FROM AN INSTITUTIONAL PERSPECTIVE. 14*(1). https://www.tandfonline.com/doi/abs/10.1080/10811680802577665

Porlezza, C., & Schapals, A. K. (2024). AI Ethics in Journalism (Studies): An Evolving Field Between Research and Practice. *Emerging Media*, *2*(3), 356–370. DOI: 10.1177/27523543241288818

Porlezza, C., & Splendore, S. (2019). From Open Journalism to Closed Data: Data Journalism in Italy. *Digital Journalism (Abingdon, England)*, *7*(9), 1230–1252. DOI: 10.1080/21670811.2019.1657778

Poynter Institute. (2025). In *Wikipedia*. https://en.wikipedia.org/w/index.php?title=Poynter_Institute&oldid=1286699137

Prachi, N. N., Habibullah, M., Rafi, M. E. H., Alam, E., & Khan, R. (2022). Detection of fake news using machine learning and natural language processing algorithms. *Journal of Advances in Information Technology*, *13*(6). Advance online publication. DOI: 10.12720/jait.13.6.652-661

Pramod, D., Patil, K. P., & Bharathi, S. V. (2025). Is it really unreal? A two-theory approach on the impact of deepfakes technology on the protection motivation of consumers. *Cogent Business & Management*, *12*(1), 2461239. Advance online publication. DOI: 10.1080/23311975.2025.2461239

Prochazka, F., & Obermaier, M. (2022). Trust through Transparency? How Journalistic Reactions to Media-Critical User Comments Affect Quality Perceptions and Behavior Intentions. *Digital Journalism (Abingdon, England)*, *10*(3), 452–472. DOI: 10.1080/21670811.2021.2017316

Pusztahelyi, R. (2020). Emotional AI and its challenges in the viewpoint of online marketing. *Curentul Juridic, 81*(2), 13-31. Retrieved July 01, 2025, from https://ideas.repec.org/a/pmu/cjurid/v81y2020p13-31.html

Qiu, S., Liu, Q., Zhou, S., & Wu, C. (2019). Review of Artificial Intelligence Adversarial Attack and Defense Technologies. *Applied Sciences (Basel, Switzerland), 9*(5), 909. DOI: 10.3390/app9050909

Ramsälv, A., Ekström, M., & Westlund, O. (2024). The epistemologies of data journalism. *New Media & Society, 26*(11), 6307–6324. DOI: 10.1177/14614448221150439

Rana, M. S., Nobi, M. N., Murali, B., & Sung, A. H. (2022). Deepfake detection: A systematic literature review. *IEEE Access : Practical Innovations, Open Solutions, 10*, 25494–25513. DOI: 10.1109/ACCESS.2022.3154404

Reddy Sure, T. A. (2023). Ethical implications of deepfake technology in user interfaces. *International Journal of Computers and Technology, 10*(2).

Reinsel, D., Gantz, J., & Rydning, J. (2018). *The Digitization of the World From Edge to Core*. IDC.

Reisdorf, B. C., & Blank, G. (2021). Algorithmic literacy and platform trust. In *Handbook of digital inequality* (pp. 341–357). Edward Elgar Publishing. DOI: 10.4337/9781788116572.00032

Ribes, D., Henchoz, N., Portier, H., Defayes, L., Phan, T. T., Gatica-Perez, D., & Sondereger, A. (2021). Trust indicators and explainable AI: A study on user perceptions. In *Proceedings of the 18th IFIP conference on human-computer interaction (INTERACT)* (pp. 662–671). Springer. DOI: 10.1007/978-3-030-85616-8_39

Rocha, Y. M., de Moura, G. A., Desidério, G. A., de Oliveira, C. H., Lourenço, F. D., & de Figueiredo Nicolete, L. D. (2021). The impact of fake news on social media and its influence on health during the COVID-19 pandemic: A systematic review. *Journal of Public Health*. Advance online publication. DOI: 10.1007/s10389-021-01658-z PMID: 34660175

Rodrigues, C. (2023). Evidence and transparency in Open Data Journalism: A case study on British and Brazilian news agencies [PDF]. DOI: 10.7275/CPO.1880

Romero Moreno, F. (2024). Generative AI and deepfakes: A human rights approach to tackling harmful content. *International Review of Law Computers & Technology, 38*(3), 1–30. DOI: 10.1080/13600869.2024.2324540

Roszell, O. A. (2021, November 8). *AI Learned How to Generate Fake News, and It's Terrifying Fake News, Deep Learning and Machine Learning Technology Changing the News.*

Rubin, V., Conroy, N., Chen, Y., & Cornwell, S. (2016). Fake News or Truth? Using Satirical Cues to Detect Potentially Misleading News. *Proceedings of the Second Workshop on Computational Approaches to Deception Detection*, 7–17. https://doi.org/DOI: 10.18653/v1/W16-0802

Ruhanen, L., Weiler, B., Moyle, B. D., & McLennan, C. J. (2015). Trends and patterns in sustainable tourism research: A 25-year bibliometric analysis. *Journal of Sustainable Tourism*, *23*(4), 517–535. DOI: 10.1080/09669582.2014.978790

Russia "meddled in all big social media" around US election. (2018, December 17). https://www.bbc.com/news/technology-46590890

Rusu Mocăna u, D. (2020). DETERMINING THE SAMPLE SIZE IN QUALITATIVE RESEARCH. *International Multidisciplinary Scientific Conference on the Dialogue between Sciences & Arts. Religious Education (Chicago, Ill.)*, *4*(1), 181–187. DOI: 10.26520/mcdsare.2020.4.181-187

Ryan, M. (2020). In AI we trust: Ethics, artificial intelligence, and reliability. *Science and Engineering Ethics*, *26*(5), 2749–2767. DOI: 10.1007/s11948-020-00228-y

Saeidnia, H. R., Hosseini, E., Lund, B., Tehrani, M. A., Zaker, S., & Molaei, S. (2025). Artificial intelligence in the battle against disinformation and misinformation: A systematic review of challenges and approaches. *Knowledge and Information Systems*, *67*(4), 3139–3158. DOI: 10.1007/s10115-024-02337-7

Sağlam, F., & Cengiz, M. A. (2023). Sosyal Bilimlerde Veri Bilimi Kullanımı. *Avrasya Sosyal ve Ekonomi Araştırmaları Dergisi*, *10*(4), 1375–1407.

Sample, I. (2020, January 13). *What are deepfakes – and how can you spot them?* The Guardian: https://www.theguardian.com/technology/2020/jan/13/what-are-deepfakes-and-how-can-you-spot-them

Sanchez-Acedo, A., Carbonell-Alcocer, A., Gertrudix, M., & Rubio-Tamayo, J. L. (2024). *The challenges of media and information literacy in the artificial intelligence ecology: deepfakes and misinformation.*

Santos Silva, M. (2022). Nudging and other behaviourally based policies as enablers for environmental sustainability. *Laws*, *11*(1), 9. DOI: 10.3390/laws11010009

Sarı, E. (2025). Sosyal Medyada Dezenformasyonla Mücadelede Yapay Zekâ: Olanaklar ve Sınırlılıklar. *Van Yüzüncü Yıl Üniversitesi Sosyal Bilimler Enstitüsü Dergisi*, (67), 49–61. DOI: 10.53568/yyusbed.1583326

Schiffrin, A. (2021). AI, automation, and the future of journalism: Report. *Center for International Media Assistance*. https://www.cima.ned.org/

Schmalz, S. (2024). Varieties of digital capitalism and the US–China rivalry: The rise of competing technological spheres. *Critical Sociology*. Advance online publication. DOI: 10.1177/08969205241291645

Schmitt, M., & Flechais, I. (2023). Digital Deception: Generative Artificial Intelligence in Social Engineering and Phishing. SSRN Electronic Journal. DOI: 10.2139/ssrn.4602790

Schudson, M. (2008). *Why democracies need an unlovable press*. Polity Press.

Semetko, H. A., & Valkenburg, P. M. (2000). Framing European politics: A content analysis of press and television news. *Journal of Communication*, *50*(2), 93–109.

Şener, N. K. (2020). *Yapay Zekanın Habercilikte Kullanımı: Olanaklar ve Sakıncalar. F. Zengin, & B. Kapır (Dü) içinde, Yapay Zeka ve Medya*. Doruk Yayıncılık.

Shah, M. U., Rehman, U., Parmar, B., & Ismail, I. (2024). Effects of moral violation on algorithmic transparency: An empirical investigation. *Journal of Business Ethics*, *193*(1), 19–34. DOI: 10.1007/s10551-023-05472-3

Shanbhogue, R. (2024, 15 Kasım). *Yapay zekâ için karar anı*. The Economist, The World Ahead 2025.

Shannon, C., & Weaver, W. (1963). *The Mathematical Theory of Communication*. University of Illinois Press.

Sharadga, T., Tahat, Z., & Safori, A. (2022). Journalists' Perceptions towards Employing Artificial Intelligence Techniques in Jordan TV's Newsrooms. *Studies in Media and Communication*, *10*(2), 239. Advance online publication. DOI: 10.11114/smc.v10i2.5749

Simon, F. M. (2022). Uneasy bedfellows: AI in the news, platform companies and the issue of journalistic autonomy. *Digital Journalism (Abingdon, England)*, *10*(10), 1832–1854. DOI: 10.1080/21670811.2022.2063150

Sisman, B., Yamagishi, J., King, S., & Li, H. (2021). An overview of voice conversion and its challenges: From statistical modeling to deep learning. *IEEE/ACM Transactions on Audio, Speech, and Language Processing*, *29*, 132–157. DOI: 10.1109/TASLP.2020.3038524

Söderlund, K., Engström, E., Haresamudram, K., Larsson, S., & Strimling, P. (2024). Regulating high-reach AI: On transparency directions in the Digital Services Act. *Internet Policy Review, 13*(1). Advance online publication. DOI: 10.14763/2024.1.1746

Stanford, H. A. I. (2025, January 15). *Artificial Intelligence (AI)- Information about AI: how to use, evaluate, and learn more*. Ball State University- University Libraries: https://bsu.libguides.com/c.php?g=1395427&p=10320854#:~:text=Artificial%20 intelligence%20(AI)%2C%20is,like%20playing%20chess%2C%20but%20today%2C

Stencel, M., Luther, J., & Luther, M. S. and J. (2020, April 3). Update: 237 fact-checkers in nearly 80 countries ... and counting. *Reporters' Lab*. https://reporterslab .org/2020/04/03/update-237-fact-checkers-in-nearly-80-countries-and-counting/

Stromer-Galley, J., McKernan, B., Zaman, S., Maganur, C., & Regmi, S. (2025). The Efficacy of Large Language Models and Crowd Annotation for Accurate Content Analysis of Political Social Media Messages. *Social Science Computer Review*.

Sun, S., Yujia, Z. S., & Yibei, C. (2020). Newspaper coverage of artificial intelligence: A perspective of emerging technologies. *Telematics and Informatics*, *53*, 101433. Advance online publication. DOI: 10.1016/j.tele.2020.101433

Sunstein, C. R. (2017). *Republic: Divided democracy in the age of social media*. Princeton University Press. DOI: 10.1515/9781400884711

Sütcü, C. S., & Aytekin, Ç. (2018). *Veri Bilimi*. Paloma.

Swart, J. (2021). Experiencing algorithms: How young people understand, feel about, and engage with algorithmic news selection on social media. *Social Media + Society*, *7*(2), 20563051211008828. DOI: 10.1177/20563051211008828

Szczepański, M., Pawlicki, M., Kozik, R., & Choraś, M. (2021). New explainability method for BERT-based model in fake news detection. *Scientific Reports*, *11*(1), 23705. DOI: 10.1038/s41598-021-03100-6 PMID: 34880354

Tagle, F. (2025). Why Radio is More Reliable Than Television During Social Protests: An Explanation Through Framing Theory. *Journal of Radio & Audio Media*, 1–15.

Tai, R. H., Bentley, L. R., Xia, X., Sitt, J. M., Fankhauser, S. C., Chicas-Mosier, A. M., & Monteith, B. G. (2024). An examination of the use of large language models to aid analysis of textual data. *International Journal of Qualitative Methods*, *23*, 1–14.

Tandoc, E. C.Jr, Lim, Z. W., & Ling, R. (2018). Defining "fake news" A typology of scholarly definitions. *Digital Journalism (Abingdon, England)*, *6*(2), 137–153. DOI: 10.1080/21670811.2017.1360143

Tau. B. (2025). Researchers link DeepSeek's blockbuster chatbot to Chinese Telecom banned from doing business in US.

Tejedor, S., & Vila, P. (2021). Exo Journalism: A Conceptual Approach to a Hybrid Formula between Journalism and Artificial Intelligence. *Journalism and Media, 2*(4), 830–840. DOI: 10.3390/journalmedia2040048

Tellan, T. (2022). *Yapay Zeka, Robot Gazetecilik ve Dijitalleşen İletişimin Doğasını Tartışmak. 9.Uluslararası İletişim Günleri.* Üsküdar Üniversitesi.

Teodorescu, D., Aivaz, K. A., Vancea, D. P. C., Condrea, E., Dragan, C., & Olteanu, A. C. (2023). Consumer trust in AI algorithms used in e-commerce: A case study of college students at a Romanian public university. *Sustainability (Basel), 15*(15), 11925. DOI: 10.3390/su151511925

Than, N., Fan, L., Law, T., Nelson, L. K., & McCall, L. (2025). Updating "the future of coding": Qualitative coding with generative large language models. *Sociological Methods & Research, 54*(3), 849–888.

Thaware, N., & Agnihotri, N. (2018). AI gone rogue: Exterminating deep fakes before they cause menace. *Blackhat. com/eu-18/Thu-Dec-6/eu-18 Disponible en.*

The Telegraph. (2020) Doctor Audio Evidence used to damn Father in Custody Battle. In: The Telegraph Newspaper. https://www.telegraph.co.uk/news/2020/01/31/deepfake-audio-used-custody-battle-lawyer-reveals-doctored-evidence/. Accessed 14 July 2024

Thompson, S. A. (2024, September 17). *California passes election 'deepfake' laws, forcing social media companies to take action.* The New York Times. https://www.nytimes.com/2024/09/17/technology/california-deepfakes-law-social-media-newsom.html

Thompson, J. B. (2008). *İletişimin küreselleşmesi.* Phoenix Yayınları.

Thormundsson, B. (2024, June 19). *Artificial intelligence (AI) worldwide - statistics & facts.* Statista: https://www.statista.com/topics/3104/artificial-intelligence-ai-worldwide/#topicOverview

Timur, T. (2017, May 22). *Suyun üzerinde yürümeye çalışan papazı timsahlar yedi iddiası.* Teyit.org: https://teyit.org/analiz/suyun-uzerinde-yurumeye-calisan-papazi-timsahlar-yedi-iddiasi

Toğaçar, M., Eşidir, K. A., & Ergen, B. (2021). Yapay Zekâ Tabanlı Doğal Dil İşleme Yaklaşımını Kullanarak İnternet Ortamında Yayınlanmış Sahte Haberlerin Tespiti. *Journal of Intelligent Systems: Theory and Applications, 5*(1), 1–8.

Topsümer, F., Durmuş, Y., & Yılmaz, B. A. (Eds.). (2023). *Media and Communication in the Digital Age: Changes and Dynamics*. Özgür Yayınları., DOI: 10.58830/ozgur.pub234

Törnberg, P. (2024). Large language models outperform expert coders and supervised classifiers at annotating political social media messages. *Social Science Computer Review*, *0*(0), 1–15.

Tosyalı, H. (2021). Dijital Çağda Siyasal İletişim: Algoritmalar ve Botlar. Communication and Technology Congress – CTC 2021, 12-14 Nisan, 2021 – Turkiye, İstanbul. https://web.archive.org/web/20210616092152id_/https://ctc.aydin.edu.tr/wp-content/uploads/2021/06/10.17932CTC2021ctc21011.pdf

Tsukamoto, S. (2006). Social Responsibility Theory and the Study of Journalism Ethics in Japan. *Journal of Mass Media Ethics*, *20*(1), 55–69. Advance online publication. DOI: 10.1207/s15327728jmme2101_4

Tufekci, Z. (2015). Algorithmic harms beyond Facebook and Google: Emergent challenges of computational agency. *Colorado Technology Law Journal*, *13*, 203-218. Retrieved July 16, 2025, from https://ctlj.colorado.edu/wp-content/uploads/2015/08/Tufekci-final.pdf

Tünalp, B. F. (2024). Yapay Zeka Sistemlerine Etik Değerlerin Entegrasyonu-Kavramsal Çerçevede Bir Tartışma. *Uluslararası Akademik Birikim Dergisi*, *7*(5), 1041–1052.

Turing, A. (1950). Computing Machinery and Intelligence. *Mind*, *59*(236), 433–460. DOI: 10.1093/mind/LIX.236.433

Türkmen, B., & Koçlu Maman, S. (2024). Yapay zeka destekli haber metni üretimi ve çevirilerinin karşılaştırmalı bir analizi: ChatGPT-4o örneği. İstanbul Üniversitesi Çeviribilim Dergisi, 21, 212-229.

Ufarte, R. M. J., Verdú, F. J., & Túñez-López, J. M. (2023). Use of artificial intelligence in synthetic media: First newsrooms without journalists. *El Profesional de la Información*, *32*, e320203. Advance online publication. DOI: 10.3145/epi.2023.mar.03

ULAKBİM. (2025). *Bibliyometrik Analiz*. https://cabim.ulakbim.gov.tr/bibliyometrik-analiz/

Ulaş, T. (2024). Yapay Zekâ Ve Haber Doğrulama Konusunda Yapılan Araştırmalar Üzerine Bibliyometrik Bir Analiz. *Pamukkale Üniversitesi İletişim Bilimleri Dergisi*, *3*(2), 247–267.

Understanding Information disorder. (n.d.). First Draft. Retrieved May 25, 2025, from https://firstdraftnews.org/long-form-article/understanding-information-disorder/

UNESCO. (2021). *Recommendation on the ethics of artificial intelligence*. https://unesdoc.unesco.org/ark:/48223/pf0000379939

Usage policies. (n.d.). Retrieved May 21, 2025, from https://openai.com/policies/usage-policies/

Uth, B., Badura, L., & Blöbaum, B. (2021). Perceptions of Trustworthiness and Risk: How Transparency Can Influence Trust in Journalism. In Blöbaum, B. (Ed.), *Trust and Communication: Findings and Implications of Trust Research* (pp. 61–81). Springer International Publishing., DOI: 10.1007/978-3-030-72945-5_3

Vaccari, C., & Chadwick, A. (2020). Deepfakes and disinformation: Exploring the impact of synthetic political video on deception, uncertainty, and trust in news. *Social Media + Society*, *6*(1), 1–13. DOI: 10.1177/2056305120903408

Van Dalen, A. (2012). The algorithms behind the headlines: How machine-written news redefines the core skills of human journalists. *Journalism Practice*, *6*(5–6), 648–658. DOI: 10.1080/17512786.2012.667268

van der Sloot, B., Wagensveld, Y., & Koops, B. J. (2021). *Summary Deepfakes: The legal challenges of a synthetic society. In the Tilburg Institute for Law, Technology, and Society*. Tilburg University.

Van Drunen, M., Zarouali, B., & Helberger, N. (2022). Recommenders you can rely on: A legal and empirical perspective on the transparency and control individuals require to trust news personalisation. *Journal of Intellectual Property, Information Technology and E-Commerce Law, 13*, 302. Retrieved July 16, 2025, from https://heinonline.org/HOL/LandingPage?handle=hein.journals/jipitec13&div=29&id=&page=

Vaswani, A., Shazeer, N., Parmar, N., Uszkoreit, J., Jones, L., Gomez, A. N., ... & Polosukhin, I. (2017). Attention is all you need. NeurIPS.

Vecchietti, G., Liyanaarachchi, G., & Viglia, G. (2025). Managing deepfakes with artificial intelligence: Introducing the business privacy calculus. *Journal of Business Research, 186*, 115010. DOI: 10.1016/j.jbusres.2024.115010

Verma, D. (2024). Impact of Artificial Intelligence on Journalism: A Comprehensive Review of AI in Journalism. *Journal of Communication Management (London)*, *3*(02), 150–156. DOI: 10.58966/JCM20243212

Vishnupriya, G., & Jeriel, K. A., RNS, A., Ajay, G., & J, A. G. (2024). Combating Fake News in the Digital Age: A Review of AI-Based Approaches. *2024 IEEE 9th International Conference for Convergence in Technology (I2CT)*, 1–6. https://doi.org/DOI: 10.1109/I2CT61223.2024.10544008

Vosoughi, S., Roy, D., & Aral, S. (2018). The spread of true and false news online. *Science*, *359*(6380), 1146–1151. DOI: 10.1126/science.aap9559 PMID: 29590045

Vu, T., Iyyer, M., Wang, X., Constant, N., Wei, J., Wei, J., Tar, C., Sung, Y.-H., Zhou, D., Le, Q., & Luong, T. (2024). FreshLLMs: Refreshing large language models with search engine augmentation. In *Findings of the Association for Computational Linguistics* (pp. 13697–13720). ACL.

Wang, S., Cao, L., Wang, Y., Sheng, Q. Z., Orgun, M. A., & Lian, D. (2021). A survey on session-based recommender systems. *ACM Computing Surveys*, *54*(7), 1–38. DOI: 10.1145/3465401

Wazid, M., Mishra, A. K., Mohd, N., & Das, A. K. (2024). A secure deepfake mitigation framework: Architecture, issues, challenges, and societal impact. *Cyber Security and Applications, 2*.

Weidinger, L., Mellor, J., Rauh, M., Griffin, C., & Uesato, J. (2021). Ethical and social risks of harm from language models. *arXiv preprint*. https://arxiv.org/abs/2112.04359

Weikmann, T., Greber, H., & Nikolaou, A. (2024). After deception: How falling for a deepfake affects the way we see, hear, and experience media. *The International Journal of Press/Politics*.

West, D. M. (2019). *The future of work: Robots, AI, and automation*. Brookings Institution Press.

What Is Deep Learning? | IBM. (2024, June 17). https://www.ibm.com/think/topics/deep-learning

Whittaker, J. P. (2019). *Tech giants, artificial intelligence and the future of journalism*. Taylor & Francis. DOI: 10.4324/9781351013758

Wiener, N. (1989). *The Human Use Of Human Beings: Cybernetics and Society*. Free Association Books.

Winner, L. (2020). *The whale and the reactor: A search for limits in an age of high technology*. 2. Baskı. University of Chicago Press. DOI: 10.7208/chicago/9780226692685.001.0001

Winter, S., Maslowska, E., & Vos, A. L. (2021). The effects of trait-based personalization in social media advertising. *Computers in Human Behavior, 114*, 106525. Advance online publication. DOI: 10.1016/j.chb.2020.106525

Wu, T. (2016). *The attention merchants: The epic scramble to get inside our heads.* Alfred A. Knopf.

Xu, K., Zheng, H., Zhan, X., Zhou, S., & Niu, K. (2024). Evaluation and optimization of intelligent recommendation system performance with cloud resource automation compatibility. *Applied Computing Engineering*, *87*(1), 228–233. DOI: 10.54254/2755-2721/87/20241620

Yapar Gönenç, A. (2012). Medya ve Haber. İstanbul Üniversitesi İletişim Fakültesi Dergisi, 14, 77-89.

Yasar, K., Barney, N., & Wigmore, I. (n.d.). *What is deepfake technology?* WhatIs?: https://www.techtarget.com/whatis/definition/deepfake

Yeles Sinem, S. (2024). *Yalan Haber ve Medya Okuryazarlığı: Medya Okuryazarlığının Medya Önyargıları Üzerindeki Etkileri*. Graduate of Social Sciences.

Yenduri, G., Ramalingam, M., Selvi, G. C., Supriya, Y., Srivastava, G., Maddikunta, P. K. R., Raj, G. D., Jhaveri, R. H., Prabadevi, B., Wang, W., Vasilakos, A. V., & Gadekallu, T. R. (2024). GPT (Generative Pre-Trained Transformer)—A Comprehensive Review on Enabling Technologies, Potential Applications, Emerging Challenges, and Future Directions. *IEEE Access : Practical Innovations, Open Solutions*, *12*, 54608–54649. DOI: 10.1109/ACCESS.2024.3389497

Yeung, K. (2017). 'Hypernudge': Big data as a mode of regulation by design. *Information Communication and Society*, *20*(1), 118–136. DOI: 10.1080/1369118X.2016.1186713

Ye, X., Yan, Y., Li, J., & Jiang, B. (2024). Privacy and personal data risk governance for generative artificial intelligence: A Chinese perspective. *Computer Law & Security Review*. Advance online publication. DOI: 10.1016/j.clsr.2023.105753

Yıldız, E. (2021). İletişim Alanındaki Yapay Zeka Konulu Tezlerin İncelenmesi. *İstanbul Aydın Üniversitesi Sosyal Bilimler Dergisi, 13*(3), 605 - 618.

York, C., Ponder, J. D., Humphries, Z., Goodall, C., Beam, M., & Winters, C. (2020). Effects of fact-checking political misinformation on perceptual accuracy and epistemic political efficacy. *Journalism & Mass Communication Quarterly*, *97*(4), 958–980. DOI: 10.1177/1077699019890119

Yu, F., Liu, Q., Wu, S., Wang, L., & Tan, T. (2017). A convolutional approach for misinformation identification. *Proceedings of the 26th International Joint Conference on Artificial Intelligence*, 3901–3907.

Zamith, R. (2019a). Transparency, Interactivity, Diversity, and Information Provenance in Everyday Data Journalism. *Digital Journalism (Abingdon, England)*, *7*(4), 470–489. DOI: 10.1080/21670811.2018.1554409

Zengin, F., & Kapır, B. (2021). *Yapay Zeka ve Medya*. Doruk Yayımcılık.

Zewe, A. (2025, 17 Ocak). *Explained: Generative AI's environmental impact*. MIT News. https://news.mit.edu/2025/explained-generative-ai-environmental-impact-0117

Zeydan, İ. (2024). Yapay Zeka Pazarlama Entegrasyonu: Örnek Uygulamalar. *International Journal of Management Economics and Business, 20*(ICMEB'24 Special Issue), 423-446.

Zhai, Y., Yan, J., Zhang, H., & Lu, W. (2020). Tracing the evolution of AI: Conceptualization of artificial intelligence in mass media discourse. *Information Discovery and Delivery*, *48*(3), 137–149. DOI: 10.1108/IDD-01-2020-0007

Zhang, L., Qiao, T., Xu, M., Zheng, N., & Xie, S. (2023). Unsupervised learning-based framework for deepfake video detection. *IEEE Transactions on Multimedia*, *25*, 4785–4799. DOI: 10.1109/TMM.2022.3182509

Zhao, W. X., Zhou, K., Li, J., Tang, T., Wang, X., Hou, Y., . . . Wen, J. R. (2023). A survey of large language models. arXiv preprint arXiv:2303.18223.

Zhou, W. (2024). Dilemma and coping strategies of news communication based on artificial intelligence and big data. *Heliyon*, *10*(3), e25398. DOI: 10.1016/j.heliyon.2024.e25398 PMID: 38352794

Zhou, X., & Zafarani, R. (2021). A Survey of Fake News: Fundamental Theories, Detection Methods, and Opportunities. *ACM Computing Surveys*, *53*(5), 1–40. DOI: 10.1145/3395046

Zhu, L., & Lerman, K. (2016). Attention inequality in social media. *arXiv*. https://doi.org//arXiv.1601.07200DOI: 10.48550

Zinderen, İ. E. (2024). *Yapay Zeka Gazetecilik İlişkisi. Y. Bayram (Dü.) içinde, Temel Gazetecilik-Kavramlar, Teknikler, Yenilikler*. Akademisyen Kitabevi.

Zou, L., Xia, L., Du, P., Zhang, Z., Bai, T., Liu, W., Nie, J.-Y., & Yin, D. (2020, January). Pseudo Dyna-Q: A reinforcement learning framework for interactive recommendation. In *Proceedings of the 13th international conference on web search and data mining* (pp. 816–824). Association for Computing Machinery. DOI: 10.1145/3336191.3371801

Zuboff, S. (2019). *The age of surveillance capitalism: The fight for a human future at the new frontier of power*. PublicAffairs.

About the Contributors

Bünyamin Ayhan is currently employed on a full-time basis as a professor at Selçuk University's Faculty of Communication. Ayhan holds a bachelor's degree in sociology, a master's degree in the same subject, and a PhD in research methods. He has worked in post-Soviet countries for many years and was a visiting scholar at Goethe University in Frankfurt am Main, Germany. His research interests include the sociology of communication, media studies and news.

Zehra Özkeçeci was fortunate enough to receive her bachelor's, master's and doctorate degrees from the University of Vienna. She is currently working in the cinema department of Necmettin Erbakan University. Her fields of study are media studies, communication sciences and social media.

***

Sana is an interdisciplinary researcher in Media and Cultural Studies, Journalism, and Human Rights. Her research focuses on how media narratives shape cultural identities, social perceptions, and public discourse, particularly in South Asian contexts. She explores the role of digital media, journalism, and popular culture in constructing meanings around gender, childhood, and marginalized communities.

Duygu Dumanlı Kürkçü was born in 1985 in Istanbul. She graduated from the Department of Communication Arts at the Faculty of Art and Design, Istanbul Kültür University, in 2009. In the same year, she started working as a research assistant in the same department. She completed her master's degree in 2011 at Marmara University, Institute of Social Sciences, in the Department of Public Relations. In 2015, she earned her Ph.D. in Journalism from the Institute of Social Sciences at Istanbul University. She began her academic career at Istanbul Arel University in 2014 as a lecturer. Between 2015 and 2021, she served as an Assistant Professor in the Department of Journalism at the Faculty of Communication, Istanbul Arel

University. In February 2021, she was awarded the title of Associate Professor in the field of Journalism and Media Studies by the decision of the Interuniversity Board (ÜAK). She currently works as an Associate Professor in the Department of Journalism at the Faculty of Communication, Istanbul Arel University, and has been serving as the Head of the Journalism Department since 2021. She is the author of the books "New Media and Youth" and "Hashtag in Communication Studies", and the editor of "Communication Studies on New Media" and "Journalism Studies on New Media". Her academic research interests include new media, online journalism, social media, and artificial intelligence, through which she continues to produce publications and projects.

Ashutosh Koirala is an undergraduate student pursuing a Bachelor of Science in Information Technology (BSIT) under the academic affiliation of Westcliff University. Mr. Koirala focuses on the intersection of Artificial Intelligence and Marketing, studying how intelligent technologies support content production, marketing, and overall community management. He has contributed to various marketing and communication initiatives that have strengthened his understanding of strategic content development and audience engagement. A strong advocate for the ethical and thoughtful use of AI in marketing, he actively engages in academic exploration and writing on these emerging subjects.

Murat Mengü graduated from Middle East Technical University with a degree in English Language and Literature in 1988 and completed his master's degree at Marmara University's Atatürk Faculty of Education in the Department of English Language Education from 1993 to 1995. Between 1998 and 2004, he earned his PhD from Istanbul University, Faculty of Communication, Department of Radio-TV-Cinema. He became an associate professor in Communication Studies in 2017 and a full professor in 2022. He has lectured on Media Literacy, Intercultural Communication, Communication Sociology, Cinema Theories, Criticism in Cinema-Television, Social Behavior, and Protocol Rules, as well as Communication Theories. He is currently working at Istanbul Arel University in the Faculty of Communication, Department of New Media and Communication.

Duygu Neşeli began her journalism education in 2006 at the Aydın Doğan Anatolian Vocational and Technical High School of Communication. In 2010, she was admitted to the Department of Journalism at Marmara University's Faculty of Communication and graduated in 2015. In the same year, she started her master's degree in the Department of Journalism, in the field of Contemporary Publishing and Publishing Management at Marmara University. She spent some time in London for language education and successfully completed her MA in 2019 with a thesis titled “Book Publishing in Turkey and Wattpad Publications.” In 2020, she began her academic career as a research assistant in the Department of Journalism at Istanbul Arel University. That same year, she started her PhD in the Department of Journalism, Media Economics and Management Program at Marmara University. Before pursuing an academic career, Neşeli worked in the media industry as a reporter, web editor, and digital content writer. She is currently continuing her doctoral studies at Marmara University and working as a research assistant at Istanbul Arel University. Her academic interests include journalism, new media, and media economics.

Sinem Yeles Karaman is an academic specializing in media, communication, and the societal impacts of emerging technologies. She serves at Konya Technical University, where her work focuses on media literacy, AI-driven communication environments, digital ethics, and misinformation studies. Her research critically examines topics such as social media addiction, media literacy and fake news, the impacts of artificial intelligence on communication practices, and, more recently, climate journalism and environmental literacy. In particular, she investigates how AI transforms contemporary media ecosystems and influences public information flows. She has contributed to various national and international academic projects and has served as a reviewer for scholarly publications. Her current research interests include AI-supported journalism, fake news detection, socio-technical systems, and ethical frameworks for responsible technology use. Dr. Yeles Karaman prioritizes developing interdisciplinary education and research models aimed at strengthening critical digital awareness in the face of rapidly advancing artificial intelligence technologies.

Index

A

B

C

D

E

F

H

J

L

M

N

O

P

R

S

T

www.ingramcontent.com/pod-product-compliance
Lightning Source LLC
LaVergne TN
LVHW080858300926
849162LV00003B/469
* 9 7 9 8 3 3 7 3 2 9 6 0 4 *